INTRODUCTION
to ACTION
RESEARCH 2nd Edition

We dedicate this book to the best learning partners of all:
Pilar Fernández-Cañadas Greenwood and Turid Sand Levin.
Much of what is good about this book has been learned from them
and without the space they created to make our collaboration possible,
this book would not exist. Davydd Greenwood would also like to acknowledge
that Morten Levin, whose idea the book was to begin with, has exceeded all
reasonable expectations for a colleague and friend. Were it not for his selfless support
over the past year, the current revised edition would not have been completed.

INTRODUCTION *to* ACTION RESEARCH 2nd Edition

Social Research *for* Social Change

Davydd J. Greenwood
Cornell University

Morten Levin
*Norwegian University of
Science and Technology*

SAGE Publications
Thousand Oaks ■ London ■ New Delhi

For information:

Sage Publications, Inc.
2455 Teller Road
Thousand Oaks, California 91320
E-mail: order@sagepub.com

Sage Publications Ltd.
1 Oliver's Yard
55 City Road
London EC1Y 1SP
United Kingdom

Sage Publications India Pvt. Ltd.
B-42, Panchsheel Enclave
Post Box 4109
New Delhi 110 017 India

Printed in the United States of America on acid-free paper

Library of Congress Cataloging-in-Publication Data

Greenwood, Davydd J.
Introduction to action research : social research for social change / Davydd J. Greenwood, Morten Levin. — 2nd ed.
    p. cm.
Includes bibliographical references and index.
ISBN 1-4129-2597-5 or 978-1-4129-2597-6 (pbk.)
    1. Action research. I. Levin, Morten. II. Title.
HM571.G74 2007
300.72—dc22

                                                    2006014042

07 08 09 10 11 10 9 8 7 6 5 4 3 2 1

Acquiring Editor:	Lisa Cuevas Shaw
Associate Editor:	Margo Crouppen
Editorial Assistant:	Karen Greene
Production Editor:	Sanford Robinson
Copy Editor:	Pam Suwinsky
Typesetter:	C&M Digitals (P) Ltd.
Indexer:	Julie Sherman Grayson
Cover Designer:	Glenn Vogel

Contents

Preface to the Second Edition   ix

Preface to the First Edition   x

Acknowledgments   xiii

PART 1: WHAT IS ACTION RESEARCH?   1

1. Introduction: Action Research, Diversity, and Democracy   3
   Action Research Defined   3
   Why General Overviews of Action Research Are Hard to Find   4
   Action Research, Applied Research, and Qualitative
       Versus Quantitative Research   5
   Action, Research, and Participation   6
   Action Research, the Disciplines, and Coverage   7
   Our Take on AR: Pragmatic Action Research   9
   The Plan of the Book   11
   Our Assumptions About the Readers of This Book   11
   Notes   12

2. A History of Action Research   13
   Industrial Democracy   14
   "Southern" PAR, Labor Organizing, Community
       Organizing, and Civil Rights   29
   Human Inquiry and Cooperative Inquiry   32
   Conclusions   34
   Notes   34

3. Action Research Cases From Practice: The Stories of
   Stongfjorden, Mondragón, and Programs for Employment
   and Workplace Systems at Cornell University   35
   Stongfjorden: Village Development in Western Norway   36
   Mondragón: Organizational Problems in Industrial Cooperatives   42
   Cornell University's School of Industrial and Labor
       Relations: Research and Extension   48
   Conclusions   51
   Notes   52

PART 2: SCIENCE, EPISTEMOLOGY, AND PRACTICE
    IN ACTION RESEARCH   53

 4. An Epistemological Foundation for Action Research   55
    Defining Scientific Research   55
    General Systems Theory   57
    Pragmatic Philosophy and Action Research   59
    Epistemological Foundations of Action Research   62
    The Action Research Inquiry Process Is Thus
        Inevitably Linked to Action   65
    Credibility and Validity in Action Research Inquiry   66
    Readdressing the Action Research Processes   71
    Political Economy and the Social Structure of Science   73
    Conclusions   74
    Notes   75

 5. Scientific Method and Action Research   76
    Can Action Research Produce
        Scientifically Meaningful Results?   77
    Physical and Biological Science as Iterative
        Cycles of Thought and Action   80
    Science Is Humans in Action   86
    Conclusions   87
    Notes   87

 6. Social Science Research Techniques, Work Forms,
    and Research Strategies in Action Research   89
    Conventional Social Research and Action Research   90
    The Cogenerative Model   93
    Action Research Is Not Merely "Qualitative Research"   98
    Workability and Explanation   100
    Conclusions   101
    Note   101

 7. Knowledge Generation in Action Research: The Dialectics
    of Local Knowledge and Research-Based Knowledge   102
    Local Knowledge and Professional Social
        Science Research Knowledge   103
    The Knowledge Generation Process   106
    Writing Up Action Research   109
    Conclusions   113

 8. The Friendly Outsider: From AR as a Research Strategy
    to the Skills Needed to Become an Action Researcher   115
    Not Trying to Overcome an Unruly World   115
    Creating Possibilities Rather Than Reinforcing Limits   116

Linking Theory and Local Understanding: Being Scientific,
        Counterintuitive, and Technically Competent   119
Practices and Skills of the Action Researcher   121
The Friendly Outsider   124
Becoming an Action Researcher   129
Conclusions   130
Note   130

**PART 3: VARIETIES OF ACTION RESEARCH PRAXIS:
        LIBERATING HUMAN POTENTIAL**   **131**

 9. **Pragmatic Action Research**   **133**
    Constructing Arenas for Dialogue   135
    Searching   136
    Preparing for the Search   143
    Planning and Executing a Search   144
    Conclusions   150
    Notes   150

10. **Power and Social Reform: Southern PAR, Education,
    Feminism, and Action Research**   **151**
    Participatory Research and Southern PAR   153
    Educational Strategies   158
    Feminist Analyses of Inequality and Development   163
    Conclusions   166
    Notes   166

11. **Educational Action Research**   **168**
    Frameworks   168
    Reforming Education in the North   170
    Adult Education Approaches in Industrialized Countries   173
    Corporate Classrooms   175
    Adult Education and Community Development   176
    Conclusions   182
    Notes   183

12. **Participatory Evaluation**   **184**
    The Authority of Evaluation   186
    The Emergence of Participatory Evaluation   186
    Modes of Participatory Evaluation   187
    Action Research in Evaluation Practice   192
    Conclusions   192

13 **Participatory Rural Appraisal, Rapid Rural Appraisal,
    and Participatory Learning and Analysis**   **194**
    Participatory Rural Appraisal in International Development   195
    Participation and Sustainability   199

The Specifics of Participatory Rural Appraisal 200
Critiques of Participatory Rural Appraisal 204
Participatory Rural Appraisal and Action Research 205
Conclusions 206
Notes 207

14. **Varieties of Human Inquiry: Collaborative,
    Action, Self-Reflective, and Cooperative** 208
    Central Perspectives 209
    Human Inquiry 211
    Action Inquiry and Self-Reflective Inquiry 215
    Cooperative Inquiry 218
    Conclusions 221

15. **Action Science and Organizational Learning** 223
    Action Science 223
    Organizational Learning 232
    The Skills Required for Action Science
       and Organizational Learning 234
    Conclusions 234
    Notes 235

**PART 4: ACTION RESEARCH, HIGHER EDUCATION,
AND DEMOCRACY** 237

16. **Educating Action Researchers** 239
    General Considerations 241
    AR Praxis in Higher Education 243
    Some Possibilities for Current Undergraduate AR Teaching 244
    Ph.D. Training in Action Research 249
    Situating Action Research Within the University 251
    Conclusions 254
    Note 254

17. **Action Research, Participation, and Democratization** 255
    Participation 256
    Democratization 261
    Venues for Participation and Democratization 262
    Conclusions: Action Research and Democratic Processes 265

References 266

Index 278

About the Authors 301

Preface to the Second Edition

We are gratified to have had the opportunity to revise this book. In the years since we published the first edition, the book has become a common reference work for those attempting to gain a perspective on action research (AR). Our strategy in writing it was to mix both an essay structure to introduce readers to the intellectual, scientific, and political economic foundations of AR with a brief survey of the major variants of AR. This continues to seem to be a good idea and a unique feature of the book. In the years since its original publication, we have both learned a good deal more about AR, deepened our epistemological understandings, and broadened our grasp of the diverse practices of AR. All of this should improve the second edition. Perhaps the major emphasis of our work in the past 8 years has been the analysis of the problems and the integration of AR into institutions of higher education and their practices. Seen as a key, not just to the future of AR, but to the future of higher education institutions in what seems to be an endless period of retrenchment, this emphasis is perhaps the most notable dimension of this second edition.

Preface to the First Edition

D avydd Greenwood and Morten Levin met for the first time in 1986 at a planning meeting for the Einar Thorsrud Memorial Conference, and our cooperation started half a year later. Levin spent his sabbatical in 1987 at the School of Industrial and Labor Relations at Cornell, working at the Program for Employment and Workplace Systems. Greenwood was also affiliated with this group at the time, and gradually we got to know each other better. Our laughter, irony, politics, and professional interests resonated. Levin made frequent trips to Ithaca, including other sabbatical leaves in 1994–95 and 2005 at Cornell.

In 1986, Levin was already well established in action research (AR), whereas Greenwood was in the final year of his first major AR project in the industrial cooperatives of Mondragón in the Spanish Basque Country. For Greenwood, the planning conference was an interesting event for two reasons. He met some of the important figures in the European, American, and Australian AR movement, and he got his first dose of the process of participatory planning Scandinavian style. Levin had already been engaged in teaching AR theory and models at the Norwegian University of Science and Technology in Trondheim for some time. Greenwood would not take AR into the classroom until 1990, and had not yet thought through the teaching issues that AR would raise.

Our real collaboration began with students present, and our collaboration has been sustained by our concern with teaching. In 1989, Morten Levin and Max Elden invited Greenwood to Trondheim to give a set of seminars on the Mondragón work to the first group of doctoral students of AR in Trondheim's innovative graduate program. The opportunity and effort to explain a complex, 3-year process of AR to a group of knowledgeable students left Greenwood convinced that he had to take AR into the classroom at Cornell. He began this process in 1990 with a seminar that changed his teaching practice forever. The story of that very first seminar is documented by the participants in a coauthored monograph about the experience (Elvemo, Grant Matthews, Greenwood, Martin, Strubel, & Thomas, 1997). Levin and a group of his students visited Cornell at the end of that first seminar, and Greenwood's students and Levin's students had a spirited discussion of AR.

Subsequently, Greenwood and Levin exchanged visits frequently. Greenwood was invited regularly to advise Levin's group of doctoral students and to serve on a pair of dissertation defense committees. Then Levin appointed Greenwood to the Norwegian Enterprise 2000 Program module he directs to serve as a kind of AR consultant and provocateur for Levin's AR team. During some of those visits, we also lectured together at the university. Levin coached Greenwood carefully on the design of Greenwood's first search conference.

Greenwood and Levin served with Hans van Beinum, René van der Vlist, Kjell S. Johannessen, and Claude Faucheux as staff members in the Scandinavian Action Research Development Program, which brought about 30 professional action researchers together for additional training to improve the quality of their research and writing about AR over a 2-year period. We were stunned to learn how difficult it was for practitioners of AR both to communicate research findings in writing and to get a firm handle on epistemological issues.

These experiences led us to recognize our common commitment to teaching and our similar political and ethical views. In the process, we became close friends. But these experiences also caused us to recognize that we share many ideas that add up to a rather different view of AR from the ones we commonly read about. Although the methods we employ are not new, our concerns with the political relationship between AR and conventional social research, the passive social role of universities, and the general lack of epistemological ambition and methodological attention in much AR writing told us that we had a view of AR enough at variance with other views that it would be worth articulating in writing.

Levin proposed we write this book, using his sabbatical leave in 1994–95 as the time to plan it together. As we got into the process, we not only had a wonderful time, we deepened our conviction that our view of AR is different from the dominant views. We also had a number of chances to try out these views on both students and colleagues, including through some coauthored papers. This book emerged out of the challenges of teaching about AR and a common desire to increase the quality and reputation of AR by charting an extremely ambitious epistemological and political agenda for AR within universities.

Our students have been with us throughout in this process. They have taught us how to teach (and not to teach) about AR; they have critiqued most of the ideas in this book; they have constantly held us accountable with their tough questions deriving from the existential dilemmas they face as action researchers. We have been their colearners in the process of creating this book.

So the present book has emerged out of an 11-year dialogue between Greenwood and Levin in which students of all kinds and ages have been active participants. Our commitment to these students, combined with our belief that we have something new to say about AR, caused us to write the book.

The book is unique in a number of ways. It lays out an epistemological agenda for AR, one that reaches well beyond the aspirations of many practitioners and that issues a head-on challenge to the conventional academic social sciences on both epistemological and ethical grounds. It is also unique in trying to map out the diversity and complexity of the intellectual and political streams that feed into AR. We do not try to reduce this complexity to one ideal model. Rather, we want readers to understand something about the different approaches to AR practice.

We took this approach intentionally. We do not think there is one right way to do AR, even though we have practices that we prefer personally. AR is both context specific and linked closely to the skills, background, and interests of the practitioner. We have learned through our teaching that we cannot predict how particular students will connect to AR issues. We know that good pedagogy requires an open and diverse approach that enables students to find their own points of connection.

Though a completed book, this remains a work in progress, an invitation to dialogue and debate in a field that has not seen enough of it. Our aim and hope is that the book will encourage the reader to reflect critically on AR praxis; we invite you to join us in this project.

Acknowledgments

W e would like to acknowledge the initiative and enthusiastic support we have received from Lisa Cuevas Shaw at Sage Publications, on whose initiative this revised edition of the book was created. The reviews she commissioned helped us refashion the book, as have the many journal reviews since its initial publication. Pam Suwinsky's copyediting was superb.

Part 1

What Is Action Research?

This book presents action research (AR) as a set of collaborative ways of conducting social research that simultaneously satisfies rigorous scientific requirements and promotes democratic social change. We introduce the reader to the epistemological and the technical issues raised by AR, and we paint a broad picture of the varieties of AR found around the globe. In Chapter 1 ("Introduction: Action Research, Diversity, and Democracy"), we introduce AR as a research strategy and reform practice. We view AR as a way of working in the field, of utilizing multiple research techniques aimed at enhancing change and generating data for scientific knowledge production. AR rests on processes of collaborative knowledge development and action design involving local stakeholders as full partners in mutual learning processes.

AR is a set of self-consciously collaborative and democratic strategies for generating knowledge and designing action in which trained experts in social and other forms of research and local stakeholders work together. The research focus is chosen collaboratively among the local stakeholders and the action researchers, and the relationships among the participants are organized as joint learning processes. AR centers on doing "with" rather than doing "for" stakeholders and credits local stakeholders with the richness of experience and reflective possibilities that long experience living in complex situations brings with it.

AR emerged from a variety of sources and gradually converged in a currently multidimensional strategy for social change. Because of the diversity of AR approaches, we seek in Chapter 2 ("A History of Action Research ") to provide a broad overview of the field as well as detailed in-depth arguments for AR. We posit that for many years AR has presented powerful arguments regarding the way the social sciences can and should operate but that this position has been both ideologically and institutionally suppressed. In our view, at present it is vitally important to show how AR can revitalize the social sciences, whose future seems to us increasingly in doubt because of the joint onslaughts of globalization, the commodity production view of knowledge generation and dissemination, and the reconstruction of universities as corporate industrial parks and vocational schools.

The major sources of AR are the original political economy tradition out of which the contemporary social sciences developed, American "pragmatic" philosophy, social and experimental psychology, community development and adult education, industrial democracy work, human inquiry, action science, action learning, reflective practice, participatory rural development, and liberation theology. What brings all these approaches together is the belief that there is no substitute for learning by doing.

One result of this is that cases and case narratives occupy a central place in the learning processes associated with becoming a competent AR practitioner. Therefore we end the first part of the book with the presentation in Chapter 3 ("Action Research Cases From Practice") of three descriptions of AR cases to show the rich texture, the challenges, pitfalls, and possibilities. One case emerges out of Spanish experiences in the Mondragón cooperatives, another was located in a small village of western Norway, and the last takes place within the walls of Cornell University.

1

Introduction

Action Research, Diversity, and Democracy

A ction research (AR) can help us build a better, freer, fairer society through collaborative problem analysis and problem solving in context. In this book, we offer a general overview of AR, including a comprehensive philosophical justification for it, a review of some commonly used methods, case examples to contextualize it, and a review of a variety of different approaches to AR praxis. Throughout, we advocate AR and its social change agenda vis-à-vis other forms of social research that do not contribute as actively and directly to processes of democratic social change and the simultaneous creation of valid social knowledge.

Our advocacy rests on two distinct but related bases: democratic inclusion and social research quality. AR democratizes research processes through the inclusion of the local stakeholders as coresearchers. AR also produces better quality social research than that arising from professional expert social research strategies. Thus, AR is central to the enactment of a commitment to democratic social transformation through research, analysis, and action design.

Action Research Defined

Action research is social research carried out by a team that encompasses a professional action researcher and the members of an organization, community, or network ("stakeholders") who are seeking to improve the participants' situation. AR promotes broad participation in the research process and supports action leading to a more just, sustainable, or satisfying situation for the stakeholders.

Together, the professional researcher and the stakeholders define the problems to be examined, cogenerate relevant knowledge about them, learn and execute social research techniques, take actions,[1] and interpret the results of actions based on what they have learned. AR rests on the belief and experience

3

that all people—professional action researchers included—accumulate, organize, and use complex knowledge continuously in everyday life. This belief is visible in any AR project because the first step professional action researchers and members of a community, organization, or network take is to define a problem that they seek to resolve. They begin by pooling their knowledge. AR democratizes the relationship between the professional researcher and the local interested parties.

Because it is a research practice with a social change agenda, AR involves a critique of conventional academic practices and organizations that assert either the necessity or desirability of studying social problems without trying to resolve them. Although AR views academic and professional knowledge systems that do not engage practice direction as wrongheaded, action researchers neither reject formal research methods nor ignore the epistemological issues that necessarily undergird the development of valid social knowledge. To the contrary, action researchers, precisely because the results will affect the lives of the stakeholders, have a profound interest in the validity of the generated knowledge. These issues are dealt with in greater detail throughout Part 2 of this book, particularly in Chapters 4, "An Epistemological Foundation for Action Research," and Chapter 5, "Scientific Method and Action Research."

Why General Overviews of Action Research Are Hard to Find

We decided to write a general overview of AR because of our experience with university students and practitioners encountering the subject for the first time. In our experience, students and novice practitioners generally lack access to a sufficiently comprehensive and balanced way to learn about the diverse origins, theories, methods, motives, and problems associated with this complex field. Although there is an extensive bibliography of works on AR, including a number of introductory works and a handbook that provide overviews of various approaches (we cite these throughout), we felt that another kind of general book is also needed. Existing works are compendia, focus on a particular variety of AR to the exclusion of others, or do not link the history, philosophy, and practice of AR to a sufficiently broad set of philosophical, scientific, and political issues. The present book tries to overcome some of these limitations.

Gaining such an overview of AR is difficult, in part because of the organization of AR praxis. Action researchers are found in social service agencies, nongovernmental organizations, international development agencies, planning departments, and industry and are spread around the disciplines in academic institutions (for example, education, planning, communications, social services, program evaluation, sociology, anthropology, organizational behavior). Almost nowhere in academia is there a "department" of action research. Rather, networks of colleagues from diverse disciplines share an interest in AR. One result is that AR practitioners have very little common knowledge, read different journals and books, and often write in ignorance of relevant contributions of others in AR from other fields.

We do not believe that creating a university department of AR is the answer to this dilemma. Indeed, we view the departmentalization of the social sciences as one of the ways in which the social reform agenda of the fields emerging from political economy in the 19th century was eliminated. However, we do not let academic institutions off the hook, and the final part of this book (Part 4) deals with these issues.

We want the reader to understand that what follows is not an overview of a discipline in the making. It is a presentation of a diverse and often divergent set of practices centered on putting social research to use for democratic social change. To that end, we try to include representation of many different approaches to AR and offer some references to allow readers to follow their own interests. What we include is limited by our own experience, our judgments of the different approaches we know about, and our own epistemological, methodological, and political agendas. Still, our goal is to give an honest and broad-minded presentation of the field of AR from our point of view. We are fully aware that the map is not the territory, and we know that knowledgeable AR practitioners will find gaps and idiosyncrasies in our choices.[2]

Action Research, Applied Research, and Qualitative Versus Quantitative Research

Action research refers to the conjunction of three elements: action, research, and participation. Unless all three elements are present, the process may be useful but it is not AR. Put another way, AR is a research strategy that generates knowledge claims for the express purpose of taking action to promote social analysis and democratic social change. The social change we refer to is not just any kind of change. AR aims to increase the ability of the involved community or organization members to control their own destinies more effectively and to keep improving their capacity to do so within a more sustainable and just environment.

AR is not applied research, and AR explicitly rejects the separation between thought and action that underlies the pure/applied distinction that has characterized social research for a number of generations. This theoretical/applied pseudo-split, in our view, has been a key mechanism by which the social sciences have become deformed. It creates a useless dance between disengaged theorists and engaged actors, a dance that liberates both sides from the need to generate valid understandings of the social world and its change processes and to hold themselves accountable to both meaningful social consequences and solid methodological and theoretical groundings.

We believe that valid social knowledge can only be derived from practical reasoning engaged in through action. As action researchers, we believe that action is the only sensible way to generate and test new knowledge. The widespread belief that being a "true" social scientist means not being engaged in social action is, to us, so peculiar and counterintuitive that we devote a considerable amount of space to explaining this phenomenon in Part 2 of this book.

We reject a widespread tendency for people to believe that AR must be qualitative research rather than quantitative research. This unjustifiable assumption probably arises from the belief that action-oriented work cannot be scientific (precisely because it involves action) and the additional assumption (erroneous in our view) that quantitative research must be more scientific than qualitative research. Because we see no merit in these assumptions and because we use both quantitative and qualitative methods ourselves, we reject the notion that AR is qualitative research only and argue that action researchers are obligated to be competent in all major forms of social research.

Action researchers can accept no a priori limits on the kinds of social research techniques they use. Surveys, statistical analyses, interviews, focus groups, ethnographies, and life histories are all acceptable, if the reason for deploying them has been agreed upon by the AR collaborators and if they are used in a way that does not oppress the participants. Knowing exactly how much heavy metal is in the groundwater somewhere may be as much a part of an AR project as knowing how people make sense of the future. Formal quantitative, qualitative, and mixed methods all are appropriate to differing situations.

Action, Research, and Participation

Despite the significant differences among AR practitioners and their life situations, we believe that several important commitments link most of us. AR is composed of a balance of three elements. If any one of the three is absent, then the process is not AR. This is not to say that all non-AR processes are meaningless but to distinguish AR from other kinds of research and application activities.

1. *Action.* AR is participatory because AR aims to alter the initial situation of the group, organization, or community in the direction of a more self-managing, liberated, and sustainable state. What is defined as a liberated state varies from one practitioner to another. Some use AR to create a kind of liberation through greater self-realization. Others emphasize more political meanings of liberation, and these vary among themselves regarding how strong a political

liberation agenda they advocate. Still others believe that AR occurs in any kind of research activity in which there is participation by some members of the organization being studied. Although a few practitioners try to link AR and revolutionary praxis, by and large, AR practitioners are democratic reformers rather than revolutionaries.

2. *Research.* We believe in research, in the power and value of knowledge, theories, models, methods, and analysis. We believe that AR is one of the most powerful ways to generate new research knowledge.

3. *Participation.* We believe in participation, placing a strong value on democracy and control over one's own life situations. These values permeate our arguments and create a strong general commitment to democratizing the knowledge generation process. AR involves trained social researchers who serve as facilitators and teachers of members of local communities or organizations. Because these people together establish the AR agenda, generate the knowledge necessary to transform the situation, and put the results to work, AR is a participatory process in which everyone involved takes some responsibility.

All these different approaches are further subdivided by the kinds of topics they deal with: community development, change in educational systems, economic development and liberation in the Third World, participatory change in core institutions of society (companies, administrative bureaucracies, and so on). Many of these different approaches to AR are incompatible. Some rest on Marxist notions of political economy and social transformation; others are rooted in pragmatic philosophy; still others build on a particular brand of social psychology; and a few simply advocate that, whatever the question, participation is the answer. We take seriously the obligation to make the reader aware of these differences, but we harbor no illusions about reconciling them.

Action Research, the Disciplines, and Coverage

As noted earlier, AR is not a discipline. It involves practitioners from anthropology, development studies, education, engineering, gender studies, human services, psychology, human services, social work, sociology, planning, civil engineering, and many other fields, including many forms of nonacademic practice. Consequently, students will not find AR presented in introductory disciplinary courses in most departments. Academic disciplines use introductory courses to recruit neophyte disciplinarians and to enhance enrollments to satisfy the demands of university administrations in return for which the departments get additional resources. These courses generally do not aim to attract scholars and practitioners who share particular views about democracy, participation, and the creation of useful knowledge. This is the case despite the fantasies of U.S. neoconservatives who imagine the social sciences and humanities in U.S. universities to be hotbeds for the promotion of left-wing ideologies.

In a higher education environment, AR is not an easy way to work, because disciplinary enrollments and boundaries are the tools used in academic competition and administrative command and control. Yet, we encounter increasing numbers of students from diverse fields who come to us to learn about AR. Some come in reaction to their unsatisfying experiences of the abstractions and social passivity of their home fields, others because of their rejection of the instrumentalism of many so-called applied fields, and still others because of their experiences with other approaches that are critical of "canonical" disciplinary systems (for example, feminism, neo-Marxism, critical theory). The teaching challenge with such heterogeneous groups is how to present an introduction to people who are searching for something, to provide them with enough background to permit them to continue learning about AR independently, and, at the same time, to build as directly as possible on the experiences that moved them to explore AR in the first place.

After thinking through this problem and teaching AR courses over the past 20 years, we decided that the best approach is for us to develop a consistent historical, philosophical, and ethical argument for AR, provide some cases of AR practice, and then introduce a variety of AR approaches. To fulfill the conditions of this design, we develop a philosophical argument for AR as scientific activity and a view of the links of AR to many different kinds of reform movements in the sciences, engineering, and social sciences. We couple this with a political economic argument that accounts for the suppression of praxis-oriented social research in academia. Because we intend to bridge theory and praxis, we also develop discussions of methodologies and tools useful in AR. Then, to evoke some of the diverse visions among AR practitioners, we provide a general overview of some of the main AR positions (including our own), knowing well that many of these positions ignore one another in practice.

This general overview will most likely be criticized by other AR practitioners because it is not truly comprehensive and because we express our own views about each approach we review. AR has many proponents, and several different groups would like to claim they know the "right" way to do AR, whereas others reject the name entirely, preferring (often for sensible reasons) another term (such as *participatory research, human inquiry,* or *action science*). Occasionally, some practitioners are ignorant or intolerant of each other's work. Although we are well aware that our review is not likely to win us friends in all groups, we persist in presenting our own view of the field as our intellectual and political right and invite others to present alternative views and critiques of ours. The first edition of the book did provoke some reactions, but, as yet, no comprehensive alternative view of the field of AR has been proposed.

Our Take on AR: Pragmatic Action Research

Our experience is predominantly, though not exclusively, in industrial, community, and higher education settings in Europe and the United States. Davydd Greenwood is an anthropologist and Morten Levin is a sociologist with a background in engineering. Greenwood, a professor at Cornell University, a large combined state and private institution, has served as an academic administrator of large multidisciplinary centers for more than 20 years while continuing to teach anthropology. His main research has taken place in Spain, in upstate New York, and recently in the international, comparative study of universities. He has been active in a number of AR programs in Norway and Sweden, including an AR Ph.D. program led by Morten Levin. Levin is a professor at the Norwegian University for Science and Technology (NTNU) at Trondheim and has been the leader in the creation of combined engineering and AR programs there, as well as the leader of a number of national work-life development programs. He has also conducted AR in the United States and Canada and is the founder and leader of a Ph.D. program in AR sponsored by the Norwegian social partners and anchored at his university.

We have made a good-faith effort to become knowledgeable about many different approaches, but we are aware that there are many gaps in our backgrounds. We do not intentionally slight other approaches by writing from our own knowledge base. The longer-term solution to problems of balance found here is for others to write their views of these subjects and be critical of what we have offered. We will respond, and hope thereby to open up a dialogue that broadens our collective sense of the scope of AR and enhances discourse on the democratization of knowledge creation and action. Our hope is that this book can encourage a long-needed critical discourse on the foundations and praxis of AR.[3] Our aim is to present one consistent strand of thought, integrating a philosophical, methodological, and political economic position with a consistent praxis supported by suitable methods and tools, while keeping the different kinds of AR practice and visions in sight.

As we mentioned previously, we are both mostly experienced in the use of AR in industrial and community development in Western industrialized countries. We share a strong commitment to the democratization of knowledge, learning, and self-managed social change. We are reformers, not revolutionaries, however, and we are social scientists, not psychoanalysts. We do not believe that we have the wisdom or the right to "lead" others to the "correct" social arrangements "for their own good," as some of the more liberationist practitioners do or as some of the more "therapeutic" approaches to AR advocate. Rather we believe in trying to offer, as skillfully as possible, the space and tools for democratic social change.

We refuse to guide such change unilaterally from our positions as action researchers. We consider ourselves participants in change processes in which democratic rules guide decision making. We bring to the table certain skills and knowledge, and other actors do the same, bringing their own capacities and experiences to bear on the problems. This is why we call our own particular variety of AR practice "pragmatic action research."

Our views on democracy and liberating situations are relevant, and we want to clarify them. Democracy is a concept with such a multiplicity of meanings that attempts to be clear about it are extremely controverted (see Dahl, 1989, for an excellent review). To some, especially many North Americans, the term often evokes egalitarianism. For others, it involves participation, whereas for others it conjures decision making by consensus, and for still others, decisions by majority rule. For some, democracy implies a homogeneous community and for others, arenas for lively debate. All these meanings have their associated genealogies, theories, politics, and ethics.

Our own view of these matters equates democracy with the creation of arenas for lively debate and for decision making that respects and enhances the diversity of groups. We explicitly reject both the distributive justice and the consensus models of democratic processes. We take the diversity of skills, experiences, ethnicities, gender, and politics as the most valuable source of potential positive changes in groups. Consequently, we reject the dominant political view of democracy as majority rule, accepting Iris Young's (1990) critique of this view of democracy as one that rests on the oppressive actions of welfare state capitalism to reduce social justice to a limited redistribution of goods to those defined as disadvantaged. That view of democracy neither respects diversity nor seeks to enhance the capacity of the disenfranchised to act on their own behalf. For us, AR aims to enable communities and organizations to mobilize their diverse and complex internal resources as fully as possible.

Consequently, we are suspicious of approaches to AR that seem to privilege the homogeneity of communities or consensus-based decision making, believing that such approaches open up great potentials for co-optation and coercion. One does not have to look far for documentation of these problems. At various points in recent history, such as 1968, the democratic critique of capitalist business as usual was embodied in attempts to create so-called alternative social forms. Many of these took the form of intentional communities, cooperatives, and open schools, and many tried to abolish social and cultural differences and to substitute consensus decision making for majority rule. A wonderful ethnographic portrait of such an organization is given in Jane Mansbridge's (1983) *Beyond Adversary Democracy.* To obliterate oppression of minorities by the majority, these architects of social change tried to substitute absolute consensus for majority rule. The effect, as Tocqueville (2001/1835,

1840) saw generations ago, often was to create a tyrannical demand for consensus that eventually undermined the belief in democracy through the experience of group pressure and self-censorship.

We believe that diversity is one of the most important features of human societies. Diversity is a biological fact, continually reproduced in each generation, regardless of anyone's intentions. Diversity is also a cultural product. Anyone who takes the trouble to look closely discovers that, even in the most homogeneous-appearing groups, there are wide differences in knowledge, interests, experience, and capabilities. We view these differences as a rich social resource that, when effectively mobilized, gives a group or an organization a much greater capacity to transform itself. We view democracy as an open system that should be able to welcome and make humane use of these differences. From our perspective, the aim of democracy is to give rise to societies and organizations capable of emphasizing, mobilizing, and energizing the differences within them.

We view liberating situations as those in which social change is possible and can be influenced by the participants. Further, we see a group or organization as being on a liberating trajectory when it is increasingly able to tolerate, use, and reward the diversity of viewpoints, capacities, and experiences within and if it is increasingly possible for a greater and greater proportion of members to affect the future directions of the collectivity. Finally, in a liberating situation, a group increasingly welcomes change as an opportunity for group enhancement and growth.

The Plan of the Book

Part 1 of the book continues with Chapter 2, a history of AR, and three cases presented in Chapter 3. Following this, in Part 2 ("Science, Epistemology, and Practice in Action Research"), Chapters 4–8 present the philosophical and methodological arguments for AR as a form of scientific inquiry that better meets scientific standards than what is currently called "social science" in academia. We provide an explanation of the marginalization of AR activities in academia through a brief historical political economy of academic institutions in advanced capitalist societies. In Part 3 ("Varieties of Action Research Praxis"), we move on to Chapters 9–15, on different approaches to AR, beginning with our own approach. We close, in Part 4, with Chapter 16, on the education of action researchers, and Chapter 17, a broader look at AR, participation, and democracy. Throughout, we advocate our views strongly, but with the intention of encouraging the reader to consider them, not to accept them without debate.

Our Assumptions About the Readers of This Book

We assume that our main audience has some previous experience either in formal social research or in social change-oriented action. We aim to present AR to readers who are seeking what they hope will be more appropriate and productive ways of conducting social research. We do not ask you to ignore your prior experience; we encourage you to use it as a point of reference as you learn about AR approaches. As in our classrooms and AR projects, we see the relationship between the reader-participant and the author-researcher as a collaborative one.

Notes

1. Sometimes the professional action researcher is engaged in the actions deriving from the AR process and sometimes not. This depends on the situation and the needs of the stakeholders.

2. The existence of the *Handbook of Action Research,* edited by Peter Reason and Hilary Bradbury (2001a), helps remedy this problem, and that work can be turned to with profit for an enormous array of perspectives and extensive bibliographies. A second edition is in the works and due out in 2007.

3. A useful exchange of this sort recently was published in the *International Journal of Action Research* (then named *Concepts and Transformation;* Greenwood, 2002, 2004a).

2

A History of Action Research

History can be written in many ways, and no one ever writes *the* history. Our intention in this chapter is to present a genealogy of action research (AR) that centers on the way we have learned to understand it during our own years in the field. We do not believe that it is possible to present an objective account of the development of AR. Attempting to create a history of a specific phenomenon often has an underlying assumption that it is possible to draw one historical line that connects the different elements in the field. This is not the case in AR or probably anywhere else. The diversity of activities today identified as "action research" cannot, in an obvious manner, be linked to each other. A striking example of this situation occurred in 1991, when two important books were published simultaneously with similar elements in their titles: Fals Borda and Rahman's (1991) *Action and Knowledge: Breaking the Monopoly With Participatory Action Research* and Whyte's (1991) *Participatory Action Research*. Both books use similar elements in their titles, but as Levin (1998) pointed out, they hardly acknowledge each other. In their bibliographies, they share only three references relating to the practice of action research.

This situation has changed over the past 15 years. *The Handbook of Action Research* edited by Reason and Bradbury (2001a) indicates, by gathering many of the strands of thinking in the field into one volume, that a more ecumenical view of the recent development in AR is developing. Shared references are found to the classic works of Karl Marx, John Dewey, Kurt Lewin, Jürgen Habermas, Hans Georg Gadamer, and Richard Rorty, for example. What is lacking from Reason and Bradbury's volume and from the field in general, however, is a critical discourse between different conceptualizations of AR or a contrast between different practices and findings. Rather the unspoken intention of the different contributors in Reason and Bradbury (2001a) seems to have been to present a specific position, not to map that position onto other strands of thinking. We hope that the next stage in the international network of AR professionals will be the creation of this kind of engaged, multiple, critical discourse that provides a more meaningful map of the varieties and trends in AR.

Despite this, it would be a mistake to draw the conclusion that the diverse activities called AR lack the features of an intellectual and social movement.

AR, as a whole, embodies a broad and diverse movement within which there are many similarities in values, approaches to the empirical field, and commitments to mutual learning between problem owners and researchers. The diverse practitioners in the field now do have encounters at conferences, write chapters in the same handbook (Reason & Bradbury, 2001a), and publish in the same journals. But, this activity has not yet resulted in sufficient communication so that it is easy for a reader starting in one corner of AR to find her or his way to other corners.

The many different strands of thinking could be subdivided into more precise categories, but for our purpose here, it is sufficient to focus only on creating a more general historical overview. Later, in Part 3 of this book, we present the historical origins of major approaches to AR as we introduce each. From our viewpoint, the history of AR necessarily contains more than one narrative, and each narrative adds necessary elements of the larger historical picture.

In constructing the history of action research, we begin with and pay most attention to the Northern tradition of industrial democracy. The Northern experiences in industrial organizations were a primary and fertile ground for the development of AR, and we devote most of the space in this chapter to the Northern, Western tradition because the reader needs to know where we are coming from. This should not be construed as an exclusionary strategy but rather as an articulation of our own situatedness. Next we provide a presentation of the liberationist movement in poor countries because it is a vital part of the history of AR, even though it is not as much a part of our personal itineraries. (In later chapters, Southern participatory action research (PAR) and other liberationist approaches are given a more nuanced treatment.) The eventual rapprochement (without mutual assimilation) is a necessity for the future of AR, given the forces arrayed in both the North and the South against democratization. It was one of the primary practitioners of Southern PAR, Orlando Fals Borda, who understood this best and who reached out to all positions in the world of AR when he chose to organize the world conferences that he titled "Convergence" in Cartagena, Colombia, in 1977 and 1997. We conclude the chapter with a brief overview of the human inquiry/collaborative inquiry approach.

Industrial Democracy

The emergence of what came to be called the "industrial democracy" tradition or movement refers to the first systematic and reasonably large-scale AR effort in Western industrialized countries. Its roots trace back to Kurt Lewin's early work in the United States (first at Cornell University and later at MIT). His ideas recrossed the Atlantic and found fertile ground at the Tavistock Institute of Human Relations in London. Though there were a number of activities in Great Britain, the major source of large-scale AR projects turned out to be in Norway in the Industrial Democracy Project. Many of these ideas were reinvented in the form of industrial management strategies in Swedish and U.S. industrial firms; later, they reached Japan as well. This very widespread diffusion of ideas developed through AR is a success story about the dissemination of AR, but it is also a story about the way fairly radical ideas for social change can be appropriated as management tools aimed at producing more efficient, rather than fairer, organizations.

Our central claim is that the basic ideas of the industrial democracy movement are today accepted as state of the art in the organization of work. No sensible industrial leader in the West fails to take account of team-based work organization or the training of skillful and responsible workers able to engage in continuous innovation (improvement) processes at the shop-floor level. These ideas are so widely accepted now that their relatively recent origins in the industrial democracy movement are largely forgotten.

One consequence of this is that the concept of industrial democracy has lost its initial meaning. Some practitioners and companies apply the term *industrial democracy* in a co-opted form, giving the typical control strategies of management a socially euphonic name while still working in Tayloristic ways.[1] Although we see this as a problematic situation, it is what one always sees when new ideas appear in industrialized settings. We can also see the same domestication processes in the other two approaches to AR we discuss in this chapter. Within the liberationist tradition, for example, the work variously called "Rapid Rural Appraisal," "Participatory Rural Appraisal," or "Participatory Learning Analysis" (Chambers, 1994a, b, c) unintentionally made participation into a commodity that was built into development strategies as a technique instigated by the funding agencies. This process is quite parallel to the co-optation of industrial democracy. Likewise, it is possible to trace elements of the same sort of domestication taking the form of quick fixes in organizational settings without the learning perspectives advocated by Heron (1996) and Reason (1994). Co-optation always exists alongside more genuine efforts to democratize society. The challenge for the AR community is not to retain its "purity" but to figure out strategically how to open up new ground for democratic work organization and to retain the democratizing momentum that makes AR worth doing.

THE EARLY WORK OF KURT LEWIN

The spread of Nazism in Germany led the psychologist Kurt Lewin to leave Europe and seek refuge in the United States. Lewin was trained as a social psychologist, and his central interest was in social change, specifically questions about how to conceptualize social change and how to promote it. Although accounts on this matter differ, Lewin is generally thought to be the person who coined the term "action research" and gave it meanings quite close to those we use in this book.

In AR, Lewin envisaged a process whereby one could construct an experiment in a holistic social and material situation with the aim of achieving a certain goal. For example, in the early days of World War II, Lewin (1943) conducted a study, commissioned by U.S. authorities, on the use of tripe as part of the regular daily diet of American families. The research question was to what extent American housewives could be encouraged to use tripe rather than beef for family dinners. Beef was scarce and was destined primarily for the troops. Thus, the authorities were looking for resources to substitute for beef in domestic consumption.

Lewin's approach to this research was to conduct a study in which he trained a limited number of housewives in the art of cooking tripe for dinner. He then surveyed how this training had an effect on their daily cooking habits in their own families. In this case, AR was synonymous with a so-called natural experiment, meaning that the researchers in a real-life context invited or forced participants to take part in an experimental activity. This research approach still fell very much within the bounds of conventional applied social science, with its patterns of authoritarian control, but it was aimed at producing a specific, desired social outcome. Lewin's thinking about experimentation in natural settings became the main strategy for the Norwegian Industrial Democracy Project. Lewin was trained as a social psychologist, and thus had a strong professional concern with behavioral modification that became one of the core issues in the early stages of Norwegian efforts to improve working conditions.

Two other strands of Lewin's thinking had an important influence on the development of the industrial democracy tradition. First, Lewin conceptualized social change as a three-stage process: dismantling former structures (unfreezing), changing the structures (changing), and finally locking them back to a permanent structure (freezing). Second, his work on group dynamics, identifying factors and forces important for development, conflict, and cooperation in groups, led to the concept of T-groups, which has had a rich subsequent history (see Gallagher, 2001).

Lewin's conceptualization of change as a three-stage process is still an influential model. Lewin's major idea is that social change can be identified as sequential and discrete processes, using a thermodynamic metaphor of unfreezing, floating, and freezing matter. The core of Lewin's model is the notion of the existence of stable social states, those preceding a change and those established after the change has taken place. The action intervention (that is, the change process) is an episode and, in the end, the social system will return to a stable state. This conceptualization of change as intermittent had a dominant influence in the early days of AR and still prevails in the conceptualizations of many U.S.-based organization development practitioners (Levin, 1994). The model was attractive because it legitimated short-term interventions, a concept developed mainly among social psychologists in the 1970s. It also played a major role in framing the thinking behind consultation practices in the field of organizational development, that is, a planned and systematic effort to create participative change in organizations (Cummings & Worley, 2001) without necessarily engaging in long-term change processes.

In our view, this is a very limiting and mistaken position. We argue in favor of modeling AR as a continuous and participative learning process, not as a form of short-term intervention. For us, the change process has an open starting point and often no absolute ending point. Moreover, because the core idea in our own practice is to create sustainable learning capacities and to give participants the option of increasing control over their own situations, predefining the processes as short term is inconsistent with what we take to be good AR practice. Short-term goals (quick fixes) might be relevant if they are woven into a broader web of continuous change.

These criticisms of Lewin's view of AR do not undermine the basic idea of AR; they only show the limitations in his own deployment of the approach and the rather convenient use made of his concept of short-term change processes by consultants who took advantage of the early prestige of AR to turn organizational development into a profit-making enterprise. In contemporary AR, a major shift away from the Lewinian formulation can be seen in the ways change processes are now characterized. Contemporary formulations emphasize ongoing dialogue a great deal more (Gustavsen, 1992) and cogenerative learning as a vehicle for sustained change (Elden & Levin, 1991).

Kurt Lewin's work had important effect in another area: the field of group dynamics. Group dynamics is a set of methods and praxis strongly shaped by Lewin's focus on creating groups that could withstand the tensions of developmental processes, rather than breaking down as the tensions arose. Among the most famous of these approaches is the T-group technique. The *T* in the name suggests the structure of the group. In this initial form, the outside facilitator plays the key social role in the group, sitting at the top of the T. The facilitator encourages practice by taking on a role of both not being in command and still being present. With such an authority figure present but not operating in the normal authoritarian way, the members of the group are put in a dilemma and forced, occasionally through painful struggles, to come to terms with their own approaches to authority, and eventually to try to make the group work in a new way.

T-group praxis began what became the road to sensitivity groups, providing experiential learning about interpersonal interaction as a path to deeper

personal development. This is a much-criticized approach to human development that involves high risks of creating sustained harm to participants (Filley
& House, 1969). The National Training Laboratory at the University of
Michigan still teaches people group dynamics by means of this methodology,
but with less emphasis on the issues that were central to the initial sensitivity
training model and more on group dynamics and social interaction skills
needed to build teams.

Lewin is also credited with coining a couple of important slogans within
social sciences. They are so widely known and interesting that they bear repe-
tition here: "Nothing is as practical as a good theory" and "The best way to
understand something is to try to change it." These mottos resonate with AR
practitioners because they privilege praxis and value theory only insofar as it
guides praxis well, clearly a position that sets them against conventional social
researchers. In AR, we believe that the way to "test" a theory is to show how it
provides in-depth and thorough understanding of social structures, understanding gained through planned attempts to invoke change in particular
directions. The commitment of the local stakeholders to the change processes
and the resulting appropriate changes are the demonstration of the utility of
the theory.

Lewin's work is a fundamental building block of what today is called AR.
He set the stage for knowledge production based on solving real-life problems.
From the outset, he created a new role for researchers and redefined criteria for
judging the quality of an inquiry process. Lewin shifted the researcher's role
from being a distant observer to involvement in concrete problem solving. The
quality criteria he developed for judging a theory to be good focused on its
ability to support practical problem solving in real-life situations.

THE TAVISTOCK INSTITUTE OF HUMAN RELATIONS

In Great Britain after World War II, rebuilding the industrial base was a
major political goal. During the years of the war, this industrial base had been
severely damaged and national efforts were launched immediately to revitalize
the economy. The Tavistock Institute of Human Relations in London was
called on by the British government to support various parts of this effort.

The Tavistock Institute (called "the Clinic" by its members) was an intellectual environment shaped by psychoanalytic thinking and an action orientation. Its rise to importance began with a pathbreaking study done in the
English coal mines, where the introduction of new mechanized equipment had
not led to the expected increase in productivity. The board overseeing the coal
mines commissioned research on this issue, and Tavistock got the contract.
The resulting, and now famous, study by Trist and Bamforth (1951) shows how
production technology and work organization are linked inextricably. These

authors show that the lack of improved performance can be explained by the incompatibility between the demands created by the technology and what is beneficial for the workers as a group of interacting human beings. Breaking up the work cycle in fragments on each shift caused suboptimization on the shifts and lessened overall productivity. The insight based on Trist and Bamforth (1951) represented a break with the conventional Tayloristic approach to work, where research is always focused on finding the most technically efficient way to organize workers into separate, responsible groups dealing only with a clearly identifiable and bounded element of the production cycle. These insights shaped the emergence of the industrial democracy movement.

Tavistock brought Lewin's work on the concept of natural experiments and AR (Gustavsen, 1992) back from the United States, and Tavistock committed itself to doing direct experiments in work life. The relationship between employers and trade unions in Great Britain was such that it did not allow for experimentation on the organization of industrial work there. However, at this very moment, Einar Thorsrud, a psychologist and former human resource manager of a Norwegian industrial company, was in the process of creating a link to Tavistock. This link eventually led to the hoped-for real-life experiments in industrial democracy, but in Norway rather than in Great Britain.

In cooperation with key Tavistock researchers Eric Trist and Fred Emery, Thorsrud sketched out a Norwegian program very much in line with Lewin's approach (Gustavsen, 1992). The major strategy was to begin several experiments at the same time, all focusing on improving democracy at the shop-floor level. Through what was called the "sociotechnical reorganization" of work, semiautonomous groups were created to provide increased motivation for the workers and to open up participation in decision making at the shop-floor level.

Thorsrud and the Tavistock professionals managed to convince the Norwegian Confederation of Employers and the Trade Union Council to support the Industrial Democracy Project. The first stage of the activity was a European study of industrial democracy in general, focusing on whether representative or participative models of democracy really gave a high degree of employee control over work (Emery & Thorsrud, 1976). Not unexpectedly, the conclusion was that participative approaches to work organization are necessary for increasing industrial democracy.

The Norwegian Industrial Democracy Project was carried out as a set of experiments in different companies engaged in different types of production and located in both rural and urban areas. Of the six field sites in this project, probably only one can now be identified as a long-term success, in the sense of there still being a clear impact on a particular company. The other experiments gave rise to short-term successes, proving that group-based production is both feasible and efficient in industrial settings. These altered work systems clearly outperformed conventional Tayloristic organizational systems.

Three major conceptual schemes emerged through this work. The first is "sociotechnical" thinking, that is, building direct links between technology and work organization. The sociotechnical approach became a design criterion for all interventions. Second, the design of work was done according to a concept called "psychological job demands." Third, by linking sociotechnical thinking with fulfillment of psychological job demands, the idea of "semiautonomous groups" was created. The psychological job demands could be fulfilled if a group of workers took on the responsibility for production. Learning, the needed variation, and self-control could be achieved within such groups. Industrial technology could be reorganized to give greater freedom to workers and to offer greater possibilities for both human and industrial development by linking more jobs together.

We provide some brief examples of the central concepts. The sociotechnical interrelationship argument (meaning "joint optimization") affirms the possibility that the adjustment process can move in either direction, from social organization to technology or vice versa. Given a specific technology to be used, one would have to recruit or train workers with the necessary skills for operating in that technical environment or design the technology with particular kinds of behaviors and group organizational features in mind.

The core principle in sociotechnical design is to make these two adjustments at the same time, seeing technological and organizational design as inseparable elements of the same web of relationships. It is impossible for a worker to operate a lathe unless the worker has skills to understand how to set the piece in the chuck, how to choose the appropriate cutting speed, and how to match the cutting depth. The skill requirement could be further specified, but it is enough to point out that a lathe creates requirements for operational skills. A worker without the necessary skills would certainly be a catastrophe in grinding any product.

A parallel example from the organizational side is a conveyer belt production system. An ordinary work cycle in a car assembly line is usually less than 1 minute. Under these conditions, it is hard to conceive how work can create learning opportunities and personal freedom. Unless the conveyer belt system is totally redesigned, there are few possibilities for organizational change. It is doable to produce cars through group-based work, using long work cycles and providing relatively high degrees of freedom to the workers. Volvo, in both the Kalmar and the Thorslanda factories, created such systems. In both examples, it is obvious that a joint social and technological design created an effective production system.

Psychological job demands turned out to be a central design criterion in the sociotechnical tradition. Emery and Thorsrud (1976) formulate them as in Figure 2.1. The criteria suggested in Figure 2.1 guide the design of work.

Optimum Variety of Tasks Within the Job

A meaningful pattern of tasks that gives to each job the sense of a single overall task

Optimum length of work cycle

Some scope for setting standards of quantity and quality of production and suitable feedback of knowledge about results

The inclusion in the job of some of the auxiliary and preparatory tasks

The task included in the job should entail some degree of care, skill, knowledge, or effort that is worthy of respect in the community

The job should make some perceivable contribution to the utility of the product for the consumer

Provision for interlocking tasks, job rotation, or physical proximity where there is a necessary interdependence of jobs

Provision for interlocking tasks, job rotation, or physical proximity where the individual jobs do not make an obvious perceivable contribution to the utility of the end-product

Where a number of jobs are linked together by interlocking tasks or job rotation, they should be grouped

Provision of channels of communication so that the minimum requirements of the workers can be fed into the design of new jobs at an early stage

Provision of channels of promotion to supervisor rank that are sanctioned by the workers

Figure 2.1   Psychological Job Demands

SOURCE: Emery & Thorsrud (1976), pp. 103–105.

Another important aspect of sociotechnical design is the application of Philip Herbst's (1976) concept of "minimum critical specification." His idea is that we should shape technology and organizational structures in a way that they render as much choice in organizational design as possible. By introducing as few constraints as possible in modes of operating tools and machines or in organizational structures, more freedom can be given to the workers to design their own working conditions. Thus, by specifying the minimum conditions for operation, one can achieve a higher degree of participative control at the shop-floor level. This, of course, also relies on assumptions about both the knowledge and motivations of the workforce.

Another important concept applied in sociotechnical design is Emery and Trist's (1973) "redundancy of functions" and "redundancy of tasks." In a system with redundancy of functions, a worker is able to handle more than one job, whereas in a system designed according to redundancy of tasks, the organization is built on having workers easily substitute for each other because they all have such limited and narrow competencies. Here the aim in following the principle of redundancy of functions is to design work in such a way that every member of the organization is able to handle more than his or her own immediate work task, and this, of course, assumes that workers are quite capable of managing multiple skills sets. If problems occur at any stage in the production system, someone else will be capable of stepping in to help. This creates greater flexibility and potential freedom for the people responsible for production. It also enhances the workers' opportunities for learning because they are trained to manage more than one job. This, in turn, gives them increased understanding of the total production system and their place within it.

Sociotechnical thinking is the major conceptual outcome of the industrial democracy tradition. In Trist and Bamforth's (1951) study of coal mining, interrelationships between technology and work organization were already articulated. This represented a major shift from Tayloristic thinking, where technology and management control are totally dominant, or from human relations thinking, where organizational, social, and psychological factors are considered independent of technological influence (Herzberg, 1966; Maslow, 1943; Mayo, 1933). In these approaches, organization and technology are considered two distinct and separate spheres, whereas the sociotechnical view argues that no technological or social design could be done independently of the other. This, in turn, rests on a more integrated and comprehensive view of workers and work organizations as multidimensional human systems.

Trist (1981) summarizes the relationship between old paradigms of work organizations with new (sociotechnical) paradigms, as shown in Table 2.1.

There is little doubt that sociotechnical thinking has had a major effect on organizing industrial work. Sociotechnical design has involved efforts to break away from Tayloristic modes of organizing work and has been important in pinpointing the interrelationship between technology and social life. It has argued effectively that an exclusive concentration on technological change or on the social organization of work will not create good work systems. Yet the proponents of the sociotechnical approach certainly overestimate its influence (for example, Van Eijnatten's 1993 book with the bombastic title, *The Paradigm That Changed the Work Place*).

The Norwegian Industrial Democracy Project had a strong democratic and idealistic dimension. Participation at the shop-floor level was a value in its own right. Labor leaders and action researchers advocated this position. A remarkable example is the blunt and unconditional statement from one of the lead researchers, Philip Herbst (1976), that democratizing workplaces is the first step to enhancing democracy in society at large. This ideological element

Table 2.1   Old and New Paradigms of Work Organization

Old Paradigm (Scientific Management)	New Paradigm (Sociotechnical Design)
The technological imperative	Joint optimization
Man as an extension of the machine	Man as complementary to the machine
Man as an expendable spare part	Man as a resource to be developed
Maximum task breakdown, simple narrow skills	Optimum task grouping, multiple broad skills
External controls (supervisors, specialist staff)	Internal controls (self-regulating subsystems, procedures)
Tall organization chart, autocratic style	Flat organization chart, participative style
Competition, gamesmanship	Collaboration, collegiality
Organization's purposes only	Members' and society's purposes
Alienation	Commitment
Low risk taking	Innovation

SOURCE: Trist (1981), p. 42.

gradually dissipated over the years in Norway and was also lost from view in most of the process of diffusion of the ideas beyond Norway.

It is important to note that the ideas from the Industrial Democracy Project did not immediately spread in Norway. To the contrary, the ideas were treated as interesting, but most of Norwegian industry was not willing to act on them. Initially, these ideas had more effect outside the country. Only in a longer time perspective is it possible to identify how the Democracy Project gradually impacted Norwegian production systems.

THE DIFFUSION ROUTE: FIRST EAST AND THEN WEST

The core ideas in industrial democracy—semiautonomous working groups and work designed according to psychological demands—were picked up by key industrial enterprises in Sweden. Volvo, Saab-Scania, and Alfa Laval saw the potential in these ideas and soon redesigned some of their production systems around these concepts. The Saab engine assembly plant in Skøvde and the Volvo car assembly factory in Kalmar soon won international reputations for their ingenious ways of redesigning work. But efficiency was emphasized in praising and justifying these projects, and the ideas about the democratization of work as a goal in itself were left out. An organization, *PA rådet,* that emerged from the ranks of the Swedish Confederation of Employers, became the leading change agent working near the border between AR-based approaches and conventional consulting. It did a respectable job of communicating the ideas and practices and convincing Swedish industry to take on ideas produced through the Industrial Democracy Project. But one consequence was that industrial democracy gained a reputation in industry more as an efficient way of organizing work in assembly line production than as the path to a more just system. It outdid to a certain degree conventional Fordist ways of organizing work in economic terms, but the motivation that led to its creation involved a broader social change program than this.

The transfer of sociotechnical thinking to the North American continent was almost equally fast. Louis Davis, a professor at the University of California in Los Angeles (UCLA), picked up the ideas and soon set up a teaching and consultation program in sociotechnical design (Davis & Taylor, 1972). Davis's thinking was completely separated from any ideological connection to the value of democracy in itself. Instead, sociotechnical design was converted into a design tool for high-performance industrial production. The design concept focused on joint optimization of technology and social systems, indicating that as the only way to generate a really effective production system to properly match technology and people.

Morten Levin participated in a workshop held by the UCLA group in 1980. The UCLA group organized a 14-day training program in Toronto, bringing together people both from Canada and the United States. Levin was amazed to learn that the social system dimensions of work were described and analyzed according to Talcott Parsons's (1951) positivist pattern variables. Because the Parsonian model is one of the most abstract and nonbehavioral constructions in the field of role theory, it was a singularly inappropriate bridge between technology and social systems analysis. More fruitful was the use of social psychological models and analysis of psychological job demands, but, even then, Levin noticed that the joint optimization of technology and work was simply ignored as a concept. As an interesting coincidence and perhaps relevant, Levin noticed that a union-busting firm also was running a 14-day workshop at the same hotel to train managers how to keep the unions out of their companies. Clearly these counterposed training programs highlighted the difference in the political and economic context between Scandinavia and North America.

In the Scandinavian context, union busting is an inconceivable strategy for running any business. The change projects centering on Scandinavian work life have almost always been joint ventures between trade unions and management. Thus, the lack of attention to many of the internal social justice dimensions of sociotechnical systems work in North America appears to reflect clearly the broader, more adversarial political economy of industry there.

The industrial democracy thinking also inspired other national movements. Japan was looking for ways to organize its industrial production that would secure both high productivity and excellent quality. Two U.S. scholars who specialized in quality control, J. M. Juran (1980) and W. E. Deming (1983), played an important role in the Japanese reindustrialization process. Their models for obtaining quality production were easily picked up by Japanese companies. In fact, the Japanese were much more receptive to them than were their U.S. counterparts. "American" ideas (even though some were imported from Great Britain and Scandinavia) helped make the Japanese production miracle work. This story might appear to be a sideline but, in fact, it runs parallel to the industrial democracy movement. The central themes of industrial democracy found fertile ground in Japan because collective work had a strong cultural base in Japan and the ideas of groups taking on joint problem-solving and operational responsibility were easily picked up.

In Japan, these activities first appeared in the form of quality circles, problem-solving groups created to handle emergent issues in the production system (Ishikawa, 1976). The aim was to have workers and engineers work together to solve production problems. These quality circles were mostly organized separately from daily work routines. The groups often met on unpaid time in the evenings, working for free to solve company problems. In the Japanese cultural context, this made sense. Later, new concepts of production control, such as *Kanban* (the Toyota system of production management; see Monden, 1983) and "just-in-time" (production without unnecessary waste and temporary storage; see Womack et al., 1990) demanded a different approach to the organization of work. A high degree of autonomy and local responsibility, combined with the ability to learn ways to improve performance systematically, became a core element in the mode of organization. These efforts were in line with the major sociotechnical design principles emanating from the industrial democracy tradition. Thus the overall diffusion route was complex and surprising, from Great Britain to Norway to Sweden, then to the United States, Japan, and finally worldwide.

The diffusion route is itself an interesting phenomenon because research networks also play an important role in this process. The diffusion to Sweden and then subsequently to the United States was made possible by communication between researchers. Part of the mission of academics is to work and play with ideas. Though this does not always happen, in the case of industrial democracy, ideas created within academic circles soon gained a foothold in industrial praxis. In the early phases of the Norwegian Industrial Democracy Project, this effort was located at the Norwegian Institute of Technology (later renamed the Norwegian University of Science and Technology) in Trondheim, creating a locus for links to the international scholarly networks. Tavistock, on the other hand, was not a university-based institution, but it had a high profile among work researchers interested in organizational change, and thus was well known internationally. And the researchers at Tavistock communicated widely through intellectual networks as well, which facilitated the fairly rapid diffusion of sociotechnical ideas in academic contexts.

But it makes no sense to overestimate the academic role in this process. Certainly, academics did not "sell" these ideas and practices to the private and public sector. Rather, the widespread proliferation of this thinking must ultimately be attributed to the success of the design principles grounded in industrial democracy in shaping effective and profitable production systems. That is, the ideas diffused because they "worked" and met strongly felt social needs.

The sociotechnical perspective gradually developed into a broader perspective on participation. The next generation of work researchers changed from what Elden (1979) identified as the "sleeping bag generation" (the experts who came to town, told people what to do, and left) to the later generation of researchers who understood their role as providing long-term support for local companies' ability to manage change processes increasingly by themselves. This movement toward greater in-company participation created an interesting democratic paradox. In the first, expert-driven phase, democracy was an explicitly stated value. But as the practice of change moved in the direction of increasingly self-managed change processes, the focus on democracy as a concept and a value evaporated while the practices themselves were more collaborative.

This change in general approach to action research in industry also created a movement away from a theoretical position based on sociotechnical thinking to a focus on mutual learning or discourses between the organizations' problem owners and the involved researchers. This relationship was modeled in two ways. One was built on an operationalization of Habermas's (1984) ethics of ideal speech. Bjørn Gustavsen (1985, 1992), in particular, has published extensively about how development work can be understood as discourses among equal participants (members of the organization and researchers). Other key figures in this mode of working are Øyvind Pålshaugen (1998) and Per Engelstad (Gustavsen & Engelstad, 1986). The main emphasis in this work was on constructing dialogues that enabled participants to create a language describing their own life world, a language that subsequently would lead to organizational change.

A different take on the discursive mode of doing action research was presented by Elden and Levin (1991) in the early 1990s. In this work, the research process is conceptualized as a mutual learning process involving problem owners and researchers, where their diversity and differences are considered as major constituting factors needed for the knowledge generation process. The participants have different power positions, just as the power of the researchers is different from that held by the local problem owners. In this approach, action research emerges from an ongoing process of experimentation and reflection, in which mutual learning is the driving process both for sustainable change and for knowledge generation.

THE INTELLECTUAL CONTENT OF THE INDUSTRIAL DEMOCRACY TRADITION

The major reason for attaching the label "industrial democracy" to the tradition starting with AR efforts in the United States, intellectually extended during the Tavistock period, and fully emerging in the Norwegian Industrial Democracy Project is that all these approaches sustain a central focus on shaping alternatives to conventional hierarchical organizations. As noted earlier, only a modest element within all this activity really claims democracy as a major concern, but still, it does not make sense to overlook the participatory dimensions of these approaches to organizational change even when they have not been connected to the democratization of ownership.

Industrial democracy focused on the ways research results manifested through redesigned organizations would improve the participants' ability to control their own situations. Industrial democracy also began the first reflections about designing research processes that redefined the relationship between participants and researchers toward a much greater degree of mutuality. The second generation of research practice within the Norwegian Industrial Democracy Project opened up even greater possibilities for participant control (Elden, 1979).

Carole Pateman's (1970) book, *Participation and Democratic Theory*, forcefully presented the argument for democracy in organizational settings, and this book played a major role in creating a theoretical backdrop for participatory industrial democracy efforts. Pateman drew a genealogy from Rousseau's and Mill's thinking to the modern debate on democracy at the shop-floor level. Her work offers a well-argued model of democracy that takes as a point of departure the ability of workers to control their own work situations. In her argument, immediate control over the work situation replaces numerical (that is, representative) models of democracy as the key to shaping a successful democratic society. Pateman did not discuss the relationship between representative and participative democracy, an issue that soon emerged as a vital point in the European debate on how to promote democracy in work organizations.

Individual influence through direct participation soon confronted collective power created through systems of workplace representation, an issue that greatly concerned trade unions. This debate soon focused on the degree to which trade union power was undermined by individual and direct control over the immediate working conditions and it is still a vital question in the discourse on industrial democracy (see Chapter 17, "Action Research, Participation, and Democratization").

Despite this, the strongly idealistic democratic content of the first decade of the industrial democracy tradition within AR gradually lost ground. Initially, the dominant argument was that democracy was an ideological imperative. It was gradually replaced by pragmatic arguments that softened the questions regarding political economy that industrial democracy raises. In this process, the rhetoric shifted from a focus on democracy to an emphasis on empowerment, from participation as the key to democracy to participation as a necessary move to motivate workers to shape a more effective, efficient (and, perhaps, profitable) organization.

Indeed, it seems to us that *empowerment* is a term that substitutes for the more ambitious and clearer concepts of participation and democracy. We think the language of empowerment, which has inevitably hierarchical dimensions, represents a step backward, and certainly a step away from the concepts that began the industrial democracy movement. This point is illustrated in one of the standard textbooks on organizational development (Cummings & Worley, 2001), where empowerment, used as an ill-defined concept, was substituted for democracy. The first edition, published in 1975, took a stronger position, but by 2001, it had weakened greatly.

Another dimension of the link between industrial democracy and the early work of Kurt Lewin is reliance on an overly simple change model (unfreezing-change-freezing) and his notions about the experimental design of change processes. Both elements were prominent in the early development of the industrial democracy tradition in AR. Experimental design drawn from the Lewinian tradition became the way ideas were acted on. The researchers made their analyses, recommended new organizational designs, and structured processes by which changes were implemented. The core idea was to make the changes and then let the organization develop a stable state incorporating the changes. Consultation with the local participants was minimal.

This remained the "expert" model in action and did not evolve into AR as we understand it now. In the early stages, researchers within the tradition of industrial democracy played a clear-cut expert role. They made their analysis of a situation in the specific context, and they worked out their recommendations for a new design. The next step in their activity was to have these ideas implemented in a way that involved workers who were affected by the changes. In this way, the researchers created an experimental situation in a natural setting to test whether their ideas were fruitful or not. They did not become collaborative researchers in any broader sense, however.

In the contemporary version of this approach, a lot of emphasis is put on involving employees in the change processes. Usually, the participation is enabled through different types of conferences where participants can exercise influence over the development of the actual process. "Search conferences" (Emery, 1982, 1998) are a well-developed tool, and a somewhat different approach named "dialogue conferences" has a stronghold in Scandinavia (Gustavsen, 1992; Pålshaugen, 1998).

"Southern" PAR, Labor Organizing, Community Organizing, and Civil Rights

A second major strand in the historical development of AR is another hetero-geneous combination of democratizing efforts that take place under conditions of overt oppression. Just as the industrial democracy movement is not a single activity, these "liberationist" approaches exhibit many internal differences in politics, aims, and methods—too many for us to document here. Rather our aim is to be sure readers are aware of these major approaches and some of the most prominent varieties.

Many of the activities discussed here antedate the terms *Southern participatory action research* (PAR), *Participatory Research,* and *Participatory Community Development,* and this is an important element in understanding how they have developed. These approaches to AR emerged initially out of the conditions created by some of the most undemocratic situations humans have created: massive colonial exploitation of Africa, Latin America, and Southeast Asia, the genocide/ethnocide of American Indians, the impoverishing of generations of Europeans who immigrated widely, and the enslaving of Africans in the West. All of these conditions gave rise to circumstances of highly institutionalized and consolidated inequality, exploitation, and human misery. The advent of inde-pendence movements, the civil rights movements in various parts of the world, and general attempts to achieve some world standards for basic human rights seemed to promise potential solutions to these long-term evils.

Unfortunately, decolonization has been followed by recolonization in the form of sustained inequalities carried over from the colonial period and the creation of new inequalities through globalization and what has been called the "development of underdevelopment" (Gunder Frank, 1970) that has made it clear that it is not colonialism but endemic structures of advanced capitalism that cause these inequalities to persist.

It seems to us that the realization that the struggle for equality had to take on a new shape emerged with exceptional vigor with the ferment that finally exploded in the events of 1968.[2] From that point on, many of the strands of this struggle against structural inequality came to be known under the rubrics of Southern PAR, Participatory Research, and the civil rights movement. The loci for this work have been worldwide: rural communities and urban slums in poor countries, rural communities and urban slums and small towns in the industrialized "North." The focus has been on oppressed categories of people: the landless, women, subjects of racism and genocide, the disabled, the elderly, the orphaned, the homeless, and many others.

No single thread of argument, analysis, or method runs through all the approaches in this arena, but certain frameworks are found frequently. Much of the thinking has been stimulated by the literature of revolution and rebellion, by the organizing movements of trade unionists, the community organizing strategies of adult educators and organizers, liberation theology and ecumenical Catholic Action, and the feminist movements. Given the complexity and diversity of the participants, a single historical genealogy is impossible for us to create. Rather we will simply provide a few exemplars to guide the reader onward.

THE "SOUTH"

So vast an area is obviously more heterogeneous than any characterization we can make of it. The core thematic unity is massive, structured inequality and class-related violence in both rural and urban areas. In this approach to AR, there can be no presumption of a disposition to share power or to see to the welfare of the poor and marginalized. These regimes are financed by the exploitation of the poor, and participatory schemes are understood to be attempts to undermine authoritarian regime control systems. Thus AR is an inherently political activity with the attendant dangers and patterns of division.

To commit to AR in these circumstances is to affirm solidarity with the oppressed and to declare an adversarial role toward the powers that be. As a result, in this kind of AR, the holders of power themselves are rarely included. Much of the activity—be it education, organizing, mobilizing—involves building structures and confidence among the poor to enable them to confront the powerful in sufficient numbers and with clear enough plans so that they have some likelihood of success. This work is always risky because the AR practitioner can be seen as an *agent provocateur*.

These approaches to AR differ, not in the issues they address, but in the strategies they use for confronting or "speaking the truth to power." Paolo Freire's "conscientization" (1970) relies on adult education strategies of dialogue and group analysis of oppressive conditions coupled with learning the power of changing ideas and words to reveal rather than to hide oppression. The stakeholders are moved from passive to active voice, from a sense of powerlessness and worthlessness to an understanding that is designed to lead to confronting power through redescribing society as it is experienced by the downtrodden rather than as it is said to be by the beneficiaries of their suffering. And, in Freire's approach, the oppressed ultimately must also liberate their oppressors from the inhumanity of the systems from which they benefit.

In many situations, these approaches and allied ones practiced by Orlando Fals Borda and many promoters of community action involve trying to take on some kind of "natural" coalition of stakeholders—a squatter community, a union, a religious group, a cooperative, and so on—and build its strength and reach. In other situations, the work involves creating the conditions through adult education, public projects, and so on that bring people together so that they can be organized and an AR process of self-reflection, social critique, and the design of agendas for change can take place. In other situations, such as those where Participatory Rural Appraisal is practiced (Chambers, 1997), the external agents arrive with a set of techniques that promote multilateral dialogues among community or organization members, and the results of these dialogues lead to action planning and change efforts.

In the poor countries of the South, the governments are often adversaries of these efforts but multilateral agencies or nongovernmental organizations may be on the scene helping local people to push back against their governments. However, it is not unusual for the powerful outsiders to become as much a part of the problem as a part of the solution.

THE "SOUTH" IN THE "NORTH"

Were the South only in the South, the world would not be as unequal. This kind of AR is as much at home in the North as anywhere, because the structured inequalities of capitalism see to it that a great majority of the people in the wealthiest countries in the world live in misery. (The "South" also refers to poverty zones in the North; it is a code word for poverty and disempowerment.) As a result, there has been significant AR activity in the United States in Appalachia (Belenky, Bond, & Weinstock, 1997; Gaventa, 1982; Hinsdale, Lewis, & Waller, 1995; Horton, 1990), in the deindustrialized areas of the Northeast (Reardon, 1997; Schafft & Greenwood, 2003), and in urban slums all over (Benson, Harkavy, & Puckett, 2000). These activities are a complex mixture of rural development efforts, community organizing, labor organizing, intercommunity networking and coalition building, civil rights activism, feminism, and advocacy for those who fall below the poverty line.

For some, like Myles Horton, who founded the Highlander Research and Education Center in Tennessee, the people had the power but did not know or believe it. Horton thus operated by gathering people together and encouraging them to share their problems and their analyses. His contribution was to facilitate the conversations, add his experiences to the mix, and encourage people to design their own actions. He felt that he would not "organize" people because they were capable of organizing themselves when given a little support. Others working in the same area have had a more interventionist framework and have engaged in purposely goal-driven efforts (Belenky, Bond, & Weinstock, 1997; Maguire, 1994, 1996).

Other AR practitioners have decided to "dig where they stand" and have gone to work in the communities immediately around them. Such is the case of the Center for Community Partnerships at the University of Pennsylvania, where Ira Harkavy, John Puckett, Lee Benson, and others over decades have moved the University of Pennsylvania into a more collaborative and supportive relationship with the West Philadelphia community, a notorious slum (Benson, Harkavy, & Puckett, 2000). Others have been called into action by their university being held accountable to its "land grant mission" to serve the people of the state they are located in. This is how the East St. Louis redevelopment project came about (Reardon, 1997). Still others have focused attention on those who fall through the many holes in the welfare system—the homeless, the injection drug users, sex workers, the elderly, the orphaned. By building the capacity and confidence of such groups through AR, some successes have been achieved (Lather, 1991; McIntyre, 2004; Maguire, 1994, 1996). Parallel activities emerged in Scandinavia, especially with a support of the trade union education organizations.

These approaches share certain elements, despite their significant differences. Their activities are understood to be first and foremost political activities. They are also willing to be directive, to take action in order to provoke a response among the poor and passive. They place a strong emphasis on building community and solidarity among the stakeholders to prepare them to confront the powerful and oppressive. And their aim is to equalize power relations and to redistribute resources from the rich to the poor.

Human Inquiry and Cooperative Inquiry

Human inquiry or cooperative inquiry approaches can be traced back to a research group formed in London in 1977. The New Paradigm Research Group had the stated goal of developing alternatives to conventional social science approaches that do better justice to the humanity of the participants. (Reason & Rowan, 1981). This group was set up by John Heron, Peter Reason, and John Rowan, and they met every 3 weeks for 3 years. The New Paradigm group probably had a clearer picture of what they wanted to get away from than a clear vision of where they would go. In fact, an interesting and strong value in those research circles has been openness to new ideas and a lived understanding of being "on the road" to create alternative research to the dominating orthodoxy. A core value focus for this group was to do research *with* people instead of *on* people. The initial framing was the interest in shaping "humanness" in research. Participation became a vital element, since the researchers' engagement converted them into insiders in the ongoing knowledge generation processes.

Four researchers have been dominant in human inquiry or cooperative inquiry. First and foremost, there is Peter Reason. He has authored or coauthored many of the significant books in this strand of thinking. His research center at University of Bath has been the academic stronghold in this tradition. At Bath, Reason has managed both to set up a center for action research and to combine that with training future practitioners both at master's and Ph.D. levels. Together with Hilary Bradbury, Reason undertook the huge effort to edit a *Handbook of Action Research* (Reason & Bradbury, 2001a) and managed to convince Sage Publications to publish the *Journal of Action Research*, which, together with *Systemic Practice and Action Research* and *Concepts and Transformation* (now the *International Journal of Action Research*), are the leading journals in AR.

Human inquiry is a mode of doing research in which the researcher gradually involves him- or herself in the research process, connecting emotional and tacit insights to the conventional explicit reflections that are the conventional point of departure. Through engaging all stakeholders in the inquiry, the distinctions between outsiders and insiders are gradually wiped out. The Bath group has done a lot of research in the area of health care; doctors and nurses have been the prime cooperative partners. The work with medical professions was, in fact, the first arena where they worked. These steps were taken together with the British Postgraduate Medical Federation linked to the University of London.

The initial members of the group have managed to stay together while still following independent intellectual itineraries. John Heron has played an important role both through his practice and his publications. The book *Co-operative Inquiry* (Heron, 1996) includes a particularly thorough discussion of the epistemological foundations of his mode of doing participative research. On the American continent, William Torbert (1991, 2001) has been a key figure, and he brings an even stronger focus on personal and emotional aspects of human inquiry.

An important strength of this tradition is its openness to other modes of thinking within AR and the ability to integrate new ideas into the body of knowledge that characterizes human inquiry. These practitioners have always been visible at international conferences on AR and at the special interest group meetings at the U.S.-based Academy of Management annual meetings.

Conclusions

This partial history of AR provides the background for some of the perspectives that have influenced the writing of this book. Other histories underlie other AR practices, and they are given some attention in Parts 2 and 3 of this book, but we repeat that AR cannot be described and analyzed as a unified development. It is better understood as a field in which there are many competing strands of thinking that historically have been developed quite independently. In our account of the history of AR, we have included three different approaches. Industrial AR received the dominating place simply because that is where the authors come from. Southern PAR and similarly political approaches are important because this strand of activity probably is the biggest, both in terms of engaging broad cadres of participants but also because it deals with pertinent and highly conflictive social problems. Human inquiry or cooperative inquiry shows how AR can support knowledge creation by bringing explicit, tacit, and emotional knowledge together to improve organizations and the welfare of individuals.

We have now said enough to have anchored our approach in a set of relevant institutional and historical contexts, but the main "project" of this book is to present where we hope AR will go, not merely to recount where it has been.

Notes

1. "Taylorism" refers to the industrial organization approach that involves the maximum division of labor in production through the division of tasks into narrow specialties that are integrated by senior management and production engineers who do all the design and thinking. It is called Taylorism because the author who most clearly captured and promoted the practice of what he called "scientific management" was Frederick Winslow Taylor (1911).

2. See, for example, Fals Borda (1969).

3

Action Research Cases From Practice

The Stories of Stongfjorden, Mondragón, and Programs for Employment and Workplace Systems at Cornell University

This chapter provides three evocations of action research (AR) processes: one in a small community, another in a group of industrial organizations, and the last at a major university. These portraits precede the more abstract and detailed discussion of AR that follow in Part 2. In narrating these cases, our aim is to convey the complexity, challenges, and excitement of doing AR. It is also important to show that even projects that fail to reach desired action goals create rich learning opportunities. The three cases present AR in very different contexts to emphasize our point about the heterogeneity of AR situations. The Stongfjorden project was aimed at supporting local community development in a small rural community in Norway, whereas the work in Mondragón was focused on organizational problems in industrial cooperatives in the Spanish Basque Country. The work at Cornell was aimed at reforming the relationship between research and extension in the School of Industrial and Labor Relations.

All cases are based on the authors' longtime involvement in these local settings. AR is about specific action-reflection processes in particular contexts, so the cases are an appropriate starting point. We emphasize how projects develop and change over time and how the reflection processes involved follow, to different degrees, the unique patterns of the emerging projects. We also use these cases to alert readers to AR's strong emphasis on case narratives in all AR approaches.

Stongfjorden: Village Development in Western Norway

Sailing south along the Norwegian coast and passing the westernmost reach of the mainland, one sees a narrow, short fjord reaching 3 miles inland. Stongfjorden is surrounded by low mountains cascading straight down to the water. At the shoreline, some scattered houses can be seen, along with an industrial building, a small school, a grocery store, a tennis court, and a waterfall, partly dried up by the hydropower plant that channels the water into turbines. Small farms encircle the fjord. In all, 217 people inhabit this village, most of them over the age of 40.

The village was isolated from inland Norway until the early 1960s. Although a road linked residents to a community center, besides that, going on the main road required the use of various ferries. Sea-based communication was dominant, but in the mid-1960s the inhabitants decided to improve their road links, and through collective action they built several miles of road over difficult mountain terrain, linking the village to the mainland highway system. The "people's road," as it was named, illustrates the community's solidarity and ability to solve problems of common interest. This activity caught national attention as an illustration of how a small community could reverse public decisions simply by making things happen on its own.

Stongfjorden was "discovered" by an aristocratic Englishman who was salmon fishing there in the late 19th century. One day in early summer, this man, who also was the chairman of the board of British Aluminum, was impressed by the sight of the local waterfall found at the base of the fjord. As an industrial entrepreneur, he immediately saw an energy potential, and the process leading to the creation of the first aluminum smelter in Norway began. He bought the rights to use the waterfall, built a hydroelectric power station, and started on the construction of the aluminum smelter. The power station was finished in 1908, and the smelter was completed in 1913. A company town was created, on the model of English industrial communities. A tennis court nicely completed the picture of a class-divided town. Management built their houses on the sunny side of the fjord, whereas the workers' quarters rested in the shadows. Infrastructure, such as schools, doctors, and technical support, was created by the company, and soon the village had one of the best public schools and health care systems in the whole of western Norway.

The industrialization of Stongfjorden met with several obstacles. The first challenge came during the first winter the smelter was in operation. The waterfall did not deliver enough power to keep the smelter going. Consequently, the first high-voltage transport line was constructed to link the community to the mainland power distribution system. The smelter produced aluminum until the end of World War II. The end of the war also meant the closing of the aluminum smelter, and the workers were offered jobs in a smelter some 300 miles north of Stongfjorden. There is a very moving and powerful story of how families left the village on the same boat to settle and work at this new aluminum smelter. Some years later, even after a local knife producer took over the facilities and started production of knives and cutlery for home use and the food processing industry, the downturn of the fortunes of Stongfjorden had already begun. Great numbers of industrial jobs were lost, and houses and public facilities in the village deteriorated. In many ways, the village seemed to be preparing for its own funeral as the social structure dissolved.

In late 1970s, the Norwegian Ministry for Environmental Protection and Land Use launched a program to support municipal activities aimed at increasing local participation in and control over community affairs. Towns, neighborhoods, or municipalities could apply to the program. A group of "burning souls" (Philips, 1988), under the leadership of a very capable woman, applied for money through this program. This local task force sent in the application without following the formal procedure of sending it through the municipal government. Even so, Stongfjorden was accepted as one of 60 sites that participated in this revitalization program.

As outside consultants, Morten Levin and a group of collaborators from Trondheim were linked up with this task force in Stongfjorden through the administrator of the national program. Sociologists Levin and Tore Nilssen made up the AR team leaders and worked with Ivar Brokhaug as the research professionals. In addition, two students were engaged the first year. The project involved the Department of Organization and Work Life Science and the Institute for Social Research in Industry at the Norwegian University of Science and Technology.

Getting to Stongfjorden from the office location in Trondheim was complicated. Flying there required the use of at least three different planes and the rental of a car. The time spent in air transport matched the 12 hours spent driving the whole distance, but the driving also involved crossing three mountain passes and driving on roads cut in the steep slopes that drop straight into the fjords. At first the team flew in, but later they turned to cars as the major form of transportation.

The first meeting with the task force was productive. Task force members presented their view of the situation and articulated their interest in preserving their home village. The team suggested running a search conference (see Chapter 9, "Pragmatic Action Research") to initiate the development process. The team had several reasons for suggesting the search conference as the first move. At that time, the team was ideologically committed to this kind of consensus model for local community development. The team also saw a need to mobilize the village as broadly as possible, and believed that a development effort would never succeed if only a handful of people became involved. It was easy to convince the task force that a search conference was a good idea.

Planning the conference brought us back to the community a couple of times over the next 1 1/2 months. In planning the conference, the team wanted to get acquainted with as many of the potential participants as possible, and, at the same time, we wanted to convey what a search conference was. A new task force was established, incorporating more people than the original applicants for the grant. The search conference staff consisted of three researchers from Morten Levin's home institution and one from the National Institute for City and Regional Planning, an overstaffed situation that inadvertently led to internal staff conflicts. The person running the conference refused to cooperate with other staff members. Still, the search conference worked out very well, which tells us a lot about the robustness of the design itself.

Several new task groups were formed. One took on the responsibility of building new road lights, another focused attention on constructing a new sheltered harbor for small craft. The third group planned the reconstruction of houses and roads. One of the old houses, formerly inhabited by several working-class families, was given to the local activists, and the task force organized the work to restore it and then used it for community purposes. A kindergarten was established, and a workshop for textile production was created.

In the first year after the search conference, we organized two follow-up conferences. The goal was for the participants in the different task forces to present their work and thereby share possibilities, successes, and problems with the other participants. Thus, the follow-up meetings functioned as tools for sustaining the group elements of the developmental effort, encouraged collective reflection, and supported mutual learning between researchers and activists. In addition, the follow-up meetings forced the task forces to make clear commitments to their own aims and to revise their plans for further activities. These follow-up meetings were invaluable in creating feedback loops. It was advantageous to start a reflection process on the previously stated goals and to identify what had been achieved and what remained to be done.

The task forces generally were quite successful in achieving their goals. The group aiming at rebuilding the road lighting made a series of smart moves in applying for municipal, county, and power company money. Most of the expenses for the lighting hardware were covered by these funds, whereas the work itself was done collectively. This built on a strong tradition of collective work in Stongfjorden that relates to the Norwegian concept of *dugnad*, which is inherited from early farming and fishing cultures where people had to cooperate to resolve issues of mutual interest that could not be dealt with in households alone. In the beginning, the work was done fast and effectively, with good support from many people. The task turned out to be quite demanding, involving a lot of individual commitment, and, as time passed, the group was gradually reduced to just a few of the original "burning souls."

Other tasks were dealt with quickly. The tennis court, a symbol of former wealth, was soon fixed up. A few people played tennis there, but mostly it was used as a children's play area. The clean-up activities were generally very successful. Roads and houses were restored, and the general look of the village was improved.

One task that did not turn out to be so successful was the construction of a harbor for small craft. To be able to finance it, the task force had to establish a nonprofit company. Everyone who wanted a slip for a boat had to pay the money up front. The task force then signed a contract with an entrepreneur, but this person was unable to deliver the harbor. His machines were not suitable for the work, and he could not finish the job without buying new equipment. Because he was living in the village, this created tension. Some thought the entrepreneur had cheated the boat owners, but others saw and understood his miscalculations. The task force wanted to take the matter to court, but the problem was settled before it came to that.

The team continued our work in the community until 1986. In the later stages of the process, activity focused more on entrepreneurial efforts and on relationships with political and administrative bodies of the municipalities. The central local woman who had moved the project along over the years gradually burned out. She had devoted enormous time and energy to it, but because she felt her energy was no longer sufficient, leadership was handed over to a very creative local entrepreneur. He initiated a fishing venture centering on marine crawfish, developing the technology and a fishing strategy and creating a market. He started building high-tech wooden boats using state-of-the-art gluing and mantling techniques. He started farming black grouse. In addition, he successfully created a tourism business, running his own campground and renting out several cabins.

Every activity was high risk, but always with the promise of making a lot of money. Through the project, the local entrepreneur developed the marketing ability and initiated cooperation with other campgrounds in the neighborhood to enable the development of a foothold in the German market. To a high degree, this turned out to be a successful activity. Over the later years of the project, we cooperated closely with him, and we were kept informed about his entrepreneurial work, but we did not become directly involved in it.

Another major issue we were involved in over the last year of the project was an effort by the village to convince the municipal government to support the reconstruction of roads and the public quay in Stongfjorden. The local activists had long been interested in rebuilding the public quay (a long, large platform along which many boats tie up) in the fjord because the old quay had almost fallen down, and there was no money available for building a new one.

The municipal government resisted spending money on this refurbishing project, arguing that there would not be enough traffic over the quay to make it profitable. Ship berthing had been reduced drastically over those years, a process that the municipal administration felt was caused by a structural transportation change from ships to trucks. The Strongfjorden people argued that a reduction of transportation volume at the quay came about because the quay itself was in such bad shape. Thus, they were stalemated.

Local people had contacted the Ministry of Environment for help and had received all kinds of support. Through the contact person in the ministry, the team was asked to help the local group negotiate a solution with the municipal authorities. The team traveled to the community, set up meetings with the municipal administration, and ran roughshod over them because we had the requisite skills in framing arguments and the explicit support of the ministry. The money was granted, and the quay was refurbished. After this, our relationship with the local community slowly wound down. The grants from the ministry ceased, and we pulled out after 3 ½ years in Strongfjorden.

Over time, the researchers' roles had shifted a great deal. The researchers started as facilitators for the fairly narrow task of running a search conference, and we worked on that for some months. As the project shifted, the roles changed to supporting particular efforts and to encouraging collective reflection on the ongoing activity. During this period, the team also brought in two students both to support the activity and to give them an opportunity to learn about AR. Through their work, the researchers were able to describe and analyze the social structure of the village, learning about the 13 different local missionary groups consisting of women knitting for a Christmas auction, thereby making money for missionary work domestically and abroad. The team also learned about family structures, kin relationships, and how the inhabitants were linked through other kinds of networks. This middle phase involved a lot of analytical work, though that was coupled with facilitating the ongoing change activity. During this period, the researchers also took on the task of running a search conference for the local knife factory. This company was clearly the dominant employer in the municipality, and the search aimed to develop new markets for knife-related products. This was a reasonably successful activity, even though no great economic market breakthrough emerged for the company.

In the later part of our work, the researchers took on a much more direct and active role. We played the activist role and nearly dominated local activity in handling external interest groups. This was an unpleasant role, and involved many serious ethical questions. In retrospect, the researchers should never have taken on the power role in the negotiations with the municipal government. The team entered the scene as resourceful "friendly outsiders" (see Chapter 8) able to mobilize our professional networks to support the Strongfjorden activists. The researchers should have taken on a conflict-handling role in at least an initial effort to make the conflicting parties find solutions by themselves.

In Stongfjorden, the researchers had a very powerful partner in the "burning souls." Some of these individuals burned out in the process, but mostly they stayed through the whole project. These people, four men and one woman, had the inner strength and ability to perform concentrated work on important goals. This group operated as a fairly closed unit. Only the campground entrepreneur and the local knife factory manager later entered that group. The manager was active for a couple of years, but when his company demanded greater attention, he dropped out. The entrepreneur became the lead person during the later phase of our engagement. Although we occasionally had contact with other members of the local community, these persons never became central and key activists. Still, it seems reasonable to believe that the core group had the backing of a large proportion of the village population. When *dugnad* was called for, people showed up.

Over the course of the project, several different arenas for communication were constructed. The researchers started with the search conference. This activity was followed up by a series of meetings in which stock taking and collective reflections on the process development were central. These meetings created knowledge both for the local people on reengineering their activity to reach desired goals better and for the outside researchers on understanding more about the challenges in local community development.

Two issues became cornerstones in our intellectual research efforts. The first major question was related to understanding the complex social structure. The team was struck by how fast information spread in the community. Basically, the whole village knew everything, even though they were sure that they had communicated with only a few people. The initial research question then focused on the integrating factors in the social structure. Through the students' work, the researchers eventually spotted the effect of the 13 missionary clubs, the choir, the boat harbor, and all kitchen table coffee-drinking groups. These closely nested networks created the possibility for the very efficient distribution of information. These findings were reported in the students' work.

The most important published research resulting from this work focused on understanding why certain inhabitants become "burning souls." How could it be explained that a person gets up from in front of the TV set and takes on the workload and the responsibility for leading local development activity? The initial framing of this question was done during the work in Stongfjorden. Several discussions with local activists created some preliminary understanding of the mobilization question. This preliminary insight shaped the research question for a master's thesis (by one of the students) focusing on the early phases of local community development. Eventually this work was published by Morten Levin (1988) under the title *Local Mobilization.*

Mondragón: Organizational Problems in Industrial Cooperatives

The Mondragón Cooperatives in Spain are one of the most successful examples of industrial democracy anywhere and are the subject of worldwide attention and debate. As a group of labor-managed businesses, the cooperatives have been at the center of a great deal of debate focusing on the ability of democratic organizations to compete successfully in advanced capitalist societies (Bradley & Gelb, 1983; Kasmir, 1996; Thomas & Logan, 1982; Whyte & Whyte, 1991). The project described briefly here involved 4 years of AR by a team drawn from the cooperatives and a number of professional researchers from outside, and resulted in a number of reforms in the cooperatives and the book about the research by members of the research team (Greenwood et al., 1992).

Mondragón is located in the Spanish Basque Country, one of the most densely populated and highly industrialized parts of Spain. The region is known because of the Basque nationalist political movement and because the Basques speak a language unrelated to any other language currently spoken in the world. As a focus of Spanish industrialization since the 19th century, the Basque Country has been a major destination for internal migration and has a non-Basque population drawn from the rest of Spain of more than 24 percent. After a long period of growth, the region experienced industrial decline due to the aging infrastructure, the high costs of doing business, and increased national and international competition. At the time the project began, the overall unemployment rate in the region hovered around 25 percent. Mondragón itself is an industrial town of about 27,000 with a much lower unemployment rate. The Mondragón Cooperatives employ about 50 percent of the active population of the zone and account for this radically lower rate of unemployment.

The cooperatives were founded as a single cooperative, Ulgor, in 1956 by 5 leaders and 13 coworkers. There are now nearly 200 cooperatives employing more than 30,000 worker-owners. Through worldwide recessions, the cooperatives have remained generally solvent, and they have successfully managed the transition to competing effectively in the European Union. They manufacture industrial robots, machine tools, semiconductors, computer circuit boards, refrigerators, dishwashers, stoves, microwave ovens, electrical and plumbing supplies, and also retail food; have a variety of service cooperatives such as janitorial and cooking; and run a variety of schools, including an accredited university. They export in excess of 30 percent of their production.

The cooperatives were founded on principles of industrial democracy and embody the principles of worker ownership and participation. To join, a person must pay an entrance fee that is the equivalent of a year's wages. This becomes the basis of one's own capital account and part of a personal stake in the cooperative's success. As pay, members receive a distribution of the profits and increments to their capital accounts. The amount distributed back to the members depends on anticipated economic performance and future capital requirements based on the cooperative's business plan. These distributions and plans are voted on annually by all the members. The pay distribution is made according to the functional classification of the job the member holds. At the time of the study, the pay differential was 1 to 6, the lowest-paying jobs receiving one-sixth the compensation of the highest-paying jobs.[1]

Cooperative managers, who because of this compensation scheme receive much less income than they would in a private company, are elected from among the membership for 4 years and are subject to recall. Elaborate internal governance structures provide freedom of information and strong checks and balances in decision making. The cooperative system also has its own health and retirement system, a major research and development cooperative, a major cooperative bank, and a wide variety of schools, ranging from primary to university level.

Within this system, until a subsequent reorganization realigned the entire structure and created a single overall Mondragón Cooperative Corporation, the Fagor Cooperative Group was the largest and best-known cooperative group and contained the founding cooperative, Ulgor. The AR project took place within the then Fagor Group.

The project began when William Foote Whyte, a well-known professor of industrial and labor relations at Cornell University, decided to write a comprehensive history and structural analysis of the cooperatives. After a research visit in 1982 to complete gathering data for the book, he offered a seminar on what he had seen to his hosts. He made a number of critical observations about certain practices within the system and, to his surprise, the Fagor director of personnel, José Luis González, stood up, thanked him, and then asked how Whyte would propose to help them solve the problems he had identified.

Whyte returned to the United States and involved Davydd Greenwood, a Cornell anthropologist with years of fieldwork and historical research experience in the Basque Country, in the project. Together with González, the three developed proposals for funding that lasted 2 years.

As González stated the aims of the collaboration, and he took the lead in doing so, the goal was to develop the internal social research capacity of the Fagor Group, bringing it to a level of sophistication comparable to that already achieved in internal economic research. This kind of thinking embodied González's own understanding of the necessary equilibrium that the cooperatives have to maintain between their economic and social dimensions. Nevertheless, the underlying motives for the research, the identities of the local partners, and the actual agenda of activities were not clear to the outsiders.

The AR process began with mutual visits, followed by a 1985 summer course in AR taught by Greenwood to about 15 members of the Fagor Group. This course ended with the cowriting of a preliminary monograph on crises in the history of Fagor. On the basis of this monograph, the group and the Fagor management decided to continue the project. Then followed an extensive interviewing project, another summer course, a series of focus groups, and a lengthy cowriting process by which two books about the project's findings were written (Greenwood et al., 1990, 1992).

The cooperative participants were primarily drawn from the central personnel department of the Fagor Group. They did not represent the founding generation, but rather the next generation of cooperative management. These people expressed a deep and authentic concern that the future of the cooperatives was by no means assured. In particular, they worried that the many new members being recruited were not committed to cooperative values and that, under stress, the system would not be able to adapt.

To address these concerns, the AR team developed an analytical perspective that stressed understanding cultural systems as dynamic webs of meanings that generate both contested meanings and complex and often contradictory practices. We read the books written by outsiders and insiders to the cooperatives and articulated our critiques of them. We explored the constant use of dichotomies to stereotype desired and disapproved behavior in the cooperatives and to contrast the cooperatives with ordinary businesses.

Over time and through training, we developed a team attitude and set of techniques that permitted the coresearchers to get into more direct touch with reality as conceived and experienced by cooperative members and to link abstract cultural formulations back to institutional structures in their organizational and historical contexts. The aim became to gain a differentiated, dynamic understanding of the state of the cooperatives and to do so by means of research processes that were, like the cooperatives, self-managed, open ended, and practically useful. The project began in an analysis of the feared loss of cooperative values, but gradually evolved into a full-scale AR project touching on the members' deepest fears and hopes about their collective future.

The research process that took place was unusual. The beginning July 1985 seminar opened with a colossal mismatch of expectations. The Fagor Group members clearly expected and thought they wanted academic lectures on organizational culture. Greenwood came believing that most social research fails to produce useful new knowledge and that, if the cooperatives really were the self-managing organizations they seemed to be, a successful self-managing group like this should also be able to self-manage research processes and learning. Greenwood therefore refused to prepare a neat course and relieve members' anxieties by handing over a set of tools for them to use. Rather, his goal was to develop a research mindset through which members could learn new things about themselves, find counterintuitive information, and develop action plans that linked these findings to appropriate actions. Greenwood was unwilling to teach social research tools until the group was willing to define the problems and concerns that brought it together. Greenwood believed that standard social research, with its parametric assumptions and shallow positivism, would produce no useful outcomes and that no cooperative resources should be wasted in this way. He believed that the members of the Fagor Group were already researchers, but that he might be able to help them to learn counterintuitive nonparametric approaches to social research and learn to be "falsificationist" researchers. He was particularly concerned that they be alive to the complexity and diversity of the scene, because he was aware that members intended to act on their findings.

As a result of these beliefs, Greenwood came to the seminar with no prepared lectures, and the members of the Fagor Group were duly upset. The effect of this mismatch of expectations was to create a T-group[2] atmosphere. Greenwood was not willing to teach research techniques until the group had taken responsibility for identifying the issues that should be studied and considering the ethical dimensions of collaborative research within the cooperatives, where all members, in principle, are equal.

After struggling for a period with the authority dynamics this created, Greenwood suggested that the group could begin to discover what it wanted to know by finding out how others viewed the cooperatives. The group engaged in a critical reading of the professional social science literature and insider books on Mondragón. The coresearchers disliked this literature a great deal because they felt it misrepresented them and their experiences. Building on this notion of misrepresentation, Greenwood argued that they had to take control of and responsibility for the development of a view of themselves if they intended to have an ongoing social research effort that met their objectives. The project developed from there.

As time went by, the group did learn many techniques of social research and developed its own view of the cooperatives. Central to this view is a vision of culture as complex and dynamic. In particular, the team came to believe that organizational culture in Fagor set the terms of conflict and contradiction in the group, and that the strength of the system was not found in absence of conflict but in commitment to broad goals and a set of rules of debate. There was no absence of prolonged disagreement about how to achieve strongly desired goals.

As the team developed its own research and interpretations, each new view was subjected to reality testing through continued research and feedback sessions with other cooperative members. Greenwood and González insisted on keeping open the possibility of terminating the project at any time it ceased to be deemed useful.

Because the cooperatives are a success story and these successes are well known, the team decided to concentrate its attention on diversity, dissension, debate, and disagreement within the cooperative system. Throughout the process of conducting surveys, through a long series of interviews with members who were felt to be the most alienated in the system, and through focus groups, the research team stressed paying attention to the heterogeneity of viewpoints, sought out conflict and contradiction within the system, and tried not to flinch in dealing with the most threatening questions about the possible future of the cooperative system. The formal research process closed with a series of focus groups in which the team members subjected their most important values about cooperative life to open questioning: participation, solidarity, and freedom of information.

This research process sought and found conflict and contradiction, but we also discovered a great deal of strength within the system, including among newly recruited members. Gradually, it became clear that there was no fundamental crisis of cooperative values, that the initial premise of the research itself had been wrong, and that the most common explanation for perceived problems in the cooperatives was simply wrong. Yet the sense of anxiety about the future remained, and the research had produced lots of information about dissatisfaction with many dimensions of cooperative operation. The coresearchers thus began to look for other factors that could help them to understand the evident tensions within the system. In particular, they began reflecting on their own role and practices as part of the cooperatives' personnel system in creating negative conditions.

The cooperative members recognized that their initial formulation of the problems of the cooperatives as a lack of commitment by new members to cooperative values was self-serving. It became clear that they had developed a distrust of new members, who they did not feel were as committed to the cooperatives as this group of longtime members was.

Because of the decision to do extensive interviewing of disaffected members, the team began to notice that many of the complaints were about the practices of personnel departments themselves. The disaffected members gave examples of situations in which personnel departments were guilty of applying rules impersonally to cooperative members rather than embodying cooperative principles and direct personal treatment of affected parties in their work. Thus, the team members began to see themselves as part of the problem that they wanted to solve.

Reflections also proceeded at a broader level. The coresearchers had enough case material and enough sense by this time that there were significant negative dynamics in the system to begin to reflect on larger processes in the system. They noticed that when some kind of problem surfaced in a workplace and a complaint was lodged, the local managers and the personnel departments often took the matter directly to the cooperative governance apparatus rather than trying to find a solution in the workplace. As this view was developed, the coresearchers came to recognize a dangerous institutional dynamic within the cooperative system. Rather than struggling to democratize the workplace, the cooperative system had developed a strong tendency to extract all conflicts from work relations and treat them as matters of governance, to be dealt with by the governance system (rules, statutes, procedures). This made the cooperatives both unresponsive to individual claims about justice and increasingly bureaucratic. It is a beautiful example of Argyris and Schön's (1996) Model O-I organizational behavior that responds to error by reproducing the conditions that make the error recur. One result was the truncation of the ongoing growth and development of workplace democracy.

Support for this view was found in one interview after another. The coresearchers began to understand better the complaints heard from members about the tension that existed when operating in a largely undemocratic work environment while simultaneously voting on the annual business plan, being able to recall management, and participating in general assemblies of the cooperative group that often restructured the whole cooperative system in fundamental ways. To put it another way, the members articulated an existential contradiction between their lives as workers and their lives as managers. The insider members of the research team found this result to be quite convincing because the team members were able to recount numerous episodes from their own experience in which these very contradictions were augmented by their actions as personnel managers.

Another, more abstract, dimension of reflection also characterized this phase of the research. One of the main ways the literature on Mondragón explains the success of the cooperatives is to attribute it to strongly shared values that unite the members. Either elements of Basque culture (solidarity, egalitarianism, and so on) or simply a strong organizational culture imposed by the priest-founder of the system and his collaborators is used to explain how, in a capitalist world, successful democratic industrial organizations can prosper in northern Spain but not in London, Detroit, or Singapore. The coresearchers' close reading of these analyses, coupled with their own experiences and the research process they had undertaken, invalidated these viewpoints.

The AR carried out in the cooperatives showed that every core value in the system was contested and that existential tensions abounded. Though it became clear that cooperative members shared high levels of agreement about what an ideal cooperative would be like and the kind of process rules that should govern cooperative life, they suffered significant tensions and disappointments over the daily failure of the system to live up to these values. They also had very different takes on the ways to solve these problems. Thus, the organizational culture of these cooperatives was indeed a strong one, but its strength was not to be found in its uniformity. The culture of these cooperatives is a culture of contestation, debate, and dialogue about a certain basic set of organizational principles and ethical ideals. The coresearchers came to formulate their own conception of a strong organizational culture as one that does not glue individuals together in a uniform matrix but that creates ongoing dialogue and debate over the ways to embody certain important and shared values. This view of organizational culture was quite novel in the academic and consulting literature on the subject at the time, and was a direct result of this AR project.

Having reached this point, Greenwood suggested to the AR team that it should write a book to tell others about its results. This was a long and arduous process, both because team writing is difficult and because writing a book initially was a very threatening notion for most of the team members. Despite their gains in competence and confidence as social researchers, the insider members of the AR team initially did not feel qualified to write for an outside audience. At the very end of the process, during a final session of reflections, the coauthors (Greenwood et al., 1990, 1992) agreed that the process of reflection that writing demanded was the richest part of the whole learning experience.

Parallel to the writing, AR as an approach to problem solving was also institutionalized in a limited way within the Fagor Group. Some 40 people had received training in these approaches over the 3 years of the project. Five pilot projects had been undertaken in particular cooperatives, with members of the AR team serving as AR team leaders in the new venues. A number of the team members quickly were given major management responsibilities within the system, three becoming general managers of cooperatives in the years immediately following the project and another two becoming central figures in the cooperative training system for new members and retraining for existing members. The book that emerged from the project (Greenwood et al., 1990) is now used in training courses. One of the pilot projects resulted in a fundamental reorganization of one cooperative that is now among the most successful in the system.

All in all, this case shows how AR can be linked to organizational reflection, training of organizational insiders, and organizational development efforts, while also reaching intellectual goals that go well beyond the limits of the particular case.

Cornell University's School of Industrial and Labor Relations: Research and Extension

During one period in its history, Programs for Employment and Workplace Systems (PEWS) in the Extension Division of the School of Industrial and Labor

Relations at Cornell University sought to enhance its connections and reputation among the resident faculty in the academic departments. It was having limited success because of deeply held beliefs among the resident faculty that "applied" work was intellectually uninteresting. Greenwood became involved with PEWS through the efforts of one of its founders, William Foote Whyte. As he participated in discussions at PEWS, Greenwood was struck by the radically different mindsets of the PEWS members and the resident faculty at Cornell. PEWS members were attracted to and driven by the needs of their client organizations, whereas the academic faculty were attracted to and driven by the paradigms and the struggle for acceptance within their professional research communities. As a result, a regressive division of labor ensued. Action agents were not expected to write much or to think theoretically, and academic faculty were not expected to write or think in terms of the application of knowledge.

During the period that Greenwood worked with PEWS, he suggested that PEWS try a reconciliation of these positions by attempting to suffuse its client-centered processes with research dimensions that would make use of faculty expertise and interests. As an AR experiment to model this approach, PEWS undertook a pilot project at a nearby manufacturing plant. This plant faced problems implementing new manufacturing systems (manufacturing cells, total quality, statistical process control, and just-in-time production).

As an experiment to increase PEWS' effectiveness, the participants overlaid the early stages of a typical consultation process with a research perspective. First, PEWS gained access, basic familiarity, and an initial contract with the plant. Well into the process, Greenwood, operating as a professional social researcher, accompanied the PEWS staff (Peter Lazes and Ann Martin) to the plant for 2 days as a participant-observer. During that time and in written analysis afterward, he raised questions and pursued the issues raised by his observations. This helped make the intervention process accessible to others not directly involved.

Next, Greenwood and the staff members joined other PEWS members and Jan Irgens Karlsen, who was visiting the School of Industrial and Labor Relations, to ferret out the research issues relevant to this plant. This provided an opportunity for the PEWS personnel to inform the others about the plant's problems and to raise questions. The question-and-answer process refined the issues for all involved. An array of important research questions emerged, along with an inventory of further information about the plant that the PEWS consultants needed.

The process pointed in two directions. First, the consultants to the plant with Greenwood and Karlsen identified the larger theoretical issues that the events in the plant embodied. Two large families of issues emerged: the organizational effect of new manufacturing systems and models of organizational change involved in creating manufacturing cells. These, in turn, raised issues about the larger social meaning of the new manufacturing. They also referred to the difficulties organizations face in modeling organizational change.

Second, Greenwood and Karlsen identified what the research literature contained on these issues that could be useful in the plant. This involved forays into the literature on organizational learning, models of organization, and new manufacturing systems. Third, they suggested that the PEWS staff develop the basic data needed to address these questions via study-action teams composed of plant employees. Experience with such teams has shown that they can become very knowledgeable quickly. They often become a positive part of the change process themselves.

Finally, they organized and collated these research materials. These provided good theoretical and methodological perspectives for the PEWS staff to deploy at the plant. The social research issues were as clear to the AR group as were the client's needs. Comparative research through library and fieldwork on elements of the new manufacturing systems deployed at the plant was possible. This kind of research would have been exciting to the academic faculty both for its research value and its utility in providing materials for teaching. In reality, PEWS and other extension programs continually face problems at the cutting edge, where their clients live. A body of research built on these experiences could serve as a tracking device for students of industrial society. But the initiative stopped at this point.

What prevented it from going forward? Organizationally, it would have required major changes in both PEWS and the School of Industrial and Labor Relations. The PEWS members would have had to balance their commitments to their clients with the disciplines of research by devoting time to reading, writing, and communicating with resident faculty. Resident faculty would have had to be willing to invest time ferreting out the larger issues in the cases, organizing the relevant literature, and engaging themselves with projects in which action was an element. Although the lack of incentives for academic faculty to do this was clear, it was less clear why action agents did not wish to change the structure they were working in.

Thus, a successful AR model was deployed within the organization, provided uniquely useful results, was replicable in other cases, and was never deployed because of the combined division of labor between academic faculty and extension staff at Cornell University (and elsewhere) and because AR made the job of extension staff both harder and more time consuming than the standard pattern of behavior. The project disappeared without a trace, despite its apparent success, because the initiators did not have the resources and political clout to take it to the next level.[3]

Some years later, as a sequel to this process, the resident faculty moved aggressively to eliminate PEWS entirely, many of its key personnel left, and the rift between extension and research has grown even deeper. While PEWS survives in a modest form, it is certainly clear that doing the right thing, doing it well, and gaining a great deal of external credibility in no way guarantees the success or survival of AR in many academic settings where conventional social science and its concepts reign supreme.

Conclusions

Though the richness of the three experiences cannot be evoked in such brief presentations, we have aimed to characterize what we have in mind when we use the term *action research*. These cases shed light on some of the potential diversity of AR. There are clear differences in the focus of the AR in these cases. The Stongfjorden case started from an action point, whereas the Mondragón case was rooted in a more abstractly analytical research design. The PEWS case emerged from felt needs within a university extension group for increasing their intellectual prowess and anchoring their work in the relevant theoretical and methodological literatures. The important point is how the discourse between researchers and local group members gradually shaped a mutual learning situation, affecting both research and actions. Stongfjorden moved from an activist community to one that learned how to research issues related to the mobilization of resources effectively, whereas Mondragón shifted from a strong research focus on organizational culture to inclusion of actions to solve important challenges for the Fagor Group. PEWS attempted to modify the political conditions under which it operated by demonstrating the success of integrating academic and practice elements.

AR is a complex, dynamic activity involving the best efforts of both members of communities or organizations and professional researchers. It simultaneously involves the cogeneration of new information and analysis together with actions aimed at transforming the situation in democratic directions. AR is holistic and also context bound, producing practical solutions and new knowledge as part of an integrated set of activities. We hope that we have conveyed an understanding that AR is not a method as method is conventionally understood. AR is a way of producing tangible and desired results for the people involved, and it is a knowledge generation process that produces insights both for researchers and the participants. It is a complex action-knowledge generation process. In the three cases presented, the immense importance of insider knowledge and initiatives is evident, marking a clear distinction from conventional research that systematically distrusts insider knowledge as co-opted.

Notes

1. It is difficult to characterize this dimension of the cooperatives accurately now. For many years, the differential was 1 to 3, and it was gradually expanded to 1 to 6, though it is one of the thorniest subjects the members debate. More recently, different cooperatives have adopted different scales, a few permitting as much as a 1 to 20 differential and others holding the line at 1 to 6.

2. The T-group technique was developed to enhance group dynamic learning. The idea is to train the members to take responsibility for their own learning and development of social relationships. The concept of T-groups is presented in Chapter 2.

3. This experience is written up in Greenwood (1989).

Part 2

Science, Epistemology, and Practice in Action Research

Action research (AR) belongs to the class of knowledge construction processes that should be identified as scientific knowledge generation. Our core argument is that AR is a stronger research strategy than is conventional social science. AR utilizes all relevant social science methods, but these methods are integrated in a larger research strategy in which local participants play a key role in acquiring new knowledge, negotiating its meaning, and testing its validity in action. Research problems are chosen based on the issues that are pertinent in the local context, and efforts are launched to concretely solve these problems directly and to evaluate the adequacy of the outcomes and the analytical understandings arrived at.

AR is not "soft" or "qualitative" research. It is multi-method research, and its validity is tested in action. In contradistinction to the conventional social sciences, action research rejects the superiority of professional researcher knowledge over the practical knowledge of local stakeholders. It asserts the value of both kinds of knowledge and the need to bring them together. AR is based on a rejection of a privileged position for "knowing that" and privileges instead "knowing how" as the path to valid, credible knowledge and wise action.

AR necessarily is multidisciplinary, multi-method, contextual, and holistic, because it must respect the multidimensionality and complexity of the problems people face in everyday life. In this regard, AR seeks to orchestrate the diverse knowledge systems at our collective disposal to enable groups of different kinds of people to act in smarter ways than they ordinarily would when they privilege professional knowledge over that of local stakeholders or when local stakeholders act without the benefit of training in conducting systematic research. AR also emphasizes collaborative knowledge creation and the importance of the development of mutually understood processes of communication about the key elements of any project or experience.

Epistemologically, AR rests on the premise that reality is interconnected, dynamic, and multivariate and always more complex than the theories and methods that we have at our disposal. AR does not privilege abstract knowledge over action-oriented knowledge. In AR, knowing *how* is more important than knowing *that*, even though knowing that has its place in orienting knowing how. AR affirms that the only way to understand something is through a comprehensive, collaborative attempt to change it, placing it firmly within the neopragmatist approach.

AR is the closest of all social scientific approaches to enacting the scientific method. AR involves problem formulation, operationalization, hypothesis formulation, data gathering, data analysis, action design, action, evaluation of the action and redesign of the hypotheses, interpretations, and actions in an ongoing cycle. In this regard, its knowledge is tested in action and in context, thereby meeting the standards for scientific method more effectively than work carried out in the conventional social sciences in the library, on databases, and interpreted by professionals wholly external to the situation under study.

Building on this position, we connect AR to the current debate on the future of the social sciences that sees the privileging of knowledge creation in the context of application (Mode 2 in the model of Gibbons, Limoges, Nowotny, Schwartzman, Scott, and Trow, 1994). Mode 2 thinking has long been a cornerstone in AR, where the involved researchers engage with the problem owners in an effort to create new insights and to search for solutions to the actual problem. The researchers are not solo actors, but join with local actors in team-based research.

Working in solidarity with local stakeholders does not mean that action researchers themselves become "one" with the local people. There is a clear value in the action researcher having a kind of outsider status, whether as a newcomer to a group of stakeholders or as an outsider because of experiences and training that set her or him apart from other members of the group. AR places strong emphasis on learning from diversity and on linking the diverse capabilities and needs of all participants to outcomes that respect their needs and wishes socially, politically, and ethically. Action researchers are sympathetic and committed to the welfare of the local stakeholders but are also obligated to question them, press their logics and interpretations, and help them learn for themselves how to conduct social research, how to use particular methods, and how to defend their own conclusions in real-world contexts.

We take up these issues in the following order. In Chapter 4, we deal with the epistemological foundations for AR, and then, in Chapter 5, we link this to the use of scientific methods in AR. Following this, in Chapter 6, we develop more general arguments about social science research methods in particular relation to AR. From here, we move on, in Chapter 7, to the importance of local knowledge, collaboration, and how this links to the strong use of narrative forms in AR. Finally, in Chapter 8, we explore the status of the action researcher as both an outsider and as a participant in the local AR process.

4

An Epistemological Foundation for Action Research

What does it mean for social research to be scientific? In this chapter, we present our reasons for believing that action research (AR) is a powerfully scientific approach to social research. To do this, we touch on some issues from the general philosophy of science and then contrast positivist views of science with contemporary versions of pragmatism and hermeneutic philosophy. What follows is a modest map of a broad and challenging set of issues. Our aim is to provide enough perspective on them to stake out the positions that form the bases of our AR approach.

We begin by reviewing the connections between AR and general systems theory. Following this, we examine the contributions of pragmatic philosophy to AR and make some links to Wittgensteinian philosophy (Monk, 1990) as well. We conclude by setting our arguments in the context of political economy, and return to our original claims that AR has the potential to be the most scientific form of social research and that conventional social research does not resemble scientific research in most important particulars.

In this exposition, we assume that many readers with an interest in AR may not have an experience-based understanding of science as a form of practice. This makes it difficult to deal with the arguments for and against AR as a form of scientific inquiry. There is no simple solution to this socially produced dilemma, but it is vital for people interested in AR and for AR practitioners to develop a differentiated and realistic understanding of science and scientific practices.

Defining Scientific Research

To anchor our discussion, we define *scientific research* as investigative activity capable of discovering that the world is or is not organized as our preconceptions lead us to expect and suggesting grounded ways of understanding and acting on it. Scientific research documents both the investigative processes and conclusions arising from them in sufficient detail for other interested parties to be able to evaluate the information and interpretations offered and examine the consequences of the sequence of actions taken. Scientific knowledge is not a fixed entity but should be understood as an ongoing discourse among scientists struggling to make sense of the world. Scientific knowledge is in a constant state of transition, searching for the best possible understanding and management of specific phenomena/processes.

In the following discussion, we use the terms *logical positivism* and *hermeneutics*. For the sake of clarity, it is important to define what we mean by these two concepts.

- Logical positivism is based on the ontological argument that the world is objectively given; the epistemological effort is to apply objective techniques in order to acquire the truth.
- Hermeneutics is based on the ontological position that the world is only available subjectively and the epistemological project is to negotiate interpretations of this subjective world.

A central strategic problem we face in making this exposition is that introductory texts in most fields (including the sciences, social sciences, and humanities) do not reflect accurately the best practices or the most thoughtful views in those fields. In the often misguided effort to simplify perspectives to make them suitable for introductory students, classroom presentations regularly distort the frameworks and practices of our fields in ways that would be unacceptable to experienced professional practitioners. This can be seen clearly in the fact that few practicing social scientists would turn to an introductory textbook for guidance about the practices in their own fields. This is partly because the books are too elementary, but mainly because the books rarely reflect the best practices.

This problem is not unique to the social sciences; it afflicts the basic sciences as well. Generally, introductory instruction in the sciences gives students an idealized, ahistorical, nonbehavioral view of science either as a set of truths or as a set of rather unproblematic methods. Science's diversity and confusions, its human face, its social and historical dimensions, and, consequently, its behavioral and human excitement are often lost from view. Scientists are portrayed as disembodied minds that seek the truth behind the confusing world of appearances, with much of the complexity and excitement of their tasks washed out. In other words, the praxis and context of research are generally overlooked.

In addition, formulas and principles are presented as achieved truths. Laboratory exercises and problem sets all have one or two "correct" solutions. Unlike the real world of scientific practice, all classroom puzzles have a definite answer. In the classroom, it is made to appear that scientists know these answers, and that the students, to become scientists, must come to know them also. Of course, this is not entirely nonsensical. Respect for systematic work with principles, handling and reporting of materials, and understanding of laws whose consequences are reasonably well understood are all meaningful parts of science. But practicing scientists generally do not live science only in this narrow way.

Doing scientific work is not copying methodological blueprints written up in textbooks, but applying research methods in the complex settings of the social world (Latour, 1987). As the lecture by a chemist discussed in the next chapter points out in greater detail, scientists live in a socially complex world, chasing dynamic phenomena with limited and imperfect instruments and finite energies and budgets.

We have defined scientific research as investigative activity capable of discovering that the world is not organized as our preconceptions lead us to expect and suggesting alternative ways to understand it. Scientific research documents both the investigative processes and conclusions arising from them in sufficient detail for other interested parties to be able to evaluate the information and interpretations offered. The institutional edifices of what is called "science" today do not necessarily bear a close relationship to this definition of scientific research.

General Systems Theory

One stream of scientific ideas and concepts relevant to AR comes from a loosely integrated field that is known as "general systems theory" (GST), a field little taught to university students outside of the sciences and engineering. Having its origins in physics, chemistry, biology, and engineering in the 1920s and linked later to the development of self-correcting guidance systems for military use, GST has significantly influenced the world around us. Despite this, GST is not a household word. Partly this is because, like AR, GST is not a single discipline anchored in a particular academic department. It is a set of perspectives shared by a wide array of scientists and social reformers with diverse backgrounds and divergent political ideas.

At the core of GST is a set of holistic concepts about the way the world is organized. Rather than accepting the notion of a particulate universe made up of separate atoms, molecules, and so on that are linked together in higher combinations and structures, GST views the world (inorganic, organic, and sociocultural) as composed of interacting systems whose processes differently integrate the same basic matter of the universe to produce the immense array of things we encounter in the world of experience. The GST view argues that the differences among an inorganic, an organic, and a sociocultural system are to be understood as the product of the differences in the way these systems are organized—the kinds, sequences, and parameters of processes that take place within them.

Though GST contains complexly differentiated concepts, practitioners make a fundamental distinction between "closed" and "open" systems. These two broad classes of systems operate quite differently. Equilibria in a closed and open system are maintained by different kinds of processes, and these systems react very differently to perturbations from the environment. In GST, a system is largely interpreted as a combination of its open or closed properties and then by the history of the processes occurring within it or affecting it from the outside.

This view is radically different from the particulate view of the world that has been central to much of Western thought until recently. No system operates in isolation but is created and bounded by structures and processes linked to other neighboring systems. In GST, the units of analysis are systems, not individuals. Systems, not separate institutions, operate as wholes. Individuals operate within systems that create process environments that affect the outcomes of behavior in complex ways. The world is not a neat stratigraphic map beginning with inorganic matter, passing to organic matter, and then being transcended by sociocultural forces. Rather, the world is a complex, interacting array of systems and system processes, bumping into each other in a variety of ways. Social relationships and processes are impacted by the physical world as the physical world is transformed by social activity. The only hope of understanding any particular thing is by placing it in the appropriate system context and following the processes by which it acts. This is what Senge (1990) argues for as the "fifth discipline"—the ability to understand how elements and subsystems interact, forming a total situation.

GST has been applied to the ancient riddle of explaining the relationship between inorganic matter and organic matter and the evolution of life. Here the work of Ludwig von Bertalanffy (1966, 1968) has been fundamental. In applying these perspectives to social systems, a variety of theories of international conflict (Rapoport, 1974) and a whole tradition in the analysis of organizational behavior (see Argyris, 1985; Argyris & Schön, 1996; Flood & Romm, 1996) have been built around these notions. Finally, the pathbreaking work of Gregory Bateson (1979) on the relationship between mind and nature relies on this approach. Bateson persuasively shows that the nature-culture problem is radically transformed when we understand the relationship as an expression of processes found everywhere in nature. For Bateson, the mind is part of nature and necessarily works according to a set of organizational processes found in nature but combined in particular ways in mental activity. Thus, mind is both fully part of nature and unique as a system.

Why is GST relevant to AR? To begin with, the GST account of the world is at odds with much of what is currently called "social science." Conventional social science is still largely conceptualized in terms of a stratigraphic, particulate world, based on images of social facts that stand on their own. In particular, the recent surge in rational choice theories as some kind of "philosopher's stone" for social science shows how reductive to radical individualism and free market ideologies much mainstream social science has become (Elster, 1986; Scott, 1995). Thus, GST is a profound critique of this view and, therefore, of the scientific pretensions of conventional social researchers who are connected to it.

More important, the systems approach necessarily underlies AR in all its manifestations. Both rely heavily on an interconnected and holistic view of the world. Humans are understood to exist only within social systems, and these systems have properties and processes that condition human behavior and are in turn conditioned by that behavior. Social systems are not mere structures, but are processes in continual motion. They are dynamic and historical. They operate within material boundaries and are capable of transforming material living conditions. They are also interlinked, entwining the individual social structures and the larger ecology of systems into complex interacting macro-systems.

The relevance of GST to AR can be seen because AR is understood as an effort to transform society into ever more open systems, and also because GST identifies the relationships among the parts of a system as critical elements in the way a system as a whole operates. Indeed, some AR practitioners specifically equate increased openness with democratization (Flood & Romm, 1996). So, one thread leading in the direction of or supporting the development of AR is GST. Another is the considerably broader philosophical movements of pragmatism and neopragmatism.

Pragmatic Philosophy and Action Research

That a stereotypical view of science prevails among nonscientists does not mean that the world is or has been unaware of the perspectives we articulate here. All the elements of a more complex and humanly meaningful view of science are well known and have been articulated effectively by John Dewey (1976), Charles Sanders Peirce (1950), William James (1948, 1995), Kurt Lewin (1935, 1948), and more recently, Stephen Toulmin and Bjørn Gustavsen (1996), all writing in the pragmatist tradition. In other words, the bases for AR have been well known since the beginning of the 20th century.

John Dewey is particularly important for our exposition because his pragmatic philosophy laid out an action approach to science as a form of human inquiry and underscored its inherent connections to democracy in a way in concert with our views on AR. Dewey was born in 1859 and died in 1952. His intellectual production dates from the 1880s and continued to the end of his life. Dewey is generally viewed as having been a key influence on public education in the United States and as having been the prime mover behind one of the few rather uniquely American contributions to Western philosophy. Nevertheless, a recent intellectual biographer, Robert Westbrook (1991), shows that Dewey's was always and remains a minority view. There is little evidence that those who cite Dewey approvingly have acted on his ideas; indeed it is hard to believe that many of them have read what he wrote.

What, then, are his ideas? To render 70 years of intellectual work (his complete works run to more than 30 volumes) in a few paragraphs is impossible. We outline only a few of the key points of his approach that relate to AR and to the relationship between social research and social reform.

Dewey was a staunch believer in democracy as an ongoing, collective process of social improvement in which all levels of society had to participate. These arguments are put forward in *The Public and Its Problems* (1927/1991). In his view, the role of public education was to permit everyone in society enough training so that they could contribute their own views and experiences to the collective democratic process. In *The School and Society* (1900) and *The Child and the Curriculum* (1902), Dewey presented his arguments on the connection between democratic theory and pedagogical ideas. The important point was that democracy had to evolve through peoples' active involvement in making sense of their world and not through solutions imposed by powerful outsiders.

Perhaps the most characteristic feature of Dewey's approach was his steadfast refusal to separate thought from action. For Dewey, everything was forged in action. He saw democracy itself as an ongoing form of social action, a combination of institutional forms and ethical commitments that works toward the increasing ability of all members of society to contribute their intelligence to the greater sophistication and discernment of the whole. He believed that the only real sources of knowledge were to be found in action, not in armchair speculation. For him, all knowledge testing and proofs were, like democracy itself, ongoing experimental activities. This position was clear in his views on logic, which he treated as a theory of inquiry (Dewey, 1991).

One consequence was that schools should create environments where the students could safely confront problems that can be resolved only by using skills gained from studying the sciences, history, and the arts. Schools should not be locations where the students, seen as empty vessels, are filled with knowledge bits. This was consistent with Dewey's view that scientific judgment was not a form of esoteric knowledge. Dewey believed that all humans are capable of scientific judgment and that society could be improved to the extent these capacities are increased among all of society's members. Consistent with this, he strongly opposed the division of public education into vocational and academic tracks, seeing this as the preservation of inequality and ultimately the weakening of democracy as a whole. Everyone could be capable participants in experimental knowledge generation. He believed that limiting the learning of any individual ultimately limited society as a whole.

These ideas connect to Dewey's view of schools as environments and learning as a process of action in which the student must be an active learner and not a passive listener. Though many connect these ideas to Dewey, few students would describe the bulk of their educational experiences in these terms. Dewey is a figure simultaneously lionized and ignored. The best way to blunt a reform is to co-opt it, to state approval of it, and to act in the opposite way. This has been Dewey's fate.

One of the hallmarks of Dewey's thought is his resolute focus on diversity and conflict as essential elements in a democratic society. He viewed democracy as a process of working through conflicts, not to a final resolution but toward an improved situation. He did not hunger for the elimination of conflict in society because he genuinely respected the diversity of people and their experiences. His aim was to build momentum for democratic social reform by bringing together these conflicting experiences and by working democratically to ameliorate intolerable situations. He believed that communities (including community schools) were central to this process precisely because communities are divided and diverse. Their common stake in solutions can permit them to work through problems together.

Dewey's views on science were intimately connected to his views of a democratic society. For Dewey, scientific research was not a process separate from democratic social action. Scientific knowing, like all other forms of knowledge, was a product of continuous cycles of action and reflection (Dewey, 1991/1927). The center of gravity was always the learner's active pursuit of understanding through puzzle-solving activity with the materials at hand. The solutions achieved were only the best possible ones at that moment with materials at hand, hence the denomination of his philosophy as *pragmatism.*

Dewey remained politically engaged in a variety of democratic movements throughout his life. He was realistic about the situation he faced. He understood that the existing power structures favored having a ruling class and a duty-bound, vocationally educated populace to work for them in unreflective harmony. He was aware of the radical separation between academic institutions and the human situations he wished to change. Although he asserted that experience was an organic whole, he knew that educational practice divided it up into tiny, specialized parcels and that this process weakened the ability of the citizenry to take control of democracy in the way he advocated. Above all, he knew that conventional social science was radically opposed to his action orientation because it had come to separate thought from action and, thus, created social researchers who offered no threat to existing power arrangements.

To summarize, Dewey believed that all humans are scientists, that thought must not be separated from action, that the diversity of human communities is one of their most powerful features (if harnessed to democratic processes), and that academic institutions in general and conventional social research in particular rarely promote science or democratic social action.

Nearly his entire corpus of work can be seen as consistent with the premises of general systems theory as well, because he focused on the individual in society and societies in their environments as dynamic and open systems. His resolute emphasis on processes rather than on outcomes and the way in which society can be made responsive to the continual changes from within and from without also link him to GST. Dewey's pragmatism, with its linkage of knowledge and action, its connections among knowledge, action, community, and democracy, remains important for AR.

Epistemological Foundations of Action Research

The presentations of GST and pragmatism connect directly to AR. AR aims to solve pertinent problems in a given context through a democratic inquiry where professional researchers collaborate with participants in the effort to seek and enact solutions to problems of major importance to the local people. In doing this, AR specifically engages in systems-based, pragmatic social science. Indeed, AR is challenged to practice leading-edge science, combining the best in scientific practice with a commitment to the democratic transformation of society. Yet AR is almost universally viewed with disrespect by conventional social scientists, who see it as unsystematic, atheoretical storytelling. We, of course, believe these criticisms to be both ill founded and self-serving.

To begin with, AR generally takes on much more complex problems than do the conventional social sciences. AR focuses on specific contexts, demands that theory and action not be separated, and is committed to the idea that the test of any theory is its capacity to resolve problems in real-life situations. This focus on the world of experience, with its complexity, historicity, and dynamism, means that AR distances itself from the often purified world of conventional social research with its friction-free, perfect information and "other things being equal" assumptions that make being an academic easier, though at the cost of also being irrelevant. Conventional social researchers seem to us to be content to chop up reality to make it simpler to handle, more suited to theoretical manipulation, more suited to management by disciplinary cartels, and to make the social scientists' life easier to manage.

AR does not accept these compromises. As a result, and consistent with our presentations of GST and pragmatism, we assert that AR as a form of research has the following core characteristics:

- AR is context bound and addresses real-life problems holistically.
- AR is inquiry through which participants and researchers cogenerate knowledge using collaborative communicative processes in which all participants' contributions are taken seriously.
- AR treats the diversity of experiences and capacities within the local group as an opportunity for the enrichment of the research-action process.
- The meanings constructed in the inquiry process lead to social action, or these reflections on action lead to the construction of new meanings.
- The credibility-validity of AR knowledge is measured according to whether actions that arise from it solve problems (workability) and increase participants' control over their own situations.

Given this conceptualization of AR, several important questions emerge. What is the logic of inquiries constructed this way? What are reasonable criteria for judging knowledge to be credible in AR? How can strongly context-bound knowledge be communicated effectively to academics and other potential recipient groups? The aim of the following discussion is to present an epistemological position that supports our arguments for the value of AR.

CONTEXT-BOUND INQUIRY ON IMPORTANT LOCAL PROBLEMS

AR focuses on solving real-life problems. The focus of the inquiry is determined by what the participants consider important, what affects their daily lives. The inquiry process is thus linked to actions taken to provide a solution to the problem being examined. Of course, inquiry also can precede actions. In this case, it is a way of acquiring necessary knowledge to design actions that will resolve the pertinent issue. Inquiry can also be a way of developing reflections based on experiences drawn from prior actions that can be understood in new ways. Of course, in most real-life situations, any attempt to solve important problems involves a priori and a posteriori meaning construction.

We emphasize that the inquiry process is linked to solving practical problems. But despite the conceits of academic theoreticians, practical problems are not necessarily simple ones. Community economic development, developing new organizational structures in an organization, building a house where inhabitants in a neighborhood can meet, or collective efforts to reduce violence in the local community are all practical problems, but they are often extremely complex ones to manage.

Whether the problem is a social organizational or a material one, the results of AR must be tangible in the sense that participants can figure out whether the solution they have developed actually resolves the problem they set themselves. Here we connect directly back to pragmatic philosophy. The results of an AR process must be judged in terms of the workability of the solutions arrived at. *Workability* means whether or not a solution can be identified as solution to the initial problem or whether revision of the interpretation or redesign of the actions is required. This is not a matter of double-blind experimentation, stratified random samples, and significance levels. It is a matter of collective social judgment by knowledgeable participants about the outcomes of a collective social action. Social judgment is itself the result of a kind of democratic conversation in which the professional researcher has only one vote.

DEMOCRATIC INQUIRY PROCESSES LINKING PARTICIPANTS AND PROFESSIONALS

We frame AR as democratic processes supporting the creation of new knowledge that potentially can be liberating. Obviously, then, the inquiry process has to aim to solve problems important to the local participants, and the knowledge produced by the inquiry process must increase participants' control over their own situations. This is consistent with Freire's (1970) concept of "conscientization," which identifies the inquiry process as aimed at shaping knowledge relevant to action built on a critical understanding of historical and political contexts within which the participants act. The participants must be able to use the knowledge that emerges, and this knowledge must support the enhancement of the participants' goals.

The democratic element in the inquiry process indicates that mutualism between outside researchers and inside participants must exist. AR is a communication process where the best of both sides can cogenerate knowledge through the inquiry process. Local knowledge, historical consciousness, and everyday experience of the insiders complements the outsider's skills in facilitating learning processes, technical skills in research procedures, and comparative and historical knowledge of the subject under investigation. At the same time, we agree with Dewey (1976) that

> in all this, there is no difference of kind between the methods of science and those of the plain [man]. The difference is the greater control by science of the statement of the problem, and of relevant material, both sensible and conceptual. (p. 305)

Linking the outside researcher with insiders in a joint inquiry process eliminates the possibility of believing in Fregian (1918/1956) and Russellian (1903) logic as some kind of objective outside standard for what can be considered true or relevant knowledge. The logic of inquiry is linked to the inquiry process itself, in the struggle to make an indeterminate situation into a more positively controlled one through an inquiry process in which action and reflection are directly linked. The outside researcher inevitably becomes a participant with the insiders.

Years ago, a Norwegian philosopher titled his master's thesis *Objectivity and the Study of Man* (Skjervheim, 1974). It deals with the foundations of social science. According to Skjervheim's view, in AR, there is no doubt that the researcher is an active participant in the inquiry process. The acceptance and the active and conscious use of this position contrasts AR with conventional social science that purposely obfuscates the researcher's social role. The obvious participant status that any social scientist has in any research process is fully acknowledged in AR and is treated as a resource for the process. The construction of new knowledge is built on the premise of this mutual engagement. On the other hand, the active researcher's involvement raises important challenges of integrity and critical reflection. AR is not a mode of research that accepts researchers' co-optation by local actors or power holders either. Balancing active involvement with integrity and critical reflection is fundamental in any AR process.

DIVERSITY AS AN OPPORTUNITY

The involvement of participants in the research process creates a genuine opportunity to use individual capacities. We have argued that research involves human creativity in developing potential solutions to and explanations of the problem at issue. A purely rational argument in favor of having a diverse group of coresearchers is that the broader set of experiences and attitudes the participants bring to the research process can permit more creative solutions to develop. Lessons from research on creativity illustrate this point (see, for example, Amabile, 1996).

A second and equally important argument is the ethical position that it is important to sustain diversity as a political right in itself. AR must be constructed to gain strength from the creative potential in the diversity of the participant group, not to create solutions to problems that unnecessarily reduce diversity.

The Action Research Inquiry Process Is Thus Inevitably Linked to Action

Knowledge emerges and is evaluated through acting or as a consequence of actions. The discovery process is not purely mental, receding into the intellectual sphere at a distance from human actions. With Dewey, we argue for understanding inquiry as a process linking reflection and action in a unified process for the creation of new knowledge. This means that the logic of the inquiry process itself is the real basis that underlies human knowledge (Burke, 1994).

By linking inquiry to actions in a given context, AR understands human inquirers to be acting subjects in a holistic situation. Inquiry is not fragmented and separated; it is treated as a coherent social field. Dewey (1976) identified this as an organism-environment system that configures the holistic situation. In this view, the inquirer is also always a subject in the processes of acquiring new knowledge. AR rules out conventional positions that imagine the inquirer taking on a pseudo-neutral/pseudo-objective stance to the question under study.

AR processes do not make claims for context-free knowledge. The conventional concept of generalizability equates the general with what is universally true, context notwithstanding. Because AR is built on the notion that all meaningful inquiry is context bound, it offers a very different concept of general knowledge, one that we believe is more powerful and certainly much more useful.

We argue that AR-developed knowledge can be valuable in contexts other than those in which it is developed, but we reject the notion that the transferability of knowledge from one location to another is achieved by abstract generalizations about that knowledge. Transferring knowledge from one context to another relies on understanding the contextual factors in the situation in which the inquiry took place, judging the new context where the knowledge is supposed to be applied, and making a critical assessment of whether the two contexts have sufficient processes and structures in common to make it worthwhile to link them. We return to this issue later.

In AR, insiders and outsiders join in a mutual learning process. The enabling mechanism for this is communication. New understandings are created through discourses between people engaged in the inquiry process. For this to occur, a mutually understandable discourse is required, and this is achieved through living together over time, sharing experiences, and taking actions together. This discourse that enables communication is much like what Wittgenstein (1953) describes as "practice." Language creates meaning because it identifies actions that are meaningful for the actors. New knowledge, which we have identified as emerging from an action-reflection process, accordingly shapes a language that is relevant to describing actions and the learning arising from them. The AR process thus creates a language shared between insiders and outsiders that identifies the meaning constructed through the inquiry process.

This argument leads us not only to an understanding of the way communication processes create meanings supportive of action but also to an understanding of the reverse process. In some situations, outcomes or experiences arising from actions initiate collective reflection processes that subsequently create new meanings.

Credibility and Validity in Action Research Inquiry

Credibility and validity in conventional social science research function as the researchers' amulet. In a world of confusing information, these practitioners seem to find comfort in an elaborate methodological (and deeply ritualized) apparatus that purports to resolve these thorny problems cleanly. By focusing on methodological rules as a substitute for facing the question of whether a specific understanding is worth believing enough to act on it, it permits conventional social science to bypass the challenge of workability.

It is important to understand what the prerequisites for someone believing in meanings constructed through AR are. We define *credibility* as the arguments and the processes necessary for having someone trust research results. We can distinguish two different types of credible knowledge. First, there is knowledge that has *internal credibility* to the group generating it. This kind of knowledge is fundamentally important to AR because of the collaborative character of the research process. Its direct consequences in altered patterns of social action constitute a clear test of credibility, a test that many abstract social science frameworks lack. Members of communities or organizations are unlikely to accept as credible the "objective" theories of outsiders if they cannot recognize their connection to the local situation or because local knowledge makes it clear that the frameworks are either too abstract or simply wrong for the specific context.

A second kind of credibility involves external judgments. *External credibility* is knowledge capable of convincing someone who did not participate in the inquiry that the results are believable. This is a complex matter. Because AR depends on the conjugation of reflection and action and the cogeneration of new knowledge in specific contexts, conveying effectively the credibility of this knowledge to outsiders is a difficult challenge. Often AR reports are called "mere storytelling," an insulting attempt to disqualify the general knowledge gained in a specific AR case. Narratives are indeed central to AR. A great deal is at stake in understanding the stories of individual cases in ways that can and should have powerful general effects. Telling stories is not in contradiction to doing social science. It is fundamental to it.

We want to emphasize that the logic of scientific reasoning requires that any individual AR case that contradicts a general social theory thereby invalidates that theory and requires that a new theory be developed to take account of it. Viable theories do not have exceptions; they must be reformulated to include the exceptions in a coherent way. Thus, individual cases and stories, the stuff of many AR writings, have immense power to alter theories, and theories, no matter how complex or how prestigious a genealogy they have, cannot overrun contradictory cases.

This is the crux of the credibility-validity issue in AR. The conventional social research community believes that credibility is created through generalizing and universalizing propositions of the universal hypothetical, universal disjunctive, and generic types, whereas AR believes that only knowledge generated and tested in practice is credible. Conventional social research believes that only a community of similarly trained professionals is competent to decide issues of credibility, while AR places emphasis on the stakeholders' willingness to accept and act on the collectively arrived at results and the defining characteristic of credibility.

WORKABILITY

In AR processes, a first credibility challenge relates to the solution of the AR problem under examination locally. Here the workability test is central. We must figure out whether the actions taken in the AR process result in a solution to the problem. This is in line with Dewey's (1976) thinking on the inquiry process, where knowledge is created or meaning is constructed through acting on the environment. Johannesen (1996) develops a similar conception when he addresses the validity standard of AR. Thus, borrowing from pragmatist thought directly (Diggins, 1994), we understand the inquiry process as an integration of action and reflection and the test of the tangible outcome as workability.

MAKING SENSE

The second and complementary process in inquiry is making sense out of these tangible results. How can the outcome be integrated in a meaning construction process that creates new knowledge? Here we focus on how meaning is constructed through deliberative processes. Berger and Luckmann (1966) represent an early line in the argument that all knowledge is socially constructed. Their constructivist position does not reflect sufficiently on the quality of the socially constructed knowledge, however, because they do not attempt to scrutinize the quality of the constructed outcomes. For them, any construction is as right or wrong as any other possible one, a position antithetical to AR.[1] In AR, we use processes in which chains of arguments can undergo some kind of testing procedure. We can describe two possible processes for such deliberations: Habermas's (1984) ideal speech situation and Gadamer's (1982) hermeneutics, though many more formulations exist.

The Habermasian (1984) ideal speech situation counterfactually characterizes a process free from domination, where the actors involved in meaning construction exchange arguments without coercion. In this idealized situation, each participant seriously and honestly judges the arguments presented to him or her and comes back with the best judgment he or she can make in the response argument. This process leads to an understanding that is characterized as a legitimate truth when no further arguments are able to overturn those already stated.

The credibility of this line of argument emerges out of this ideal situation when no better explanation can be offered. This is not a one-shot affair but more a continuous process in which new experiences or new arguments continually challenge what is already thought of as credible knowledge. Scientific knowledge is then easily understood as an ongoing discourse searching for the best interpretation of certain phenomena. The Habermasian (1984) ideal speech situation is alluring in its strict logical and rational reasoning, but it leaves out emotions, power, and inequality as key determinants of all communication processes, a critique that has been widely made (see, for example, Flood and Romm, 1996).

Gadamer's (1982) major work, *Truth and Method,* resists facile synthesis. He treats Habermas's (1984) ideal speech situation as a piece of naive idealism, advocating instead a more complex combination of dialogue, mutual interpretation, and eventual (but never final) "fusion of horizons." Gadamer respects the historicity of the knowledge, interpretations, and experiences the participants bring. Gadamer, unlike those who have tried to convert hermeneutics into an academic parlor game, insists that hermeneutics is a form of acting, not merely a method for thinking.

TRANSCONTEXTUAL CREDIBILITY

At a still broader level, there exists the possibility of transcontextual modeling of situations, and this can be explained historically and causally. This is vitally important because it is precisely here that conventional social scientists usually invoke the canon of generalizability and try to move social research toward what they view as objectivity and away from what we understand as scientific research.

Our view, paralleling that of François Jacob (1982) on the possible and the actual, sees every situation containing more possibilities than those that are acted on. We understand that all current situations could have been different but were not. A particular outcome was realized through the intersection of environmental conditions, a group of people, and a variety of historical events, including the actions of the participants.[2]

From this perspective, all explanations of present situations are actually accounts of historical moments and particular causes acting on particular organizations in specific contexts. In this way of thinking, theory does not predict the outcomes of a particular situation. The role of theories is to explain how what happened was possible and took place, to lay out possible scenarios for the future, and to give good reasons for the ones that seem to be the probable next outcomes. This latter move, of course, relies precisely on analogizing outcomes from other cases and contexts in a coherent way.

These practices are science at its best, and our previous example was drawn from evolutionary biology. Are there examples in the social sciences? We believe there are, but that they are generally ignored. One such example is the structure of thinking underlying the work of Max Weber. He built a wide variety of ideal types to deal with the diversity and complexity of the issues he studied: bureaucracy, charisma, legitimacy, authority, religion, urbanization.[3] In every case, he created an abstracted list of transcontextual characteristics after the painstaking study of many historical cases. He then used these characteristics to develop explanatory strategies.

Weber's (1958) rarely cited work on cities presents a particularly clear example. He gathered all the evidence he could from all over the world about the phenomenon of cities. On the basis of this broad reading, he developed a synthesis of the traits he found in each major example of cities in different places. He then took this list of traits and arrayed the traits together until he had a list of all the major features that he could find in the cities of the world. The total list of major traits made up the basis of his ideal type of city.

This was only the beginning, however. Armed with this list, Weber returned to each world area, to each context, to examine what traits were present or absent in each situation. When he found particular complexes of traits present or absent in a location, he reexamined the history of that area to explain the presence or the absence. Gradually, he developed what he calls a "causal interpretation of history" that helped him understand why particular features were present or absent in particular situations, built over the backdrop of a general knowledge of the phenomenon of urbanization.

Weber's way of examining particular situations and environments by closely gathering traits from those situations, listing and analyzing those traits, and then returning to the particular situations helped him understand why particular features were present or absent. This is how knowledge developed in one AR situation is to be transferred to other situations. AR does not generalize through abstraction and the loss of history and context. Meanings created in one context are examined for their credibility in another situation through a conscious reflection on similarities and differences between contextual features and historical factors. They are moved from the context where the understanding was created through a collaborative analysis of the situation where this knowledge might be applied. Based on the historical and contextual analysis, AR judgments are made about the possibility of applying knowledge from one situation in another. This is also the proper way to develop AR approaches, through the in-depth analysis of the use of a variety of techniques and processes in multiple contexts.

Thus, we believe that detailed attention to cases, context, and history is essential to the development of science in general. It is the most meaningful way to proceed in developing a social science that respects the diversity of situations while also developing an understanding of the processes found in many situations and that can be used to explain what happened in each case.

Readdressing the Action Research Processes

We argued that relevant actions to solve the problem at hand are the first out-come of an AR process. We also argued that the meaning construction process linked to solving practical problems is the major knowledge generation ele-ment in AR. Finally, we discussed the situations that transfer learning from one context to another and how to develop historical and causal interpretations of what has happened in each particular situation.

To reflect on why all this is not so obvious as to be banal, we have to return to the broader epistemological debate that forms the backdrop. Though we have concentrated on Dewey, it is important to recognize that Dewey's ideas developed in discourse with many colleagues, including Charles Sanders Peirce and William James, who were also at work on the pragmatist framework for philosophy. They were very well known and respected for a long time, and then eclipsed almost completely. The eclipse of pragmatism is the subject of a controversial and important work, Richard Rorty's (1980) *Philosophy and the Mirror of Nature*. A broader meta-commentary on these issues is found in John Diggins's (1994) *The Promise of Pragmatism*. These works deserve attention from anyone interested in AR because their analyses provide an analytical and historiographical structure into which the vicissi-tudes suffered by AR can be fitted.

For Rorty (1980), the pragmatists, contemporary hermeneuticians (for example, Gadamer, 1982; Taylor, 1985), linguistic philosophers such as Willard Quine, the Frankfurt school, Wittgenstein, Martin Heidegger, some existentialists, and some of Rorty's colleagues aim at the repudiation of what he calls "the epistemological project." Though Rorty defines this project in a variety of ways, at base, he means to criticize modern philosophy's pretensions to create a system of analysis that would permit philosophers to distinguish between "correct" and "incorrect" knowledge—a view of philosophy as a kind of self-appointed supreme court of knowledge to which everyone would have to submit.

Rorty counters the epistemological project by distinguishing between *systematic philosophy* as the search for an absolute reality determined by philosophical experts and *edifying philosophy*, which he views as an ongoing conversation involving methods and debates that attempt to bring people into some kind of state of communicative clarity. Rorty clearly advocates the latter but notes that the edifying philosophers are peripheral to contemporary phi-losophy, specifically mentioning Dewey, Wittgenstein, and Heidegger as exam-ples (Rorty, 1980, pp. 367–368).

In praising Dewey, Wittgenstein, Heidegger, and others like them, Rorty points out that they make fun of the classic picture of man, the picture that contains systematic philosophy and the search for universal commensuration in a final vocabulary. They hammer away at the point that

> words take their meanings from other words rather than by virtue of their representative character, and the corollary that vocabularies acquire their privileges from the men who use them rather than from their transparency to the real. . . . The point of edifying philosophy is to keep the conversation going rather than to find objective truth. Such truth . . . is the normal result of normal discourse. (Rorty, 1980, pp. 368, 377)

These arguments are central to the structure of AR as we view it. AR is, first and foremost, a way of "keeping the conversation going." AR's methods aim to open horizons of discussion, to create spaces for collective reflection in which new descriptions and analyses of important situations may be developed as the basis for new actions. This is what we mean by *cogenerative learning.*

This is directly relevant to the intellectual and social project announced by Hans Georg Gadamer (1982) as well. His emphasis on the interpretive, dialogical, and practice-oriented character of all human knowledge includes a powerful argument that these dimensions are present in all the sciences: the physical, biological, and social sciences, and, of course, the humanities and the arts. He emphasizes the ongoing, ever-provisional character of interpretations and points out that hermeneutics is a form of action, to use Rorty's (1980) language, a way of keeping the conversation going. That AR practitioners have not carefully examined the work of Gadamer and that of other contemporary hermeneuticians is hard to understand and contributes to their vulnerability to improper but energetic criticism from conventional social researchers who are well ensconced in their academic bunkers.

Elements of pragmatism and democratic political critiques of existing social arrangements are also closely connected. One of the most interesting points emerging from Diggins's (1994) analysis is his linkage of Henry Adams's and John Dewey's scathing critiques of education. Quoting a letter from Adams to R. Cunliffe written August 31, 1875, Diggins reproduces Adams's words describing the Harvard professorate and their students:

> They cram themselves with secondhand facts and theories till they burst, and then they lecture at Harvard College and think they are the aristocracy of intellect and are doing true heroic work by exploding themselves all over a younger generation and forcing up a new set of simpleminded, honest, harmless, intellectual prigs. (Henry Adams, quoted in Diggins, 1994, p. 307)

Academic institutions are seen as centers for the promotion of knowledge without action, reflection without commitment. This directly parallels Adams's and Dewey's critique and links back to the common ground between pragmatism and AR in asserting that the truth is not a thing to be acquired but rather an aim of an endless process of collaborative social inquiry.

Diggins (1994) also makes persuasive links among pragmatism, hermeneutics, linguistic philosophy, the Frankfurt school, and deconstruction. Although these seem like odd bedfellows, if one takes the critique of the epistemological project as the centerpiece, they all contribute key elements to it. More important for our purposes is that these schools are also the inspiration for a significant amount of AR thinking. Thus, AR is not on some side road. AR is neopragmatism in social research, an attempt to keep the conversation going and to democratize our society further. Like pragmatism, AR has met with the unflinching resistance of the epistemological project and positivist social science for whom taking pragmatism seriously would bring about the end of the academic world as they know (and profit from) it.

Political Economy and the Social Structure of Science

Underlying what we have said is a set of ideas about power relationships in our society. AR is about the transformation of power relationships in the direction of greater democracy. Yet most of the experience we have of the world is of authoritarianism, command and control systems, bureaucracies, narrow specializations, separation of reflection and action, and sanctions against those who oppose these systems. John Dewey posed the issue well when he affirmed that life, thought, and action are all part of one larger whole, but everyday experience makes it appear that the world is composed of a pile of independent, self-serving atoms that continually crash into each other.

What makes an integrated whole system appear to be a set of independent bits and pieces? The answer AR gives is that the cause is power relationships and, thus, without an analysis of power relationships, AR is impossible. The political economy of capitalist societies, of science as an activity, and of academic institutions are all necessary elements in any attempt to understand the dilemmas that AR seeks to overcome. It also explains the continual effort by power elites to marginalize AR activities in all social arenas.

AR explicitly seeks to disrupt existing power relationships for the purpose of democratizing society. It also instrumentally seeks to incorporate the great diversity of knowledge and experience of all society's members in the solution of collective problems. AR asserts that societies, because of authoritarianism, use only a tiny portion of their knowledge and capacities to confront important problems. The reasons for this are the desires of the few who currently control key resources to retain that control and the fundamental lack of respect that elites have for the capacities of nonelite members of society. Given these interests and the resources at their disposal, these elites create and maintain reasonably loyal bureaucracies that operate by categorizing the citizenry in infinite ways (deserving/undeserving, criminal/good, heterosexual/homosexual, male/female, black/white/yellow/red, and so on). According to these classifications, the resources controlled by elites are then doled out to the categories, who in accepting them, are accepting the elite's hegemonic definition of them. This kind of bureaucratic distribution in the pseudo-name of welfare creates a dyadic relationship between the subordinate individual and power structures, discouraging rebellion and collaboration among the receivers of this largesse.

This political economy affects science and the academy. Science now is largely paid for by the governments and by large corporations, and conventional social science would die without governmental grants. As the funders, they decide the topics and methods of the research and create a policing process of peer review that guarantees that, like welfare recipients, scientists are unlikely to be very collaborative among themselves. In the social sciences, this kind of funding has created socially disengaged, statistically oriented "disciplines." As a result, these disciplines end up mainly documenting the workings of bureaucratic control structures. They rarely promote or envision an active process of social change, and they assuage their consciences by affirming the self-serving notion that they are doing science and that social action or even modest application of their knowledge is not their responsibility. When they do promote reform, they often pay a very severe political price (see Price, 2004).

Thus, social research and social reform are sharply separated by these mechanisms and each new generation of students that arrives at universities after having competed ferociously with others like them is quickly taught to accept this separation. As an ideology to retain power in the hands of the powerful while employing a vast number of bureaucrats and their academic minions, this has been notably successful. The participants discipline each other, and the hand of power is rarely seen.

In this context, AR is branded "unscientific" because of its social and ethical engagements and thus it is deprived of funding and institutional support. It is also cut to ribbons in academic and other bureaucratic structures because AR is inherently a system activity with the fundamental multidisciplinarity this implies. By dividing the disciplines and creating structured interests that guard against any territorial incursions, schools, universities, and other bureaucracies strangle the social project of democratization that is the heart of AR. Finally, by demanding that social research be separated from the context of application, power holders assure themselves that social scientists will study nothing significantly controversial in society. In the end, the answer to the question of why AR is currently so marginal is to be found in the general lack of commitment to democratic social change in our societies and universities, not in AR's inherent weaknesses as a form of scientific inquiry.

Conclusions

In the subsequent chapters of Part 2, we spell out the details of the various strategies AR uses to keep the conversation going and we summarize in very general terms our overview of the map on which AR fits. In our perspective, AR lies at the very center of human life. It is constituted by a series of communicative actions that take place in dialogical environments created by communities or other organizations for the purpose of the cogeneration of new knowledge, the development and implementation of plans of action, and the democratization of society. Unlike the epistemological project, it rejects both unquestioned authority and realism-positivism as reasonable approaches to social learning and social change. Unlike local activism, it also rejects pure relativism and an uncritical commitment to the group it serves. It is a form of discussion, of critical communication that generates new and often painful knowledge.

AR processes create an arena in which the forces of authority and community, realism and relativism, meet in communicative situations that are structured to open up all positions for scrutiny as well as for positive contributions. AR is open to all and aims to keep the conversation going.

Notes

1. For an overview of the ontological, epistemological and methodological positions, see Guba and Lincoln (2005).
2. See Chapter 8 for a more complete discussion.
3. The concept of ideal type is incompetently treated in most social science literature. According to the dominant view, ideal types are a form of primitive modeling in which variables are not formulated in dynamic relationship to each other. A major contribution of current social science has supposedly been to get beyond ideal types to create models of dynamically connected variables that then yield predictions that can be tested. Not only do we see no evidence for the superiority of this method, we believe that the destruction of social science connections to context and history is part of the contemporary domestication of social science analysis.

5

Scientific Method and
Action Research

The mantle of science is highly prized in many quarters among contemporary social researchers.[1] For those seeking it, being deemed "scientific" confers financial and ideological support and offers social prestige to theories, conclusions, and recommendations derived from research. The genesis of this situation, the "trust in numbers" (Porter, 1966) that often supports it, and the long-term splitting of the positivistic and normative dimensions of social research is well known. The upshot of this situation is that if action research (AR) can be categorized as unscientific or "soft," then the hegemonic powers both in academia and in society at large feel free to ignore our results. Of course, this is especially convenient when our findings are critical of existing power relations and when our methods require social researchers to abandon their offices and libraries and engage cogeneratively with the world beyond their own institutions.

For our purposes, we take the political economic and cultural conditions awarding this prestige to science as a given. The hegemony of the idea of science itself requires an explanation, but addressing it would take us beyond the purposes of this chapter and book. We want to clarify that we do not have anything against science; it can be carried on as an activity aimed at generating new knowledge and can serve as the basis for emancipatory processes. Whether or not this is true depends on how science is socially embedded and deployed.

In this chapter and the next, we make a simple but bold claim. We assert that AR is much closer to the practices of physical and biological sciences than are any of the mainstream varieties of conventional social research. We affirm this not because we want to sanctify AR with the name of science, but because we want to show that AR is far more likely than conventional forms of social research to produce reliable information and interpretations of social phenomena and that this information is directly actionable. The conventional social sciences (economics, psychology, sociology, political science, and, to a lesser degree, anthropology) have situated themselves in academia hegemonically as the social sciences. They treat all other forms of social research as being something else and something less, for example, management studies, planning, education, AR, and so on. Thus, by this kind of power move, they make it appear that these other practices, such as AR, necessarily are not scientific.

We agree that the praxis of AR is fundamentally different from that found in most conventional social research, but we argue that AR proceeds by methods quite likely to produce valid and actionable research results, while conventional social research rarely produces results whose validity can be tested in action.[2] In Chapters 7, 16, and 17, we explain why the current structure of conventional social research exists and marginalizes AR in academic institutions.

Can Action Research Produce Scientifically Meaningful Results?

We begin with a review of the standard criticism that AR is unscientific. Some of our AR colleagues address this issue by accepting the idea that science itself is necessarily inhumane and alienating. They are proud to be called unscientific. We disagree with them vehemently and argue instead that AR can, does, and should produce valid and meaningful social research results.

In academic circles, AR, applied research, and most qualitative research are generally denigrated as "unscientific." Although conventional social science researchers occasionally admit that some AR is useful, they generally argue that AR findings are anecdotal, based on telling stories rather than on doing science. Indeed, most conventional researchers behave as if they believe that useful work is, by definition, scientifically trivial. In these circles, doing science is equated with being objective and rigorous, using statistical tests, using at least quasi-experimental controls, and staying away from the world of application. In this regard, they throw their entire weight behind what Nowotny, Scott, and Gibbons (2001) call Mode 1 knowledge production—"reliable knowledge"—while AR produces knowledge in the context of application or Mode 2 knowledge that is "socially robust."

It is not as if we are inventing criticisms that have never been leveled at the social sciences. The conventional social sciences have been criticized over the years for their often-questionable scientific practices. Critics of the contemporary social sciences often claim that these fields erred in accepting classical physics and chemistry as the model of science (see Clifford & Marcus, 1985; Geertz, 1973; Porter, 1995; Rabinow & Sullivan, 1987). For some of these critics, the proper response is to repudiate science and to advocate perspectives that challenge the very existence of generalizable knowledge. Others argue for various reforms in social science practice, such as doing more "relevant" research, but without understanding that a serious engagement with relevance requires a fundamental change in social research approaches.

Many critics say that the social sciences have been captured by some kind of mechanistic and ritualistic error in conceptualization (for example, Barnes & Shapin, 1979; Mills, 1959), to be remedied by a variety of cures ranging from hermeneutics to structuralism to deconstruction. According to this view, the social sciences have become derailed from methods appropriate to them. This is a "tragic" narrative, and it usually argues that the social sciences have not paid sufficient attention to the dimensions of social phenomenon that do not exist in the sciences (for example, intersubjective understandings, language). Of course, a particular academic agenda emerges from these criticisms, including a struggle for power and influence in the academy, a struggle that is increasingly intense as we see in battles between the rational choice positivists and the cultural studies practitioners in the social sciences.

We do not dispute the need to change the agenda, but this imagined history of the social sciences does not correspond to the findings from research on the history of the conventional social science disciplines nor to the situations we have experienced. This is not the place to rehearse the purging of engaged and reformist work from the core social sciences (see Madoo Lengermann & Niebrugge-Brantley, 1998; Messer-Davidow, 2002; Ross, 1991) and their retreat into jargonized irrelevance, but this is a significant part of the story. The other part of the argument that we wish to concentrate on arises from a misunderstanding of science itself.

Research in the physical and biological sciences does not match the stereotype of scientific research that these critics unknowingly (we suppose) use. Rather, we believe that much research in the sciences can best be understood as a successful and disciplined form of repeated cycles of testing and reformulation and on a clear relationship between thought and action. In other words, the sciences indeed are radically different from the contemporary social sciences, but only because the contemporary social science practices have very little to do with scientific practices.

One mistaken notion, incorrectly borrowed from the sciences, is that social scientists should be completely disengaged (actually and intentionally) from the phenomena they study. Equating social disengagement with objectivity, impartiality, and the requirements of scientific practice, these practitioners systematically distance themselves from their research subjects. Having achieved a distance from which it is all but impossible to understand human actions, they then further insist on separating science from action. This move severs the connection between thought and action that permits the testing of results, making the conventional social sciences quite unlike either the physical and biological sciences and quite unlike AR.

We do not take on the larger issues about the meaning of science itself and simply assume that it is useful to consider the physical and natural sciences to be scientific in some meaningful sense.[3] Our focus is that AR's pursuit of constant and disciplined interactions between thought and action resembles research in the physical and biological sciences far more closely than do the practices of conventional social science.

At the heart of this problem is the tremendous emphasis conventional social scientists place on their claim that being scientific requires researchers to sever all relations with the observed and to avoid being co-opted by the seduction of their own prejudices. Such social scientists equate objectivity with disengagement from the phenomena under study and demonstrate both arrogance about their own capacities to understand other human beings and about the incapacities of their research subjects to offer conceptual analyses of their own behaviors and situations. This belief and practice undermines the argument that conventional social science practices scientific methods precisely because biological and physical scientists do not disengage themselves from the phenomena they study to be objective. The experimental method requires just the opposite—it requires engagement, albeit on particular terms. The scientific method and its experimental apparatus are a form of praxis on and in the world, though certainly not one oriented around democratic social change.

Viewing social research this way is not a new idea, but it has been suppressed as conventional social scientists and the social interests their work serves have turned away from social engagement and social reform. Kurt Lewin, the social psychologist we introduced earlier (Chapter 2) and an early proponent of AR, operated with a view of social research as both scientific and socially engaged. As we stated there, his view of the matter is summed up in the two often-repeated statements attributed to him: "Nothing is as practical as a good theory" and "The best way to understand something is to try to change it." He articulated these views in the 1930s and 1940s, echoing the earlier ideas of the famous pragmatist philosopher of democracy and education, John Dewey.

We make a fuller presentation of these arguments in Chapter 6. What is important about Lewin and Dewey in the present context is that their approaches to social research are in concert with the way contemporary scientists think and behave, and Lewin understood clearly the link between AR and the scientific method.

Rather than pursing the contention about AR and scientific method in the typical manner of such discussions (that is, through more pronouncements), we make the case by narrating an episode that illustrates our claims.[4] Our purpose is to clarify the implications of our argument that AR is more capable of producing valid results than is conventional social science[5] and then to examine why conventional social science has deviated from this course.

Physical and Biological Science as Iterative Cycles of Thought and Action

The episode that we recount here happened to Greenwood 25 years ago. He has retold the story often enough that, in the way of narratives, his recollection of it is as much tied up with the retellings as with the original episode. He did not document the episode with anything other than lecture notes because only on reflection over the years did the larger meanings become clearer. Still, Greenwood feels that he is being true to the episode that he participated in.

At the time this occurred, Greenwood was the chair of the Biology and Society Major at Cornell University. A program for students in their first 4 university years in the U.S. higher education system, this multidisciplinary, multicollege major was designed to link the basic biological and physical sciences with the social sciences and the humanities. It provided opportunities for students with a strong interest in the basic sciences to explore the social sciences and the humanities systematically. Greenwood was responsible for the core, upper-level courses that included an overview of the relationship between biology and society as well as discussions of science and scientific method.

Having taught this course several times, Greenwood discovered that good, advanced undergraduates with strong backgrounds in mathematics, physics, chemistry, and biology had very little in the way of concrete, behavioral under-standing of the scientific method. They were sophisticated enough at using the appropriate language to describe the rules of the scientific method, but they did not understand the scientific method as a form of knowledge-generating and reflective behavior. Instead, they used their notions about the scientific method mainly as a way of advocating scientific values about truth, objectiv-ity, and replicability.

On reflection, Greenwood realized that it was not really surprising because, by their third year at the university, most students had done only rote science work in the introductory courses they had taken. They had very little experience of science as a form of discovery and interpretation in a laboratory setting.

Although this situation was understandable, Greenwood found it unac-ceptable for the Biology and Society major. Many of the majors were preparing for careers in medicine or in other branches of health care in which their understanding of the scientific method as a form of behavior would have direct consequences for thousands of patients. He cast around to find some way to deal with the problem. He knew that, despite his good relations with the students, as a cultural anthropologist, his views about the scientific method would have little credibility to them. He thus decided to invite a Nobel Prize-winning chemist from Cornell to come to the class and lecture on the scientific method. He made this choice partially because he knew the scientist and partly because this professor was known to be an extraordinarily good and committed teacher of science.[6]

The lecture given by the chemist lasted the standard 50 minutes, and the students were on the edge of their seats throughout. The prestige of this individual, combined with his congenial and down-to-earth manner, made the lesson effective for most present. It was clear at the outset that the students expected a very abstract and theoretical lecture from this eminent scientific intellectual. They apparently equated great science with great abstractions, very general laws, and big theories. What they got was something different. The chemist chose to describe his activities as a scientist and to bring the students into his world through a behavioral perspective, particularly through the perspective of the principal investigator in charge of a scientific research project.

He began by pointing out to the students that the first issue in any scientific inquiry is to generate a problem to study. He explained that this is not a simple process. It was evident from the students' reaction that they had not been asked previously to think about how scientists come up with questions to ask, probably because students are generally given a set of predigested questions to address in their class work. The chemist pointed out that there are many problems in the world and many more suggested in the scientific literature. Some of these are interesting to the researchers in question; some are not. What is interesting, he argued, is partly a matter of personal preferences and histories. Also, some problems require equipment and funding that are not available; others touch on elements of previous experience that make them attractive or unattractive. Occasionally, an anomaly picked up through observation generates a questioning process and a review of the literature that eventually causes a group of people to decide it has a problem worth studying.

It was already clear at this point that the students were hearing ideas new to them. Most had not considered the matrix of ideas, experiences, organizational structures, and histories that provide the context in which scientists ask questions. Yet the chemist's statements accord well with studies carried out in the philosophy of science (Kuhn, 1962) and the social studies of science (Barnes, 1977; Barnes & Shapin, 1979; Latour & Woolgar, 1979; Rabinow, 1996; Traweek, 1992; Zabusky, 1995). There are few convincing accounts of the scientific problem generation process. The exception is a study by Paul Rabinow (1996) that addresses this issue effectively in relation to one particular discovery in recombinant DNA work. This subject is now a central concern of the field of science and technology studies (for example, Hess, 2001).

Problem selection tends to be bracketed under the headings of "individual creativity," "genius," and so on, converting science into a story of individual heroes that, we note, is a story with a hierarchical and authoritarian moral to it, a story of a few leaders and many followers. The lecturer pointed out that this process turns on the creativity of an individual or team in thinking up and defining problems well enough so they can be studied. The individual and team operate in a social context locally, through the scientific literature, and through their ongoing contacts around the world that place problems in a complex social, intellectual, and spatial web.

The chemist then asked the class how anyone could know that a selected problem is worth studying. Again the students were puzzled. He pointed out that there are many rational tests of the consequences arising from particular subjects, but none guarantees that the problem itself is worth the effort. Whether or not a researcher or a team becomes committed to the study of a problem is a matter of individual preference, intuition, insight, and the availability of the required resources, including money. It often is also the result of a chain of previous work in which this particular activity forms a link.

Having defined a problem and decided it is important enough to pursue, the next issue for researchers is to figure out how to study it. The group must ask itself what would be potentially relevant data for the study of the selected problem. The professor problematized this deliberately by showing that it is often not obvious what data might be relevant for a particular problem. In his view, much valuable effort often goes into trying to decide what data could bear some reasonable relationship to the problem and other researchers would find convincing.

Again the students were surprised. The ambiguity of what constitutes data, the amount of social processing that goes on in a scientific research team, and the dependence of local researchers on their wider networks and on the limitations of local equipment and funding were all dimensions of science that their introductory science courses had not revealed to them. They had been given a view of scientific method primarily as an individual encounter with a world of facts and individualistic formulations of hypotheses, research strategies, experiments, and reports. That is, they had been given the heroic, radical individualist view of science, and they were listening to a scientific hero who was giving them an antiheroic narrative of science, yet one that was filled with a profound respect for the activity of scientists.

They seemed particularly bewildered by the notion that the data also are determined, to an extent, by the kind of equipment available at the research site. What is at hand plays some role in what data are thought to be relevant and the way data might be collected. Greenwood could see the students were uncomfortable with this, as if it was a form of cheating because of the idealization of scientific processes they were familiar with.

The chemist also emphasized the large number of decisions about how to document the information being collected and organizing the activity among a team of researchers to make it efficient and reasonable. The notions that a Nobel Prize chemist would have to be a team leader, an accomplished grant writer, and a social actor skilled in organizing and motivating groups were surprising to the class. That compromises would be made to design an activity that would not cause the research group to run out of resources before the data collection was completed was also new. Of course, this is not the students' fault, because few had ever faced the need to write grants, collect resources, and conduct experiments within a budget.

Having emphasized the intellectual and social embeddedness of all the elements in the scientific process, the chemist then argued that it is difficult to decide when data collection is complete. He pointed out that deciding how much data are enough often is a pragmatic matter, not always justifiable in abstract terms. It may be a decision based on fatigue; the exhaustion of financial, physical, or temporal resources; or the sense that there are enough data to say something others will believe about the problem in question. The students realized that this was a much more indeterminate view of the closure of the data collection phase of a scientific process than they had expected.

At this point, the chemist moved on to the second phase of hypothesis or question formulation. He pointed out that, although the activity is initially guided by a sense of a particular problem and possibly by a hypothesis, once a body of data has been collected and is examined, the issue becomes how to account for the array, or the distribution, or the structure of the data at hand. In the physical and natural sciences, this part of the process often is a group activity. A variety of hypotheses is often formulated by a brainstorming activity through interaction influenced by a reading of the literature, flurries of e-mail, interpersonal and interunit relationships, and other interactions.

The chemist then asked the class members how they would know when they had formulated enough hypotheses. The students were mystified, because hypothesis formulation as a form of behavior is apparently not often discussed in science courses. The chemist's sober answer was that hypothesis formulation is over when you cannot think of any more hypotheses or when you are too tired to go on. The students initially thought he was joking, but it became clear that he was not. He wanted the students to understand that science is not an activity that takes place in some idealized metaphysical space with perfect information, infinite resources to spend, and perfectly rational human beings in attendance. Science is a form of human activity that combines a set of pragmatic compromises between all the elements present at any given moment.

Beyond the pragmatics of the situation, the chemist also wanted to make a deeper point. We believe he was arguing that there is no rational way to know when one has formed enough alternative kinds of explanations for the array of data in question. The world is more complex than our apprehension of it can be, and thus we will always be approaching this complexity through a series of imperfect compromises. Being trained in a particular institution with a particular group of scientists is likely to have a powerful effect on judgments about how many hypotheses are sufficient. The appetites for complexity and other characteristics of these groups will, probably, socialize a young scientist to a particular standard. However this occurs, the chemist was pointing out that one can never know that all the relevant, possible ways of accounting for the data have been formulated. Science, as powerful as it is, is not a means for transcending the human condition.

Having completely perplexed his audience, the chemist then moved on to the next step: the process of testing questions or hypotheses against the data. Doing prestructured experiments with finite solutions in laboratory exercises did not prepare the students very well for what he said. In the students' experience, all the puzzles had specific answers, and they would receive grades for solving the puzzles with a specific set of resources and in a limited amount of time. They knew the answers were there, and they simply had to uncover them. These scientific training practices did not prepare them for the chemist's much less determinate view.

He pointed out that translating hypotheses into testable propositions and matching data to hypotheses are complex, ambiguous, and creative activities. Chains of assumptions and definitions are required to link data and hypotheses, and these chains have to be built so they are capable of convincing others that the reasoning and research process gone through is sensible and, therefore, that the results are acceptable. Doing this in laboratory situations is often a group process with rapid brainstorming and much trial and error, eminently social activities.[7]

Once the group has inventoried all the questions or hypotheses it can think of against the data collected and organized, the lecturer said that the best possible outcome is that the group has not invalidated all the explanations that it initially developed. The hope is that it would have at least one left. Quite often, this does not happen, and the group must return to the process of hypothesis formulation because none of the hypotheses is left standing. Alternatively, the data may not provide the basis for choosing among alternative explanations, and the experiment has to be redesigned.

At this point, the students were relieved because this began to sound like the sort of science that they could identify with. At the end of the process, the group has a validated explanation. But the chemist was not through. He explained that not having invalidated all the hypotheses did not mean that the remaining hypotheses had been proved true.

In making this argument, he was not being perverse. Having pointed out that the initial process of hypothesis formulation is indeterminate, in the sense that there always exists the possibility of hypotheses that the group did not think of and that financial and human resources are finite, he was being consistent. If a single hypothesis were left after the testing procedures were complete, one could only say that, of the hypotheses thought of, at least one had not yet been invalidated. It might be invalidated in the future, but other better hypotheses might be formulated to account for the data in the future. Thus, the remaining explanation could not be said to be correct. It is simply the only one left of those thought of.

The 50 minutes were over. Greenwood's class seemed stunned, though appreciative. Rather than making the usual quick and noisy exodus, they wandered out of the room silently. The chemist had given a master class, but more important, he had conveyed a view of science as a form of human action involving complexity, ambiguity, creativity, group dynamics, and many pragmatic concessions to the limitations imposed by the time and resources available. Rather than diminishing or demystifying science, this view helps us understand that science is a way of behaving, a way of acting in relation to the nonhuman and human worlds that has resulted in remarkable improvements in our understanding of how those worlds work and our ability to change the state of those worlds. Good scientific practice centers on constant cycles of thought and action.

Something the chemist did not mention at any point was prediction. Although it was clear that a good explanation could be used to generate a prior idea of the way the data should be arrayed if the explanation were to hold, he did not stress prediction itself as a core element in science. Rather, he emphasized explanation. Yet, commonsense views of science almost always equate science with prediction. We believe the chemist was right to deemphasize prediction as a fundamental criterion for science.

Scientists seek to explain arrays of data. Predicting the expected array of data under given conditions is a powerful way of testing explanations, but the goal is having an explanation that makes sense. Another way prediction is productively used is when engineers, in attempting to solve an important problem, design an apparatus or system that they "predict" will solve the problem. Here the prediction is the vision they have of the ideal outcome that guides their developmental process.

Prediction is a tool to be used in this effort, and its use varies a great deal with the conditions. Under some conditions, prediction, in the ordinary sense, is out of the question, as in the historical studies of evolution.[8] Under other conditions, predictions take the form of statistical generalizations about huge populations and cannot accurately capture what is happening in particular segments of those populations. In other situations, predictive activity takes the form of intervening in the phenomenon under study to change its state in a desired direction. This is precisely what the experimental method in science does and what AR aims to achieve in the social world.

The chemist's view matches closely with our experiences of scientists and engineers at work. It puts them, as human actors, at the center of the combined social-research activity that is science. He made it clear that scientists and engineers are not the enactors of some abstract, perfect, determinate system. The chemist conveyed to the students that scientific method is a form of social behavior, a form that is not foolproof, but one that uses human capabilities to pose questions and attempts to examine those questions through rational but fully social inquiry. He stressed the need to recognize the significant gaps and imperfections in any process of this sort, and he affirmed that human judgment, creativity, and social interaction are an intrinsic part of the process.

Repeatedly, he emphasized that science is a collective activity carried out by members of research teams within a larger scientific community. The larger community provides the literature on which the research is built to some degree, as well as the resources used to carry out the research. The research team and the laboratory form a complex, dynamic social system of people acting on phenomena and sharing their thoughts within the pragmatic limitations set by the availability of key resources and the dynamics of the human relationships involved.

Science Is Humans in Action

There is much to learn from this story, but we want to stress the social and cultural dimensions of scientific activity that are revealed by this way of presenting the scientific method. Not only do the scientists go out and get grants, often writing collaboratively to do so, but the laboratories in which they work are social systems involving teamwork and divisions of labor (see Adams, 2004; Latour, 1987; Latour & Woolgar, 1979; Zabusky, 1995). Their activities are often characterized by cogenerative problem solving because they work in groups and use both present records that they create themselves as well as written records of data from others. Brainstorming is a common activity in these settings, and data collection is often also a product of teamwork. Question formulation often takes place in groups, with people interrogating one another. Good science is an eminently social activity, as the field of science and technology studies has clearly shown.

Science is also quite often an interventionist activity. Most experiments are some form of intervention designed to discover principles and causes by managing or disturbing them in some way and predicting how they will change as a result of the intervention.

And science is a highly iterative and dynamic activity involving repeated action-reflection-action cycles. The amount of time spent cross-referencing resulting data with expectations, checking and rechecking for fit, and acting on the data to assess the effects of particular actions in relation to expectations about how the data will behave is a dominant characteristic of science. Thought and action cycle around each other repeatedly, as they necessarily do in any kind of AR.

AR is very similar in its use of thought-action cycles and the testing of understandings collaboratively generated through actions that then become part of the next cycle of thought and planning. By contrast, conventional social science, which is purposely separated from the world of action, is not like this.

This matters, not as an exposé, but as a call to reconsider the history and development of social research. Our experience of collaborative cycles of thought and action in AR corresponds well to the chemist's presentation of his experiences as a scientist. We encourage you to pause and wonder why conventional social science is hegemonic in our societies, has claimed the mantle of science, and yet does nor resemble what scientists do.

Conclusions

In this chapter, we have developed a systematic comparison between the way the scientific method is deployed in the physical and biological sciences and the iterative cycles of reflection and action characteristic of AR, using a narrative of a lecture on science as the centerpiece. We have pointed out that the conventional social sciences resemble neither the physical or biological sciences nor AR because they sever the relationship between reflection and action. In the next chapter, we turn to more detailed philosophical arguments about AR as a form of social science.

Notes

1. One may object that deconstructive, interpretive, and postmodern approaches to social research in the current generation have turned their backs on the prestige of science. We think, rather, that most such endeavors are built on a poor and stereotypic understanding of science and therefore constitute a retreat that is portrayed as an advance. Some exceptions are Fuller (2000), Latour and Woolgar (1979), Rabinow (1996), and Zabusky (1995).

2. One common reaction to our argument from readers interested in AR has been to view this as bad news. Apparently, as part of the process of becoming alienated from conventional social science, many practitioners become alienated from the idea of science as well. We believe this is an error. Being scientific is not tantamount to being inhumane. Social action is more likely to be inhumane when it is based on poor research practices and a weak understanding of local situations. We believe that many of the inhumane and authoritarian trappings of conventional social research are elements that prevent it from discovering the causes of and solutions for most social problems.

3. Readers who reject this point need read no farther because we reject the radical relativist position that all knowledge is equally flawed.

4. Because one of the main criticisms of AR by conventional social researchers is that we are just storytellers, we think that narrating a story with a very sharp moral for conventional social scientists is appropriate here.

5. This claim closely echoes the view espoused by Chris Argyris, Robert Putnam, and Diana McClain Smith (1985) in *Action Science*. For those interested in a view of these issues deriving from a very different approach, see our Chapter 15, "Action Science and Organizational Learning," and the extensive writings of Chris Argyris.

6. The lecturer was Roald Hoffman, the Frank H. T. Rhodes Professor of Humane Letters at Cornell University. Greenwood takes full responsibility for any inaccuracies in his rendering of the lecture Hoffman gave.

7. One relevant dimension of science as a form of action that was not touched on in the lecture is the sheer amount of trial-and-error experimentation and troubleshooting that goes on in any scientific work. Most experienced scientists know that science is composed of a few insights and discoveries and a vast amount of routine, tiresome, and often frustrating laboratory work. Troubleshooting, false positives, false negatives, and confusion are all part of the daily routine of scientific work.

8. Occasionally the term *retrodiction* is used to refer to an attempt to build a prediction about past processes out of a theoretical formulation and then compare the predicted result with what happened historically. This seems to us simply another meaning of prediction, albeit a useful one.

6

Social Science Research
Techniques, Work Forms,
and Research Strategies
in Action Research

We take an approach to thinking about action research (AR) that argues
for understanding AR as a research strategy that uses many conventional social science techniques but that orchestrates the overall research
process in distinctive way. To articulate our position, we now situate AR within
the broad array of general social science practices. Of course, we invite those
action researchers who believe AR is a completely unique approach to research
to articulate their views in writing and to respond to our way of framing these
issues.

The idea that AR is separate from all existing approaches to social research
cannot be justified empirically, since a reading of much of the AR literature
shows us the deployment of a great many conventional social science methods.
The conception of AR as an independent research practice is also historically
false. The social sciences themselves began as a form of engaged political economy aimed at social betterment. Only as the social sciences were split out into
the various existing conventional disciplines and subjected to harassment and
purges because their social activism offended the rich and powerful did the social
sciences become separated from action. Thus AR is much closer to the form and
orientation of the original social sciences than the current autopoietic conventional social sciences. We view these conventional social sciences as an impoverished derivative, albeit a methodologically and theoretically sophisticated one, of
the original social sciences to which we think AR is the legitimate heir.

Another defect that arises from considering AR to be a separate kind of
research is that it permits action researchers who assert the uniqueness and isolation of AR to claim that they do not have to become competent in the use
of the full panoply of quantitative and qualitative methods found in social

research generally. We think this is a serious matter because we believe action researchers must be competent in all major social research techniques and theories, as well as the few methods and work forms (such as search conferences, dialogue conferences, and variation matrices) that are strongly associated with particular schools of AR. Action researchers have to be more broadly trained than their conventional social research colleagues, and treating AR as a unique approach to research obfuscates this requirement.

Conventional Social Research and Action Research

To organize this discussion, we begin by paralleling our treatment of conventional social science with our presentation of AR. We say much less about conventional research because we assume the reader's familiarity with it, but we use the contrast to highlight both similarities and differences between conventional social science and AR.

We find it useful to talk about varieties of research as research strategies rather than trying to reduce them to a set of particular postulates, techniques, and aims. All forms of research involve, at minimum, individual techniques, work forms, and research strategies anchored in a set of epistemological, theoretical, and methodological assumptions.

What we discuss next would typically be captured in other books under the heading of "method" or "methodology." A standard definition of *methodology* is presented in Schwandt (1997a):

> [Methodology is the] theory of how inquiry should proceed. It involves analysis of the principles and procedures in a particular field of inquiry that in turn govern the use of particular methods. The study of methodology includes topics in philosophy of social science (*e.g.* explanation, theory, causality and so on) and philosophical anthropology (the study of human nature). (p. 93)

However, such broad philosophical orientations toward methodology are so extensive as to be impossibly vague and they also separate methodology from values. In view of this, we abandoned the notions of method and methodology and have organized our discussion differently.

We introduce three concepts and orient them specifically for use comparing AR with conventional research and in articulating core characteristics of AR. We choose to identify the concrete practices in social research as "techniques" (for example, the standard social science techniques found in conventional methodology handbooks), the linking of these techniques in the construction of learning arenas as "work forms," and the overall process of orchestrating these techniques and work forms in AR into research projects as "research strategies." Thus, we use the term *research strategy* to identify the overall approach taken, including, techniques, epistemological positions, and the values advocated or embodied in the inquiry process. In what follows, we make a brief comparison of the deployment of techniques, work forms, and research strategies in conventional social research and in AR.

CONVENTIONAL SOCIAL RESEARCH STRATEGIES

Techniques

Conventional social research relies on techniques that, in one way or another, center on epistemologies that posit the radical separation between the researcher and the subject of the research. This separation is asserted to be possible but to be desired. The researcher is given a superior status to the research subjects by virtue of theoretical and methodological training and an education that also permits the conventional researcher to interpret what is going on in a situation on a much deeper level than any local stakeholder presumably could. This kind of interpretive autonomy of the researcher is not less true for social constructivists than it is for logical positivists.

Work Forms

This vision of conventional social research creates hermetic communities of professional social researchers and converts the rest of the world into potential research subjects. These ideas are made clearly visible in the work forms that typify this kind of research. Local stakeholders are not supposed to influence the selection of topics, techniques, hypothesis formulation, data gathering, interpretation, or the representation of the results in print. Conventional researchers, as individuals or in teams, orchestrate all dimensions of the "scientific" work process. And, by dint of the exclusion of the local stakeholders from the epistemology and work forms, the conventional researchers "own" the results because the data have been extracted from the subjects and only become meaningful when handled by the research professionals.

Research Strategies

In conventional research, there is ongoing reflection as the research process proceeds. These processes are primarily oriented around maximizing the efficiency, effectiveness, and defensibility of the data collection and analysis processes. If the reflections are shared at all, they are shared among similarly trained professionals. At the end of the project, conventional social scientists do reflect on the larger meaning and implications they think it possible to draw from the project, again in the context of a community of similarly trained professionals. They are under no obligation to deliver the results to the research subjects themselves and generally assume that most research subjects would neither be interested in the results nor capable of understanding them. In this regard, it is particularly interesting to us that even the social constructivists have no trouble taking this relationship of superiority over the research subjects for granted.

ACTION RESEARCH STRATEGIES

Technique

In AR projects, all known social science methods are applicable, as long as they are set in a context that aligns them with the values of participative and democratic knowledge construction. From this perspective, all the social science textbooks on methodology are sources of tools to choose from.

Work Forms

AR is constituted by both social science techniques and work forms that enable the cogenerative construction of learning arenas. Action researchers regularly turn to the literatures and praxis in organizational development and change (see Cummins & Worley, 2001) and to what we already have identified as techniques generated by AR itself (for example, search conferences, dialogue conferences, and variance matrices). In Levin and Klev (2000), these approaches are identified as work forms for the construction of learning arenas.[1] In AR, we consciously make the work forms and technical methods interact throughout the entire AR project to create mutual learning opportunities for the insiders and outsiders. Technical social science methods are used to inform the choices made in learning arena construction, and analytical research methods are used to make sense of the learning emerging from the concrete change activity and to support the meaning construction process. This dialectical process between change and reflection based on social science methodology is a core dynamic of the AR research strategy.

Research Strategy

When we construct an AR project, we not only select methods but we must plan comprehensively for the social change and learning processes that will occur throughout the project. AR processes aim to create learning both for the involved problem owners and for the professional researchers. This knowledge construction, which is expected to create gains for both sides, is based on using any and all of the social science research methods available as well as the knowledge and experience of all the stakeholders in a well-managed process of cogenerative learning. This mutuality is a core democratic value in AR, and it specifically gives voice to the participants and establishes the freedom, the right, and the obligation of the participants to take part in the knowledge generation process. It confers joint ownership and representation of the jointly created knowledge and action designs.

The Cogenerative Model

AR can be thought of as a process consisting of at least two analytically distinct phases. The first involves the clarification of an initial research question, whereas the second involves the initiation and continuation of a social change and meaning construction process. This does not mean that the problem definition process is ever final; in fact, a good sign of the learning taking place in an AR project is when the initial questions are reshaped to include newly discovered dimensions.

We can visualize the cogenerative model as shown in Figure 6.1. What follows is a thorough discussion of the elements that make up the cogenerative model.

This model identifies two main groups of actors. The insiders are the focal point of every AR project. They are the "owners" of the problem, but they are not homogeneous, egalitarian, or in any way an ideal group. They simply "own" the problem. Outsiders are the professional researchers who seek to facilitate a colearning process aimed at solving local problems and to make contributions to the scientific discourse. Insiders and outsiders are both equal and different. They are different because most insiders have to live directly with the results of any change activity in a project, whereas most outsiders can leave. Another difference is that the insiders have the central influence on what the focus of the research activity should be.

PROBLEM DEFINITION

The question to be researched must be of major importance to the participants or the process will go nowhere. Once it is established, we can gain additional leverage by using relevant bodies of professional knowledge in the field, as in the case of the organizational culture literature in the Mondragón project (see Chapter 3).

We have argued that an AR process deals with solving pertinent problems for the participants. In this respect, the whole research process emerges from demands arising outside the academy. This contrasts with conventional social science, where research problems are defined as much by developments within the disciplines as by external social forces. Yet AR professionals do not just

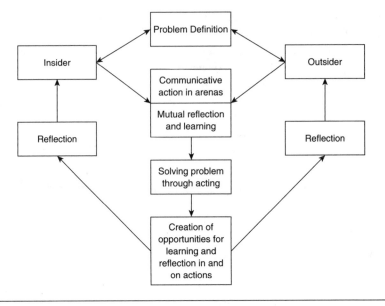

Figure 6.1   The Cogenerative Action Research Model

blindly accept any problem formulation forwarded by the local participants. We view the problem definition process as the first step in a mutual learning process between insiders and outsiders. To facilitate a process in which insider knowledge is clarified in relation to outsider professional knowledge, communication procedures must permit the development of a mutually agreed-on problem focus. These procedures include rules of democratic dialogue, which involve openness, mutual support, and shared "air time." A first working definition of the problem under study comes out of a discourse through which knowledge held by insiders and outsiders cogenerates a new, mutual understanding through their communication with each other.

COMMUNICATION ARENAS

Central to the cogenerative process in AR is its ability to create room for learning processes resulting in interpretations and action designs that participants trust. To this end, the "arena" for communication between the groups of actors must be properly configured. (See Figure 6.1.) These are locations where the involved actors encounter each other in a material setting for the purpose of carrying on AR. The arena can be a meeting between two and more people, a team-building session, a search conference, a task force meeting, a leadership group meeting, or a public community meeting. The key point is that an arena allows communicative actions to take place in an environment structured for cogenerative learning and research.

The central challenge in any AR project is to design adequate arenas for communication about the problems of major importance to the local participants. Arenas must be designed to match the needs at issue. There is no "one-size-fits-all" approach. If the challenge is to engage a whole organization in an organizational development process, it generally is smart to gather everyone in a large room to work out the plans for a new project. However, dealing with conflicts between managers in an organization might better be addressed in a leadership group format. Selecting and structuring proper arenas depends on the professional skills and experience of the AR facilitator, and good and appropriate choices are vital for a successful AR project.

In arenas, communication between insiders and outsiders aims to produce learning and open up a process of reflection for the involved parties. These discussions and reflections are the engine for ongoing learning cycles. The initial problem focus suggests a design for an arena for discourse. The subsequent communication produces understandings that help move toward problem solutions, creating new experiences for both the insiders and the professional researchers to reflect on.

The discourses that take place in these arenas are inherently unbalanced. The insiders have a grounded understanding of local conditions far beyond what any outsider ever can gain, unless he or she settles in that specific local community or organization to live. Likewise, the outside researcher brings with him or her skills and perspectives often not present in the local context, including knowledge about how to design and run learning and reflection processes.

The asymmetry in skills and local knowledge is an important force in cogenerating new understandings as the parties engage each other to make sense out of the situation. The democratic ideals of AR research also mandate a process in which the outsider gradually lets go of control so that the insiders can learn how to control and guide their own developmental processes. These ideals also promote the development of the insiders' capacities to sustain more complex internal dialogues with a more diverse set of participants than would have been the case without this set of learning experiences.

The asymmetrical situation between outsiders and insiders (Markova & Foppa, 1991) lies at the center of complex social exchanges. The outsider designs training sessions that make transfer of knowledge possible and uses his or her influence to direct the developmental process. The professional researcher necessarily exercises power in this process. Though the outsider does not have a formal position in the local organizational hierarchy, she or he exerts influence through participant expectations that she or he play a major role in designing and managing the change processes. Dealing honestly and openly with the power those expectations grant to the researcher is a central challenge in AR change processes. This has a significant effect on the development of local learning processes, and this power is easy to abuse.

At the beginning of a research process, the outsider makes decisions and teaches and trains local participants on topics that both consider important. At the same time, the outsider is responsible for encouraging insiders to take control of the developmental process. The professional researcher's obligation to let go of the group near the end is sometimes difficult to live up to, but often this is easier to achieve than the development of the local participants' capability to control and direct the ongoing developmental process according to their own interests.

For participants to become active players in a change process, they must exercise power. The initially asymmetrical situation between insiders and outsiders can be balanced only by the transfer of skills and knowledge from the professional researcher to the participants and the transfer of information and skills from the local participants to the outside researcher. In the end, to be sustainable, the process must be taken over by the local participants. The AR process cannot fulfill its democratic obligations unless the main thrust of the process is to increase the participants' control over ongoing knowledge production and action. Standard training in conventional social science research and the whole academic reward system focus strongly on retaining control over both the design and the execution of research activities, treating this control as a hallmark of professional competence.

The struggle to solve important local problems shapes the ground for new understandings, hence the double feedback loops in Figure 6.1. That is to say that, through actions taken as a result of the cogenerative processes, the participants learn new things about the problems they are facing, often revising their understandings in fundamental ways. The outcomes of this collective process of action and reflection support the creation of new shared understandings. The larger this shared ground is, the more fruitful the communication has been and the greater the likelihood is that further insights can be developed through reflection and actions based on this shared knowledge. This in turn can open up new ways of formulating the AR problems and thus result in ongoing learning for all parties, including the professional researcher.

FEEDBACK

The feedback loops are similar for both insiders and outsiders, but the interests they have in and the effects they experience from the communication can be quite different. For insiders, it may be central to improve their action-knowledge capabilities, whereas the outsiders may, through the reflection process, produce meaning (publications or insights) for the research community. Both of these reflective processes are then fed back into the communicative process, further shaping the arenas for new dialogues aimed at either redefining the initial problem statement or improving the local problem-solving capacity. Cycles like this continue throughout the life of a project.

CREATING ARENAS

A major challenge in AR is to find a good first question that is at least partly shared among the involved parties, particularly at the outset. There are several obstacles to overcome. The conventional training of academic researchers generally makes them experienced debaters with lots of practice in managing conceptual models. This can create a situation of communicative domination that undermines the cogenerative process. This situation has been called "model monopoly" by Bråthen (1973). He identifies and analyzes situations where one side dominates and, through skills in communication and the handling of certain kinds of conceptual models, constantly increases the distance between insiders and outsiders. In addition, the professional's social prestige and years of formal training may convince people to accept a particular point of view too easily. When this happens, it is a serious threat to the AR process because it distracts attention from local points of view that are central to the initiation of any AR process. Skilled action researchers develop the ability to help articulate and make sense of local models and are sure they are well articulated in the communicative process.

Thus, AR is a strategy for orchestrating a variety of techniques and change-oriented work forms in an intentionally designed process of cogenerative learning that examines pressing problems, designs action strategies based on the research on the problems, and then implements and evaluates the liberating forms of action that emerge. While conventional social research is oriented around professional enlightenment, AR is oriented to achieving particular social goals, not just to the generation of knowledge to satisfy curiosity or to meet some particular professional academic need.

WHAT ACTION RESEARCHERS MAY NOT DO

Though we have asserted that any kind of social research techniques and processes are deployable in AR, there are constraints on how action researchers can operate. Certain kinds of "double-blind" methods are unacceptable if they involve purposely depriving some group of stakeholders of support or information that affects them in important ways. Controlled processes solely for the purpose of advancing professional social sciences or of satisfying the curiosity of outsiders with no benefit to local stakeholders are not permissible. Action researchers may not make demands of local stakeholders that they are not willing to make of themselves. If disclosure of interests and aims is part of the structuring of the arena, the action researchers must also disclose their interests and aims in the situation. Action researchers may not extract or expropriate the intellectual property created in the AR process. All results are co-owned in this cogenerative process, and complex negotiations about the handling of the generated results in public and in print are a sine qua non of AR.

Action Research Is Not Merely "Qualitative Research"

We asserted at the outset that it is wrong to think of AR as "qualitative" research, yet a great many conventional researchers and far too many action researchers make this error. It is clear to us that limiting AR to qualitative research approaches is entirely unacceptable and is inconsistent with the AR enterprise itself. An AR process must use qualitative, quantitative, and/or mixed-method techniques wherever and whenever the conditions and subject an AR team deals with require. If the task at hand requires counting, sampling, factor analysis, path analysis, or regression analysis, then these techniques will be used. If issues of voice, community story, the logico-meaningful universe of discourses and culturally constructed human situations are central to an AR project, then the collaborative research will make use of the appropriate qualitative methods. Text-based database analyses (formal, informal, IT-assisted), narrative analysis, life histories, autobiographies, focus groups, interviews of all sorts, documentary analyses, and many other methods can and will be used, and many of these will be learned by and executed by nonacademic members of AR teams.

There is no logic whatsoever in claiming that AR is more in one method-ological camp or another. AR is resolutely a mixed-method research strategy, so long as we understand that the particular mix of methods is contextually determined. While this might sound appealing as a principle, this places action researchers in a difficult situation because, while there have been significant improvements in the development of procedures and epistemological defenses of mixed-method research, the epistemologies and methodological discussions of mixed-method research are still relatively underdeveloped (see Miles & Huberman, 1994).

Thus AR makes heavy demands on professional social researchers. While it would be absurd to argue that action researchers must be fully competent in all social research methods, this actually is the ideal. Anything you don't know, any competence you lack and cannot learn easily is something that cannot be transmitted to the local stakeholders for use in the arena. So, realistically, action researchers must cultivate openness to all methods, make the effort to learn about them, and learn to be supportive of their deployment in AR projects whenever necessary.

Living with this sense of our own limitations is one of the key features of being a professional action researcher. As troubling as this might be, we find it infinitely better than the self-satisfied cultures of professional expertise in the conventional social sciences, where narrow mastery of some particular technique confers prestige and professional rewards. Doing AR is a constant exercise in humility.

Action research is research, not just doing "good": too often people engaged in meaningful participatory and democratizing change processes claim they are doing AR but one looks in vain for the "research" element in their projects. Participation and collaboration are often there, but there are no definable research objectives beyond data gathering and mobilization efforts. Conventional social researchers, looking at AR reports and projects, have often called attention to this (see Sørensen, 1992).

Not surprisingly, if something is to be called research, then we think it actually should *be* research. We expect the knowledge generated through an AR process to have "the texture that displays the raw materials entering into arguments and the local process by which they were compressed and rearranged to make conclusions credible" (Cronbach & Suppes, 1969). This involves a transparent process of data analysis that eventually will lead to credible knowledge, a core aim of scientific knowledge generation. The research process must be convincing for the persons that access the communications from the research. So doing good does not make a project an example of AR. There must be action and research held in a close relationship to each other in a cogenerative arena for a project to deserve the name of AR.

There clearly is a built-in tension here. AR projects owe their first allegiance to the local stakeholders and their issues. But, for AR to continue to develop and for AR research strategies and learning about effective AR to develop, the processes and results have to also take the form of credible knowledge that can be shared effectively with practitioners, researchers, and stakeholders elsewhere.

While this might sound impossible, it certainly is not. The apparent impossibility of reconciling these aims is mainly an artifact of the autopoietic and self-interested ways conventional social science has been pursued for a number of generations. In practice, the topics, complexities, techniques, interpretations, and strategies of AR projects touch on all of the major issues in the social sciences, including the major epistemological, theoretical, and methodological issue that are regularly debated. The difference is that AR does not carry on about these issues in an academic "hot house" but plays them out in the context of application with knowledgeable local stakeholders. We create socially robust knowledge of precisely the sort that current major figures in the social sciences claim as the necessary goal of the renewed endeavors of 21st century social science (Nowotny, Scott, & Gibbons, 2001).

Workability and Explanation

While many of the techniques used in AR and some of the operations that take place in AR projects are familiar to experienced social researchers, the similarity ends when it comes to workability—for example, judging the adequacy of an interpretation according to how well it works when acted on in a local context. Conventional social research shows no concern with workability at all. Instead, hermetic professional tests (statistical probability, replication, peer critique) are used to assess the quality of the results. Here, a chasm yawns between conventional research and AR, because a central focus in AR is to create trustworthy knowledge and use it to design and guide actions and evaluate the results. Workability is the central aim of any AR project, most particularly from the point of view of the local stakeholders.

This focus on workability often seems to conventional researchers to be anti-intellectual. We believe it is just the opposite. Postulating grand theories and polishing fancy methods that have no workability hardly seems to us an intellectual accomplishment. But, by the same token, what works in context is not therefore fully understood. Put another way, successful workability does not automatically create a credible understanding of why something worked; it only shows that it did work.

So when a successful a solution (or an unsuccessful solution) has been reached regarding a problem, there may well remain a set of interpretive puzzles to solve in order to make sense of the workable outcomes and to build on them both locally and for AR practitioners elsewhere. In other words, workability is a key data point, but not the endpoint of an AR process. It does, however, show that you provided a practical solution to a particular problem. Moving from workability to credible knowledge that can be shared beyond the local project requires subjecting the workable outcomes to a variety of counterfactual analyses, to searching the literature and known cases for other approaches that create similar outcomes. If other cases can be found—a clear responsibility of the professional in AR—then the local AR interpretation of why actions were taken and why they had the effects they did can be contrasted with other possible interpretations that might account for the results. In this way, an interaction among cases is created that is a core feature of the development of the professional research side of AR.

Though it might appear that this only benefits the action researcher, this is not the case. When the local stakeholders and professional researcher engage in mutual reflection and discussion about this broader credibility, they both have a stake in the process. The professional researcher needs to understand what has been learned and how to communicate it transcontextually. The local stakeholders need to be able to defend their outcomes and understandings to people outside their project whose support, financing, or understanding is necessary for the continuation of the process they have engaged in. Both need to expand their understandings beyond the immediate context.

Conclusions

We have argued that AR is not a method but a way of collaboratively orchestrating social research processes to enhance liberating social change processes. We asserted that AR can use almost any research technique found in the sciences, social sciences, and humanities when such a technique is contextually appropriate to a collaboratively orchestrated research process. Quantitative research, qualitative research, mixed-method research, and hermeneutic dialogues all can form part of AR projects. The only research techniques ruled out in AR are those that either do not help or that actively harm the local stakeholders in the AR project. We argued that acquiring AR competence involves learning a broad array of research techniques, work forms, and learning to manage or facilitate collaborative research processes and to assist in the process of documentation and synthesis of the results and action implications. Finally, we pointed out that workability and transcontextual credibility are central features of an AR process.

Note

1. Levin and Klev (2000) devote a whole section to this discussion.

7

Knowledge Generation in Action Research

The Dialectics of Local Knowledge and Research-Based Knowledge

This chapter embarks on a more complete discussion of the knowledge generation process in action research (AR). Referring back to the cogenerative model presented in Chapter 6, the crux of the AR knowledge generation process is the encounter between local insights and the understanding that the outsider brings to the table and the fusion of these insights into a shared understanding that serves as the basis for solving practical problems. These two forms of knowledge both connect and are quite distinct. One way to understand the relationship between local knowledge and outsider knowledge is to conceive of the connection between them as a dialectical one. An affirmation or proposition from one of the parties (the thesis) is brought forward and is met with demanding and challenging questions and counterpropositions (antithesis), and out of this friendly encounter of points of view an understanding (synthesis) will gradually evolve.

It is important to conceptualize this process of dialectical knowledge generation as context bound and strongly linked to practical problem solving. Local understanding is challenged by research-based knowledge, and theoretic understanding is evaluated by its ability to make sense of everyday incidents. From a perspective of context-bound knowledge, local knowledge is informed by research-based insights and theoretical knowledge. But these outside perspectives must have the capacity to explain local and context-bound phenomena to the satisfaction of the local stakeholders. The dialectical process is of course what takes place in the constructed areas for learning. These are processes that were described in Chapter 6 in our discussion of the cogenerative model.

With this background we move on to a discussion of the bases of knowledge generation in AR. Despite a tendency to presume that AR-based knowledge should reflect a consensus, nowhere in AR is there a basis for a rule that the knowledge that emerges should reflect a consensus among local participants and researchers. Quite to the contrary, it is vital to build new knowledge on the diversity of knowledge and experience among the local participants and outside researchers. This is precisely why we conceive of this relationship as dialectical and dynamic. The cogenerative learning process is a rolling discourse, an ongoing dialectical cycle.

In such a view, "truth" is understood to be the best reasoned knowledge that can be accepted by the parties at a particular point in the collaborative process, and it will always be provisional, always challenged by new experiences that alter prior results of the sense-making efforts. New positions taken by one actor or group can challenge or support already existing knowledge and can motivate further movement in this dialectical process.

To close the chapter, we deal with how to communicate or write about the knowledge generated in AR projects. All too often the writing we have seen has fallen into the false abyss between local knowledge and the scientific community. We often find either theoryless case descriptions with little to offer either to the research community or to the local people's practice, or we find texts so inscribed with scientific jargon that the AR-related elements have disappeared. Finding a voice that keeps the core elements of AR intact is quite a challenge. The sophisticated use of narratives is part of the solution, and so is writing up in experiential learning circles.

Local Knowledge and Professional Social Science Research Knowledge

In AR, professional social researchers and insider community, organization, or network members are cosubjects and coresearchers in the research process. Both contribute many kinds of knowledge and actions to their joint enterprise. The conventional social sciences have no difficulty with the idea of expert social researchers, but they generally reject the idea that local people, untrained in the theories and methods of conventional social science, can make valuable contributions to both the form and the substance of a social research process. AR is based on the affirmation that all human beings have detailed, complex, and valuable knowledge about their lives, environments, and goals. This knowledge is different from scholarly knowledge because everyday knowledge is embodied in people's actions, long histories in particular positions, and the way they reflect on them. This kind of knowing is different from much conventional scientific knowledge because practical wisdom, practical reasoning, and tacit knowledge are its central characteristics (Carr & Kemmis, 1985; Schwandt, 1997b).

AR centers on a cogeneratively structured encounter between the worlds of practical reasoning and those of scientifically constructed knowledge. We do not assert the superiority of either type of knowledge, but we do believe in the inherent superiority of combining these kinds of knowledge in the study and resolution of complex problems. That is what we have termed as the "dialectical relationship" between local knowledge and professional knowledge. AR processes bridge these knowledge worlds by integrating practitioners and professionals in the same knowledge generation process that we call "cogenerative learning." Through these collaborative processes, the quality of the research can be enhanced because the insiders are able to contribute crucial local knowledge and analysis to the research, and can comment effectively on external interpretive frameworks as well. The practical reasoning guiding the insiders' actions can be enhanced and reformulated through accessing and transforming scientific knowledge for use in dealing with everyday problems.

We do not see any fundamental difference between local knowledge and scientific knowledge in the sense that they both are social constructions but warranted under different "regimes." A local theory is context bound and makes sense in the context of years of local processes matching interpretations with concrete experiences. These processes are thoroughly described in Berger and Luckmann's *The Social Construction of Reality* (1966). The authors make it clear that social construction processes create understanding on various levels, from rudimentary everyday theories to formal scientific understandings. These models of knowledge are differentiated by the structure and content of the social processes shaping the conditions under which they are constructed.

In AR, the central intent is to generate knowledge that bridges these two "knowledge worlds." This is a position that accords fully with Dewey's argument that there is no significant difference between how laypeople approach knowledge generation through active manipulation to solve pertinent problems and how scientists solve their scientific problems.

We believe that local people often act skillfully on the basis of appropriate valid knowledge, that local knowledge systems are complex, differentiated, and dynamic, and that, without formal training, it is possible for people to develop warrants for action based on good analyses. Therefore, local stakeholders are essential partners in any social research activity. Obviously, we reject the notion that valid knowledge can be produced only by "objective" outsiders using formal methods that supposedly eliminate bias and error.

It should not be necessary to point out that when local stakeholders take action, they prefer to produce their desired outcomes skillfully. To think of everyone but trained social scientists as amateur social actors is an unacceptable academic conceit. Precisely because local stakeholders take action in their own environments, the consequences of errors are both significant to them and often rapidly apparent. Conventional social researchers, who have severed the connection between research and action, rarely know whether they are right or not, as their findings seldom are acted upon and the practical results from their research rarely have direct consequences for them.

Despite the importance of local knowledge, the AR literature does not offer many clear statements about it. Some action researchers repeat the term "local knowledge" like a mantra rather than evaluating it critically. For these action researchers, local knowledge is "true knowledge" in opposition to the false and class-interested knowledge imposed by hegemonic outsiders. Others among us treat local knowledge as a mixed bag of analyses and information, some useful, some not, some helpful, some perhaps even dangerously wrong. The view taken on local knowledge depends partly on the action researcher's system of beliefs and views of human nature and the human condition generally exist prior to any AR activity. It also partly depends on the action researcher's experience in the field where she or he has experienced local knowledge in action and the consequences of its deployment in change processes.

For some action researchers, local knowledge simply means insider knowledge, the knowledge that people in the community or organization have. For others, local knowledge is understood to be detailed and complexly organized knowledge of local situations. In the second view, local knowledge belongs mainly to insiders, but outsiders can also develop varieties of local knowledge through ethnographic research based on local engagement over the long term. Each of these views has very different consequences, both ideologically and methodologically.

Our own understanding of local knowledge centers on viewing it as practical reasoning in action and local reflections by participants on their actions. This conception of knowledge can be traced back to Aristotle's concept of *phronesis:* "the ability to spot the action called for in any situation" (Toulmin, 1996, p. 207). As Eikeland (1992) and Schwandt (1997b) point out, this is a different type of knowledge from that used in recent generations to develop social scientific theories. Part of the aim of AR is to create a research process that reveals and values the local combinations of practical reasoning and socially constructed meaning (Berger & Luckmann, 1966). AR then bridges local knowledge and scientific knowledge through cogenerative learning in a process that creates both new local knowledge and new scientific understandings.

No matter which view of local knowledge an action researcher has, it is clear that local knowledge in AR is generally understood differently from knowledge in conventional social science. Despite a number of recent moves toward social constructivism and forms of discourse analysis and a stronger emphasis on qualitative research approaches, the dominant conventional social science practices generally reserve to the researcher the right and power to create the structures into which knowledge is put. Most conventional researchers do not question their ability or right to create separable units of "objective" knowledge that can be intercorrelated, subjected to formal manipulations and comparison, hypothesized, synthesized, and theorized outside of the local context. Even when the conventional social scientist is not a logical positivist of this sort, he or she generally reserves the right to formulate and express what the subjects think, how they think, and what import their thinking has without checking these conceptions against the local knowledge of the relevant stakeholders. What is valid, interesting, important, and trivial is treated as the professional researcher's decision, not to be second-guessed by amateurs.

This conception of the generation of social research knowledge makes social science research production and local knowledge production antithetical to each other because local knowledge is built in and conveyed through a wide variety of context-bound formats and often is rendered in extended narrative structures. From ethnographic fieldwork and from AR experiences, we know that the narrative structures of local knowledge are often key components in the way it is constructed, learned, and applied. Because AR privileges local knowledge, AR necessarily works with the role of narrative in the research process, as well as in the writing up of the results. For most logical positivists and those using formal qualitative techniques, the strong presence of narratives is taken to show that AR is hopelessly "unscientific" and incapable of producing valid knowledge.

We have already discussed the validity question in Chapter 4. Here we want to emphasize that the validity question generates some of the most unproductive debates between conventional social researchers and action researchers. Many conventional social scientists equate local knowledge with invalid or at least subjective information. They want to believe that untrained people cannot produce valid knowledge because they lack the methods, training, and commitment to transcend bias and self-interest in their interpretive processes. By contrast, some action researchers appear to equate local knowledge with valid information and to believe that only those natives uncontaminated by the capitalist system are able to see things clearly. Neither position is persuasive. If one believes that local people are always right or never right, there is no need for theories, methods, or much else—a clear sign of a polemical position rather than a concern with doing social research.

We will leave these polemics aside and focus on the extent and ways local knowledge is historically constructed and how it can be mobilized, relied on, acted on, and interpreted, and to learn how research results based in part on local knowledge can be communicated and contextualized effectively beyond the local situations where it was generated. New knowledge is created in debating the fracture lines between local knowledge and professional knowledge.

The Knowledge Generation Process

We argue that AR, in addition to generating valid knowledge and effective social action, embodies democratic ideals in its core practices. This democratization is involved in both the research process and the outcomes of the research. In AR, the research process must be democratic in the sense that it is open, participatory, and fair to all the participants. In addition, the outcome of AR should support the participants' interests so that the knowledge produced increases their ability to control their own situation. We have summarized this double meaning of democratization by referring to AR as "cogenerative research."

Central to the effort to democratize research is changing the roles of the researched and the researcher. Democracy in inquiry cannot be promoted unless the local participants, however selected, are enabled to take charge of the meaning construction process. At the same time, trained researchers cannot make sense of local social life without secure communication links to these local participants. The dynamic tension between insider and outsider knowledge is the basis for this cogenerative process.

In AR, we believe that the whole of the communicative process can be greater than the sum of the parts. The outside researcher is assisted enormously in learning things he or she does not know or immediately perceive through dialogue with insiders and through experiencing and understanding shared actions. The insiders reformulate and revalue their own knowledge in response to queries from the outsider. Both sides gain understanding from their interactions. Both sides have a complex web of intentions and interpretations of the structures and processes they are engaged in. These can be made available, at least in part, to each other through the cogenerative process.

MAINTAINING DIFFERENCES

In AR, the insiders and outsiders are treated as having equal integrity because both are expected to behave in accordance with their backgrounds and knowledge bases and both have an equal right to be heard. It is important that the AR professional not try to pretend to become an insider. A professional researcher will always be an outsider, situated in an institutional and professional setting that creates particular demands on the professional praxis and ethical standards of behavior.

The cogenerative challenge in this unbalanced situation is to take advantage of the differences between the parties. Together, insiders and outsiders can create the ground for new learning for all participants, their differences being one of the main contributions they bring to the process. Reducing differences is detrimental to AR processes. Learning to appreciate differences and to build comprehensive actions that take account of the common ground among different stakeholders is the central process in AR. Thus the synthesis in this dialectical process is not a reduction of the differences among the participants.

AR TAKES TIME

Any AR process builds on communications and actions between involved parties. From the research literature and from everyday experience, we all know that engaging in mutually interesting dialogues demands time for learning about each other and the creation of a language that is mutually accessible. AR processes accordingly demand time investments in the form of sustained communications and interactions that shape a common ground of understanding. There are no meaningful "drive-by" or one-shot AR processes, and any AR approach that promises quick results should be treated with suspicion. It is a common saying that one never knows exactly when an AR project starts and ends; it emerges out of social relationships and it concludes as social relationships are dissolved.

PRACTICAL AND CONTEXT-BOUND PROBLEM SOLVING

It is important to emphasize that in an AR process, the knowledge is generated through conscious attempts to solve practical problems. The workability of these solutions will accordingly create the platform upon which new knowledge can be constructed. In this respect, there is no other social science research strategy that links the knowledge generation more strongly to everyday practice of the actors involved in the knowledge generation process than AR. On the other hand, knowledge generation in engineering, for example, is not so radically different, since no new engineering insight is considered to be valid unless the technology created serves its purpose adequately.

CHOICE OF TECHNIQUES AND WORK FORMS

One size does not fit all in AR: as important as local knowledge, narrativity, and the cogenerative approach are, there is no blueprint for combining them in the design of an AR process. The knowledge produced in AR is linked to the context of the work. Techniques and work forms are chosen to fit the problem focus of a particular context. The cogenerative approach thus is a framework for thinking through how to choose appropriate techniques and work forms—not a simple recipe. It is fully and necessarily compatible with the deployment of a wide variety of research techniques and agendas.

The design of these communicative arenas (see Chapter 6) and the use of particular group processes must always result from an assessment of the particular situation. Thus, where a neighborhood has an overriding common interest in economic and social survival, techniques based on consensus building might be appropriate. The use of a search conference methodology (see Chapter 9, "Pragmatic Action Research") might be helpful. By contrast, in a situation where opposing groups have manifest and latent conflicts, for example, regarding the use of natural resources, a conflict-bridging strategy might be more useful. A skillful AR practitioner must be able to read and make sense of specific situations and use this insight to suggest ways to design the AR process; in each case, there are different combinations of local and social science knowledge, actors, and processes.

We are emphatic in rejecting a one-size-fits-all approach to AR because doing AR means engaging in a codetermined process of mutual action and reflection. The skillful professional practitioner continually reflects on experiences from the field, seeking what is necessary to help a change process keep moving and to track what is being learned. Just what combinations of techniques, work forms, and local stakeholders will emerge is always context dependent, as befits a process that involves both reflection-in-action and reflection-on-action (Schön, 1983, 1987; see also Chapter 15, "Action Science and Organizational Learning"), and it is a core feature of the praxis of AR.

Writing Up Action Research

A secondary effect of applying the concept of a dialectic as a way of conceptualizing knowledge generation in AR is that it introduces the dynamics of the knowledge generation into the picture. Knowledge is not constructed once and for all but results from a sequence of dialectic encounters (theses meeting antitheses to generate new syntheses). Each sequence produces knowledge that is the best available at that point in time, but it is understood by both the insiders and outsiders in the cogenerative process that it is always provisional, always capable of being developed and improved by new challenges. Accordingly, the knowledge generation process will evolve dialectically for as long as the engagement among the actors is sustained.

Given the nature of this knowledge generation process, the write-up cannot adopt the form of conventional social science. The change process that gave rise to the knowledge must be conveyed well and made clear from the inside. To do this, the participation in the process and the perspectives on the project and its development held by the various stakeholders must be conveyed from the involved actors' positions.

AR needs a genre for writing that faithfully reflects the dynamic and developmental nature of AR, that recreates for the reader key elements in the experiential learning cycles. The reader might not need to understand all learning sequences, but the reader needs to have a clear access to the major learning history in a project. This demand would integrate a narrative style into experiential learning cycles.

NARRATIVES

As we see it, narratives are generally the most promising way to write up AR experiences. Of course, this does not mean that action researchers should write up endless stories that do not provide a link between theory and practice. Indeed, the challenge is to create a persuasive connectedness between theory and practice. The most obvious solution to this problem is to create a text that has meaning both for practitioners and for scientists. This does not rule out the need to write for different audiences, ranging from academic journals to newspapers. The point is that these texts generally will have to be built in the narrative mode to create transparency about the actual project. Of course, audience also matters, as we explain below. As a result of all this, AR writing often takes the form of case studies, with detailed discussions of the processes that the group went through in generating the knowledge that is being communicated and acted on. As a result, most AR follows many of the rhetorical conventions of narrative writing.

Most conventional social scientists are, despite many gestures toward constructivism and postmodernism, positivists with a narrow view of what constitutes meaningful professional standards. For them, narratives are incomprehensible, uncontrollable, trivial, and probably just a little scary. Now, quite unfortunately in our view, with the increasing vogue for rational choice models, these once defensive positivists have regained momentum—right in tune with the neoconservative turn in the global system—and the environment in conventional social science for narrative analysis is not particularly favorable.

AR gains much of its power through narratives because narratives are inherently particular, revealing specific histories, processes, commitments, battles, defeats, and triumphs, the core of the cogenerative dialectic. Though the narratives may fall into broad types, each narrative refers to a specific situation and a specific set of connections between elements (people, organizations, and events). But writing narratives is not opposed to making scientific contributions. As we took pains to point out in Chapters 4 and 5, if the narrative developed in a particular AR project tells a story that is at variance with a major social science generalization, the major generalization is either wrong or must be modified to cover the case. Narratives are scientifically powerful.

For example, the dominant generalization among economic theorists is that cooperatives cannot compete successfully with noncooperative businesses. The study of Mondragón (Greenwood et al., 1992) demonstrates that the cooperatives are considerably more successful than their direct competitors. Subsequent events have amply confirmed this. Thus, the narrative of Mondragón means that the generalization about the noncompetitiveness of cooperatives, as stated, is wrong; it is invalid, even if the rational choice gang does not like it.

Over the past 15 years, a renewed appreciation of narrativity has developed through the recognition that, like all human action, social research is a set of socially constructed understandings built out of discursive structures. These structures have narrative properties, and these narrative properties themselves must be analyzed to understand how the structures of the discourses them- selves create local meanings, become hegemonic, or seek to persuade.

Not long ago, what we have just written would have seemed an outrageous, woolly minded approach and would have been dismissed. But the conventional social sciences have been undergoing a variety of crises of their own making. Though they still get grants, it is clear that some important part of the public has lost faith in what passes for conventional social science, finding it unintelli- gible, self-serving, and, where it is understandable, either banal or wrong. The worried efforts by the American Sociological Association and the American Anthropological Association in the past couple of years to claim a "public" value for their disciplines is a defensive reaction to this loss of relevance.

THE NARRATIVES OF EXPERIENTIAL LEARNING

The narrative is, as we have argued, an important and powerful tool to write up (in a systematic and deep manner) the experiences from activities in an AR project. But that does not quite make it a good text for communicating the process and the insights in AR. We need something more. Let us start by recapitulating the vital elements in AR. The activity revolves around cycles of active experimentation, reflection over outcomes, and sense making of what has produced or created those outcomes. These constructions of meaning, which of course integrate problem owners and outside researchers, lead to pos- sible new actions that could better meet the aims of the project. In this way the AR process can be conceptualized as a sequence of processes that experiments, learns from the outcomes, and creates a new insight that leads to new actions. This is a process through which both insiders and outsiders cogenerate this knowledge that leads to actions. In writing up AR, it is important to capture these sequences of learning. Some of the sequences are short and simple, and some are long and complex; some had little impact on the project while others were vital in determining the outcome.

Writing up AR will in this perspective demand a conscious judgment of what sequences of learning were the determining ones for the current status of the project and which were not. In a narrative form, these sequences should then be the way the events in the project are communicated, in a way that is transparent and has enough texture to enable a critical and engaged reading. With this perspective, the reader would have the opportunity to make her or his own judgment of the research process, the practical and tangible outcomes, and the contribution to the body of literature that is claimed by that specific text.

Following this recommendation, it is clear that the AR text actually breaks with the linear form of a conventional research-based publication. The knowl- edge that is generated in the project will be conveyed to the reader following the same basic logic as it was achieved in the real project. This allows the reader to see how context and political economy stage the outcomes of the project. From this perspective, this type of spiraling text is much closer to real-life development than a linear writing and will accordingly shape a much richer understanding and perspective of the AR process.

CONVENTIONAL PUBLICATIONS

Conventional research publications can result from AR when the researcher learns something of relatively little interest to the local participants but that may address a major issue in the research literature. We believe, however, that even these conventional research results are formulated on a much more solid basis than most conventional social science results because of the long-term engagement and shared understandings developed with insiders in AR.

JOINT WRITING

Communications to the scientific community can be produced jointly by insiders and outsiders in AR projects (see the Mondragón case in Chapter 3 and Levin, 1988; Levin et al., 1980a, 1980b). Although this process is complex and creates a variety of new issues about authorship, intellectual property, and so on, it is undeniable that insiders and outsiders together can communicate effectively with the professional research community.

And there are many options in between. Sometimes two reports are produced, one for the local stakeholders and another for AR practitioners. Sometimes only a local stakeholder report is produced. And so on. The permutations depend on the context and aims of all the stakeholders in the project.

INSIDER'S REFLECTIONS

Coproducing reports with outside researchers is one way of introducing laypeople to the tool of writing as a form of reflective learning. The writing process, which involves many of the tools of scientific reflection (working with data, analysis, and conclusions), can bring new dimensions to local knowledge production. Although this way of structuring the reflection process is no substitute for everyday practical reasoning, it can be a very useful tool for local organizations and communities to have at their disposal. The insiders also enhance their practical reasoning through sharing experiences and learning from the actions they take as members of the AR team. Such processes often run independently of the outside researcher's efforts, and yet are part of the AR process.

HOW GOOD IS GOOD ENOUGH TO CALL A PROJECT AR?

We are conscious in this writing process and in our classroom experience that when we assert high ideals for AR, we can overstate the case and make it appear that transcendentally high standards must be met in AR. AR is not an ideal process, happening like neoclassical economics in an environment of perfect information, *ceteris paribus,* and other absurd nonexistent conditions. It is a real process, happening in real-time contexts with real people, and it has all the contingencies, defects, and exhilarations of any human process. Dialectics may sound attractive, but often, as a lived experience, they are exhausting and even enervating.

Most AR processes often necessarily start with a quite limited problem statement, modest collaborative intentions, and without all the relevant parties at the table. The key in good AR practice is to design and sustain a process in which important reflections can emerge through communication and some good practical problem solving can be done in as inclusive and fair a way as possible. With some initial successes, the initial problem can be refined and reformulated, just as hypotheses are reformulated and refined in laboratory science (see Chapter 5), and the composition of the initial group can be changed to reflect a broader set of problem owners more adequately. How far in the direction of an ideal AR process a particular project goes depends on the resources, energy, and skills, and other elements of the situation in which the project takes place.

We emphasize this point because we often find action research practitioners or those who are aspiring to do AR very apologetic about their projects. We cannot count the number of times we have been told about a project with the preface, "Well, my project is not a 'real' AR project, but . . ." We think this mindset is extremely destructive. AR projects are long-term, complex processes built by patient steps in a process of cogenerative knowledge construction and developing mutual awareness, and they also depend on many events in the local context over which the stakeholders have little control. From the point of view of perfection, the bulk of AR projects do not live up to the ideal. We are unapologetic about this and hasten to point out that we have never seen a conventional social research project that was not filled with compromises and defects. As it is said, "Let him who is without sin cast the first stone."

Conclusions

The theme of this chapter has been to discuss the knowledge generation processes in AR at the learning system level. In Chapter 6, where the cogenerative model was presented, we discussed learning and knowledge creation at the social and actor level; in this chapter, we have moved to the analytical level of knowledge.

None of this should seem particularly threatening to professional researchers, so why is the conventional social scientists' reaction to AR so hostile? What do conventional social scientists have to fear from us? We think they react intuitively to the threat AR poses to their comfortable professional lives and to the threat that, if AR were to become dominant, they would be called upon to demonstrate the social value of their work in real-world contexts in front of knowledgeable stakeholders.

8

The Friendly Outsider

From AR as a Research Strategy to the Skills Needed to Become an Action Researcher

The lens in the previous chapter was focused on the local stakeholders; here we emphasize the professional researcher more. As always in action research (AR), however, the two are always linking through cogenerative learning processes.

Not Trying to Overcome an Unruly World

As we defined it earlier, action research is a cogenerative process through which professional researchers and interested members of a local organization, community, or a specially created organization collaborate to research, understand, and resolve problems of mutual interest. AR is a social process in which professional knowledge, local knowledge, process skills, research skills, and democratic values are the basis for cogenerated knowledge and social change.

Conventional researchers attempt to make a sharp separation between a research design that they determine in advance of initiating the research and endeavor to control throughout the research (carefully noting any deviations from the original plan) and the analysis of results of the research, which are developed and reported largely after the research actions are completed. Conventional researchers seldom take on the responsibility of producing socially applicable research results or being involved in the application of their research. Some do claim that their research is useful because all improvements in social knowledge are useful or because the topics they study are socially important.

These behaviors lead us to believe that for conventional researchers, the world appears to be an unruly place that attempts to fool them into believing what is not true. Their response to this unruly world is to do all they can to gain control of its unruliness through reliance on impersonal techniques of data generation and manipulation and through self-discipline. Research techniques are important insofar as they impart control, distance, and objectivity to the researcher so that any other similarly motivated researcher can reproduce the same results using the same techniques.

Action researchers reject this view on a variety of grounds. Although many action researchers recognize how easy it is to believe whatever we prefer about the world, we do not accept that it is possible to separate the research process from its human dimensions or to separate the process from the results. AR seeks to bring the process and the results into the closest possible relationship, and builds research on fundamental respect for and trust in human capacities. AR also emphasizes democratic values and processes by co-creating knowledge applicable by the local stakeholders in their efforts to increase control over their own situations.

Creating Possibilities Rather Than Reinforcing Limits

The dominant imagery in conventional social research comes, for very good historical and political economic reasons, from the language of bureaucratic organizations. These organizations constantly seek control, objectivity, classification, and replicability, all essential features of a bureaucratic and authoritarian mindset. But before we go too far down this line, it is worth remembering that bureaucracy, despite fashionable antibureaucratic ideologies in academia, is, among other things, an embodiment of attempts to build public structures and decision-making criteria on an abstract notion of social justice. Rather than making decisions about allocation of public resources on personalistic grounds, bureaucrats were supposed to develop objective criteria for classifying clients and problems in such a way that the allocation of public resources was beyond the reach of personal choice. By developing and employing "impartial" norms and methods, bureaucrats were supposed to make fair and unbiased decisions on important issues and allocate social resources justly. The vastness of the failure of this attempt hardly needs emphasis in a world of international cartels, war profiteers, and pork barrel politics, but it nevertheless left an indelible imprint on conventional social science.

Underlying the ideology and practices of bureaucracy are notions that humans are strongly given to self-deception and that the unruly world has to be brought under rational control. Bureaucrats are taught to set themselves apart from other people, using their rational minds to solve problems that others react to personally and emotionally. They also accept radical differences in social power and intellectual ability, with bureaucrats having the power and resources, their clients being active only in as much as they must press their claims for assistance. This bureaucratic ideology mirrors the basic belief system and professional practices of conventional social research.

Action researchers reject this framework on theoretical, methodological, political, and moral grounds. On theoretical grounds, action researchers assert that those who face social problems have much of the information and analytical capacity needed to solve them. Action researchers attribute much more weight to the knowledge of local people than do conventional researchers or bureaucrats. Action researchers are deeply skeptical about the transcendence of professional knowledge over all other forms of knowing and that "Father/Mother knows best."

Methodologically, action researchers argue that shared decision making about methods, collaborative case analysis, and teaching analytical techniques to a group of research partners produces superior research results in the quality and amount of information gathered and in the depth and quality of the analyses made. Politically, action researchers argue that research results should be useful for the local partners in gaining increased control over their own situations and that the research questions should be influenced by all parties involved in the research. Morally, action researchers reject the imposition of research on other human beings. We do not believe that social research is a professional right. We promote research methods that enable nonprofessional researchers to enhance their own control over their lives and their social situations.

AR thus is a process comanaged by the interested parties, not a technique applied by a professional researcher to other people. This means that action researchers visualize research processes in unique ways and use these visualizations to help keep the processes moving in useful directions without imposing an overall direction from above. One of the visualizations of this kind of process that best captures our collective experience of AR is that provided by the French biologist, François Jacob (1982), in his book *The Possible and the Actual.*

Jacob (1982), one the foremost evolutionary biologists of the contemporary generation, was not writing about AR. He was trying to communicate to a general audience a clear sense of the open-ended, dynamic, and diversifying character of evolutionary processes and was criticizing the ever-present tendency to try to reduce evolution to some kind of preordained and directed optimal process. To this end, he wrote about evolution as a process built on a constant dialogue between the possible and the actual.

Jacob's (1982) analysis of the physicochemical and biotic universe was built on the view that what exists at any moment in history always contains many fewer objects and beings than could possibly have existed. Although this may sound odd, it is quite logical. Jacob observed that physicochemical and organic matter are capable of yielding an immense number of possible combinations: all those that have existed and that currently exist, plus many more that are possible but have never existed.

The reasons why certain combinations exist or do not exist are fundamentally historical. History intervenes because, at each point in the Earth's development, particular conditions exist. At those moments and under those conditions, only certain of the physicochemical or biotic capabilities of matter are acted on, leaving the other possibilities forever untouched in ongoing evolutionary processes. In other words, what happened simply is what happened, not everything that could have happened. As time goes on, only some of the new possibilities generated are acted on at the next turning points (or selection events, in biological parlance).

This argument is paralleled in the work of Latour (1987). An important claim Latour makes is that a fact becomes a fact when actors decide that it is true. This is conveyed through the metaphor of closing the black box, meaning that when and how the box is closed depends on which actors participate, their power and interests, and the context under which the box is closed. When the box is closed, the fact has become true. With new constellations of actors, the black box can be reopened and new "truths" or possibilities can be produced.

This perspective argues that the relationship between the possible and the actual is a historical and contingent relationship and that the history of the process itself is a causal agent. According to Jacob and the evolutionary biologists, our world is not Pangloss's best of all possible worlds, but rather a possible world that was actualized historically, leaving others unrealized. This is precisely what the concept of evolution means, despite repeated attempts to domesticate the notion by making it a directed, teleological process (see Greenwood, 1985).

Thus far, we have been discussing so-called blind evolutionary processes, that is, those in which self-aware beings have not intervened. When dealing with humans, the situation becomes more complicated, because the dialogue between the possible and the actual continues to operate but the human ability to conceptualize alternative pasts and futures opens up a much wider range of possible-actual relationships. Thus, the relationship between the past and the future in human affairs is a combination of the physicochemical and biotic possibilities and historical conditions and the variety of visions of the past and the potential futures that humans conceive as they determine the actions they will take.

Like other teleological, antievolutionary forces, bureaucratic control systems and existing power holders expressly attempt to gain control over the way the relationships between the past and future are conceptualized to be able to determine the direction the future will take. Against this, AR specifically aims to reopen the dialogue between the possible and the actual and to counter attempts by power holders and their bureaucratic agents to pretend that the future is predetermined. Thus, a core belief in AR is that there are always more possible futures than appear at first to be open, and thus there is a significant effort in all AR processes to reanalyze the past, projecting what happened against other possible outcomes, and a consequent division of the future into what is likely to come about if no self-conscious action is taken and what other, possibly more desirable, futures may be available.

To be an action researcher is to believe that other, better situations are possible than those currently existing. Action researchers aim to reopen the possibilities for change, enhance a sense of responsibility for the direction of the future, and emphasize that human agency, not impartial control systems, is the centerpiece of social change. One consequence of this perspective is that action researchers do not "apply" techniques to a situation. Rather, we bring knowledge and skills to a group of people who collaboratively open up the possibilities for self-managed social change. Nearly all the AR approaches we discuss in this book, in one way or another and in very different languages, revolve around this basic vision.

Linking Theory and Local Understanding: Being Scientific, Counterintuitive, and Technically Competent

In conventional social research, expert knowledge is the basis of the high status of the researcher and his or her ability to impose controls and methods on a research situation. As we said in Chapters 6 and 7, action researchers obviously must have expert knowledge, but this knowledge is not treated as a source of unilateral power. Rather we view it as our contribution to a social situation in which we participate as contributing human agents.

The knowledge demands on an action researcher are heavy and keenly felt. To assist a group of collaborators in resolving some kind of important social problem, the action researcher must have some kind of substantive appreciation of the particular issues involved. If the problem is a polluting industry, the action researcher must know or learn about the industry, the pollution, and some of the possible solutions. Unlike the case of the conventional social researcher who systematically distrusts local knowledge, however, this contextual knowledge is not a unilateral responsibility of the professional expert. The action researcher can and must rely on local knowledge to a considerable degree.

The local interested parties have a great deal of information (or access to such information) about what is going on and long experience with their situation. Action researchers actively seek out this knowledge as an element in the research process. This contrasts strongly with conventional researchers' claim that the universal applicability of their research methods and techniques makes such substantive knowledge minor and considered an unreliable and co-opted source of information.

Precisely because the outcomes of an AR project are likely to be applied in specific human situations, the action researcher must master the scientific method. Perhaps AR has an even higher standard to meet here, because conventional social research rarely entertains responsibility for the application of its results to human situations.

Professional action researchers must be adept in the use of the scientific method with its insistence on the systematic attempt to discover the unexpected and counterintuitive explanations often hidden from view by assumptions and other elements in cultural training and social systems. This is one fundamental contribution that the action researcher makes to an AR situation. The ability to ask counterintuitive questions, to approach issues from the "outside," and to question pet explanations is a role that the action researcher must know how to play well.

The action researcher must also bring a set of analytical frameworks to the process—among them, views on political economy, social structure, discursive strategies, change processes, and ideology. These analytical frameworks are important to the conceptualization of the relationships between the past and the possible futures. Some work in the social sciences has developed perspectives and methods that can assist in making these structures clear, and action researchers must be knowledgeable about them.

All humans have views about all of the matters mentioned. Such views are necessary equipment for living, and they form part of local knowledge. Social science research adds some analytical techniques and comparative frameworks that are generally unavailable or not often entertained in local knowledge systems. Having analyzed these matters from around the world and over long periods of time, professional researchers have developed a sense of where the local systems fit into a larger range of variation. This broader contextualization is useful in AR because many groups suffering from acute problems feel stuck in a particular view of the situation and have a difficult time developing a sense of alternative courses of action. By setting the local situation in the context of these broader comparisons, a professional action researcher can assist the local group in opening up its sense of the situation and some options for the future.

Though we strongly believe that the views on political economy, social structure, and ideological systems that professional action researchers bring to local situations are of critical importance, we do not believe that there is one correct approach to each of these subjects that is monopolized by the professionals. We, the authors, have our own views on these matters, but we recognize that there are many different kinds of analyses of political economy (Marxist, neo-Marxist, Gramscian, neoclassical, reformist, revolutionary, trade unionist, and so on), just as there are of social structures (Parsonian, constructivist, and so on) and ideational systems (structuralist, deconstructivist, constructivist, and so on).

Though no one system of analysis is correct, some approaches can make no meaningful contribution to AR. Frameworks that are blind to the play of economic and social power or triumphalist about the overall beneficent direction of history have no place in AR. The analysis of power relations, the role of ideology, and the direction of history necessarily animate all AR projects and must be on any research agenda as problematic phenomena to be dealt with.

Practices and Skills of the Action Researcher

Up till now we have portrayed the situation of the professional action researchers in fairly abstract terms. From here forward, we become more concrete.

KNOWING HOW, TACIT KNOWLEDGE, REFLECTION-IN-ACTION, REFLECTION-ON-ACTION

Academia generally trades on a narrow notion of competence and expertise that limits intellectual capacities and training. AR challenges this position, building on a long tradition of philosophical discourse about skills, competence, and knowing. Gilbert Ryle (1949) argues for an important distinction between *knowing what* and *knowing how*. Knowing what is the main activity of conventional intellectual life in academia, and stresses the ability to know why a certain issue exists and what its definition is. A competent expert in knowing what is one who verbally can argue in favor of what he or she thinks, not one who knows how to do anything in particular.

Ryle (1949) rejects this framework by arguing that intelligence is more manifest in the way we act than in the way we think. Knowing how is manifest in intelligent actions that apply whatever capacities and knowledge a person has; it emerges through the application of knowledge in a given context. The definition of competence and expertise is knowing how to do something appropriately.

Framing the issue this way, Ryle (1949) anticipated and laid the groundwork for later efforts on the subject of competence. For example, the philosopher Michael Polanyi (1964, 1966) argues that competence is gained through the tacit dimensions of human behavior. Human beings know a great deal more than we can put into words, and unspoken (tacit) knowledge is a key component in competent human action.

Polanyi's (1964, 1966) most powerful illustration focuses on how children are able to learn to speak. If we limit ourselves to a view of knowledge as only expressible in language, then, by definition, children would be unable to learn to speak. Polanyi resolves this problem by arguing that language conveys only part of what we perceive and know and that another, major part of our knowledge is expressed in our actions. Thus, children learn initially from tacit knowledge, which eventually permits them to join the community of language speakers, though they always retain the tacit dimension as well.

Building on this framework, we conceptualize the complex activities underlying intelligent actions as human skills, complex combinations of knowing how, tacit knowledge, and other kinds of knowledge (knowing what, language, and so on). We believe that conventional academic knowledge (knowing what) about AR is important for future practitioners, but we assert that such knowledge is never sufficient to train an AR practitioner.

Given this framework, we argue that skills are a fundamentally necessary component of AR and that they emerge only through intelligent actions, not merely from abstract and passive intellectualization. At the same time, we emphasize that skills can and must be developed. We do not believe that such skills are inherited human traits. Throughout life, all humans develop new and enhanced skills. A central aim of this book is to support the development of skills for AR practitioners. Skills in AR are certainly based on intellectual mastery of concepts (called by some "theory"), but skills express themselves in actions taken to facilitate AR processes, and the process and skills focus is an essential part of learning about AR.

In this regard, we strongly support the perspectives on reflective practice developed by Donald Schön (1983, 1987, 1991). In his work, Schön introduces the concept of reflective practice to analyze the way in which professional competence is developed through training. Focusing on the analysis of a number of teacher-student interactions, he develops a conceptual apparatus that highlights the role of linked reflection and praxis in the development of professional skills. Knowledge is not imparted simply through the passage of concepts from a teacher to a student, but rather through the interactions between them and their collaborative efforts to solve certain problems together through their actions.

Schön's (1983, 1987, 1991) argument is directly in line with Ryle's (1949) knowing how and Polanyi's (1964, 1966) notions about tacit knowledge, but he takes the issue farther because he is concerned with how to educate these reflective practitioners. These concerns are stimulated both by his readings of John Dewey and psychoanalytic theory and by his long experience in organizational consulting. Schön's response is to identify two reflective processes. The first is "reflection-in-action," the ability to mirror a reflective process in the action itself that is a way of assessing actions in the process of acting. The second is "reflection-on-action," consisting of working through experiences gained from actions after the fact. Both of these processes are greatly enhanced when the professional is engaged with other people in interactions in which mutual reflections are used to enhance understanding. Schön develops his arguments about reflection-in-action much more thoroughly than his views on reflection-on-action.

As a result, in developing and presenting his framework, Schön privileges the master-apprentice relationship as a key means of improving the professional's skills. Working with an experienced master, following him or her through daily work processes, and engaging together in reflective processes, the apprentice accesses the master's skills as they are embodied and explicated in actions. This is accompanied by the dialogical processes of reflection between master and apprentice.

One consequence is that skillful actions are not developed in isolation. We agree that a logical first step in acquiring skills can be the gathering of intellectual knowledge by reading texts and taking classes, the road usually open to university students. But this is only a beginning phase in a much longer process. The development of expert AR skills is a process involving many stages.

Over the years, Levin has run several Ph.D. programs training graduate students to do AR. The main idea in all this training has been to combine theoretical knowing with practical skills in knowing how. The way to achieve this has been to have students work with experienced researchers. Projects are run with students working with senior faculty. They share the responsibility for the project and engage the research issues together. These professor-student dyads are further combined in a group structure that creates a community of action researchers colearning and developing skills together.

These relationships are more complex than a master-apprentice dyad might suggest. Dreyfus and Dreyfus (1986) list five stages in the development of expert skills: novice, advanced beginner, competent, proficient, and expert. Skillful human activity gradually reaches different levels, and practitioners operate differently on each of these levels. The novice follows analytical rules applied without much recognition of context and, like the conventional researcher, feels detached from the process. Gradually, the ability to read a context and to understand possible implications for actions moves the novice practitioner to the level of advanced beginner. Building on one's own experience is key to this development; a history of actions taken is much more important as a source of learning than the forms of explicit and analytical communication so prized in academia.

A competent practitioner has the ability to shift between context-free (for example, analytical) and contextual components in a particular intervention situation, but her or his involvement in the activity is limited to trying to influence the outcome. Finally, an expert bases professional activity on full involvement in the local situation and makes many suggestions on the basis of experientially informed intuitions about reasonable options drawn from previous work: "Intuition or know-how, as we understand it, is neither wild guessing nor supernatural inspiration, but the sort of ability we all use all the time as we go about our everyday task" (Dreyfus & Dreyfus, 1986, p. 29). Dreyfus and Dreyfus's (1986) developmental schema is summarized in Table 8.1.

Whether or not we accept the particular models of skill development in Schön (1983, 1987, 1991) or Dreyfus and Dreyfus (1986), we want to be

Table 8.1   Stages of Skills Acquisition

Skill Level	Components	Perspective	Decision	Commitment
Novice	Context-free	None	Analytical	Detached
Advanced beginner	Context-free and situational	None	Analytical	Detached
Competent	Context-free and situational	Chosen	Analytical	Detached understanding and deciding. Involved in outcome
Proficient	Context-free and situational	Experienced	Analytical	Involved understanding Detached deciding
Expert	Context-free and situational	Experienced	Intuitive	Involved

SOURCE: Reprinted with the permission of the Free Press, a Division of Simon & Schuster, from *Mind Over Machine: The Power of Human Intuition and Expertise in the Era of the Computer* by Hubert L. Dreyfus and Stuart E. Dreyfus. Copyright © 1986 by Hubert L. Dreyfus and Stuart E. Dreyfus.

clear that such skills are a major component in the competence necessary to become a good AR practitioner. Professional practice involves more than explicit rules imparted abstractly in academic settings. Knowledge is context bound, intuition and tacit knowledge play important roles, and the acquisition of skill is mainly achieved through reflection in and on action. Learning from one's own experience is a core element in the development of AR practitioner skills, and there is no substitute for it.

The Friendly Outsider

In addition to the general orientation to skills we have articulated, we wish to point briefly to certain specific skills that AR practitioners must master to be effective. A professional action researcher must know how to be "the friendly outsider." This role is vital in AR because the external perspective is a key element in opening up local group processes for change. But this outsider is friendly in a special sense. He or she must be able to reflect back to the local group things about them, including criticism of their own perspectives or habits, in a way that is experienced as supportive rather than negatively critical or domineering. Good professional action researchers achieve a balance of critique and support through a variety of actions, including direct feedback, written reflections, pointing to comparable cases, and citing cases from the professional literature where similar problems, opportunities, or processes have occurred.

The friendly outsider must also be expert at opening up lines of discussion, a kind of good Socratic teacher. Often local organizations or groups are either stuck in positions that have hardened or they have become pessimistic about the possibilities for change. A variety of methods, discussed in Part 3, is used to reopen the possibilities for change. Flexibility and opportunities for change are pointed out to local people, along with encouragement in the form of moral support and information from other cases where similar problems existed but change turned out to be possible.

Another key role of the friendly outsider is to make evident the tacit knowledge that guides local conduct. This can be in the form of critical reflections or supportive comments about the extent of local capabilities. The outsider, who is not used to the group and to the local scene, is ideally placed to notice this kind of tacit knowledge, whereas it is often invisible to insiders. Often this takes the form of encouraging local people to realize that they have a valuable store of knowledge that is relevant to solving the problems they face. Occasionally, it takes the form of criticism of particular local modes of thinking that cause groups to shut down or to cycle unproductively over issues without resolving them.

Related to this is the role of speaking the locally unspeakable. Local people, because of their history together, because of local social structure and economic relationships, or simply because of decorum, often are unable to tell each other uncomfortable things that they clearly are aware of. Human groups are like this everywhere (Argyris & Schön, 1996). No human group operates with every member giving every other member absolutely honest feedback, but social change processes require the development of more open feedback to generate possibilities for action in particular social arenas.

In this context, the friendly outsider does not speak up on every unspeakable matter. The effort is to seek out and examine those tacit agreements not to discuss certain things, the local silences that constitute obstacles to positive change for the issues at hand. This is a judgment the action researcher must make carefully. Too much feedback can block a group; too little can prevent the group from moving ahead.

Another role of the friendly outsider is to help local people inventory and assess the local resources available for a change project. Although local people are far more expert about the local scene than the outsider will ever be, their history together can lead them to overlook some important resources for change. This may simply be a matter of not appreciating that they have a store of knowledge somewhere that they are not thinking about using. It may be the matter of insisting that a particular local person or group must be included in the process, despite a history of either bad relations or distrust. Sometimes this takes the form of the outsider insisting on the presence of representatives of opposed political factions or other kinds of ideological groups. Or it may require the outsider to insist on a better gender, class, or ethnic balance in the working group.

One of the outsider's principal resources in doing all this is precisely being an outsider. The outsider's links to the outside world—universities; state, national, and international agencies; unions; philanthropic groups; professional consultants—may be of considerable practical value to the local project. In this regard, the outsider is also a resource for the local project and must be able to deliver on these relationships effectively. These outside links also lend certain legitimacy to the views of the friendly outsider, however, and this legitimacy has to be managed carefully to enhance the possibilities for local change.

THE FRIENDLY OUTSIDER'S PROCESS SKILLS

The friendly outsider is a coach, not a director or a boss. The last thing most local groups who are stuck in difficult situations need is someone else telling them what to do. The coach counts on local people to be the talented players and helps them improve their skills and strategies. The boss takes over the direction, management, and control of subordinate local groups and acts for them, further disempowering them in most cases and usually guaranteeing that whatever changes are produced will not continue to produce locally initiated changes over the long run.

Self-Confidence and Integrity

The outsider must be self-confident in social situations and he or she must demonstrate integrity in action and reflection. The outsider can and may need to express doubts about what to do and how to do it, but the outsider should have a kind of basic optimism about herself or himself and about the collaborators. Not a form of arrogance, this confidence is expressed in open-mindedness, a lack of concern with maintaining rituals of status superiority over local people, a willingness to celebrate the capacities and actions of local people, and an active appreciation of the possibilities for change that exist locally. This also involves an ability to appreciate the skills of others to articulate this appreciation tactfully. The outsider's interest in the success of a local project and community must be authentic. Local people are very good at sensing the sincerity of those who come to them from the outside.

The outside researcher does not wish to "go native." Building a cogenerative learning process does not imply that one should lose sight of professional and ethical values. Quite to the contrary, in a cogenerative learning process, it is important to be aware of the need for integrity, because that integrity will be the basis upon which real cooperation can be built. "Erasing" oneself is not a feasible strategy for cooperation that is built on diversity and the ability to cooperate to learn and act together. Integrity is, of course, as important for the local insiders as it is for the outsiders. Cogenerative learning can only take place when it is founded on the integrity of the participants and their joint processes.

Risk Taking

The outsider must also be a risk taker. Unless the outsider is willing and able to risk personal failure by supporting a local group that may or may not succeed, she or he will not provide the necessary moral support and confidence to people who are trying to persuade themselves to take risks as well. Most academics and bureaucrats are trained to avoid risks and to try to look good, no matter what happens. The friendly outsider must be willing to be implicated in the success or failure of local projects, as a professional and as a human being who is taking some responsibility for the lives of other human beings.

Irony

Finally, a kind of playfulness and irony[1] is an indispensable tool for the professional action researcher. Someone who is unremittingly serious and dour and carries the burdens of the world on his or her shoulders energizes no one. Humor and playfulness have an important role in social change processes. This is because AR projects attempt to suspend business as usual and try to produce unlikely but positive outcomes. In these contexts, the powers of irony, absurdity, and humor are considerable precisely because they cause ordinary thought to stop momentarily, creating juxtapositions that can provoke both amusement and openness to change.

Strictly speaking, the trope of irony centers on affirming in words facts or situations that are precisely the opposite of what the listener understands them to be. Irony is a kind of displacement, a viewing of the world in reverse that often provokes humor but also is capable of opening up patterns of thought to new possibilities.

Humor also evokes tacit knowledge; it provokes people to respond and to become active themselves. It can also equalize statuses by turning many participants into commentators on the local scene rather than reserving the right to definitive judgments to the professional outsider and powerful insiders.

There is a strong connection between irony, humor, and achieving a sense of Jacob's (1982) world of the possible versus the actual. Irony and humor look at the world from the vantage point of the possible, making the actual only one of the possible outcomes. The outsider's use of irony and other forms of displacing humor and commentary can induce local participants to do the same, opening up groups to brainstorming and the play of ideas that is a necessary part of prefiguring a possible new future.

Security

In addition to a willingness to face the complexities of learning a great variety of social research approaches, action researchers necessarily must have a certain mindset and personality, an ability to be themselves in the context of a group of local stakeholders. Action researchers must be personally secure enough to admit ignorance and uncertainty and yet be able to advocate their own understandings and hopes. This must be done sensitively and requires a capacity for empathy, integrity, and involvement.

Operating this way involves being open-minded, curious about and respectful of the experiences and knowledge of others, and a certain degree of playfulness that allows processes to develop in an unpressured way. It also requires an ability to be truly open to other people in a way that many academics find difficult.

Patience

Coping with uncertainty in a patient and secure way is one of the action researcher's most important traits. Complex projects with diverse stakeholders in highly charged situations do not yield to quick fixes or magic bullets. At many points in an AR project, it will not be clear where the project is going, if it is going anywhere, or if it is going to succeed in any way. The action researcher must not only be able to tolerate this uncertainty but be able to help the local stakeholders withstand this uncertainty and the sense of risk or demoralization that often accompanies it.

Thus the standards for action researchers are quite high. Action researchers must have very broad social research training, confidence, a commitment to democracy, a willingness to live with a degree of uncertainty, a clear sense of one's own professional limitations, and good personal reasons for being engaged with the local stakeholders in a particular project. Creating trustful relationships with people in the field can not be done unless the "real" person is present.

Becoming an Action Researcher

In Part 4 of this book, we take up the education of action researchers in detail. Here, we briefly rehearse some of our central contentions.

SOCIAL SKILLS

In conventional social science, there is relatively little attention paid to the social skills of the researcher. This is in accord with the dominant positivist notion that data are independent of the researcher. Much positivist research can take place without any social relationship between the performing researchers and the respondents to the survey. All that is demanded from the researcher is technical skill in being able to prepare an instrument, to distribute or administer it and collect the data, to use statistical or formal techniques to perform the necessary analysis, and be able to write a report.

Students can be trained in these skills independent of any relationship to the field. In fact, it is quite common for professors to let new students work on datasets that the professors have collected and to steer the students' activity in the direction of the professor's interests. This is both decontextualized research and decontextualized training.

In the realm of qualitative research, training students to handle interviews or engage in deeper ethnographic research requires some attention to relating to people in their life contexts. It is impossible to become a good qualitative interviewer without the skills of empathy, without the ability to listen and to engage the interviewee in a reflection process. In ethnographic work as in AR, the need for social skills to engage and live with local people is even higher.

PLANNING AND SPONTANEITY

In AR, the planning of the intervention is very important and should be as detailed as possible. This gives the researchers a chance to be prepared for the way the research process develops. There is no excuse for not really thinking through and planning for the process.

But, plans seldom match the actual process as it evolves. The projects always take off in unexpected directions and the researcher will have to adjust to this on the fly. If participants drop out of the project, if conflicts arise between participants or with the researchers, if funding changes, or if official regulations hamper development in desired directions, the process has to be recalibrated, sometimes a little, sometimes a great deal. The challenge for the researcher is to be able to read (make sense of) the actual situation in order to understand what is at stake and how to help the group move into taking adequate new actions.

Many of these decisions will have to made on the spot, and because these actions have to take place in real time, the sense making and the creation of good responses is mainly built out of tacit knowing and skillful improvisation. A thorough reflection can and must be made on the actions taken, but no full thinking through can be done on the spot. People who cannot by character or training tolerate this kind of situation definitely should not engage in AR.

Conclusions

While the standards for an action researcher are high and the multiplicity of forms of substantive knowledge and of skills needed is great, the same optimistic view of human capabilities makes it clear to us that people can be trained to become competent action researchers. They have to be trained holistically, however, and not given the compartmentalized, rote, banking-model kind of training that typifies so much conventional social science teaching. There is a great deal of substantive knowledge needed in AR and many different kinds of process skills. A combination of formal and apprenticeship training is required and we know that it works. In Part 4, we return to the education of action researchers in more detail.

Note

1. Irony is increasingly recognized as a key element in thoughtful action. See Rorty (1980) and Flood and Romm (1996).

Part 3

Varieties of Action Research Praxis: Liberating Human Potential

I n this part of the book, we provide a more detailed presentation of our particular approach to AR (pragmatic action research) and then contextualize it through a series of chapters laying out some of the other major varieties of AR. This is by no means a complete mapping of AR practices, and we use our own approach to AR as a point of reference for comparisons and contrasts. However, Part 3 emphasizes that AR is an umbrella term covering a wide variety of practices and ideological positions. After discussing our own approach in Chapter 9, we review emancipatory and liberationist approaches to AR in Chapter 10; educational AR in Chapter 11; participatory evaluation in Chapter 12; participatory rural appraisal in Chapter 13; human inquiry, cooperative inquiry, and action inquiry in Chapter 14; and action science and organizational learning in Chapter 15. As always, the map is not the territory. There are more approaches than those presented here; limitations of space and the introductory character of this text make even these presentations little more than invitations for you to find out about the approaches that you find most interesting.

9

Pragmatic Action Research

This chapter provides a more systematic presentation of our own approach, *pragmatic action research*, which was embodied in the three cases drawn from our action research (AR) experiences and methods described in Chapter 3. Although the case presentations described some of our practices, they did not explain how we conceive of our own approach to AR or provide enough information to permit the reader to compare and contrast how we work with the other approaches detailed in Chapters 10 through 15. We make no claims for the perfection of our practices. As you will have noticed from reading Chapter 3, the cases involve elements of both success and failure. Because of the way AR is practiced, valuable knowledge is co-created even when pertinent solutions to all problems cannot be found.

The three examples we gave in Chapter 3—village development in western Norway, industrial cooperatives in Mondragón, Spain, and a collaboration between an academic department and the Industrial and Labor Relations Extension Division at Cornell University—involved a wide variety of techniques and work forms. In each different context with its specific problem focus, we developed the AR process differently. In all three cases, there was not a perfect fit between an initial formulation and the development of the project, something that is true in all research and intervention situations and not just in AR. However, in pragmatic AR, the ongoing and purposive redesign of the projects to enhance cogenerative learning while they are in process is the core principle of practice. The image that guides our practice is that of the "friendly outsider" interacting with a diverse and complex group of local problem owners in a multilateral conversation resulting in the cogeneration and clarification of ideas and options and in actions. These projects never result in a single, hardline consensus to which everyone is subordinated. Rather, following Rorty's (1980) view of neopragmatism, we aim to "keep the conversation going" among the relevant parties.

In the situations we described and in many others we have been involved in, the researchers and the local participants together develop a general understanding of where they are heading and what actions to take. As action researchers, we purposely resist making these initial formulations into stringent plans. The whole AR process, viewed our way, is an emergent one until the problems have been resolved at least to the satisfaction of the local participants, the finances or energy have been exhausted, or some other event intervenes to change the direction of the process or to end it.

This is not to say that the process lacks either logic or rigor. AR, as we have described it, takes the shape of a structured and logical set of activities aimed at reaching desired results and testing in action, a planned construction of learning arenas, and a systematic choice of techniques guided by an overall AR research strategy. The direction of an AR project is guided by the learning gained through the process, not by a set of a priori norms or expectations imposed on the situation and actors. As we look across the cases derived from our own experience, we feel that this pragmatic[1] approach has yielded a set of generic characteristics common to most situations. These include:

- Construction of arenas for dialogue and mutual learning as a work form. In our work, we strive to construct arenas where participants and researchers can engage in a dialogical relationship. These arenas create the space in which reciprocal learning takes place.
- Cogenerative research. The research process emerges out of joint experiences and from mutual reflections about these experiences shared among local participants and researchers that lead to creation of new knowledge.
- The use of multi-method techniques and work forms. As stated earlier, we reject the notion that AR is a particular theory or a specific set of techniques. A great many theories, techniques, and work forms developed in the social sciences and humanities can be used in AR processes, if and when the participants decide they are appropriate and gain the requisite skills in deploying them together.

These three elements are the centerpiece of our practice of pragmatic AR. The plans, techniques, work forms, and cogenerated learning processes depend on judgments made in each concrete AR situation by the participants. This is consistent with epistemological arguments for AR that we derived from pragmatic philosophy (discussed in Part 2 of this book). Hence, we believe that AR is best understood and practiced as the use of pragmatist (or neopragmatist) philosophical positions in social research.

This approach creates problems for us when it comes to describing our practices in a single chapter. Because it is purposely fitted to local conditions, we cannot describe it in recipe terms. Yet the reader needs an introduction to the elements we take into account, some of the techniques we use, the work forms we prefer, and the overall AR strategy that emerges. What follows, therefore, is a review of some key concepts, tools, and work forms that can, and often are, deployed in pragmatic AR processes. Because we have already discussed cogenerative learning and the pragmatic approach to the choice of techniques extensively in Chapters 6 through 8, we concentrate here on our approach to the construction of arenas for dialogue.

Constructing Arenas for Dialogue

For us, the core element in pragmatic AR is the creation of arenas where discussion and collaborative research facilitate cogenerative learning. The encounter between local stakeholders and the professional researcher is the cornerstone on which mutual learning is built. Because we do not begin with a technique defined a priori, and we try to match our approach to the local situation and actors, our AR processes generally have a slow and intensely conversational opening stage. In beginning this way, with patient exploratory discussions, ours differs from most other approaches to AR.

We believe that our obligations as professional researchers are to assist the group to choose and learn whatever techniques and theories are suitable for the process they are concerned with. We do not rely on particular "recipes" that always should be followed. Such recipes mainly serve to lessen the insecurities of the professional researchers about what they should be doing, and they generally hamper the growth and development of the strength of the local stakeholder group.

We confront the local problems with all the skills and knowledge we have. What we do not know and the skills we lack may well be detrimental to the particular project, and we always wish we were smarter, more skilled, and better trained. But we advocate facing these existential and epistemological uncertainties as professional action researchers directly, rather than adhering to a particular set of recipes that would lower the demands on us personally. This is a necessary part of our integrity as researchers.

At the same time, we do not advocate casting around blindly for a way of working. We believe that in AR central skills revolve around the ability to understand and interpret social and material contexts, to decide on and configure appropriate arenas for discourse, to lead the interaction process, and to assist the participants in testing their knowledge in action and reflecting on the results. Thus, the action researcher must have the ability to interpret and reason about managing cogenerative learning processes that involve the active testing of the resulting knowledge.

A central ethical and political goal in AR is to achieve liberating outcomes. It is not easy to be precise about what a liberating outcome might look like, but we do not advocate narrowing this down to a recipe either. In our AR practice, determining what is a liberating outcome is an explicit part of the cogenerated learning process.

As a point of departure, it is possible to initiate discussion about liberating outcomes by offering an initial definition as "outcomes where local participants gain greater control over their own situation as a group." We are not referring to personal liberation or the gaining of individual power by group members, but to the increased capacity of local participants to define and manage their own collective situation.

This kind of liberation is not an abstractly quantifiable product. In highly coercive situations, a small gain may be intensely liberating, whereas in a more open situation, major changes may not be experienced as particularly significant by the participants. We believe that the change has to be real and meaningful to the local participants as a group. It is not up to the AR professional to decide if people have experienced a liberating outcome; it is up to us to pose this issue for the AR group and to keep the conversation about it going.

Searching

Although we argue strongly for pragmatic, multi-method techniques and work forms, and we have employed many different kinds of techniques and work forms in our practice, one broad and well-defined approach to cogenerative learning is particularly appropriate to our pragmatic approach to AR. It is called *searching*. We will present it *in extenso* here, not because we believe it must be used in every AR situation, but because it is a powerful approach that has proved capable of generating significant results and because presenting it in detail will give the reader a much more concrete view of our way of thinking about AR.

Searching refers to a specific kind of cogenerative learning process. The core idea of searching is to create a situation where ordinary people can engage in structured knowledge generation (from developing plans to execution) based on systematic experimentation. Participants are helped to learn by doing and by constantly searching out and trying out new ways of thinking and acting (Emery, 1993, p. 192).

SEARCH CONFERENCES

The search conference is a work form for participatory planning and design. The aim of search conference techniques is to allow for collective planning and design of actions aimed at solving problems directly relevant to the people involved. It is a collective process of inquiry, creating learning options for all those participating, moving from plans to concrete actions.

A search conference is most often a multi-day meeting of a fairly large group (15–40) of people in some kind of retreat setting. Prior to the event, the planning of a search conference begins with a process of problem identification by a planning group and the self-conscious selection and preparation of participants. Once convened, a search conference proceeds with the participants sharing their view of the history of the situation they find themselves in. Then they identify the problems they are addressing collectively through a creative process resulting in a variety of action plans for solving the problems. In the final stage of the search, participants choose among alternative action plans, making collective decisions about what to work on. Thus, a search conference integrates planning, creative problem solving, and concrete action in the same process. This integration is its most unique feature, and it is a distinctively appropriate methodology for carrying out AR.

Search conferences create many different arenas for dialogue. The structure of the events over the time a search lasts is broadly predetermined. The process moves along according to its inner logic, though under the continued guidance of a couple of search managers. Search conferences almost always succeed in tapping participants' energy for identifying and solving their own problems, so long as search facilitation is skillful. Bringing people together and providing them with the opportunity to think through and plan elements of their own future inevitably releases creative energy that is constructively channeled in the search conference process. We have not so far participated in or been responsible for a search conference that has failed, though we have often seen that the follow-up actions did not fulfill the high expectations set at the search conference.

The search conference integrates five processes. First, it creates a discourse aimed at sharing different stakeholders' interpretations of history. Second, it develops a common vision (goals) for the future and what will happen if the future is not addressed creatively. Third, it engages the participants in creative activity, searching for action plans to reach desired goals. Fourth, it facilitates a collective prioritizing among action issues; fifth, it links planning to action groups and specific actions. The outcome of a successful search conference is a set of action issues and plans that participants want to pursue collectively.

HISTORICAL ROOTS OF SEARCHING

Search conferences emerged from the industrial democracy tradition in the United Kingdom, Scandinavia, and Australia. The theoretical and methodological development of searching goes back to key researchers at the Tavistock Institute in London, Fred Emery and Philip Herbst (see Chapter 2). They had very similar professional backgrounds as clinically trained social psychologists, and they worked within the same international research network. One was located in the Southern Hemisphere and the other in the North, and together they shaped the thinking and the practice of searching in parallel. On the Australian scene, Merrelyn Emery played a crucial role in conceptualizing and developing the search process (Emery, 1982, 1993).

Another way of describing how searching developed is to see that it arose from the international networks centered on the industrial democracy movement. A major concern among those working on industrial democracy was how to integrate participatory planning in collective actions for change. The main obstacle in most models of AR at that time was domination of the processes by experts, a problem we allude to in our discussion of Kurt Lewin in Chapter 2. Change processes were often planned and executed by the action researchers, and the real involvement of the participants was limited.

A second issue emerging at the time was a concern about the failure of social innovations to spread effectively to broader groups. Many experiments in local social change had turned out to be successful, but very often these successes were encapsulated at the original site. They did not automatically spread by the sheer virtue of the promising results achieved. This led to a concern with ways to diffuse participative processes to broader strata of society.

Emery and Oeser (1958) first stated these latter concerns in a study on the diffusion of agricultural reforms in Australia. Much later, these issues were followed up in two publications in which search conferences emerge as a theme. Herbst's 1980 article in *Human Futures* presents a conceptualization of the search conference approach and communicates experiences from the first search conference in Norway, which took place on an island of Skjervøy in the north (Engelstad & Haugen, 1972; Herbst, 1980). This search became very important because it provided experience with the method to a broad group of researchers at the Work Research Institute in Oslo and because it created positive results in the local community.

In Australia, Fred and Merrelyn Emery's work on searching was first published as a working paper from the Australian National University in 1974. The Herbst and Emery publications became the pivots on which the development of search conferences turned and represented the opening of a line of developments that resulted in the widespread and respected practice of search conferences today (Emery, 1998; Martin, Hemlock, & Rich, 1994; Martin & Rich, 1994; Weisbord, 1992).

THE NORWEGIAN EXPERIENCES

The general thinking underlying the search conference fit into the Norwegian context of the early 1970s. There was an extended public debate on worker participation in a social democracy. The high-profile AR on industrial democracy created fertile ground for participative approaches to social change. In this context, the thinking underlying search conferences nicely corresponded to the issues of participative planning and the diffusion of change processes.

For example, by this time, the action researchers at the Work Research Institute in Oslo had abandoned the expert model for sociotechnical change (Elden, 1979) and were experimenting with search conference models to enhance change efforts in multiple companies at the same time. Search conferences fit suitably into this situation and led to the first major attempt to use the technique in the planning effort for the municipality of Skjervøy. Philip Herbst, one major

Norwegian link to the international networks, heavily influenced this first search. This search focused on the challenges of economic and municipal development and was seen as quite radical in the Norwegian context because it based the developmental activity on fairly broad public participation.

Applying search conferences to local community development projects became one of the major development techniques used in Norway, and searching became a central element in some government-supported local community development programs. At one point, more than 60 municipalities were engaged in community development effort, and search conferences were often used to initiate the work. The outcomes were successful enough that the Department of the Interior commissioned the writing of a manual on how to run searches (Brokhaug, Levin, & Nilssen, 1986). Although not everyone followed the suggested blueprint, elements of search methodology became widespread, showing that search conferences were a convincing method for many practitioners.

While the deployment of searching in community settings continued, parallels developed in industrial settings. The search conference was adopted as a tool for initiating change processes in industry. This methodology was successfully adapted to several different industries. In particular, the researchers and consultants connected to the Work Research Institute in Oslo focused a lot of attention on searching as a way of initiating change processes (Hanssen Bauer & Aslaksen, 1991, p. 202). These Norwegian experiences were a major inspiration for the U.S.-based private consultant Marvin Weisbord, who spent part of 1987 learning about searching from Norwegian practitioners. Later he took this knowledge and adapted it in his own particular way for use in U.S. business and public administration.

The Work Research Institute in Oslo developed a work form based on the search conference that let loose most of the rigid structure of search conferences and also changed the role of the facilitators. Built on "operationalization" of Habermas's (1984) ideal speech thinking, they shaped a facilitation practice that was much like policing for democratic dialogue (Gustavsen, 1985; Pålshaugen, 2000, 2002). This type of conference was given the name "dialogue conferences"; as the name indicates, the vital element is to strive for open communication among the participants. This model is heavily used in Norwegian industry, where labor and management join in for mutual enterprise developmental activity.

AUSTRALIAN EXPERIENCES

Fred and Merrelyn Emery are central in the development of search conferences in Australia, where search conferences have been widely used. Fred Emery was a key international player in the development of the search conference approach along with his role in the development of the industrial democracy movement (discussed in Chapter 2). In the Australian context, his wife, Merrelyn, has played an equally important role, and over the years has written a good deal more about searching than he did.

Many of the challenges faced in Australia parallel those in Norway. Developing social change processes and then achieving their diffusion was not very effective. When they were developed, new democratic work forms tended to remain more or less encapsulated where they were invented. Merrelyn Emery published her important monograph on searching (1982), which developed detailed arguments about participants' learning processes. She also argued for multiple searches as a way of gaining broader public momentum for participative planning. This strategy was important and was embodied in what came to be called "Searching Australia," an ambitious plan for making searching a nationwide effort at social change (Emery & Emery, 1974).

In 1989, Australian work life researchers organized an international conference called "Work Place Australia." One of the major ingredients in this event was having the participants spend 1 week involved in a search conference. Multiple search conferences (20) were organized, bringing together foreigners and locals. Though we cannot judge the effectiveness of this multiple search program, this effort created international awareness of searching as a methodology for participative design. Indeed, the success of this conference is seen in the subsequent activities of Australian researchers, who routinely travel abroad to train professionals in other countries in search conference techniques. For example, Merrelyn Emery has set up a structure in the United States to teach people how to run search conferences.

THE USE OF SEARCH CONFERENCES IN THE UNITED STATES

Searching was first brought to the United States by researchers from the Tavistock Institute. In the early 1980s, both Fred Emery and Eric Trist were affiliated with University of Pennsylvania's Wharton School of Business. During this period, Trist was actively working on a major AR project in Jamestown, New York, and Emery was invited to work with Native American groups in upstate New York. This latter activity resulted in a search focused on the future of the Seneca Indians.

A more powerful influence in the United States came through Marvin Weisbord's consulting. In one of his books, *Productive Workplaces* (1987), he collected several practical examples of search conferences carried out in a broad range of settings and cultures. Weisbord has created a significant consulting business by focusing his attention on training consultants to do search conferences. Between his training efforts and his writing, he has been the dominant influence in the United States on the development of thinking about search methods.

Although this diffusion might be welcome, it also means that a very particular view of searching has achieved broad currency in the United States. Weisbord's (1992) search conference *modus operandi* is a variant of searching tailored to fit within the given power structures of U.S. businesses. One of the principal ways Weisbord's approach differs from those we have discussed is that he accepts certain parameters in advance and agrees to push certain areas of disagreement into the background. Thus, he mainly uses the search as a method for shaping a shared vision and tapping some of the participants' creative capabilities. There is also little emphasis in his approach on how to sustain the development actions initiated through the search process. While some of this stems from Weisbord's own practices, and although a discussion of power and searching is presented in Ann Martin's (2000) doctoral dissertation, challenging organizational design and power structures tends to be left out of searches in the U.S. generally.

Another stream of activity centered on searching revolves around Cornell University. A program of the Cornell School of Industrial and Labor Relations called "Programs for Employment and Workplace Systems,"[2] inspired originally by William Foote Whyte, explored searching using connections to Morten Levin and the Norwegian University of Technology and Science in Trondheim (Whyte, 1994, p. 307). Given the directness of the connection, the Cornell approach is quite close to the Norwegian one and embodies a stronger link between the Norwegian tradition and U.S. academia than does Weisbord's.

SEARCH CONFERENCES AS STRUCTURED CHANGE PROCESSES

Although we obviously have our preferences, we emphasize that searching should not be equated with just one technique; there is no one right way of running a search conference. Practitioners vary in approach and skills. In addition, good practitioners are constantly developing and altering their own approaches as they learn more about the processes involved and gain more skills. There is no reason to grant any one of the founders of this methodology the honor of having the "correct" approach. We certainly do not agree with M. Emery (1993) that there is only one way of doing search conferences.

CO-OPTATION

Co-optation of searching is a real problem. Searching, like Lewinian AR and sociotechnical systems work before it, has become fashionable. Far too many processes are now labeled as search conferences that negate the necessary focus on participatory and liberating social change. Some of this is a consequence of poor planning and a lack of understanding of what a search actually is. However, some of this comes from the increasingly frequent use of search conferences to create "magical moments" for the participants by giving them an illusion of participating in real change processes while the underlying intention of the process is to reduce internal pressure for change. To help action researchers contend with this problem and to provide the reader with more detailed guidelines about search processes, we now discuss the main elements of a search conference as the approach emerged from our own practice.

WHEN IS A PROCESS A SEARCH?

In our view, six major elements must be present if a group process is to be characterized as a search:

1. Creating a shared history and letting every participant understand how the world looks according to other groups of participants

2. Creating a shared vision about what is a desirable future or solution to the focal problem of the group

3. Creating a view of what would be the probable future if nothing were done; sometimes this perspective might be integrated into the work on desirable future

4. Identifying action plans for addressing the focal problem

5. Creating a collective prioritization process in which participants choose among alternative action plans

6. Initiating concrete change activity and structuring a follow-up process aimed at sharing achievements and learning

These six elements differ in content and structure. Working on developing a history is very different from using the creativity necessary for developing new ideas for action plans. In addition, throughout a search, there is a regular interplay between plenary sessions and small group work that creates a new social structure. Another important aspect of searches is how the fairly strict structure and rules create a ritual process that helps shape valuable arenas for dialogue.

Herbst (1980) illustrates the search process as a dual track. Figure 9.1 conveys an overall conception of the search as a generative and creative process (building shared history and visions, generating creative action possibilities, reflecting on the feasibility of action possibilities, and finally working out priorities among the possible action items).

The work process in a search conference involves both plenary presentations and discussions and small group work. These small groups, either homogeneous or mixed in background and interests, are used to prepare ideas

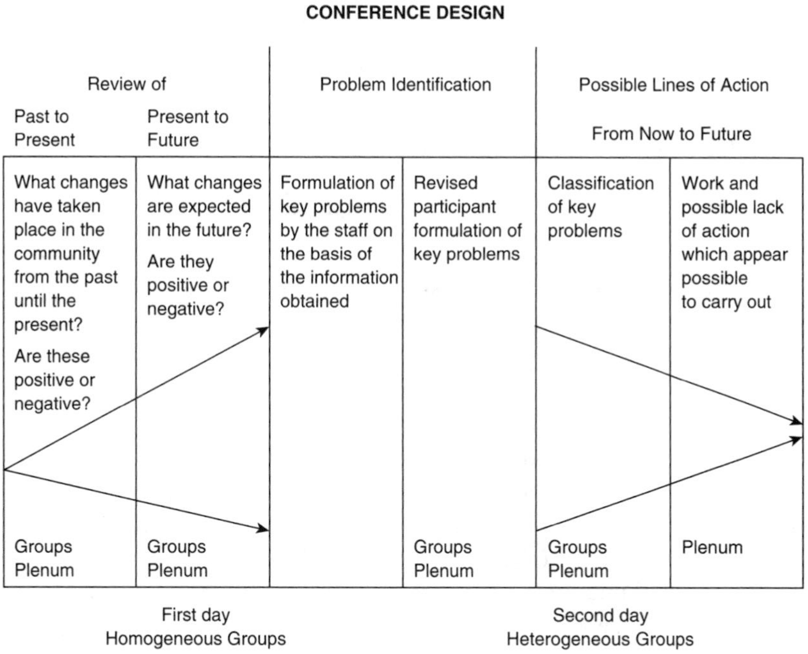

CONFERENCE DESIGN

		Problem Identification		Possible Lines of Action	
Review of					
Past to Present	Present to Future			From Now to Future	
What changes have taken place in the community from the past until the present? Are these positive or negative?	What changes are expected in the future? Are they positive or negative?	Formulation of key problems by the staff on the basis of the information obtained	Revised participant formulation of key problems	Classification of key problems	Work and possible lack of action which appear possible to carry out
Groups Plenum	Groups Plenum		Groups Plenum	Groups Plenum	Plenum

First day	Second day
Homogeneous Groups	Heterogeneous Groups

Figure 9.1   Herbst's Dual-Track Search Process

and materials for plenary discussions and, thus, to give voice to as many of the participants as possible.

Preparing for the Search

Many roads lead to a search conference. In some cases, the local actors are familiar with search conferences and accordingly know what they are looking for. In this situation, the task for the initiators is to find a facilitator to take on the job. A standard bureaucratic method is simply to call for proposals from various professional search conference managers. We think that searching as a form of AR demands skills and engagement that reach beyond the work styles of most conventional consultants, however. Thus contracting for a search conference itself is a complex matter.

Another road to a search conference is for an outsider involved in local development work to convince the local actors that a search is appropriate. In this situation, the local actors may not understand what a search is. The challenge for the outsider is to convey an understanding of the search process and to show that it potentially can help the local actors. Even so, the process of launching a search depends on mutual trust, because it is difficult to convey a fair picture of what a search is unless people have experienced one or have seen the positive effects of a search on another group.

Planning and Executing a Search

COMMISSIONING THE SEARCH CONFERENCE

The first step in searching is working with the local actors who want to commission a search. This discussion is important for many reasons. The initial question that motivates local people may not necessarily be the most fundamental one for their group or may not be stated in a way that can lead to a productive search. Because searching is a form of cogenerative learning, ample time must be devoted to discussion with those commissioning the search so that everyone has a clear idea what the process is all about.

Because the process aims to create mutual learning opportunities, the facilitator should challenge the initial problem focus and in turn be challenged by the local definitions of the problem at hand. Through this dialogue, the resulting mutual understanding will provide the definition of the search problem used to plan the search conference. It is highly advisable to have two people serve as cofacilitators or search conference managers.

IDENTIFYING THE PARTICIPANTS

The next step is to identify potential participants. For searches, an ideal size is between 20 and 40 persons, but searches have been done successfully with up to 70 participants, and recently some linked searches involving a number of groups concerned with the same issues have been carried out involving hundreds of participants (Robert Rich, 1998, personal communication; Pelletier, Kraak, McCullum, Uusitalo, & Rich, 1999; Pelletier, McCullum, Kraak, & Asher, 2003; Peters, Hittleman, & Pelletier, 2005).

The proper identification of relevant stakeholders is vital. They are identified as a function of the focus of the search. Every effort has to be made to locate individuals and groups that have a legitimate interest or say in the matter under consideration. This is a complex procedure that usually begins with the points of view of those who commissioned the search. But this group is rarely fully representative of the relevant stakeholders. The facilitator must seek to manage the process of inclusion to be certain that as many relevant stakeholder interests as possible are present.

This begins with discussions with those commissioning the search, but quickly the process of finding and inviting relevant participants becomes a form of network analysis. Starting with names and groups provided by the start-up group, each new potential participant contacted is also asked for recommendations about others or other groups who should be invited to the search. Continuing along these lines, an emergent selection of participants is established. Often the scope of those included expands and contracts a few times until a tolerable balance has been achieved.

INVITING THE PARTICIPANTS

When the facilitator judges that a suitable group of people has been identified as participants and the local stakeholders agree, invitations must be made. In our opinion, the best way to do this is to combine the invitation with an interview. If the invitations are made by the facilitators, the facilitators can, through the interviews, gain more knowledge about the participants, their backgrounds, and their institutional contexts, which will help the search facilitators be more effective. The interview provides the facilitator with an understanding of the persons and the situation that enables the facilitator to make knowledge-based decisions regarding the structure and process of the search while it is taking place. At the same time, this invitational interview is valuable as a way of informing participants about what a search conference is. This can both inform and motivate the potential participants. Occasionally, constraints require delegating this task to the planning group. When this is done, at the very least, participants are invited by people they know and have a chance to ask questions about the process in a comfortable environment. As in everything else, the better prepared the facilitator and participants are, the more likely the search will be successful.

LOGISTICAL SUPPORT

We will not go into detail here about the material support structures for searches, except to say that a good setting and logistical support are critically important. The search depends on a group learning about itself, so the setting must be at least somewhat retreat-like, permitting the participants to separate themselves from their daily lives briefly and focus intensively on each other and the problem at hand. This creates the opportunity for people to get to know each other socially during the moments the search itself is not running, and it creates a distance from everyday life that enhances the opportunities for reflection and concentration on the issues of the search.

It is important to find a locale that has a big enough room for plenary discussions. The room needs to be large enough for the participants to move freely around, and the walls should be filled with flip charts displaying the work in progress. The setting must also contain ample small group working spaces. An area to collect and maintain materials is important as well.

In preparing a search, close cooperation with a group of local participants is a prerequisite. This creates a good basis for inviting members and also helps members of the planning group serve as cofacilitators. This has the effect of training local people to handle future searches by themselves, but it has also an important democratic effect by giving local people a say in decisions regarding the design and management of the search conference.

STAGES IN A SEARCH CONFERENCE

A typical search process takes about 2 days, though the length of time is flexible. The argument for using this much time is that searches depend on collective learning processes, processes that do not move fast. A shorter search might too easily fall into the trap of becoming a quick fix and violate the basic aims of creating a sustainable learning process.

The search begins with a plenary on the shared history of the problem being dealt with, followed by sessions on the ideal and probable futures. This usually ends the first day. The second day begins with the development of action strategies, the creation of task forces, and the search ends with the planning of future meetings.

CREATING A SHARED HISTORY

The first step in searching is to create a shared history. This is not to say that a unified understanding of the group's historical roots must exist. Rather, the focus is that all participants should be aware of the other actors' understanding of the relevant history. The core idea is to show how multifaceted and heterogeneous the history is; this will be obvious after all points of view have been heard. Most groups at a search already have a history together, but the search-generated history is different because it actively seeks out the experiences and views that are often overlooked or actively suppressed in everyday life.

One common way to initiate the search is to have a well-respected member of the group draw up a kind of broad-view historical sketch. Then each group of participants is given the opportunity to work out its own version of the history. These are combined in plenary sessions until together the whole group has developed a more heterogeneous position that satisfies it as a whole.

Another way to develop a shared history is based on the creative use of drawing and writing. In the plenary room, a wall area is covered with paper to write and draw on. It can be a line of separate sheets or a long sheet of butcher-block paper (Martin & Rich, 1994). On this surface, a very rough timeline is drawn, starting on the left with an initiating point and continuing up to the present. Participants are then given the opportunity to add drawings or events anywhere they have something to contribute. After this, the whole group listens as each person who has added something explains it. Through this approach, participants can learn and build on each other's interpretation of history, and the whole process creates a new cogenerated history.

CREATING A SHARED VISION

The general aim of this part of the search process is to create a shared position about a desirable and feasible future. This is built from the contrast between an ideal future and a probable one. An ideal future can be a vision of how the local community or organization should look by the end of the next decade. The core issues here are to have the participants surface their views and share their sense of what a desirable future is. This is again a collective process, where participants engage in a discourse using both small groups and plenaries to create a sort of consensus. What often emerges is a general agreement that allows room for individual interpretations and actions.

Although absolute consensus is not necessary or desired, there must be a tolerable level of mutual understanding and agreement. A search conference can produce useful results only where there is a minimum common understanding and consensus on goals. Martin (1995) argues a harder line, claiming that strong differences about the ideal future make it less likely that a search conference will produce practical results.

One way to carry out the process of defining the ideal future is to start with small, relatively homogeneous groups and to ask each group to identify 5 or 10 important goals to reach on the search issue. Each group then presents its view in plenary, and this creates the basis for a discussion among all the participants. The search facilitators must see to it that the plenary discussion gradually focuses on issues that participants can agree on. This working consensus is important because it will be the reference point for the later action teams.

The probable future is arrived at by the same technique. The groups are asked to develop their sense of what will happen if they do not take action to improve their future. This part of the process is sensitive because the negative view of the future is usually easier to articulate and often corresponds to the participants' worst fears. We think groups must deal openly with these fears because naming their worst fears contributes to the sense of the need for real change.

Once the search group has identified the probable future, the kind of bubbling energy that is often associated with the history and ideal future seems to evaporate. This reality check is part of the process, and the facilitators should do nothing to make it easier or more tolerable. Indeed, we believe that it is important for each participant to experience directly the implications of not taking action. This is the basis for making a subsequent commitment to action. To reinforce this, usually the day ends at this point, with the participants left to their own ruminations about the ideal and probable futures. Alternative endings are possible. The time available, the kinds of issues, and the group dynamics often suggest modifications in the segmentation of the time.

IDENTIFYING ACTION PLANS

Given an overall understanding of desirable goals and the results of no action, the task is to develop action ideas and strategies that support the attainment of valued goals. This process builds on the creative capacity of the participants. It is important to encourage participants to let their creative capacity come out in the open. Too often in everyday life, we experience very low demands on our personal creativity; in a search, it is a good investment to devote plenty of time to encouraging this kind of creativity.

To do this, certain rules must be observed. Criticism of the ideas of others is not permitted. Participants may ask each other for clarification, but all ideas are treated as worthy of consideration. No one is permitted to dominate the airtime or to shut others down. The facilitator must be alert to gender, age, race, and ideological differences and try to keep the dialogue as open as possible. One good way to encourage creativity at this point is to set up small groups of participants who differ in experience and position in the local community or organization. Members work on developing strategies and action plans that are subsequently presented in the plenary session. In the plenary, the participants are encouraged not to criticize the ideas presented, though they are free to ask for clarification.

PRIORITIZING IDEAS

If the creative process has worked, by this time the assembled group has generated many options for action from which to choose. All these aim to reach the ideal future. It is in the nature of the creative process leading up to this, however, that these ideas are not in any particular order. To be worked with in the large group, they must be ordered in some way. We believe this is a task for the search facilitators.

In many searches, the first day is coming to an end at this point while in other searches, the day ends with the participants facing their worst fears. When options for action have been generated, the facilitators can use the late evening to work on creating categories of action items that can be grouped together. This is a very important task because it shapes the ground for the prioritization process. This is one of the key skills the facilitators bring to the process. Facilitators must have the ability to understand the local culture, to be intellectually capable of distinguishing between alternatives, and to understand similarities. Although the facilitators' synthesis is never final, it provides the basis for the next day's prioritization process.

The next day begins with the presentation of the facilitators' organization of action items. After questions of clarification and modification have been addressed, an open plenary discussion ensues to create some understanding of how diverse the participants' views are. If common core issues easily emerge, the move toward setting priorities will be straightforward. If no clear and unified view emerges in the plenary, it then makes sense to redivide the participants into small groups to work on the issues. Each group, for instance, might be given the task of developing a list of the three to five most desirable action issues. This will then be presented in plenary, and the group as a whole can see if a possible road to making collective decisions has emerged.

CONCRETE CHANGE ACTIVITY
THROUGH VOLUNTEER ACTION TEAMS

The final stage of the search is the creation of action teams responsible for addressing the agreed-on action issues. This is the acid test of the prioritization process. Here participants vote with their feet by signing up on sheets on which the key action items have been listed. Usually, some of the issues identified by the participants as important will not attract any sign-ups. Although reflecting on these is worthwhile, the purpose of a search is to define not an ideal world of action but a world in which people are willing to commit to concrete actions to solve problems. There are always more plans than energy or courage to deal with them.

To conclude the search conference, the newly created action teams have a brief planning session. Each develops a plan for the first part of their work. This plan should integrate a specification of the goals for the group, a detailed schedule including concrete meeting dates, and the selection of a temporary convener of the group. The participants as a group also must commit to specific general follow-up meetings. An ideal situation is to have the process, including the search conference itself, last for a year. General follow-up meetings every 2 to 3 months keep track of the development process by allowing participants to share the results of the different task forces. This can lead to increased learning opportunities for everyone, creating collective ownership and control over the change effort.

We want to reinforce the point that search practices can vary considerably. The length of the phases, the numbers of facilitators and participants, the configurations of small groups, the degree of emphasis on the rules of discussion all differ because facilitators differ or because the same facilitator skillfully adjusts the approach to the developing dynamics of particular groups. Thus, searching is not a recipe but a highly skilled, cogenerative AR process. Efforts to treat it as a recipe result in ineffective action and processes that are misrepresented as participatory.

Conclusions

Search conferences are only one of the methods that can be used in pragmatic AR processes, but by making an extended presentation of the search conference, we have emphasized the key characteristics of our approach. It involves gradually developed multilateral conversations with the local stakeholders, the progressive refinement of a problem focus, and a process of inclusion. Then more structured cogenerative learning arenas are created, in which the relation between thought and action is emphasized in a multilateral, teamwork context.

Many of the other dimensions of our approach were presented in Chapters 4 through 8. Of course, the whole toolkit of social research is available, if a community or organization cogenerates a need for social research techniques. Quantitative techniques, qualitative techniques, mixed methods, particular techniques (T-groups, group dynamics exercises, simulations, force field analyses, variance matrix analysis, participatory design workshops, role playing, scripting, narrating) can be effective, but are appropriate only if they are deployed within the context of a collaboratively defined set of objectives and if the local participants are helped to deploy them and to analyze the results critically.

The core of the pragmatic AR strategy is to respect the combined research, action, and democratization goals of AR and to keep the conversation going with the participants. This also is one of the lessons emerging from the review of the cases presented in Chapter 3. As powerful and valuable as we think searching is, and as good as other tools can be in particular contexts, we doubt that pragmatic AR can be used to mediate situations in which some of the participants are committed to the ruin of some of the other stakeholders. Pragmatism alone is an insufficient weapon against authoritarianism.

Notes

1. We are using the term *pragmatic* in two ways. We intend it to refer to the philosophical traditions of pragmatism and neopragmatism discussed in Part 2, but we also intend to evoke the ordinary language meaning of *pragmatic*, which is "practical" or "practically useful."

2. Discussed in Chapter 3.

10

Power and Social Reform

Southern PAR, Education, Feminism, and Action Research

Introducing a complex and diverse field briefly and in broad outline inevitably courts caricature. This is particularly apparent to us as we address an enormous array of approaches to action research (AR) that are focused on issues of power, social reform, community development, and confronting oppression. Feminists, liberation theologians, labor activists, community organizers, nongovernmental organization (NGO) leaders, governmental officials, ethnic group leaders, and a small number of professional social scientists located in the academy all find a place under this rubric. United in concerns with power and fundamental social reform, they are divided in a hundred ways by differences in method, ideology, and focal issues of concern to them. Some would place all these approaches under the rubric of "Southern PAR" because of the enduring concern with power relationships and oppression, and this would not be wrongheaded. However, we take pains to identify the various streams within Southern PAR to not lose sight of the significant diversity among the approaches and their quite different ideal designs for social reform. We take them up together both to introduce them and to provide some guidance into the literatures they produce.

We also do so in order to portray the broader differences between these practitioners and other action researchers who are less focused on structural reform of society and more on improving social learning, organizational design, and general individual well-being. These two broad tendencies in action research amount to a significant divide that has been bridged only by a few practitioners. Both sides have tended to be both ignorant of each other's work and intolerant of their broad ideological differences regarding AR. At worst, the power-oriented action researchers view the action researchers who work in academia, industry, the public sector, and local governments as too willing to compromise their ethics to power elites. Their opposite numbers often view the power-oriented researchers as authoritarian, too sure of the rightness of their views while being perpetually condemned to marginality because they insist on their peripheral status as a badge of honor.

Such intransigent stances, fortunately, are rare, but there are nevertheless significant ideological and often methodological differences between the practices of these two broad groups. We believe that anyone doing AR has the right to approach the subject according to their own lights, but we believe that all sides can gain a great deal if they try to learn from each other and work to keep each other honest. This is, after all, what they claim to do in their own AR practices, and it is inconsistent to argue for respecting the knowledge of others and then to reject the knowledge of whole groups of AR practitioners.

What generally unites the practitioners discussed in this chapter is a view of power and power relationships as the central problem that any AR project must deal with. The greatest evils stem from power imbalances, and without the rebalancing of power relationships in a fair or a more egalitarian way, no real social change is likely. By contrast, the action researchers on the other side do not deny the existence of power differentials but believe that much can be done to improve the quality of life and functioning of organizations and that these improvements are also liberating. Many believe that without these changes in the core institutions of advanced industrial societies, the goals of participation and democratization will never be reached.

In this chapter, we blend the discussion of Southern[1] participatory action research (PAR), adult education, and contemporary feminism because the approaches share a number of common issues. But they are not the same, nor do they coexist without strong cross-currents. Some feminists, for example, have been appropriately critical of Southern PAR's androcentrism (Maguire, 1996). Recently, the work of Paolo Freire, a charismatic leader of the participatory research movement in Brazil and eventually around the world, has been subjected to harsh critique from within this very Southern tradition (Bowers & Apffel-Marglin, 2004; see also Chapter 11, "Educational Action Research").

We think that bringing the approaches together is useful, however, because they share a number of major underlying features centering on the analysis of political economy and praxis. We particularly privilege feminism in this mix because contemporary feminism is mainly responsible for resurrecting a concern with Southern PAR in particular and with AR in general (Greenwood, 2004b). We believe that the concerted, anticanonical, antipositivist feminist critique of contemporary social science provided the opening for the reinitiation of debates about AR in general. Feminism revitalized the politics associated with Southern PAR, and this effort has grown into a general reconsideration of AR.

We should add that this is not all good news from the point of view of some feminists, who see AR as parasitical on their efforts, viewing the discussion of AR as an appropriation or, worse, a co-optation of their efforts. This reaction is understandable for two reasons. First, there is the general co-optation that feminism has been subjected to (Messer-Davidow, 2002). In addition, feminists are often frustrated when AR practitioners announce ideas and agendas derived from feminism without realizing or recognizing their source in the long struggles of others. To further complicate matters, some Southern PAR practitioners see feminism largely as a "Northern" white woman's movement that co-opts and softens the social transformation that necessarily requires solidarity among the poor.

Neither the politics of AR nor of feminism are well served by combat among practitioners which distracts attention from the shared goals of democratic social change. We believe both groups can profit from a more sustained encounter with the methods and practices of other kinds of AR practitioners. And, given the profoundly conservative turn of the political structures in most wealthy countries, it is suicidal for a significant group of change agents who are interested in greater justice, fairness, and equity to do battle with each other rather than with their common adversaries.

Participatory Research and Southern PAR

We begin with an analysis of *participatory research* (PR) and *participatory action research* (PAR), a set of approaches that came into existence as a critique of inequality and a practice of liberation set within the framework of a model of class struggle. Though such practices and struggle exist in wealthy countries, these approaches are particularly practiced in poor countries.

The writers and schools mentioned here do not form a coherent set. These approaches differ substantially in their views of power, social stratification, and poverty. But they do share a set of fundamental disagreements with conventional and hegemonic approaches to development and the rationalization of organizational structures. They all build on a sharply political or economic analysis of power relations and the affirmation that significant social change occurs only if power has changed hands and reduced inequality. For these practitioners, simply getting along better or mediating conflicts is not enough to constitute sustainable social change.

Terminology is hard to manage here. *Southern* is an ambiguous term that has clearer moral content than it does geographical referents. In invoking the *South,* this group of practitioners symbolizes its alignment with the poor and oppressed of the world, wherever they are found. (North and South are not really geographical referents but really refer to the haves and the have nots and so there is a significant South in the North. See Chapter 2.) There are also terminological problems with *participatory action research* and *participatory research*. For some, these terms are different. For others, they are two names for the same general kinds of practice. For still others, it is necessary to add the term *Southern* to distinguish these practices from what has, unfortunately we think, been called "participatory action research" in the North, forms of practice that many believe to have been co-opted and collaborationist with power holders.[2] We have held on to the adjective *Southern* in this chapter mainly to emphasize the explicit political intentions of these forms of practice and to show our respect for these political agendas.

DEMOCRATIZATION AS LIBERATION

For many thinkers in industrialized countries, democratization is an ongoing process that furthers the inclusion of groups in self-determining political processes (that is, a standard liberal view). Others in the North and many in poor countries view the liberation of oppressed people as the sine qua non of democratization, however. Rather than seeing poverty as the result of a lack of inclusion, insufficient education, and inadequate infrastructure, these thinker-actors see poverty as the systemic outcome of the oppression of many by wealthy and powerful domestic and international elites. This view of the world rests on the belief that inequalities and injustices will not vanish simply because a group of people decides it wants something better or because a well-intentioned outsider comes in to encourage change.

From the Southern vantage point, international development projects, whatever marginal changes they may create in poor countries and poor regions, are not the road to meaningful social change. The only serious answer to poverty and oppression is a fundamental alteration in the distribution of power and money. This sharp and unshakable political focus characterizes Southern PAR approaches and, ultimately, links them closely to radical feminism.

These approaches rest on varieties of neo-Marxist views of the world that stress class conflict, the role of modes of production, the commodization of labor, and the depredations of international capitalism. These are the key ingredients in explaining and maintaining the poverty of most countries in Latin America and Africa, parts of Asia, and the miserably poor parts of most rich, capitalist countries. They also explain the current increasing gap between rich and poor in rich countries.

A logical consequence of these views is that Southern PAR approaches usually begin with a study of the distribution of wealth and the consequent distribution of exposure to risk. Existing public institutions are distrusted and generally viewed as protectors of an unjust order, unless a detailed analysis of the case shows otherwise. The suspect institutions include schools and universities, churches, governments and governmental agencies, most intergovernmental international development programs, and businesses.

Thus, work in this approach proceeds from an externally promoted analysis of the conditions of poverty and oppression to the design of interventions in local settings. This local intervention often (but not always) begins as a kind of mobilization effort, with the outsiders playing the role of consciousness raisers and catalysts for local discussions. Sometimes, this takes the form of the outsider coming in to support insiders who have already begun to take these steps. In other cases, the outsider arrives with the agenda of provoking and organizing change.

The work involves the external agent in preliminary analyses of the causes of the local situation that are fed back to local people to create the space and appetite for their own analysis of the causes of their situation. From this analysis, plans of action are derived. In some situations, Southern PAR takes the form of adult education or literacy programs in which the instruction centers on discussion and analysis of the conditions leading to local poverty and oppression. There are many other paths to follow, including working with nongovernmental organizations, churches, and many different kinds of local actors.

Unlike standard revolutionary praxis or conventional labor organizing tactics, Southern PAR values and relies much more on the knowledge, analyses, and efforts of local people. Rather than treating them only as victims (though their victimization is not denied), Southern PAR practitioners build their work on respect for the integrity and resiliency of local people and their culture. Their premise is that local knowledge of the situation is authentic, detailed, and valuable, an idea that many external organizers, who are sure they know what is good for the "people," routinely ignore. Southern PAR processes begin with a challenge that is initially addressed by bringing groups of local people together to discuss and analyze their situation. From these analyses emerge agendas for research and social change, but these agendas are the joint product of the outsider and the local people.

This focus on local knowledge is essential to Southern PAR. Although local knowledge is occasionally treated romantically in this approach, the underlying aim is to promote respect for it and, through this, to level the relationship between the outside agents and local people in a way that opens them up to collaborative efforts. That knowledge is local and grows out of intense personal experiences makes it respectable and encourages outsiders to listen to what it says and to try to build on what it offers. Put another way, this approach to local knowledge credits the poor and oppressed with having intelligence and analytical capabilities that are generally ignored. Thus, it necessarily explains their poverty not in terms of their ignorance or laziness, but in terms of oppression. In this regard, the approach is very much in line with the many other approaches to AR discussed in this book and accords with the conventional anthropological premise that all people everywhere have complex and well-organized understandings of the worlds they live in.

Building from this local knowledge and the interaction between the outsider's knowledge and local people's knowledge, a cogenerative dialogue begins that can transform the views of both. The outsider's view is necessarily abstract and often wrong about a number of the concrete impediments to local action. The insider's view is often so concrete (and occasionally homogenized by local activists) that it seems to offer only an explanation for poverty with no scope for action. The dialogue between the two perspectives can create a shared sense of locations where practical interventions are possible.

When this point is reached, the analysis often gives way to a focus on research. The outsider and the local people share some frames of reference about the problems faced and can assess and mobilize their resources for confronting them. Because ignorance (backed up by impoverishment) is one of the strongest weapons in oppressive systems, this phase frequently involves training local people in certain research methods and helping them gain confidence in their ability to investigate together the sources of their problems. They often must gather, analyze, and present evidence that supports their claims against the wishes of powerful business and political interests. Research is a weapon in this struggle, and this research is sometimes dangerous enough to have to be carried out surreptitiously.

Research training is never abstracted from the context. In the vein of adult education, the training focuses on the concrete and immediate problems that people face. Sometimes literacy training is an element in this process. In other situations, local people become social researchers by using voice recorders and video to document their conditions. No matter the form, the message is the same. Local people are intelligent, capable of rational analysis of their situation, able to conduct research aimed at improving their conditions, and they have the fundamental right to change their situations for the better. Research gives them a new voice to use in their struggles.

Throughout this process, the outside action researcher plays a mixed role as instigator, process manager, advocate for groups not yet fully included, trainer in research methods, and, often, chronicler of the activities. This is a complex, high-profile role that contains many in-built conflicts. As an educated person with the wealth to move around at will, this individual is necessarily seen as a representative of a category of outsiders with whom local experience has generally been negative and oppressive. Even when this barrier is overcome to some degree, there are still behavioral routines to be dealt with: behaviors of obeisance to educated outsiders (linked with hiding information about local situations), hostility to these outsiders, lack of confidence in local abilities, local power arrangements that are threatened by these new coalitions, racism, and so on.

As the chronicler of the process, the outsider often is in the position to influence unduly how the process is conceptualized and presented externally. The questions of voice and representation are particularly vexing in these contexts. If the insiders are at risk for attempting to change an oppressive system, the outsider may be viewed by authorities as a troublemaker, revolutionary, or even terrorist. The process is complex, often uneven, and occasionally genuinely dangerous.

Despite these difficulties, there is much to show for efforts that have been conducted in this way. One of the most important and well-known practitioners is Orlando Fals Borda. Building on his own commitments as an intellectual and an academic on the side of democratization and social justice, Fals Borda moved out of the university system into direct action in rural communities in Latin America. He has provided a public record of both his thinking and some of the many projects he and his colleagues have engaged in (Fals Borda & Rahman, 1991; Hall, Gillette, & Tandon, 1982; Park, Brydon-Miller, Hall, & Jackson, 1993). Not only do his writings document a theory of practice and a set of cases of interventions that have had desirable effects, but he has taken the attempt further by linking his own views and experiences to those of other practitioners working in Latin America, Asia, and Africa. As a result, through Fals Borda one can gain a view of the practice of liberation-oriented PAR that is applied to the lives of the poor.

Other practitioners who have written effectively for a general audience on these issues are L. David Brown and Rajesh Tandon (1993). They attempt to clarify the value of some distinctions among conventional research, participatory research, and PAR, and they base their analysis on long familiarity with concrete situations of poverty and oppression around the world. Hall, Gillette, and Tandon (1982), Freire (1970), Park, Brydon-Miller, Hall, and Jackson (1993), and Gabarrón and Hernández (1994) can all be read with profit.

NORTH-SOUTH CO-OPTATION

The reader should be aware of the problematic relationships among Southern and Northern practitioners. The recent rapid resurgence of AR in the North has caused many Southern activists to worry legitimately about co-optation of their perspectives in the North for the purpose of obscuring and blunting democratic initiatives. This is not an idle concern. We have all witnessed the co-optation of what were originally left-wing critiques and methods by oppressive forces (for example, participatory development, sustainable development, human rights, and feminism, all of which have been relentlessly subjected to efforts at co-optation and domestication).

For example, in the private sector in industrialized countries, one way of achieving the currently fashionable goal of total quality management is by involving the workforce more fully in the business. This is often framed as increasing participation, and recently, some conventional organizational development consultants have begun calling their work "participatory action research." In most cases, *participation* means only that workers and other subordinates take on greater and broader responsibilities while gaining little or no greater control over decision making. Under these conditions, allusions to participation and to AR are disingenuous because they are not built on an intention to democratize the organization or to increase social justice. One of the greatest benefits to Northern practitioners arising from interactions with Southern practitioners is to make us more alert to these processes of co-optation.

Having acknowledged the value of the Southern perspective, though, we do not accept an equation between work in the North and co-optation and work in the South and freedom from it. If we believed that all AR in the North was necessarily co-opted, we would not be AR practitioners. Our experience is that AR in core sectors of industrialized societies can engage issues of participation and democratization as seriously as in the South. In these cases, the strategies differ to a degree (reflecting different levels of literacy and poverty), the issues are focused differently (advocacy, public awareness, use of existing institutions for new ends), and the results much more often involve ameliorative rather than revolutionary change. Still, the social changes are real and the analyses of power relations and oppression are not dissimilar. Being controlled by a wealthy group of executives, even if the worker has a tolerable standard of living, is still being oppressed. To ignore or deny the rights of these oppressed people simply because there are poorer people elsewhere in the world is callous.

Of course, situations of oppression in parts of the South are terrifyingly bad in many cases. Poverty, oppression, and death under conditions of profound governmental corruption, the use of a national military to oppress local communities, the interests of foreign and domestic capital in maintaining a cheap labor force, ongoing colonialism, illiteracy, and starvation all make the problems of the North appear less severe. But the racially oppressed, the homeless, the drug addicted, the abused, and the illiterate in the North are oppressed, as are the workers in factories run by executives who use participation as a cover-up for speed-ups, downsizing, union busting, massive executive compensation, and the use of company resources to corrupt the political system, as are middle managers who are being replaced with cheaper labor that is more easily manipulated. Oppression is oppression everywhere it is found, South or North.

Educational Strategies

One of the most important and frequent paths leading people into the practice of action research (AR) has been through the field of education[3] in its various contexts. *Education,* as we use the term here, refers to everything from reforms of the formal school system, from primary to secondary schools, to universities and postgraduate work. It also includes adult education, either for re-skilling people displaced by technological and social changes or for technical education in the latest techniques in rapidly changing fields. The organizational problem we encounter with this exposition is that the broad field of education encompasses many approaches, and only some of them deal with issues of power and social change.

This diverse field can be divided up in a variety of ways. One way is by the educational arenas dealt with: primary schools, secondary schools, higher education, adult education, informal education, and continuing education. Another way is by concentrating on the multiple functions of education. Education can be viewed as having a conservative mission involving the transmission of what is known and the conservation of social arrangements. But it can also be viewed as both conserving structures and ideas and as promoting a critique of existing arrangements and the development of new ideas. In the latter case, education can be seen as involving social incorporation and mobility. Finally, some approaches to education are strongly reformist and see education as the way to change social arrangements and bring about major life course changes.

Educational efforts, formal and nonformal, have been a central field of activity for action researchers during most of the 20th century, and thus the history of the field of education criss-crosses the history of AR at many locations. John Dewey, the putative father of the U.S. public educational system, is an important figure in educationally oriented AR. His notions about the relationships between schools and society, between education and democracy, between learning forms of self-managed inquiry and being free are a powerful reminder of the potential of educational systems to engage in social change.

Though Dewey's long and constant pursuit of democratizing objectives through the schools yielded very little in the way of meaningful social change (see Westbrook, 1991), many of Dewey's ideas resonated with social change agents. Some trade union organizers saw themselves as educators, as did a host of social reformers concerned with improving the lives of the poor in the United States (for example, Alinsky, 1946; Chávez, 1975; Horton, 1990).

This wide variety of educational practices and agendas not surprisingly gives rise to quite diverse AR practices. Some of them are socially conservative, such as educational AR: classroom-based research, teacher improvement, and conventional extension work. Others are more social change oriented through promoting literacy, race/ethnic and gender sensitivity, building self-esteem, skills development, and the creation of mutually supportive communities of learners. Finally, some educational approaches are strongly reformist or even radical. These involve Freire's (1970) "conscientization," adult education in the mode of the Highlander Center, labor union study circles, and project-based work such as that done by Fals Borda. In this chapter, we deal only with the reformist and social change-oriented approaches to education. (Other approaches are discussed in Chapter 11, "Educational Action Research.")

As waves of social change sentiment have come and gone, so too have efforts at educational reform. The labor movement yielded a broad array of educational programs. The aftermath of the Great Depression created community development and education initiatives. The civil rights era did so as well. The events of 1968 caused a flourishing of educational initiatives in the classroom and beyond (Readings, 1996). Every major attempt at societal transformation has been accompanied by a set of educational changes aimed at helping people who have been treated as passive objects to become active subjects.

These educational activities are very broadly distributed internationally. The focus on education as a possible vehicle for democratization has overlapped in strategy with Southern PAR's heavy emphasis on adult education. It is difficult, even artificial, to make a sharp separation between adult education and AR in the South. Facing the staggering problems of poor people around the world, poverty created in many cases by the activities of the rich and powerful countries whose educational systems have just been mentioned, Southern practitioners have developed a strong liberatory adult education focus. This is reasonable because most impoverished adults are also poorly educated and not well prepared to take an active role in social change initiatives. Rather than focusing first on childhood education as a point of entry, many AR practitioners have felt it best to focus their resources on the development of skills, competence, self-awareness, and self-confidence among the adults to whom the task of struggling for social change necessarily falls.

Respecting this historical point of departure, we concentrate attention on the rich and diverse literature in adult education, both in poor countries and in the poor areas of industrialized countries. We review a number of education-based interventions, including labor organizing as a form of adult education, trade union education, adult education schools outside the public school system, and the potential role of educational institutions in AR. This discussion necessarily refers to a heterogeneous set of methods, ideologies, and narratives of practice, but that is just how the field is. This diversity is part of the dynamic energy that has characterized educational strategies for a long time. We are conscious that a variety of AR initiatives in educational institutions within the North, such as the work of Michelle Fine (1992), are passed over lightly.

FOLK HIGH SCHOOLS: THE ORIGIN OF POPULAR EDUCATION

There is good reason to believe that adult education as a distinctive field originated in Denmark with the work of the theologian Bishop Grundtvig (1783–1872). He initiated a fierce debate with the theological establishment regarding the scientific analysis of the Bible. His point was that the scriptures should be made sense of by ordinary people through their daily lives in their congregations. From this conflict eventually emerged a conscious effort to create a popular education system in which history, theology, and studies of cultural heritage created an integrated and context-bound knowledge system (Nørgaard, 1935). The first "folk" high school was established in 1851, and these schools soon became an important social and political factor in war-ridden Denmark. This popular education movement spread to other Scandinavian countries and was influential farther abroad. The Highlander Folk School in New Market, Tennessee, an institution that Myles Horton founded, was highly influenced by the concept of folk high schools. The Scandinavian folk high school movement is still vital and attracts many students.

TRADE UNION EDUCATION

Education has always been an integral part of trade union development, serving two purposes. Education is considered important for training union members to be efficient agents at the company level, for example, in handling bargaining and negotiating situations. The other main purpose of education is to raise the level of political consciousness. From very early on in the political struggles of trade unions, educational efforts were taken seriously. Trade unions considered it an essential union capacity to train members to become skillful actors in the company and also in the more general political arena. This broad educational strategy became very important in the social democratic movements in northern Europe and proved to be a key factor in European politics. To exaggerate the point a bit, the "Eaton" (the elite finishing school for political and business leaders) of Norway in the post–World War II era was Sørmarka, the trade union national education facility in Norway. Very few prime ministers and cabinet members came from outside the circles of Sørmarka. In the 1930s, the later prime minister Einar Gerhardsen wrote a textbook on *Becoming a Union Official* (1932), a book that is still in use.

Trade union education activities involve a combination of practical training for handling union matters on the shop floor and within the larger company, and always involve a strong component of the dissemination of union ideology. These education activities take place in the contradictory context where education for liberation and self-development is dealt with mainly by teaching a specific union ideology.

The conceptual platform for the trade union teaching effort appears to have developed pragmatically, based on specific local experiences. Based on the notion that knowledge is power, trade union education goes beyond this sort of self-evident statement by being linked closely to solving everyday practical problems. The German sociologist Oscar Negt (1977) created a conceptual platform for trade union education. In an introduction to a Danish edition of his work, the translators make the following statements:

> Negt's main interest is to give the working class the possibility, through learning processes, of creating a collective (conscious and unconscious) experience and to give them a political direction. . . . [It is important] to take as a point of departure the everyday experiences in the production process, and through information about societal relationships (information that can support the learning process through discussions, materials, analysis, etc.) train the sociological imagination, which means to teach a way of thinking that makes the individual worker capable of understanding the relationships between individual life and the societal development. (p. 7)

For our purposes here, we can accept this platform as an a posteriori synthesis of the conceptual underpinnings of trade union education. It integrated a clear and explicit ideological platform with a practical educational system. In this respect, it has much in common with Southern PAR.

POPULAR EDUCATION

The boundaries among adult education, social change efforts, trade union-type consciousness raising, and other initiatives are not easily discerned. The people involved have long been aware of each other and occasionally have worked together. No better example can be found of this than Myles Horton and the Highlander Center.

Myles Horton was a popular educator born in the southern United States into a modest family. He made it through university through a combination of talent and drive, but he never forgot his origins and was determined to use education to promote democratic social change. After learning about the Danish folk school movement, Horton decided to set up an education and social change center in the mountains of Tennessee to provide opportunities for local people to meet, reflect, learn, and organize themselves for social change.

Highlander has gone through a number of vicissitudes over the decades, including being attacked by federal agencies and being closed down at the original location, but it is still operating. It was a key partner in the civil rights movement in the U.S. South; it promoted comprehensive community-based AR projects that resulted in the curtailment of many of the most noxious practices of mining companies; and it has become a source of inspiration for generations of social change agents.

Myles Horton was well aware of a wide variety of activist social change traditions, including anarchism, trade union mobilization, civil disobedience, and AR. His own view of the process was remarkably nonauthoritarian. Horton insisted that he could not (and would not) "organize" people because people organized themselves when given a supportive environment and a chance to think for themselves. In this way, Horton set Highlander apart from more leadership-driven change approaches. He venerated local people's experience and capacity for action and communicated this confidence in a way that embold-ened generations of change agents.

The story of Highlander is well told both in Horton's biography (Horton, 1990) and in the book Horton completed with Paolo Freire just before Horton died (Horton & Freire, 1990). Highlander itself continues to be active and is a center for the promotion of adult education and AR.

Feminist Analyses of Inequality and Development

In our teaching experience over the past decade, after we have laid out the basic perspectives of AR, students ask about the relationship between feminism and AR. They correctly perceive that feminist views deal with many of the same issues found in AR: a critique of positivism, an analysis of power relations, a respect for the knowledge of the "silenced," a critique of canonical positions, and a focus on transformative praxis. They also voice fears that AR is co-opting the analyses of feminism without attribution and possibly without sufficient reformist intentions. These concerns merit attention. Without a meaningful alliance between feminists and action researchers, neither group has good prospects.

Feminism and AR are not competing frameworks. AR and feminism share underlying ethical and political commitments to democracy and social justice. It also is important to remember that AR is not a theory but a strategy toward praxis that uses any and all tools that the coresearchers find helpful. As we have said repeatedly, we view AR as a pragmatic combination of analyses and tech-niques for linking elements of participation, action, and research in concrete situations. We don't need fewer and purer tools, but more and more diverse approaches to meet the challenges of inequality and oppression.

By the same token, AR should not seek to domesticate feminism or to make polite but superficial gestures of incorporation. We are not interested in the politics of professional inclusion; we are interested in figuring out how to create a better world. AR should continue to grow, as it has in the past, by learning from feminism's profound and detailed analyses of gendered oppres-sion and efforts at gender liberation. The critiques of positivism, essentialism, oppression, and the separation of theory and practice that have been central to feminism are essential to AR as well.

Most feminists begin by viewing oppression as the usual state of affairs and build their praxis on the belief that the status quo must be overturned in favor of a more liberating set of conditions. Feminists have long struggled to gain recognition for their issues, to persuade a larger segment of the world population that the rights of women are routinely trampled on and that the essentialized gendering of human beings is a form of oppression. Feminists affirm that democratic social change—not just polite conversations about being better people—is necessary for these evils to be corrected.

In our view, feminists have done more than anyone else in the past two decades to undermine the authoritarian paradigm built into conventional social science and social programs. A good review of this contribution can be found in Iris Young's (1990) *Justice and the Politics of Difference.* Young persuasively links oppression to the welfare state, the distributive justice paradigm, and positivist social science in a way that is uniquely informed by feminism but is also directly applicable to the struggle of AR to overcome the ideological suppression of AR by conventional social research.

The feminist critique of the notion of value-free research has been devastating, because feminists have been able to reveal repeatedly how such value-free research generally embodies gender-specific values (Fox Keller, 1985; Lather, 1991). It is a short step from this notion to the general notion that value-free research covers up all kinds of oppressive social arrangements under the mask of an impartial, scientific ideology, a critique that is an essential component of AR.

Feminist approaches also stress the value of diversity. In focusing on the conditions of the underrepresentation of women, they reveal the white, male, middle-class center of gravity of most social theory and social policy. They have demonstrated this as effectively in industrialized countries as they have in poor countries (Sims Feldstein, & Poats, 1990).

Neo-Marxism and feminism have also found a useful point of contact in their focus on the actual processes of production. Feminists have worked hard to reveal the undercompensated and central role of women in the productive apparatus of society, contributing strongly to the critique of advanced capitalism and its triumphalistic ideologies (Swantz, 1985).

Feminists, dealing routinely with oppression and silencing, have developed a powerful commitment to a view from below, to hearing the voices of the silenced, and to bringing these voices to the table (Mies, 1990). Here the coincidence between feminist analysis with a strong emphasis on life history and local knowledge and AR is self-evident. Both seek to end the silencing of so many, gendered silence in one case and class-based silence in the other.

In poor countries (as well as in industrialized ones), feminists have taken a strongly actor-oriented approach to issues such as environmental protection, welfare services, and development programs. The watchword is *gender-responsible* research, in whatever sector it may be (van den Hombergh, 1993). They have persuasively pointed out that, without systematic attention to gender, the perspectives of women will be ignored in the ordinary course of events. The parallelism between this and the emphasis on local knowledge in AR, based on the experience that without the affirmation of its value, local knowledge will be discarded and oppression will continue in the same vein, is evident.

Thus, for us, the relationship between feminism and AR is complementary. Not surprisingly, we think the benefits flow in both directions. Without the feminist onslaught on the centers of power, we do not believe that the kind of space we currently occupy as action researchers would exist. At the same time, we think there is scope for both the enhancement of feminist perspectives within AR and the improvement of feminist practice through attention to the many intervention techniques that have been developed in the different AR approaches. Feminists do often engage in AR, but there are only a handful of systematic attempts to link the two perspectives. Among these, we refer briefly to the work of a few of the key writers.

Patricia Maguire (1987), in *Doing Participatory Research: A Feminist Approach,* articulates a combination of feminist agendas, participatory research practice, and the personal experiential dimension of her work. This book speaks better than most to the combination of feminism, participation, and social praxis by using issues from feminism and participation but staying resolutely focused on the social problem Maguire is trying to solve. In subsequent writing, Maguire (1994, 1996) deepens her critique of a number of kinds of AR practice, arguing effectively that the very notion of participatory research is absurd without the systematic incorporation of feminist perspectives. Though the argument is less developed, she also believes that feminist research must move into the realm of AR to extend its own scope. Thus, Maguire argues for the necessary and productive interdependence of the approaches and issues and persuasively argues for invitations to collaboration across these traditions.

Many others call for some kind of interlinking of feminism and AR. Patti Lather (1991), in *Getting Smart: Feminist Research and Pedagogy With/in the Postmodern,* argues that the principal contributions of feminism have been the critique of positivism, the demonstration that all forms of inquiry are value laden, opening up the possibility of a critical social science, pressing for the politics of "empowerment," and rising to the challenges of postmodernism. Her ambitious combination of perspectives strives to get beyond the dilemmas of postpositivism, poststructuralism, and postmodernism through an activist social science. She makes activist research a core element. Lather offers action researchers a wealth of analytical weapons and perspectives.

Other feminist thinkers advocate varying combinations of feminism and AR. Joyappa and Martin (1996) argue for a combination of feminist research and participatory research to storm the barricades of American adult education, and Reinharz (1992) explores the possibilities of what she calls "feminist action research," which links activism and scholarship. The impossibility of having a feminist perspective without a commitment to social change is what links these activists and what links them to AR more generally.

In *Disruptive Voices,* Michelle Fine (1992) links feminism, organizational interventions in a variety of organizational systems, and social activism. A number of the examples she provides move feminist research in the direction of cogenerative inquiry aimed at social change.

Many more feminist thinkers deserve mention (for example, Belenky, Clinchy, Goldberger, & Tarule, 1997; Gilligan, 1982), but we hope to have said enough to open up a broader discussion. Even this cursory review suggests the importance of increasing the frequency and detail of communication between feminist researchers and representatives of the many other approaches to AR. We share many agendas, and we think it is clear that AR is not possible without feminist perspectives. In return, action researchers can offer feminists a greater awareness of a variety of intervention and group process techniques developed in the industrial democracy movement, in collaborative inquiry, and elsewhere. These techniques can help harness the feminist commitment to activism to well-known techniques for working collaboratively in groups toward social change goals.

Conclusions

A great many more approaches to the issues of power and liberation could be mentioned. Our intention is only to say enough to persuade the reader that these perspectives can and should be linked productively and to make this assertion concrete by providing some general outlines of the perspectives that inform Southern PAR and feminism. We also hope to have persuaded the reader that there is a South in the North and that approaches to AR informed by Southern perspectives are as relevant to the different conditions in the North as they are to the South. Southern perspectives are particularly valuable in reminding Northern practitioners of the ever-present dangers of co-optation and triumphalism when participatory language is captured for nonparticipatory purposes. Finally, we argued for an intensification of the discussion about the relationship among adult education, feminism, and AR as a necessary condition for the success of all.

Notes

1. We remind the reader that the concepts of South and its opposite, North, are slippery. The South refers to people who are impoverished and oppressed. Because a greater percentage of such people exist in poor countries, the designation *South* has become a cover term for this, but there are many southern locations in the North, and initiatives such as Highlander were built on the same principles of social and economic justice as we find supporting these change efforts in the South.

2. An example of the kinds of conflicts that bedevil us can be found in Whyte and Whyte's (1991) use of the term *participatory action research* to announce the approach

to AR he was developing. Though in the book bearing this title, cases from the developing world are included, the overall politics of the approach are not informed by a liberationist framework, and the prior use of the term *participatory action research* by Southern practitioners was not mentioned. This kind of use of language inhibits communication among AR practitioners.

3. Because this field has a long history and is reasonably well organized, a number of general books can introduce readers to the major contours. Among some of the most useful general sources are Paolo Freire's (1970) *Pedagogy of the Oppressed;* Budd Hall's (1975) classic article "Participatory Research: An Approach for Change"; the many articles over the years of publication in the journal *Convergence;* Carr and Kemmis's (1985) *Becoming Critical;* John Elliott's (1991) *Action Research for Educational Change;* and a review article by Susan Noffke (1994).

11

Educational Action Research

I n the panorama of practices that relate to action research (AR), educationally centered approaches present one of the broadest and most complex
arrays, ranging from AR in the primary and secondary school classrooms and
administrative structures to AR in higher education to adult education, community development, and liberation movements. A field so broad is also internally heterogeneous, making a meaningful synthesis for the purposes of this
book quite difficult. The boundaries between education and other AR activities are also exceedingly vague, and some approaches raised in other chapters
are referred to here as well. There is no pure map, no simple guide. Our goal is
to enable the reader to make a start on this subject, find out some of the main
contours, and find her or his way to further materials.[1] The approaches taken
up here, though social change oriented, are not as sharply political as those
reviewed in Southern PAR. Here the emphasis is on organizational and behavioral change and reform of institutions.

Frameworks

Though not all AR-relevant educational work deals with adult education, one
of the peculiarities of this field is that it seems that the major intellectual syntheses and setting of the frameworks in use come from adult education rather
than from conventional primary and secondary education and higher education. These larger syntheses serve our purposes in two ways. They provide a
larger framing for the subject than do the more monographic and institutionally specific forms of work, and some of the most recent and challenging syntheses seem to us to lead inexorably to the conclusion that, as in industrial
democracy work, AR is the only sensible way to emerge from the dilemmas in
this field.

In constructing this mapping of the field, we have availed ourselves of
frameworks provided by Mattias Finger and José Manuel Asún in their *Adult
Education at the Crossroads: Learning Our Way Out* (2001) and Robin Usher,
Ian Bryant, and Rennie Johnston's *Adult Education and the Postmodern*

*Challenge: Learning Beyond the Lim*its (1997). These ambitious and thoughtful works map the field of education and social change work from the perspective of a broad view of adult education and point to some central dilemmas facing the field that will be familiar from some of the other chapters of this book.

FINGER AND ASÚN: ADULT EDUCATION AT THE CROSSROADS

Finger and Asún build their portrait of the field around a three-part classification of approaches: pragmatist, humanist, and Marxist perspectives. Under the pragmatist heading, they deal with the work of John Dewey, Kurt Lewin, David Kolb, Jack Mezirow, Chris Argyris, and Donald Schön.[2] They point out that, despite pragmatism's prosocial ideology, a theory of society or political economy is lacking in this work and the conditions affecting the possibilities for pragmatic discovery, ongoing learning, and social transformation are not explored.

What Finger and Asún call the "humanist" school includes Malcolm Knowles, Carl Rogers, and Stephen Brookfield. The centerpiece of these approaches is optimism about the potential for human growth, freedom, and self-development and owes a great deal to humanistic psychology. It is consequently also a highly therapeutic and individualistic approach to development that lacks any theorization of political economy and institutional environments.

The Marxist approach includes conventional Marxism and critical theory (Theodor Adorno, Walter Benjamin, Jürgen Habermas, and so on). This field is also developed by Paolo Freire (see Chapter 10) into what Finger and Asún call "critical pedagogy." They criticize all these approaches for conflating an epistemology that advocates the possibility of open learning processes and the politics of oppression. They do not see how the *theory* in critical theory leads to a meaningful liberatory practice, and they link this criticism specifically to what we have called "Southern PAR" in this book (Chapter 10).

Whatever one thinks of Finger & Asun's specific arguments, their assertion that, despite the differences among this wealth of approaches, they all have the same goal—"to humanize this development process by involving the people in shaping its tracks" (Finger & Asún, 2001, p. 96)—is intriguing and persuasive. Put more bluntly, despite their apparently critical stances, they see these as only limited critiques of advanced capitalism because they accept the validity of the development process and the modernization paradigm from the Enlightenment.

Finger and Asún then look to "learn our way out," and they do this by recommending a set of frameworks and practices that look to us like the very bases of AR: institutional change engaged in by all the stakeholders, sustainability, fairness. This is not a new face on the old "development" scheme, but a new cogenerated, codetermined way of living in the world in solidarity. So, though it is not quite so baldly stated, their "way out" is through AR.

USHER, BRYANT, AND JOHNSTON:
THE POSTMODERN CHALLENGE

At this point, we move to the arguments in Usher, Bryant, and Johnston (1997) because their framing of the postmodern challenge to adult education, though differently anchored from Finger and Asún's, takes us to a similar location. In their view, postmodernism, the end of modernity, links to education in a variety of ways. The hyper-individualization and the dynamism and instability of groups and systems under current conditions of globalization break the back of the modernist paradigm. But, they assert that education itself, as a concept and as a practice, is premised on certain elements of the modernist framework: development, progress, "empowerment" are all modernist notions. They believe that there is no alternative to modernism in education, that it cannot simply be abandoned. However, they also believe that postmodernism creates some very useful conditions for a new practice of modernism, and they recommend "recognizing that these are claims [modernist claims] not truths, claims which are socially formed, historically located cultural constructs, thus partial and specific to particular discourses and purposes" (Usher, Bryant, & Johnston, 1997, p. 7).

When they speak to what this means in practice, they lay out a research framework, techniques, and notions about writing that approximate those of AR. Openness, collaboration, group processes, integrated thought and action cycles, and other features provide the bases for "learning beyond the limits" of both modernism and postmodernism.

These two quite sophisticated and thoughtful syntheses deserve to be read in their own right, but, for now, they provide a kind of background around which to build our brief review of varieties of educational AR practice.

Reforming Education in the North

EDUCATIONAL AR IN THE SCHOOLS
AND TEACHING PROFESSIONS

No practice that is engaged in by hundreds of teachers and university faculty is likely to be homogeneous; under the heading of educational AR, there are many varieties. To summarize the main thrusts, we see this field as centering on primary, secondary, and higher education teachers and the university scholars who support them. These stakeholders engage in a number of varieties of AR, mainly focused on improving the quality and effectiveness of their practices as teachers and on improving the institutional environments in which they operate. There is a significant element of organizational development work in this area and many analogies to similar work done under the rubric of industrial democracy. Both approaches have drawn significant inspiration from Kurt Lewin and from the work of the Tavistock Institute for Human Relations.

In a review article, "Educational Action Research," Ken Zeichner (2001) typologizes the field as follows: a U.S.-based approach drawing on the work of Kurt Lewin and centering on Stephen Corey at Columbia University; the British curriculum reform movement (1960s–1970s) centering on the work of John Elliott and Lawrence Stenhouse; the Australian movement, which drew its main inspiration from the U.K. but had the added dimension of dealing with aboriginal education involving people like Stephen Kemmis and Robin McTaggart; the teacher/researcher movement in the United States; and, recently, higher education self-study to improve teaching.

Each of these practices differs in a variety of ways, but they mainly focus on changes in professional practice and organizational development within institutions. While they press for change in practice and organization, they are clearly reformist activities aimed less at shifting power than at improving the communication patterns and work environments for students and teachers and at making policy reforms that support those changes.

Some of these varieties of AR are heavily teacher centered and feel quite thin on participation by other stakeholders, while others are open to student engagement and to other nonteaching members of the organizations. Zeichner (2001) offers a significant bibliography on this approach (pp. 281–283). For a comprehensive synthesis and methodological guide, a good recent source is Stringer, *Action Research in Education* (2004).

ALTERNATIVES TO PUBLIC SCHOOLS

Above and beyond these varieties of educational AR, there are others that purposely take a more strongly reformist approach to the educational system. A host of specialized extra-public schools has been organized. These include special schools for music, dance, religious instruction, and cultural transmission (for example, Japanese Saturday schools in many Western countries). Here the focus is additive. These schools intend both to enrich the curriculum and to set the daily public school experience of children in the context of a larger view of the world controlled by parents and teachers.

AR WITHIN HIGHER EDUCATION INSTITUTIONS

We devote a full chapter to the education of action researchers (Chapter 16), so we will not review this subject here, except to say that a number of significant efforts are underway to create AR programs at the undergraduate and graduate levels.

One of the most ambitious and well-funded formal educational strategies for democratic social change was the development of the U.S. land grant university in the 19th century. The basic land grant system was tied to territorial conditions in the United States. Most states had a certain amount of public land at their disposal. By mandate, the states were to sell some of these public lands and use the proceeds to create a core fund. The income was to be used to build a state university (hence the term *land grant*). Each state was required to have one land grant university.

As a state university built with public funds, the land grant university's mission was to be research, education, and public service linked in a putatively seamless web. These universities were to educate the people of the state, to conduct research on subjects of practical interest to the citizens of the state, and to disseminate that knowledge directly to the people of the state. The basic formulation behind the land grant university is closely linked to AR. It involves a systematic partnership between academic and nonacademic stakeholders, a full dialogue among them about their needs and interests, and collaborative research and testing of the results. Despite this, the land grant university has not become the source of major AR initiatives.

Though there is little question that such public universities have carried out many of the required services and have prospered mightily (Lyall & Sell, 2006), over the years the land grant universities have become mainly the servants of social power rather than an avenue to the democratization of knowledge. Designed originally as institutions in which faculty would be encouraged and rewarded for their combined intellectual and practical contributions to society, these universities have become internally subdivided into high-status faculty who conduct non- and anti-applied research and extension faculty and other personnel who are much lower in status.

The land grant universities have routinely supported large farmers and powerful business interests, the substitution of machinery for labor, and other hierarchical efforts. The land grant concept is a reform idea hijacked by power, even though the legislative and economic mandate of the system should have supported a far more democratic outcome. Under these conditions, the development of a strongly reformist AR within university walls is not welcome. And yet, a few reforms manage to be undertaken; we say just a bit about them.

Within the context of the land grant university system, there is a modest movement to reconceptualize and reinvigorate this work that builds specifically on AR principles. One of the major practitioners of this approach is Scott Peters (Peters, 2001; Peters, Hittleman, & Pelletier, 2005; Peters, Jordan, Adamek, & Alter, 2005) whose commitment to land grant ideas and democracy has moved him into the study of the skillful practices of many of the unsung heroes of the extension system. From these collaborative studies, now heavily based on narratives generated in long dialogues, Peters is laying out a vision of the complexity and reform potential within these AR practices that are largely obscured by the domination of the more authoritarian and conventional models of extension as experts "doing for" rather than "doing with" stakeholders. And there are others doing this kind of work (Crane, 2000).

SERVICE LEARNING

A number of institutions develop their educational programs through various combinations of service learning, internships, and coops in which work experience and intellectual activity are integrated in the manner that Dewey (1900) envisioned. Famous for this are institutions such as Antioch College and Berea College.

Over time, this effort to engage students and faculty in internships and other forms of direct service to agencies both within and beyond the colleges and universities spawned the service learning movement (Giles, Stanton, & Cruz, 1999). In the past 20 years, this movement has grown to the point that now very few institutions of higher education lack a system at least of placements in some form of service learning. The Campus Compact in the United States (available at http://www.compact.org) organizes and promotes the efforts of more than 950 institutions and places in excess of 5 million students.

That said, and believing fully in the value of these kinds of experiences for students, we should point out that service learning can involve AR, but not necessarily. In the practices of people like Kenneth Reardon (1997), it definitely does and serves as a multi-stakeholder training ground for action researchers. But it can also be entirely external to the educational lives of students, a kind of separate "service" activity from which they might "learn" something, but they will learn it largely on their own.

Taking the service relationship into the core of higher education life and using service learning as a way of redesigning the relationships between higher education and the society beyond is much rarer. When service learning is domesticated, it becomes a way of doing "good" without changing much of anything about the operation of educational institutions. When it is taken into the institutional mission in a deeper way, it can become transformative.

Adult Education Approaches in Industrialized Countries

As we stated in the introduction to this chapter, the field of educational AR is huge and heterogeneous. In many ways, the theorists and synthesizers in adult education have gathered the many threads into an overall picture that is more synthetic than those provided by educational action researchers, who may have a more limited institutional focus. But now we move on to discuss what is more conventionally and narrowly called adult education approaches per se.

ANDRAGOGY AND TRANSFORMATIONAL LEARNING

A popular general term for adult education in industrialized countries is *andragogy;* it is heavily associated with the names of Malcolm Knowles (Knowles, 1990; Knowles and others, 1984) and, more recently, Jack Mezirow. Mezirow (1991) defines it the following way: "Andragogy is the professional perspective of adult educators. It has been defined as an organized and sustained effort to assist adults to learn in a way that enhances their capability to function as self-directed learners" (p. 199). On the European continent, andragogy is widely used as a term for adult education, with a number of universities issuing degrees that use this name.

The core of adult education is a view of learning as situated in social, cultural, and material contexts within which individual experiences are transformed into emancipatory actions through critical reflection. Mezirow's transformation theory represents a dialectical synthesis of the objectivist learning assumptions emerging from the rational modernist tradition and the concept of meaning coming from symbolic interactionism. His transformation theory focuses on critical reflection anchored directly in the structures of intersubjectivity and communicative competence (Mezirow, 1996, p. 165).

In recent years, the approach has moved much closer to a professional position parallel to AR. Later writings by Mezirow (for example, 1996) build on Habermas's (1984) critique of the scientific tradition and his work on communicative actions. The full step into the world of AR is taken by Wilfred Carr and Stephen Kemmis, both professors of education. In their book, *Becoming Critical: Education, Knowledge and Action Research* (1985), they provide an epistemological grounding for AR based on pragmatic philosophy.

A central concept in Western andragogical thinking is the focus on critical reflection and thinking. Brookfield (1987) devotes a whole book to expanding the concept of critical thinking and showing how to facilitate processes that enhance participants' ability to think critically. Brookfield identifies four components in critical thinking:

1. Identifying and challenging assumptions is central in critical thinking.

2. Challenging the importance of context is crucial to critical thinking.

3. Critical thinkers try to imagine and explore alternatives.

4. Imagining and exploring alternatives leads to reflective skepticism. (p. 7)

An important element in Brookfield's (1986, 1987) work is his focus on the facilitator as a key person in the adult education process. He points to an important contradiction between using power to have students see and reflect on specific issues and then letting go of control over the learning process when the critical thinkers are ready to take over. This contradiction or tension is also discussed in the work of Levin and Martin (1995); they argue that it is necessary to apply power in a learning situation to be able to gain emancipation.

There are some overlaps and linkages between Southern popular education and Northern andragogy. Two books, both written in a dialogical format, create a reflection on the relationship between the two positions: Myles Horton and Paulo Freire's (1990) *We Make the Road by Walking* and Ira Shor and Paulo Freire's (1987) *A Pedagogy for Liberation*. Both books show how lively and rewarding the relationship between practitioners in the South and the North can be. An excellent summary and analysis of these positions can be found in Finger and Asún (2001, Chap. 3).

Corporate Classrooms

A striking feature of late capitalism is the emergence of the corporate classroom. The trend is for many companies to create their own training and education systems. Major actors in this field are multinational consulting firms that have their own training facilities, where all newly employed consultants must go to get an understanding of the corporate culture and to learn the tools of the trade. It seems only natural that these company classrooms spread, because this structuring of education closely matches the way these consultants will work as they "educate" and advise their clients. In the United States, more than 20 years ago, it was already estimated that more hours of class were taught in classrooms created by and for major private sector corporations than in the 3,000-plus institutions of higher education in operation at the time (Eurich, 1985).

Diverse subjects are covered in these classrooms. Many areas involve technical training and retraining; others involve human relations, management education, accounting practices, self-development, and health care. Increasing numbers of such learning opportunities are available to employees off-site, through advanced information technology.

There are many different kinds of corporate classroom, and they are open to many possibilities. One interpretation is that the formal educational system does such a poor job of preparing employees that further education is necessary for them to function properly in a profitable business. Another view is that the corporate world is so dynamic and challenging that all organizations must become "learning organizations" if they are to compete effectively (Senge, 1990). It is also clear that corporate classrooms can be structured to serve the purposes of socializing and ideologically disciplining employees to the company view of the world.

This is not a small or economically insignificant activity. It is estimated that it involves $30–$50 billion spent on formal employee education in a year and more than $180 billion on less formal, on-the-job education and training (Nash & Hawthorne, 1988). How this learning is structured and imparted has not been a focus of AR work in the United States, perhaps because so few action researchers are inclined to work within the corporate environment or are even aware of the change possibilities inherent in such large and well-financed programs.

Adult Education and Community Development

COMMUNITY DEVELOPMENT

In Chapter 10, we covered a major portion of what can be classified as adult education. Community development efforts such as those spearheaded by the Highlander Center, by the various movements centering around people like Belenky, Bond, and Weinstock (1997), Freire (1970), Gaventa (1982), Hall (1975), and Hinsdale, Lewis, and Waller (1995), have already been alluded to and also logically fit under this heading here. While these movements vary a great deal in their theories, methods, and ideals, we agree with Finger and Asún (2001) that they are essentially all reformist movements taking place within the modernist model of development. As Finger and Asún would put it, these movements are mainly about putting a human face on capitalism. Some practitioners think this is much harder than do others, but they all believe in the possibilities of reforming the system. Lest we be thought to be placing ourselves above them, we emphasize that we also share this fundamental orientation, and it is certainly a central premise of our own work.

These activities can all be gathered under the rubric of adult education because they involve processes of ongoing education, capacity building, and self-determination that mainly engage adults who are already well embarked on their lives. They vary greatly in the ways they educate, in how individualized versus group-oriented the processes are, and in how strong their critique of contemporary political economy is, but they still bear some general family resemblance. The various practitioners, of course, would bridle at being lumped together, and becoming familiar with this field means reading well into the literatures in all the different varieties.

DEVELOPMENT AS A FRAMEWORK FOR AR

Though the notion that Southern PAR and popular education in the "South" is outside of the conventional approaches to international development is widespread, and at the risk of seeming to offend some practitioners of

Southern PAR, we believe that the upshot of the arguments cited earlier from Finger and Asún (2001) and from Usher, Bryant, and Johnston (1997) is that the vast bulk of these practices fit within the overall framework of modernist "development." The belief in the possibility of education to increase capacities to alter and improve society as it is does not amount to a repudiation of that society. Though practitioners differ greatly in the degree of reform that would satisfy them, nearly all of us are reformers, not revolutionaries. As a result, though it creates an uncomfortable tension or juxtaposition, we believe that it is helpful to all to understand that AR of the practitioners themselves is fundamentally a reform effort that is based on some degree of belief in the capacity of people to work together to change their life situations and institutions in positive directions.

POPULAR EDUCATION IN THE SOUTH

Probably the best-known tradition in this field is adult education and social change work in the South. This is an immense field about which numerous books have been written. We have already provided some basic views about it. It is perhaps the best known of all the AR approaches worldwide, and some of its leaders are considered the models of the AR practitioner—Paolo Freire (1970), Budd Hall (1975), Orlando Fals Borda (Fals Borda & Rahman, 1991). Because these practitioners have created effective records of their own thinking and action, they can be read in the original with great profit. Of course, their broadly similar focus should not obscure their individuality and the uniqueness of the intervention strategies they have developed. Each of them, and their many colleagues worldwide, has a unique voice and perspective to offer. For purposes of this presentation, we do violence to their individuality to make a compact presentation of the approach.

The points of departure for the popular education approach are resolutely moral and political. The moral point comes first and is never allowed to disappear from view. Humans are entitled to a decent life, free of grinding poverty and political oppression. Humans have a basic dignity and deserve respect. The political logic that follows from this moral point is simple. Because humans are entitled to be free and have the capacity to manage their own lives effectively, that they do not in so many locations must be explained. The explanation is oppression backed up by economic power and violence. Thus, the practitioners of this approach build their practices on a strongly Marxist viewpoint. They never lose sight of power and oppression, and they never consider a social change to have occurred until power structures have been overturned and more liberating structures have been put in place.

Along with the many elements of mobilization theories drawn from Marxism and trade union organizing practice, these approaches coincide in privileging local knowledge. The point of departure is that the interests and power of elites—not the poor's own ignorance or lack of ability—make people poor and oppressed. Thus, local people in communities and organizations are viewed as having detailed, complex, and valuable knowledge about their situations and the capacity to develop analyses and strategies that can mobilize this knowledge for social change.

The role of the outside expert varies from practitioner to practitioner, but almost always the outsider is a catalyst and facilitator, sometimes pressing, sometimes cautioning, but always trying to convey respect for local people and their rights. This is where the connection to adult education arises, because many of these interventions can be understood as forms of adult education and capacity building.

As the AR process continues, people often gain confidence in their own abilities and perceptions, become less willing to submit to authority, and are able to develop organizational strategies to promote social change. In some of these situations, the opponents are simply ignorant or thoughtless. In others, the opponents are truly dangerous and violent. Thus, such work can range from the development of local organizations that threaten few people to activities that would be defined rightly as insurgency.

Paolo Freire

To instantiate our discussions of this approach to AR, it makes sense to review the work of Paolo Freire briefly. Freire is one of the most widely known names associated with AR and a figure with whose work everyone in AR must have some familiarity because of its centrality to Southern PAR, adult education, formal education, and community development work.

Born in Brazil in 1921, Freire had a long and complex career. He began his work as an adult educator working with the poor but was exiled from Brazil during a military coup in 1964 because of that work. His approach is summarized in his most famous book, *Pedagogy of the Oppressed,* first published in 1970. This is one of the most widely read AR books ever published, and its messages are still relevant and exciting.

His exile from Brazil lasted 16 years, and he lived and worked in England, Chile, and spent a period working with the World Council of Churches in Geneva. He taught at Harvard from 1969 through 1979, when he was able to return to Brazil. He reinitiated his public career in Brazil in 1988 when he was appointed Minister of Education for the City of São Paulo. He had a chance to put his ideas about education into practice. Freire died in 1997.

His writing is a complex combination of neo-Marxism, Gramscian perspectives, liberation theology, and organizing, a heady mix that he brings together under the general rubric of an expansive concept of "pedagogy." Freire believed that "to speak a true word is to transform the world" (1970, p. 87). He believed in the power of speech linked to critical consciousness, a clear and disciplined action and reflection cycles. He had a complex view of the "alien-ated consciousness" that holds the oppressed in its thrall and criticized two of the most common reactions organizers have to this, verbalism and activism. *Verbalism* is talk without action (1970, p. 87), and *activism* is action for action's sake without the discipline of critical consciousness (1970, p. 88).

Freire strongly believed in the power of critical communicative action to reveal to people the conditions of their own existence and their ability to change their circumstances. Thus he saw having a voice as a central feature of liberation. Freire noted that "human beings are not built in silence" (1970, p. 88) and that reclaiming the right to speak was one of the most powerful forms of action.

Though the act of speaking might seem hostile or aggressive, Freire insisted that dialogue is an act of love and that it requires faith in humankind because dialogue rests on the hope and belief that the other can and will respond. Thus in Freire's view, authentic education is always social, "cogenera-tive" in our terminology. The notion of love and solidarity is seen in Freire's insistence that the oppressed must liberate themselves through the develop-ment of critical consciousness, what he called "conscientization," but that ulti-mately the oppressed must also seek to liberate their oppressors by the same means. To do otherwise would mean simply that the oppressed would in turn become oppressors, and the cycle would begin again.

Freire's writings are extensive (1970, 1998a, 1998b), and critiques are beginning to appear as well (for example, Bowers & Apfel-Marglin, 2004). Note again that part of this work should be situated as representative of the broad strategies of Southern PAR (Chapter 10) as well as being relevant to educational AR and parts of the human inquiry strategy as well (Chapter 14).

Much more could be said about these approaches, but enough has been laid out to encourage those interested to read more of the relevant literature. The focus on local knowledge and its value and the insistence that social change is not a mere matter of adjusting the dials but of changing systems of power are two of the most crucial contributions of the Southern PAR approach.[3]

As we have noted in Chapter 10, there is also a critical literature now emerg-ing that examines some of the shortcomings of taken-for-granted assumptions from these approaches.

INTERNATIONAL DEVELOPMENT AGENCIES

Some of the most powerful and richest agencies dealing in adult education are the arms of national governments and international institutions that fun-nel national funds into development assistance programs. This is an extremely complex topic. We deal with a very prominent part of it that links to AR in our chapter on participatory rural appraisal (Chapter 13).

These development agencies are a dominant force on the same scene where the nongovernmental organizations (NGOs) and mission organizations operate. Examples of development agencies include the U.S. Agency for International Development, NORAD of Norway, the World Health Organization, the World Bank, and the International Monetary Fund. Built largely on budgets provided by national governments, these agencies support development programs in many countries around the world.

Although it is still fair to say that the bulk of these projects fund large-scale infrastructures, are built from the top down, have generally resulted in only modest improvements in the conditions for the poor, and have not contributed much to democratization, some of the programs have had meaningful local effects. The so-called green revolution technologies in the improvement of yields of major food grains have improved the nutritional and health status of people in some world areas. Under the aegis of development programs, thousands of people from poor countries have been sent to Western industrial countries for further education, in some cases to good effect and in others never to return home at all. These very agencies, in recent years, have been active promoters of techniques such as participatory rural appraisal (with elements of AR), about which we write in Chapter 13. Most now announce their commitment to participatory development strategies, though many of us in AR view these commitments with skepticism because the record of these national efforts is extremely mixed. The funding appropriations that drive them serve national political interests, regardless of the ideological packaging they are given.

One constant feature of these programs over the past 25 years is the assertion that development requires educational and attitudinal change. A constant feature of the critiques of such programs is their failure to be knowledgeable about local people or to respect local knowledge. Although there is some attempt to improve the record on this, structurally, international development agencies are driven from the top down to meet the goals of the funders, not the local beneficiaries. When these goals are in the interests of local people, there may be room for AR processes. When they are not, AR practitioners, together with local actors, necessarily oppose them. Of course, distinguishing which kind of situation is which is always a complex judgment call.

Before we leave this topic, we point to a few other kinds of adult education efforts that might otherwise be thought to fall entirely outside the box of adult education and AR.

SUPPORT GROUPS

Though it might appear to be stretching the notion of adult education, support groups involve many of the elements of adult education and AR that we have been discussing. Support groups are intentionally created voluntary groups of individuals and families who have been affected by a shared problem: cancer in the family, spousal abuse, substance abuse. The list of support groups is endless.

These groups vary greatly in their organization and philosophies, but they do build on the notion of people coming together to share their dilemmas, solutions, weaknesses, and strengths to help each other come to terms with difficult situations. Often support groups have developed into social change initiatives through the learning acquired in the process. Organizations combating drunk driving, spouse abuse, and many other social issues originated in small support group efforts. A well-documented case that shows the connection between support groups and AR is found in the work by Chessler and Chesney (1995) on support for parents of children with cancer. The potential for significant developments of AR work in this area should not be underestimated.

STUDY CIRCLES

Much more common in Europe than in the Americas, study circles arose in the labor movement as a mechanism for bringing adults together to inquire into the conditions that affect their lives. Study circles are a very common pedagogical approach in trade union education. Many popular education movements in northern Europe use study circles as a major element in their teaching activities.

The point of study circles is to achieve adult education broadly conceived while focusing on consciousness raising and strategic thinking about specific issues affecting those participating. In one form or another, these kinds of study groups have come and gone in most industrial societies.

NONGOVERNMENTAL ORGANIZATIONS

Nongovernmental organizations in many parts of the world develop and administer extensive educational programs in support of particular kinds of social change of interest to them. Ecological education, agricultural education, sex education, health education, nutrition, and similar themes form the core of the activities of many NGOs. Though now many NGOs are immense and they are a diverse lot, they generally share a view of international development in which the people, rather than governments and monied interests, are the real agents of change. Historically, NGOs have tended to invest in people so that the people make changes and sustain the changes themselves. This view makes popular education a high priority and constant element in the activities of NGOs.

In recent years, trenchant critiques of the operations of NGOs have arisen. In some cases, they have become a hidden, nonelected government in poor countries with more disposable cash than many governmental agencies. Each pursuing its own agenda and value scheme, NGOs can be quite abusive (Mendelson & Glenn, 2002). By the same token, precisely because of their flexibility and relative freedom of operation, some NGOs can be fully and robustly focused on AR activities, involving the local stakeholders in significant social reform efforts under local control.

MISSIONS AND EVANGELIZATION

Whatever else it is, missionization is certainly an educational effort. Missionization is a reality in all the countries of the world, and it is not likely to disappear soon. Stereotypically, missionaries are viewed either as naive do-gooders or as religious fanatics. Though there are plenty who fit these images recent generations of missionaries are considerably more sophisticated. Some groups are popular educators who operate by trying to live out their ideology in local communities, contributing labor and resources to projects of value to the people. Others bring significant resources into communities and use these resources to gather people both for change efforts and for missionization. In some cases, only such religious groups have the courage, political independence, and resources to be in dangerous and divided places. Governments may be punishing the area, afraid of it, or denying the existence of problems. Thus, missionization occasionally reaches those unreached by other means.

A great array of educational strategies accompanies this process, including literacy campaigns, the formation of social groups with particular local or national change projects (see Kurt Ver Beek on the Lenca Indian mobilization in Honduras, 1996), Bible study groups, health clinics, and refugee camps. Some of these organizations promote ideologies of democratization as part of their Christian message.

Although we do not question the legitimacy of their presence, it is important to examine their practices closely. Because one element in missionization is a belief in a final or ultimate truth, there is always the possibility of the imposition of an unwanted framework on local people. When this happens, missionization is inimical to AR. But this is not always the case, and AR practitioners should keep an open mind about missionization, just as they need to be alert to the possibilities for abuse in NGOs, land grant universities, and everywhere else that democratic interventions are being attempted.

Conclusions

We hope that the vast scope of educational AR that we alluded to at the outset of this chapter is by now clear, as is the impossibility of segregating this subject neatly from a number of the other topics and approaches we present in other chapters. Perhaps what is left here is to return to the challenges raised by Finger and Asún (2001) and Usher, Bryant, and Johnston (1997). They both, from different vantage points, argue that most existing practices in educational AR are heavily influenced by the modernist development paradigm. They treat this as something of an inevitability in which some of the elements of the modernist framing are necessarily maintained by anyone who shares the optimism that education, reflection, and consequent changes can lead to more satisfying lives in improved organizations and a better society. But as they point out, this is no longer a certainty, but from a postmodern perspective must itself be understood as yet one more grand narrative.

However, understanding that something is a grand narrative does not necessarily imply jettisoning all the methods and practices associated with it or the value of democracy and participation. The challenge these researchers put to us is an important one. For educational AR to move on constructively and, by implication, for all of AR to do so, we must understand our own ideological commitments and hold ourselves accountable to more stringent standards of value transparency, consistency in the promotion of collaborative and cogenerative processes, and must remember the necessary humility that goes with collaborative inquiry rather than slipping back into being the *techne*-bound experts in the good life for all.

Notes

1. We are fortunate to have had the good counsel of our colleagues, Arthur Wilson and Scott Peters, from the Department of Education at Cornell. They helped guide us into parts of this territory that were not familiar and recommended some of the major works we have consulted. They bear no responsibility for our errors in interpretation and judgment.

2. We give ample treatment to these thinkers in our chapters on industrial democracy (Chapter 2) and on action science (Chapter 15), and our own approach is heavily indebted to John Dewey, so we will not review all this work here.

3. We have dealt extensively with this subject in Chapter 10 and refer you to that discussion for additional information.

12

Participatory Evaluation

Conventional evaluation of processes or projects is an activity that originates from the most authoritarian approaches to social management. The whole concept of conventional evaluation rests on the assumption that by coupling bureaucratic control systems with social science techniques, it is possible to present an untainted map of the activities of others—grantees, agencies, and so on—and to analyze their performance of specific activities against some kind of publicly defensible scale. This kind of conventional evaluation is built on the grounding principle that the objective and neutral expert has the capacity to make good, untainted judgments regarding specific activities independently of any values or preferences of her or his own.

Accountability to authority is the core issue here. Public and/or private funds are spent to address specific problems both in the private and public spheres, and evaluations are undertaken to understand whether the resources have been used properly. The increasing demand for accountability everywhere has made this kind of conventional evaluation the dominant response. Everyone is supposed to be held accountable, though it is not often clear exactly to whom.

Private funders, local authorities, governments, and organizational leaders nearly all require evaluations for programs that they fund either to guide or to legitimate their funding decisions or to help them keep activities that they support under their control. The utility of this kind of accountability to the funders is clear. Evaluation preserves their power position and makes it clear who is in charge.

From the perspective of those receiving the funds and who are being evaluated, accountability is not the center of their attention. They are much more interested in the quality of the outcomes of their work. Their questions are more like these: Has the program or activity improved my situation? Do I have a better life now? Am I better capable of taking care of myself? Is my work situation better now? Does my organization function better? Are we doing the right things and are we doing them right? Accountability through evaluation is highly unlikely to answer these questions. To answer such questions, it is necessary to engage the stakeholders in and clients of the organizations in their own processes of sense making about their own situations and the activities they have participated in. This inside view is what guides the conduct of those in the organization.

If evaluation is to focus on the things that matter to the funded stakeholders, then the only way to conduct it is to examine the internal dynamics, processes, and outcomes as understood and judged from inside the program or activity. The local stakeholders must be fully involved in the evaluation. As everyone knows, engaging the local stakeholders this way is exceedingly rare. Whether or not there is this kind of participant involvement is the fracture line between participatory evaluation (PE) and conventional positivistic evaluation.

An enormous range of issues have been evaluated, ranging from performance in classrooms (teachers and students both), the effectiveness of public programs, the impact of development programs, and so on. Almost no field of public or private life has been spared some kind of evaluation. The use of conventional evaluations has become the standard modus operandi for policy makers to the point that they cannot conceive of undertaking such activities differently.

Clearly, evaluation has occupied a major place in both public and private decision-making processes. Evaluation serves several political functions, legitimating decisions on the allocation of funds and creating legitimacy for particular political decisions. Evaluation is also used as a post hoc accountability argument regarding the wisdom with which money was spent. Evaluation can also be used to postpone decisions by arguing that the actual issue is under evaluation until further notice.

Given all of this, evaluation has become a lucrative professional field and a major consulting business, a true growth industry. This kind of evaluation framework cannot even begin to imagine an evaluative activity that involves the active participation of the stakeholders. The stakeholders are considered not to have the competence to evaluate their own activities and are assumed to be dishonest in representing their activities to the funders to make themselves look better than they are.

With this mindset resting so thoroughly on the putative value of distant and neutral observations and expert evaluator, unilateral sense-making processes, participative issues of engaging the "objects" of a specific activity in gathering data on their own performance and in analyzing the outcomes seem completely impossible. It not only is *not* impossible, but competent evaluators, as opposed to those who just make money doing evaluations, have gradually discovered that, if an evaluation is to have any useful impact on daily activities in funded organizations, then the evaluation process and the outcomes have to be compelling and meaningful for the local stakeholders and not just for the funders. In the wake of this insight, PE has emerged as an increasingly common practice.

The Authority of Evaluation

Being visited by an evaluator, accountant, assessor, accreditation reviewer, or any of the many other figures playing a professional evaluation role is usually experienced as being placed in a subordinate position to a person whose professional role is to review and evaluate you, your program, or your organization "objectively." Nearly all of us have experienced such evaluations, so it should be easy to conjure up the image of the objective, impartial outsider who asks hard questions in what is frequently experienced as a hostile way. Distance is supposed to be crucial in conventional evaluation; attempts to co-opt an evaluator are to be guarded against (and, of course, often engaged in). Although some evaluators are more skilled than others in managing their relationships with their subjects, conventional evaluation is assumed to center on a potential conflict of interest between the evaluator and the subjects.

The reader will probably have noticed how closely this approach to evaluation parallels the concepts of conventional social science and its links to bureaucratic impartiality. The notions of objectivity, distance, and the need to avoid bias and co-optation match closely the standard rules for conventional social research and their reliance on the complex mechanisms of sampling, statistical testing, and the like to achieve "distance." In addition, most conventional evaluations take place at the end of a project or at major intervals after some significant project activity has occurred. The purpose of the evaluation is generally to "grade" the performance of the project and its leaders, though, of course, some interim evaluations aim to produce useful information for subsequent phases of the project. One clear assumption is that the subjects should not be trusted to provide either an honest or a good-quality evaluation of themselves and that making use of the evaluation results for immediate and ongoing changes in the project is not a principal goal. Being evaluated this way gives you an experience of what it feels like to be treated as a research subject by a conventional social researcher.

The Emergence of Participatory Evaluation

Whatever else it does, conventional evaluation generally does not aim to make a positive impact on a project while the project is underway, except in cases of interim evaluations of multiyear projects. Generally, it records outcomes for a particular audience of decision makers.

Programs to fight poverty, to teach the uneducated to read, or to support rural community efforts to survive all receive the scrutiny of evaluators. Such evaluations generally result in reports that are inaccessible to the stakeholders in the programs, either because they are kept confidential or they are written in such a way as to be difficult for most nonprofessionals to understand. They also usually are not framed in actionable ways so that even the recommendations are rarely framed in ways immediately useful to the local stakeholders. They are more suitable for funder and oversight organization use.

Evaluations conducted in this fashion often have a negative effect on local participants and their autonomy as intelligent individuals. They have little say in regard to what is evaluated, how it is done, and how to make sense of the results. They are treated as the informants for the evaluators, placing them in a passive relationship to the outside and "expert" evaluators. This is because one of the most basic tenets of conventional evaluation is that the essence of evaluation is the professional evaluator's own judgment of the outcome (Scriven, 1995). The cornerstone of the profession, in this view, is to make neutral and objective judgments of the activities under evaluation.

PE rejects this detachment and disconnection as necessary, possible, or desirable. Some professional evaluators became concerned that conventional evaluations are only related to the needs of power holders and not to the needs of the local stakeholders. They also noticed that their evaluations had no local impacts other than on their own bank accounts. As a result, some reframed their professional positions and brought about the creation of PE.

This transition has been vitally important because it converts evaluations into organizational development processes that could help the stakeholders achieve improved performance on dimensions that matter to them. Stated another way, some evaluation moved away from the "court of accountability" to the engaged, value-based commitment to local program development. For this to happen, evaluators had to become involved with the stakeholders in a program or activity and accordingly have taken on a professional role as an engaged actor rather than a distant and objective judge.

The first strong voice in the evaluators' camp for this position was Ernest House (1972, 1993), who began an ethical discussion in evaluation. According to House, the different stakeholders in an evaluation having different power positions would obviously not have aligned interests. House presented evaluation as a process in which different stakeholders' or recipients' diverse values, foci, and capacities require that the evaluator move from the position of the distant observer to an involved and engaged collaborator, and this opened the way for participatory evaluations.

We should not overstate the presence of PE. Conventional evaluation, the modality of the vast bulk of evaluations, still carries on business with a rudimentary relationship to participation. For example, Michael Scriven's fourth edition of the *Evaluation Thesaurus* in 1991 does not even mention participation.

Modes of Participatory Evaluation

Within the literature on PE, we can identify at least three different approaches. These approaches to participation are built on different epistemological premises and conceptualize participation in different ways. Their on-the-ground praxis in

PE is also dissimilar. One line of thinking is represented by Guba and Lincoln's (1981, 1989) constructivist approaches. A second line is Patton's (1986, 1997) arguments for utilization-based evaluation, and the third line of thought is "empowerment evaluation" (Fetterman, Kaftarian, & Wandersman, 1995).

CONSTRUCTIVIST EVALUATION

Egon Guba and Yvonna Lincoln became interested in constructivist evaluation after becoming radically dissatisfied with the usefulness of conventional evaluation. This was a logical outgrowth of their "naturalistic inquiry" perspective; they felt that to make evaluations effective, such evaluations had to be built on the naturalistic paradigm:

> A naturalistic paradigm, relying on field study as a fundamental technique, which views truth as ineluctable, that is, as ultimately inescapable. Sufficient immersion in and experience with a phenomenological field yields inevitable conclusions about what is important, dynamic, and pervasive in that field. Ethnography is a typical instance. (Guba & Lincoln, 1981, p. 55)

The canonical text on constructivist evaluation is Guba and Lincoln's (1989) *Fourth Generation Evaluation*. In it, they introduce a constructivist approach to evaluation and link it to naturalistic inquiry by arguing that evaluation is a process of construction and reconstruction of realities. This book is a logical follow-up to their work, *Effective Evaluation* (1981), where the theme is how to make evaluation matter, and *Naturalistic Inquiry* (1985), which centers on the comprehensive development of a postpositivistic methodological stance for the social sciences. *Fourth Generation Evaluation* focuses on carving out an epistemological position for constructivist social science and forwarding detailed methodological positions for researchers who approach the field in a nonpositivistic manner.

The central theme of Guba and Lincoln's work is to urge social researchers to engage with people directly to make sense of the evaluation process and results. In this way, they make participation a central element in debates about contemporary evaluation praxis. As Guba and Lincoln say:

> The major task for the constructivist investigator is to tease out the constructions that various actors in the setting hold and, so far as possible, to bring them into conjunction—a joining—with one another and with whatever other information can be brought to bear on the issues involved. (1989, p. 142)

The constructivist approach necessarily brings the problem owners to the fore because their views are key to understanding and making sense of the processes and structures being evaluated. This means that the evaluation rests on the participants' understandings of their own situation and on how they judge the results achieved. The evaluators can support and engage in these hermeneutic processes because the processes will eventually lead to the requisite evaluative insights. The evaluation can not be completed unless the hermeneutic groundwork is done by the participants.

UTILIZATION AND PARTICIPATION

A more conventional response to the challenge of the efficiency and effectiveness of evaluations is found in the work of Michael Quinn Patton (1986, 1997). For Patton, the central question is how to shape evaluations so that the results matter to the involved stakeholders. In Patton's view, evaluation is an activity that should be designed to have an impact on the program or activity being evaluated.

Responding to the dilemma of evaluations being ignored by the stakeholders, evaluators like Patton developed participatory approaches in which the evaluator and the evaluands created a closer relationship and opened up for mutual learning. Patton was one of the first to present this different path for evaluation. In his book, *Utilization-Focused Evaluation* (1986), Patton emphasizes the use of evaluation results to improve projects as an imperative in evaluation work:

> What fundamentally distinguishes utilization-focused evaluation from other approaches is that the evaluator does not alone carry this burden for making choices about the nature, purpose, content, and methods of evaluation. These decisions are shared by an identifiable and organized group of intended users. (p. 53)

Basically, Patton aims to include every stakeholder, as defined by him. They "are people who have a stake—a vested interest—in evaluation findings" (1986, p. 43). For any evaluation, there are multiple stakeholders—program funders, staff, administrators, clients, and others—with a direct or even indirect interest in program effectiveness. Although much of Patton's (1986, 1997) attention is paid to the funders, staff, and administrators, the clients of the projects being evaluated also are included in his thinking and evaluation process.

The particular insight that local involvement is necessary for making the results of evaluations useful leads to an interest in ways the clients of the programs being evaluated themselves deal with evaluation results. These clients are in a different position from all other stakeholders as the actors who potentially should benefit most from the evaluation. Their interests are, in many situations, not the same as the interests of the program staff. They are, in a certain sense, the primary actors in any program, simply because the focus of the activity is to do something about their life situations. No other stakeholder group is in such a position, so it is a powerful move to focus attention on ways these primary beneficiaries can use the evaluation.

This is where the participatory approach to evaluation makes its appearance. Participatory evaluation aims to create a learning process for the program clients that will help them in their effort to reach their own desired goals. Participatory approaches to evaluation purposely muddy the distinction between the program activity and evaluation results because the evaluation aims to make a difference by helping program clients achieve their goals better. Such an approach often can end up going even farther and creating a situation in which it is possible not just to evaluate whether the program is doing what it is supposed to do well, but whether what it is doing is the right thing to do or whether doing something else would meet its objectives better.

A standard practice in PE is to involve the providers and clients of a program or an activity in the process of interpreting evaluation results. The most conventional way to do this is to discuss the collected data with them as a way of making sense of the findings. A more advanced form is to involve participants in the process of designing what to evaluate from the beginning of the project (for example, decide on the variables and how they are defined), to engage them in the data collection process, and to include them in making sense of the findings.

How this participatory process is structured can differ widely among evaluation practitioners. Each evaluator engages the participants in ways that are comfortable for both parties. Some construct meetings, others use group dynamic processes—search conference "look-alikes" have been used—and other participatory techniques.

Such processes, however, are not without problems. A key difficulty in using participatory approaches to evaluation for the sole purpose of achieving improved utilization is that it creates an opportunistic situation for the evaluator that easily could lead to a co-optive process in which the evaluator is effectively coaching the program clients on what they should want from a program. This can result in slighting issues of the multiplicity of stakeholder interests and the often laborious process of stakeholder goal setting.

EMPOWERMENT EVALUATION

In any participatory process, there is always a tension between participation as an instrumental means of accomplishing something and participation as an end in itself. The larger political settings involving interests and power usually play a minor role in most evaluation practices, and democratization is rarely an element in the conceptual schemes linked to evaluation. However, in empowerment evaluation, these settings are emphasized. For example, Brunner and Guzman's *Participatory Evaluation: A Tool to Assess Projects and Empower People* (1989) is an effort to see evaluation as "a methodological component of the educational development project that aims at empowering the dominated groups in a society so that they will be able to join the struggle for a just and egalitarian society" (p. 10). Weiss and Greene (1992), Patti Lather (1991), and Michelle Fine (1996) are other proponents of the empowerment evaluation approach.

Michelle Fine (1996) summarizes this work in the form of five commitments to PE research: building local capacity, evaluation and reform, an ethic of inquiry, evaluation and democratic participation, and rethinking the "products" of evaluation research. Fetterman et al. (1995) define *empowerment evaluation* as "the use of evaluation concepts, techniques, and findings to foster improvement and self-determination." They go on to say, "Empowerment processes are ones in which attempts to gain control, obtain needed resources, and critically understand one's social environment are fundamental"(1995, p. 4).

This is a radical point of departure. Empowerment evaluation is founded on a restructuring of the evaluator role that departs dramatically from the conventional detached, objectivist role and it is more proactive politically than constructivist and utilization-focused evaluation. The most striking element in empowerment evaluation is the understanding of the evaluator as an interventionist, as an activist. Active political engagement is expected.

The foundation of empowerment evaluation is to teach the participants to conduct their own evaluation. This includes an effort to help participants understand both what evaluation is and how it can be conducted. In empowerment evaluation, the stakeholders themselves are expected to be active and engaged. Here, self-evaluation is conceptualized as having a dual meaning: doing the evaluation yourself and having the evaluation done on your own situation. The professional evaluator then becomes the facilitator who works to enable the participants to commission their evaluation and also see to it that necessary learning processes are constructed to support them. In this respect, empowerment evaluation looks quite similar to good cogenerative organizational development processes.

The professional evaluator is also an advocate but is most focused on enabling the participants to conduct their own evaluation. Armed with this evaluation, the professional evaluator becomes a public spokesperson and legitimator of the insights gained through the evaluation process.

The practices of empowerment evaluation pay particular attention to illuminating (eye-opening, revealing, enlightening) experiences that can create the point of departure for a liberating development. Despite this, the broader issues of liberation are generally treated rather softly, as for example, here: "[Empowerment evaluation] can unleash powerful, emancipatory forces for self-determination" (Fetterman et al., 1995, p. 16). Liberation is seen as a secondary effect that takes place within the empowerment evaluation. Liberation is not the goal per se but a potential outcome that would be good if it happens; it is not a design criterion for the evaluation.

This is an interesting contradiction. If empowerment evaluation is not necessarily meant for the ultimate goal of liberation, what is its aim? Without clarity about this larger goal, empowerment evaluation can easily degenerate to a co-opted strategy for participation in a process that would have little or no effect on people's long-term ability to impact their own life situations. Empowerment evaluation is on the verge of falling into the same trap as did the empowerment movement in business life, in which empowerment is generally something "done to" stakeholders rather than actions taken by them.

Action Research in Evaluation Practice

Participatory evaluation strategies have a lot in common with the complexity, diversity, and specificity of action research approaches in general. PE, though a form of practice in its own right, builds directly on work from AR, and many of the authors refer directly to particular AR works as part of their intellectual repertoire. AR approaches have made significant contributions to this field by opening up the notion of evaluation to collaborative and participatory approaches. Patton (1997) makes several references to AR, but he never integrates it into his conceptualization.

It seems to us that evaluation modeled on AR has only recently had a significant impact. For example, Finne, Levin, and Nilssen (1995) call one recent AR evaluation development "trailing research." Here participatory approaches to evaluation are synthesized directly out of an AR process. The central idea of this process is to establish a continued engagement with stakeholders throughout the whole program period. The evaluators, jointly with stakeholders, decide on issues to evaluate. Then the research team usually collects relevant data and makes some preliminary analyses, and the stakeholders are involved in the sense-making processes. Out of this mutual learning process emerge redesigned actions implemented in the ongoing program to attain goals or to redirect the program toward new goals. This work is later followed by reporting from a formative evaluation where AR-like practices have been employed (Rolfsen & Torvatn, 2005).

Action research has also been used as an approach to evaluation of educational institutions. King (1998) provides an example of this type of work. It is, however, remarkable how little these approaches to evaluation are built on a well-grounded understanding of AR.

Conclusions

Although we can clearly see parallels between PE and AR more generally, there are some important differences in emphasis. PE emphasizes the participatory dimensions as the cornerstone of every move in the process, but the move from participation to active engagement in problem solving is very opaque in PE.

On the other side, evaluators, by and large, have high data collection and analysis standards and strategies, while a good deal of AR has been careless in data-gathering and analysis strategies. As the field continues to develop, a closer rapprochement between participatory evaluators and other action researchers can be valuable for both groups.

Finally, it is evident that there is a much more integral relationship between AR and evaluation activities than treating PE as a separate subject suggests. The very logic of AR projects includes the setting of problems, the choice of methods, the data gathering and analysis, the design of actions, and the *evaluation* of the effectiveness of those actions by the collaborators. Without evaluation, AR processes are incomplete. Furthermore, there is a real sense in which evaluation should be a dimension of AR projects from the first day to the end as a way of examining the processes and determining whether or not the right things are being done in the right ways, and whether or not changes in the course of the projects can improve the results. Anyone wishing to practice AR must also be proficient in participatory evaluation.

13

Participatory Rural Appraisal, Rapid Rural Appraisal, and Participatory Learning and Analysis

While participatory forms of evaluation are diverse and are applied in a wide variety of situations, they are by no means the most common form of evaluation. As we noted in the previous chapter, they rely on positive assumptions regarding the capacities and honesty of nonprofessional stakeholders. Despite strong managerialist and authoritarian tendencies in many fields, participatory evaluation (PE) techniques are making modest headway in some intractable arenas where conventional approaches have failed. One such arena is the development of multi-stakeholder sustainable environmental practices (Hemmati, Dodds, & Enayati, 2002). Another is in baseline studies and evaluation in international rural development programs, one of the few arenas where the marginal outsider status of action research (AR) does not hold, or at least, so it seems.

The practices we refer to are known under a wide variety of names, the most popular name being participatory rural appraisal (PRA), but there are many others, as we indicate below. PRA centers on participatory baseline studies and the participatory design and evaluation of international (largely but not exclusively rural) development programs. PRA is well funded, central to the operations of some of the largest international development agencies such as the World Bank, the U.S. Agency for International Development (USAID), and the Food and Agriculture Organization (FAO). Despite the importance of PRA in these key venues, being central to a set of powerful and well-financed agencies brings with it a host of problems, particularly surrounding the co-optation of AR practices for nonparticipatory ends.

The enormous diffusion of these practices and the amounts of financial and human resources devoted to them by both large multilateral international agencies and a great many nongovernmental organizations (NGOs) justifies our giving them separate treatment here.

194

Participatory Rural Appraisal in International Development

Linked to a variety of forms of participatory evaluation but occupying a very different institutional position is a collection of approaches that now generally go under the name of "participatory rural appraisal."[1] PRA is an element in overall socioeconomic development programs, mainly in poor countries. These strategies aim to develop more reliable baseline data about problems through involvement of local people in the definition and documentation of those problems. Given the proliferation of worldwide development projects and PRA at present, it is impossible to provide even a partial introduction to the literature. We simply hope to give the reader enough to get started.

The nomenclature itself is very difficult. For example, Jules Pretty and Simplice Vodouhê (n.d.) have laid out the following set of acronyms, all related to PRA[2]: AEA, BA, DELTA, DPR, FPR, GRAAP, MARP, PALM, PAR, PRM, PRAP, PTD, PUA, PfR, PD, RA, RAAKS, RAP, RAT, RCA, REA, RFSA, RMA, ROA, RRA, SB, SSM, TfD, TfT, and VIPP. There can be little doubt when seeing this alphabet soup that we are in the presence of the large international, bureaucratic agencies and a very active international consulting business in which patenting your own name for a process is a marketing strategy. To make it worse, these are not just different names for the same practices, but a variety of somewhat different practices linked to some common assumptions. Our purpose here is only to lay out some of these assumptions, remembering that there are many organizations in which a variety of participatory appraisal strategies are used and that variation in practice and conception is found everywhere.

Preeminent among the institutions promoting the use of these approaches is the Institute for Development Studies at Sussex, and the best-known person and most prolific writer in this field is Robert Chambers. We draw heavily on Chambers here,[3] but we remind you that related approaches have been developed in many locations—the International Potato Center in Peru, in some components of the Cornell Institute for International Agriculture, Food, and Development at Cornell University, and in a number of other locations worldwide. Nevertheless, Chambers is a key actor and synthesizer of what is being learned because he has been unusually thorough in documenting the work of others and is remarkably assiduous in the practice of self-criticism. We provide some additional bibliographical guidance later in the chapter.

Given the political and value positions we have articulated in this book, it is no surprise that we are not unambiguous supporters of development assistance programs as currently structured and that we are dubious about the degree to which meaningful political participation can be built into them. There are many severe constraints built into the political economy of development that prevent anything like the self-determining participation that AR seeks from moving beyond very narrow limits. But the imperfections of particular approaches and contexts should not blind us to the reality that more liberationist approaches to development have generally failed and most development work is done precisely in the kinds of agencies that PRA now is engaged with. Thus, we believe that PRA deserves a serious look from anyone interested in AR. Until workable alternative approaches to the alleviation of international poverty are developed, PRA embodies one of the development practices that has the most in common with AR.

The principal difficulties facing PRA is that the overall framing of international development work sets tight constraints around what can be done and how. International development, mainly an arm of the foreign policy and economic interests of the industrial nations, has created an immense international bureaucracy, professional societies, international institutes, academic fields, journals, book series, and a huge army of practitioners, not a few who have made nice livings by being experts on the world's poor. Add to these the worldwide proliferation of NGOs, and it appears that the poor countries of the world are nearly overrun with outsider experts.

This multibillion-dollar "development" activity gained initial momentum in the 1950s, flourished for a time, and then came under increasingly hostile governmental scrutiny from many sides. Among the donor states, governmental oversight groups began to feel that sending money abroad was a waste of resources, that developing the economies of other countries created harmful competition for national industries, and that it would be better to give money only when it was profitable for the donor nation to do so. Although these views never fully prevailed, they gave rise to extremely hierarchical systems for designing and evaluating development programs, and these systems have remained resolutely hierarchical and authoritarian ever since.

In the past 15 years or so, many nongovernmental organizations have entered the development scene as major players (Gardner & Lewis, 1996; Lewis, 2001). Not constrained by the same nationalist rationales and politics, these organizations have diversified approaches to development considerably. They are free to be more openly ideological about their goals because they are intentionally created to foment certain kinds of social, economic, and ethical practices. As a result, the present international development scene is a complex patchwork of the big international development projects of nation-states and the activities of NGOs. PRA is used in both venues.

HISTORY OF DEVELOPMENT WORK

To understand why PRA is an important departure from previous practice, it is necessary to have a brief sense of the history of international development work. There have been two major approaches since the late

1950s—liberal and Marxist—and a number of other more topical emphases that have moved across this landscape as well, including population control, capital formation strategies, feminism, environmentalism, participation, foreign debt and structural adjustment, and international human rights.

Far and away the dominant approach to development has been based on competitive individualist market theory. These views are based on a diagnosis of problems of development that treat poverty as an unfortunate and improper outcome of the workings of the world economy that can be corrected by well-targeted restructurings of incentives. A host of theories and methods has long supported this generally optimistic view of development.

One variant of this paradigm is modernization theory, in which the problem of poverty is attributed to the unfortunate continuation of a series of so-called traditional and therefore putatively irrational practices that prevent people from doing what is in their best interest. Some theorists have seen this irrationality as a characteristic of uneducated people in general. Others have seen it as the selfish exploitation of the many by a few "traditional" leaders whose positions must be undermined.

Another alternative focused on a wide variety of theories that argued that capital formation was the key to successful economic development. Just what the strategy for economic development was differed from theorist to theorist. Often it meant controlling population growth so that per capita income would become higher, or it meant learning how to use and conserve resources better so that the basic productive infrastructure would improve, or it meant an emphasis on education and communication strategies to make "traditional" people into "modern" thinkers.

Technological approaches to development have always been popular with Western industrialized nations. Building dams, roads, and schools and sending tractors, fertilizers, and other technologies have been the preferred forms of development assistance and were often quite profitable to the donor's employees. More recently, biological technologies such as the green revolution, new varieties of grain seeds and cultivation systems, and integrated pest management have become popular. Generally speaking, these technologies have been developed and often manufactured in the West and then are deployed (or occasionally imposed) on the rest of the world. They have the feature of treating world poverty as a matter to be solved by production technologies rather than by sociopolitical change and the redistribution of land and capital.

These approaches have been very powerful because governments with lots of money and political clout backed them. National development programs for a whole generation were built on these notions and the ideologies of individualism built into them, as were the agendas of international development agencies such as the International Monetary Fund, the World Bank, and the international agricultural research institutes that have been developing new and more productive varieties of basic food crops. Now NGOs have become major players on the scene, adding their particular slant to the development framework.

Counterposed to this development approach has always been a wide variety of political economy theories about the world under development. Many of these are Marxist or neo-Marxist in inspiration and understand widespread poverty as a constitutive principle of capitalism. The modern world system is unequally developed because the rich countries exploit the poor countries as a source of cheap raw materials, labor, and products. From this vantage point, underdevelopment is a product of capitalism, and international development programs are a cover for political coercion and the maintenance or expansion of the existing colonialist order.

This view of the problems leads to very different forms of practice. The principal goal is to break the dependency on the powerful and wealthy nations that master the system. Because this is both an extremely risky process and quite unlikely to succeed under current conditions, it has attracted many people ideologically as a way of explaining persistent poverty, but it has not inspired very many revolts. It has influenced the practices of a considerable number of NGOs around the world whose intervention strategies are informed by Marxist analysis and who understand economic development as requiring an intentional democratization of power structures.

PARTICIPATION IN THE CONTEXT
OF LARGE DEVELOPMENT AGENCIES

Beginning in the early 1970s, other agendas began to find their way into conventional international development thinking. One fact that deserves particular mention is that the urban and rural side of participatory work were not radically independent. William Foote Whyte and people following the labor relations and urban planning side of participation were doing related work, and Whyte himself crossed over into rural development work for a significant set of works (Whyte & Alberti, 1976, on cooperatives in Peru; and Whyte & Boynton, 1983). However, generally these threads developed independently.

Norman Uphoff, a colleague and professor of political science at Cornell, was at the center of many of these developments as the director of Cornell's Rural Development Committee. Uphoff (1992, 1996) sorts out the history of these developments in an interesting way that shows how long and complex the path to participatory approaches in development has really been.

As he frames the history, while the developments, including the transition from what was initially called rapid rural appraisal (RRA) to PRA were taking place, other efforts were being made in USAID, mainly at the initiative of Ted Owens, a USAID official who played a major role in getting USAID to mandate participatory approaches. Gathering support from the Society for International Development and people in the U.S. Department of State, they eventually garnered support in Congress for this effort, and Congress instructed USAID to put participation front and center in its program work.

To develop both academic support and credibility, Ted Owens, who had met Uphoff in 1972, provided funding to Cornell for a comparative study of rural local government, and this led to a USAID project led by Uphoff and John Cohen to define the meaning of rural development participation. Owens was interested enough in this to contract for this work after having been disappointed by the disengaged academic quality of similar work commissioned at MIT and Harvard. This Cornell project gradually placed Cornell as USAID's "mentor" on "rural development participation" under a cooperative agreement. As a component of this multidimensional and multicountry work, the group began publishing in the mid-1970s the *Rural Development Participation Review* for 3 years; this review included work of people like Robert Chambers and James Scott. It became, for a time, the central location to go to for information on rural development participation. However, the whole funding stream dried up with the advent of the administration of Ronald Reagan.

Though, by Uphoff's reckoning, many of the activities engaged in were reasonably conventional ones, they succeeded in making participation a topic that needed to be addressed and debated in development work. Some of the case work, however, moved beyond that, most notably Uphoff's major project on participatory management of irrigation systems in Sri Lanka (Uphoff, 1992, 1996).

Part of the point of this narrative is that getting participation onto the agendas of the large development agencies was a complex process involving political and intellectual networks and a long, slow, and patient process of negotiation and work. So even the vogue in the use of the term *participation* in international development itself is the product of decades of effort and should not be dismissed as cavalierly as often do the high-minded who see important deficiencies in current practices.

Participation and Sustainability

The environmental movement had a significant influence on promoting participatory approaches. Early development practice did not have a strong sense of the problems of global ecology and strongly emphasized big, energy-intensive infrastructure projects (from which many development agencies and private sector companies derived financial benefit). The emergence of the "small is beautiful" (Schumacher, 1973) and green movements also provided powerful critiques of both the liberal and the Marxist views of development and pressed for more holistic approaches to the complexities of wealth and poverty.

This coincided with the emergence of a strong movement for international human rights that went beyond arguments for a tolerable basic standard of living and included the rights to self-determination, freedom from coercion, gender equality, the rights of children and fetuses, and the rights of ethnic groups.

Together, these movements have had a leavening effect on the macro-development strategies in donor states because the states were gradually forced to pay at least lip service to gender, environment, and human rights issues to maintain any kind of ideological legitimacy. This has coincided with events within the wealthy funding countries, which are experiencing their own complex internal dynamics. These days, accountability, efficiency, downsizing, participation, and competitiveness are the watchwords of business, and these ideologies have filtered into the public sector generally and into development agencies in particular. Simultaneously, at the other end of the political spectrum, there are increasing attacks on foreign aid as a useless waste of money on people whose poverty is their own fault, an ideology that takes us back to the 1950s. Neoliberalism is alive and well in development work. These processes are not surprising since, in advanced capitalist societies, the distance between the rich and poor yawns wider each year.

At this point in history, all the lines between approaches have become increasingly blurred. Liberal and Marxist approaches were easily distinguished before, but now liberal approaches have appropriated much of the language of Marxist, feminist, and ecological analysis. NGOs have complicated the ideological scene with a huge number of agendas driven by a wide variety of ideologies, running from Christian evangelism to the rights of infants and trees. This complex situation has created an environment in which development organizations are forced to restructure themselves, redefine their methods, and try to find new modes of operation, and into this breech a few development practitioners have inserted more participatory approaches to development.

The Specifics of Participatory Rural Appraisal

Though all major social research is a collaborative endeavor, drawing on the experiences, theories, and expertise of generations of researchers, PRA, like Freire's pedagogy of the oppressed (1970), is strongly associated with the representations of it made by a single practitioner: Robert Chambers. Though by no means the only practitioner, Chambers has developed the most succinct and fully articulated statements of PRA in a series of papers (Chambers, 1994a, 1994b, 1994c), in many training workshops, in colloquia around the world, in an excellent book that summarizes the state of the art, *Whose Reality Counts? Putting the First Last* (1997), and in a number of follow-up studies on these subjects which have substantially expanded the methodological base of the work (Chambers 2002, 2005).

In Chamber's account, PRA has its origin in multiple, separate strands of activity. It draws on participatory research (what we have called Southern PAR; see Chapter 10). It also draws in elements from the diverse practices of applied or action anthropology, activities beginning in the 1950s and that have continued but rarely have a strong participatory intent. PRA also rests on a variety of schools of what is loosely called "farming systems research" and includes close observation of local farming practices from a systems perspective and also some notions of on-farm research as a proper modality for the creation of development strategies.

RAPID RURAL APPRAISAL

One of the key strategic problems that created the point of entry for PRA is a particularly bizarre and frustrating dynamic of development programs over the years: the complete lack of baseline data for the development of program strategies and the evaluation of outcomes. A whole generation of development projects was based on presumptions about what was wrong, guesses about how to fix what was wrong, and post hoc justifications of the failed strategies. Faced with a chorus of criticisms about this, the development establishment resisted baseline research as too expensive, as unnecessary, or as impossible. Greenwood himself developed an early (and judiciously ignored) position paper on this subject (1980), arguing that rapid, efficient, and meaningful baseline data could and should be collected.

Over time, the notion that quick baseline studies were necessary and possible developed and, with it, a set of strategies called rapid rural appraisal (RRA) (Belshaw, 1981; Chambers, 1981). RRA was taught at the International Institute for Environment and Development in London, and periodicals such as *RRA Notes* kept track of the developments.

Soon, RRA began to encounter a variety of other developments that were popularizing notions of participation in development work, as well as industrial and service organization restructuring. Before long, a link was forged between RRA and PRA in which RRA was modified to emphasize local knowledge and participation more fully and completely. While RRA was more expert centered and academically based, PRA gained more momentum through the activities of NGOs worldwide. It stressed local knowledge and training, power sharing, and the development of sustainable initiatives for local self-management. In the statement of its aims, PRA sounds very much like many varieties of AR discussed throughout this book.

Unlike many other forms of AR, PRA has a relatively specific set of techniques and methods associated with it. Chambers details these in his papers and books. The best way to get a flavor for these is to consult those works to get an idea of the impressive multiplicity and flexibility of the methods used. We mention a few here to give the reader a sense of the concreteness and attractiveness of these approaches.

PRA involves a number of interviewing and sampling methods and some specific group and team dynamics approaches. Among the approaches used are participatory mapping and modeling of local communities and problem areas, picking key informants as local experts, attempts to identify the different significant local groups and to make contacts with some members of each, having participants help analyze things written about them, the development of timeline and trend analyses with local information, the development of seasonal calendars including crop cycles and labor requirements, and the development of teams and team contracts. Flexibility, attentiveness to the way local people think and react, and a powerful belief in the knowledge systems of local people are key to PRA.

A couple of examples of the results of the use of these methods can be seen in Figures 13.1 and 13.2, taken from Thomson and Schoonmaker Freudenberger (1997).

RESOURCE USE MATRIX								
	GENDER		WEALTH			PROVENANCE OF USER		
	Men	Women	Richer	Average	Poorer	Villager	Neigh-bouring village	Stranger
Cropland	12	2	10	8	5	10		
Kitchen Garden Land	3	10	10	10	10	10		
Tree Wood	6	6	5	6	10	6	4	5
Tree Leaves	3	13	6	3	10	5	3	
Medicinal Plants	6	8	2	3	8	5	3	12
Grasses	10	4	9	5	2	6	4	

Figure 13.1   Resource Use Matrix

SOURCE: Thomson, J., & Schoonmaker Freudenberger, K. (1997). *Crafting institutional arrangements for community forestry*. Rome: Food and Agriculture Organization of the United Nations (Forests, Trees and People Community Forestry Field Manual 7). Available at http://www.fao.org/docrep/w7483e/2/7483e00.htm#contents

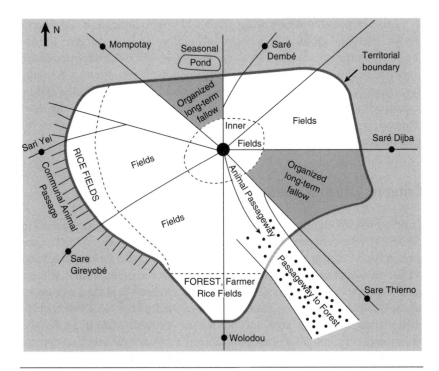

Figure 13.2   Local Community Mapping

SOURCE: Thomson, J., & Schoonmaker Freudenberger, K. (1997). *Crafting institutional arrangements for community forestry*. Rome: Food and Agriculture Organization of the United Nations (Forests, Trees and People Community Forestry Field Manual 7). Available at http://www.fao.org/docrep/w7483e/2/7483e00.htm#contents

Each PRA project involves a slightly different mobilization of the techniques depending on the expertise of the outsiders coming in, the capacities available locally, and the problems being examined. Having become massively popular, PRA is now applied in a multitude of situations, including participatory rural appraisal, the development of participatory evaluations of projects, particular topical studies, and as the source of training programs for both community members and outsiders.

PRA sounds many themes familiar from AR. Local knowledge is given pride of place. The behavior of outside experts ideally is controlled to provide space for insiders to make their own choices. The methods are not applied scattershot, and there is a kind of reasonable sequencing in the activity that moves from one kind of knowledge and team dynamics to more complex ones over time. PRA also deals with issues of validity and reliability of data, and it claims to give local people a greater right to define their own situation and act on it.

Issues of power and knowledge are joined directly, at least in Chambers's own practice. The subtitle of his 1997 book, *Putting the First Last,* gives the flavor. The assumption is that the ideas and practices of the rich and powerful will dominate in all situations unless they are intentionally subverted by "handing over the stick" to the local people, by insisting on hearing their views, and by respecting their knowledge. Development professionals are the ones who must change, learn to listen, and then take what they learn to become advocates for local people.

Critiques of Participatory Rural Appraisal

Criticism of PRA abounds because so many problems surround its practices in the large development agencies. The development establishment, at least on the surface, has welcomed it as a panacea for getting quick input for the design and evaluation of development programs, but it is by no means clear that these agencies much care about its participatory dimensions other than wishing to take advantage of the euphonic sound the word *participation* has. PRAs are now often mandated by agency fiat, and this is not necessarily a bad thing. But the larger conditions in the agencies that mandate PRAs can directly contaminate the processes, causing the practitioners to prejudge the outcome of the work and to carry forward projects that were already defined without the use of PRA.

Like any AR approach, PRA, in the hands of incompetent or malevolent practitioners, can become an empty formalism, a set of ritualized steps to go through rather than a set of tools to be deployed differently as the complexities of local situations become better understood. Of course, this co-optation of terms and practices is not unique to PRA.

PRA, often sponsored by powerful external agencies, is caught in a contradiction between espousing participatory methods while working within a coercive institutional environment. Feminists have pointed out that many PRAs fail because they do not get to the voiceless members of the community and thus create a false impression of the dynamics of local situations, especially when the outside agents are male and are dealing with male local leaders. Some of the best PRA practitioners have taken these criticisms seriously and struggle with these problems.

David Mosse (1993) points not to the failure of PRA but to its weaknesses in practice and why it should not be viewed as a panacea. He shows how PRA can unintentionally structure local knowledge to reflect existing social relationships by failing to develop the long-term and subtle sensitivity to local power relationships that an AR project would necessarily develop.

When a PRA team arrives in a community and begins a rapid process of data collection and analysis, it usually does not have the time or inclination to become aware in a detailed, subtle, ethnographic way about the nuances of local power. As a result, the coercion and collusion that dictate the public face of many communities are quite likely to be expressed in the outcomes. PRA is not immune to gender bias for these same reasons because formal representations of knowledge can inhibit women's contribution to its formulation.

At its worst, PRA is an extractive approach to information in which data are gathered for the purposes of the development agency rather than for meeting the espoused intention of having the agency's programs built to suit the needs of the community. Thus, a PRA team may come in, organize a major data-gathering effort, organize the data, and leave, designing the intervention in the local community on the basis of this rapid overview and calling the process "participatory."

Mosse (1993) points out that the participatory language of PRA also can be experienced as oppressive in some situations. When local people ask PRA teams about what should be done and the answer is that "the community should decide," local people can easily experience this as an unwillingness of powerful outsiders to reveal to the local people what their true agenda is. This creates additional insecurity and distrust, whereas in the minds of the PRA team members, they are being open and participatory.

The most sustained critique of participatory approaches to development published so far is Cooke and Kothari's *Participation: A New Tyranny?* (2001). In this book, the various contributors question the transportability of Western notions of participation to non-Western contexts. They assert that often participation is used to weaken opposition to schemes imposed from the outside, a common theme also in labor union reactions to participatory processes initiated by management. Most of all, they counsel skepticism in the face of the exaggerated claims made for participatory approaches as a panacea for problems of poverty.

Participatory Rural Appraisal and Action Research

Whatever the problems involved in its deployment, there is a clear relationship between PRA, PE more generally, and AR. Local knowledge is valued and is taken as the basis for development program design and implementation. PRA does result in some warrants for action. These approaches also contain a strong critique of urban professionalism as a key element and treat the insider-outsider relationship as a key dimension in the dynamics of the processes.

At the same time, there are dissonances in PRA when it does not match well other forms of AR practice and feminist critiques. PRA is avowedly short term, whereas AR is generally conceptualized as a longer-term relationship between insiders and outsiders. Despite Chambers's own realism about these matters, much writing and practice in PRA are insensitive to power relations, a key element in any AR approach. Though PRA has identified the problem of gender differences as they affect its method, it is clear that PRA has not been sufficiently sensitive to gender relations, and we doubt that such a short-term and rather formalistic approach can overcome these problems.

Paralleling our critique of participatory evaluation, after the initial PRA, the action plans and methodologies to be deployed are much less clearly articulated. PRA, as a short-term intervention, does not contain a clear strategy for sustaining long-term change. Although it does develop local knowledge and teams, it does not appear to be as thoughtful as many AR projects have been about working toward sustainable relationships that will keep innovations from deteriorating back to the original situation.

PRA lacks a theoretical position with regard to dealing with the intragroup conflicts that it identifies. Local people, when understood properly, have many and often divergent or incompatible interests. PRA is silent on processes that bring these differences together for the purpose of developing an acceptable and fair approach.

We see PRA as an interesting approach and a participatory one. But for now, the agenda for PRA work is still heavily in the hands of the external funders and NGOs. This opens up the possibility of changing some elements in externally imposed projects, but it does not do so in a very robust way. And by being short term, PRA is not likely to alter existing power relations to a very significant degree. All that said, PRA is a far better option than previous practices for agencies that are the plainly coercive political arms of foreign governments.

Conclusions

Whatever else one might conclude from this chapter, participatory rural appraisal and the related approaches present an unusual case for action researchers to think through. Far from being marginalized and ignored, PRA has been taken into the core of major international development agencies and deployed widely. This recognition and development has been, on the one hand, encouraging. But it has come at a cost. PRA often is deployed within deeply hierarchical agencies whose commitments to local self-determination are doubtful at best. The resource and time constraints imposed on PRA in these contexts can overwhelm the value of the approach and produce meaningless outcomes. Most of all, PRA shows that when powerful agencies adopt an AR approach, the possibility for the co-optation of the language and practices of participation is always going to be a profound problem. The general marginality of so many other AR approaches prevents this issue from surfacing, but to the degree that AR becomes more central to major institutional practices, we will have to face the very same issues of co-optation and coercion that currently affect PRA.

Notes

1. The terminology and abbreviations are hard to keep up with. PRA emerged out of rapid rural appraisal, which itself arose from a combination of baseline studies, farming systems research, and small farmer focused development initiatives. Recently, the term *PRA* is falling into disfavor and is being replaced by *participatory learning and action* (PLA). We use PRA as the terminology for the current chapter.

2. Here is the complete list provided by Pretty and Vodouhê (n.d.):

A Selection of Terms and Names for Alternative Systems of Participatory Learning and Action

AEA	Agroecosystems Analysis
BA	Beneficiary Assessment
DELTA	Development Education Leadership Team
DPR	*Diagnóstico Rurale Participative*
FPR	Farmer Participatory Research
GRAAP	*Groupe de Recherche et d'Appui pour l'Auto-Promotion Paysanne*
MARP	*Methode Accélérée de Recherche Participative*
PALM	Participatory Analysis and Learning Methods
PAR	Participatory Action Research
PRM	Participatory Research Methodology
PRAP	Participatory Rural Appraisal and Planning
PTD	Participatory Technology Development
PUA	Participatory Urban Appraisal
PfR	Planning for Real
PD	Process Documentation
RA	Rapid Appraisal
RAAKS	Rapid Assessment of Agricultural Knowledge Systems
RAP	Rapid Assessment Procedures
RAT	Rapid Assessment Techniques
RCA	Rapid Catchment Analysis
REA	Rapid Ethnographic Assessment
RFSA	Rapid Food Security Assessment
RMA	Rapid Multi-perspective Appraisal
ROA	Rapid Organizational Assessment
RRA	Rapid Rural Appraisal
SB	*Samuhik Brahman (Joint trek)*
SSM	Soft Systems Methodology
TfD	Theatre for Development
TfT	Training for Transformation
VIPP	Visualization in Participatory Programmes

3. This decision is also dictated by Greenwood's participation in a 2-day workshop on PRA given by Robert Chambers at Cornell University in the spring of 1997.

14

Varieties of Human Inquiry

Collaborative, Action, Self-Reflective, and Cooperative

The terms *human inquiry, collaborative inquiry, action inquiry,* and *cooperative inquiry* refer to but do not exhaust a group of approaches, each with a significant genealogy of its own but whose practitioners have sustained a long and fruitful dialogue with each other. We treated them together in the first edition of this book because of certain commonalities in their perspectives and because they have been interrelated directly through the efforts or Peter Reason at the University of Bath. Reason is a prolific writer (for example, Reason, 1988, 1994; Reason & Bradbury, 2001a; Reason & Rowan, 1981). In the time since 1998 and through the efforts of Peter Reason, these colleagues have become key actors in mapping and articulating the diverse elements that make up action research (AR). Peter Reason, John Rowan, John Heron, Hilary Bradbury, William Torbert, Judi Marshall, and others also form an identifiable group that uses differing mixes of elements drawn from psychology, social work, evaluation studies, feminism, action science, action learning, mediation, and meditation practices to orchestrate their own practices. But Reason has done more. He has used his approach as a way of framing and communicating to external audiences an overall perspective on AR practices as a whole.

As the central actor in this process, Reason has made great strides (in collaboration with Hilary Bradbury) toward mapping the field of AR in an intelligible way, linking practitioners from all over the world, articulating their shared and divergent interests, and creating key venues for communication among us. Reason and Bradbury's work in creating the first *Handbook of Action Research* (2001a) and his work in founding and editing the *Journal of Action Research* have benefited us all. Helping move AR from a loose network of people who knew relatively little about each other's work and used radically different terminologies and often counterposed theories to communicate about their work, Reason has brought a kind of order into the field without suppressing the differences among us. In this way, Reason and his collaborators have created a space for communication that uses AR principles of democratic dialogue to improve the quality of the field without driving wedges between different kinds of practice. This important work is by no means complete; Reason and Bradbury are in the process of preparing a second edition of the *Handbook of Action Research. Action Research* (formerly the *Journal of Action Research*) has been successful and now regularly publishes special monographic issues on topics of central importance to AR practitioners everywhere.

In view of this, understanding some of the underlying principles of Reason's work and of his major collaborators and colleagues is important to understanding AR as a whole. These perspectives necessarily affect their map of the whole field of AR and so understanding their views and methods helps us understand what their vision of AR brings to light and which dimensions of AR practice receive less emphasis. So, in addition to presenting their frameworks, this chapter also constitutes a commentary on their overall framing of the field of AR.

Central Perspectives

As framed by Reason and Bradbury in their opening chapter for the *Handbook of Action Research* (2001a), AR centers on producing knowledge that is useful to people in everyday life, that increases the well-being of individuals and communities in the context of sustainable relationships with the rest of the world, that is emancipatory in intent, and that centers on dynamic, ongoing inquiry processes (Reason & Bradbury, 2001b, p. 2). Underlying this framework is what Reason has often called a "participatory worldview." This worldview not only privileges participation but also refers to a sense of both engagement and ongoing transformation of the human situation from less liberated to more liberated states of what he calls "human flourishing" (Reason & Bradbury, 2001b, p. 1). Finally, AR produces valid results but only when validity is understood to involve an appreciation of plural ways of knowing, of the quality of the processes themselves, and of the significance of the results for the welfare of the participants and their surrounding worlds.

Together with John Heron, about whom we say more following, Reason has developed a comprehensive overview of what they call "cooperative inquiry," which means research "with" instead of "on" people. Developing frameworks they have been working on since the late 1970s, they lay out the following conditions for cooperative inquiry. It requires that all participants be fully involved as coresearchers in all dimensions of the research process. There must be a well-orchestrated interaction between sense-making activities and the results of experience and action, and validity must be treated as a central question. Validity is tested in action by the degree to which the results satisfy the participants' goals and needs.

Cooperative inquiry rests on a developed epistemology of inquiry. Reason and his colleagues distinguish *experiential knowing,* which occurs through direct action; *presentational knowing,* which communicates the results of those experiences; *propositional knowing,* which reinscribes the first two forms in words and concepts; and finally *practical knowing,* which involves knowing how, the ability to take skillful and self-conscious action. We discuss this framework in more detail following because we find it a fruitful technique for guiding AR inquiry.

In addition, this group insists strongly on making distinctions among first-person, second-person, and third-person research and practice. Torbert, in his essay "The Practice of Action Inquiry" (2001), lays out these distinctions clearly; they are used as well by Reason, Judi Marshall (2001), and a number of others. First-person research and practice involve work to discover ways to "exercise our attention" (Torbert, 2001, p. 251) and to overcome our strong tendency to shy away from the introspective dimension of inquiry. This focuses on the researcher herself and involves learning to develop habits of inquiry about her own actions and states of awareness as a key element in being present in group situations as an effective participant and researcher. As Torbert sees it, this kind of action inquiry can permit us to gain greater clarity about our ongoing experience of ourselves and thus prepare us both to participate more actively with others and to understand others better. In this regard, there are links to the work of Chris Argyris and Donald Schön (Argyris, 1974, 1980, 1993; Argyris, Putnam, & Smith, 1985; Argyris & Schön, 1978, 1996) and others for whom learning to analyze and discipline the actions of the researcher herself are centerpieces of any inquiry framework.

Torbert moves from this to identify second-person research and practice as involving the disciplines of dialogue and listening with and in the context of others. A variety of activities are central to second-person research and practice. They include attempts to "frame" the discussions and have that framing be open to response from other participants, to advocate or assert positions in a dialogical context where they can be analyzed and responded to, to offer illustrations to back up assertions, and then to inquire of the others in the situation about their reactions to the developing pattern of interpretations. These are essentially the interpersonal, dialogical context of engaged AR groups, and, again, these perspectives have a good deal in common conceptually and practically with the work of Argyris and Schön (1978, 1996) (see Chapter 15, "Action Science and Organizational Learning").

Finally, there is third-person research and practice, in which the first-person and second-person inquiries are linked into a process of organizational transformation in which power changes hands (Torbert, 2001, p. 256). These are the contexts of organizational change, organizational development, organizational leadership, and broader social change in which power and the movements of power are particularly salient.

The work of these colleagues, and many others whom they have taught and otherwise influenced, has a comprehensive framework. They rely on a basic set of epistemological positions contrasting sharply with the underlying epistemologies of conventional research. They also employ a clear set of distinctions among the variety of kinds of knowledge that are used and given weight in AR. Finally, they employ distinctions among first-person, second-person, and third-person research that keep an active tension between the personal, the dialogical, and the collective dimensions of collaborative research processes. This is a rich and well-articulated vision of AR, and Reason and Bradbury have used it to organize key dimensions of the *Handbook of Action Research* (2001a) and thus to give a certain reading to the form of the whole field of AR.

We are aware that this is very general presentation of these approaches, so we substantivize it more through the rest of the chapter by reviewing the work of four practitioners: Peter Reason, William Torbert, Judi Marshall, and John Heron.

Human Inquiry

PETER REASON ON HUMAN INQUIRY

One of the most striking characteristics of these forms of inquiry is their ongoing trajectory of development through the steady incorporation of a wide variety of perspectives and practices. The genealogy of Peter Reason's work stretches back to the late 1970s, and from then to now there is an ongoing development of an increasingly well-articulated approach. Our own favorite among his works, because of its comprehensiveness and link to case studies, is *Participation in Human Inquiry* (Reason, 1994). Here he nicely defined the central agenda as an approach to living based on experience and engagement, on love and respect for the integrity of persons; and on a willingness to rise above presuppositions, to look and to look again, to risk security in the search for understanding and action that open possibilities for creative living (Reason, 1994, p. 9).

The strong value placed on experience and engagement, a clear recognition of the emotional and ethical dimensions of relationships, a desire to have the world of experience answer back and invalidate preconceptions (against positivism), and a commitment to "creative living" are the key elements. The focus is on individual people and their organizations in their local situations, people who are attempting to live more creative lives. At the same time, there is relatively less attention paid to the larger political economy of organizations or of the broader systems of which they are a part.

The aims of human inquiry are bold. Already by 1994, Reason had laid claim to a particular epistemology, a set of techniques that emerges as a consequence of it, a history of science that backs up the epistemological claims and technical practices, and a series of social reform agendas including democratization, improvement of social services, and the incorporation of gender perspectives in all dimensions of social change. In this regard, human inquiry is among the most fully developed and complex combinations of theorization and practice in a combined social psychology-human relations framework to be found in AR.

Reason builds the work around a carefully constructed framework that insists on the priority of having a participatory worldview to match a participatory methodology. In other words, techniques alone are not sufficient to produce the kind of work desired, a point often ignored by other researchers. The techniques must be couched in a larger vision of the world and human relations that privileges participation as both a matter of principle and a matter of practice. Only then can the step be taken to transform what would be subjects in conventional research into coresearchers.

Like many of us, Reason inquires into the reasons for the domination of conventional social science by nonparticipatory and petty commodity approaches to social research and provides his own particular history. We all engage in such efforts because it is not sufficient to simply claim that AR is a better way to conduct research than is conventional social research. It is also necessary to deal with the domination of the social sciences by approaches that we claim are clearly inferior to AR.

To cope with the problem of the dominant, alienated forms of social inquiry, Reason (1994) develops a "grand narrative" about the evolution of human consciousness. His basic notion is that humans move from unconscious participation to a form of alienation created by patriarchal domination and then seek emancipation in a kind of future participation that has self-awareness and self-reflectiveness. This future participation is described as operating in a Batesonian world of pattern and form (Bateson, 1979). It involves the conscious use of the imagination, and provides for a very different experience of the self from that common to gender-divided approaches.

Human inquiry is then set in this context as a "method or a training, a set of rules, exercises, or procedures" (Reason, 1994, p. 40) that will lead to a new kind of participatory outcome. As we indicated earlier, Reason presents a classification of types of knowledge that are together the central scaffolding of human inquiry: experiential, presentational, practical, and propositional knowledge. We find this typology a particularly fruitful contribution because it calls attention to the diversity activities that necessarily form part of a broad and inclusive concept of knowledge. It also emphasizes the failure of the conventional social sciences to remember how complex and differentiated knowledge is and how knowledge is built out of sequences and combinations of different kinds of knowing and acting in context.

We also agree with Reason that the process of inquiry moves through phases in which particular knowledge forms predominate. For us, this way of understanding knowledge development in AR is one of the most fruitful parts of Reason's work. AR writing generally offers very few such characterizations to help practitioners portray and locate themselves and their collaborators within participatory processes. This framing owes something to the social psychological literature of the 1940s and 1950s but is much more effectively systematized for research purposes here. This is important because the complex combinations of first-, second-, and third-person processes and the diverse kinds of knowledge generated in AR often overwhelm the action researcher's ability to frame and explain them. In such a context, this framework serves as a useful mapping device for all forms of AR.

In human inquiry itself, these phases begin with coresearchers who are examining a subject together. For Reason (1994), these knowledge forms are mainly propositional, though there is some presentational knowledge present as well. As the process deepens, the coresearchers become cosubjects. At this point, the kinds of knowledge are mainly practical. In the next phase, the cosubjects become immersed in each other's realities and the knowledge forms are mainly experiential. Finally, the cosubjects begin to emerge from the research process together. They review, reframe, and even repudiate some ideas. At this point, the knowledge forms are mainly propositional. But elements of presentational knowledge are used to link the experiential and practical knowledge gained in the process to the propositional knowledge acquired.

This is particularly helpful because the vast majority of AR projects begin as rather conventional research or problem-solving activities. Indeed, many of our students worry about whether they are doing AR at all or not when they begin their work. There seems to be a presumption that AR projects are born fully formed in a broadly participatory and democratic way. Our experience and part of the premise of the work of Reason and his colleagues is that AR is a process that is achieved over time, one that often begins in very conventional ways. It is a process that can begin in an unpromisingly hierarchical way and then branch out into more experimental and risky forms of participation. This certainly matches our own experiences (see Greenwood, Whyte, & Harkavy, 1993).

Since AR is a process, not a thing, over the course of the process, there are a variety of opportunities to innovate by opening it up to greater collaboration and to the possibility that the partners can become real cosubjects. Just how far the process goes depends on the skills of the practitioner, the situation, the temperament and situations of the co-subjects, and other local factors. What is important is that the process begins somewhere and that the AR practitioner makes a disciplined effort at ever-greater inclusion of the subjects as coresearchers. In the process of revealing this, Reason has much of interest to say about ownership of projects, power relations, and the problems and opportunities of collaboration.

Another point that comes through clearly in Reason's (1994) closing essay is that being a good social researcher is not enough to create a good AR project. To work in human inquiry, the researcher must develop good facilitation skills and have an understanding of group processes. All the formal social science training in the world can be useful but it is not sufficient. The student of human inquiry must come to terms with group processes, must seek to develop herself as a facilitator and partner, and must continually strive to combine excellence as a researcher with ethical and political commitments as a co-subject with local partners. This is also why Reason is right to argue for the importance of having a participatory worldview to match a participatory methodology. Without an appropriate worldview, the methods take us nowhere and the moves we make will not achieve the desired outcomes.

Reason and his colleagues are also defenders of "good stories" as critical elements in this work. For far too long, action researchers have permitted themselves to be coerced by the conventional social researchers who cast aspersions on AR by claiming that we are just "telling stories." This criticism is a rear-guard attempt at justifying the masking of the alienated and jargonizing proclivities of conventional social research. As we indicated in Chapter 7, strong narratives are key to AR and essential to any kind of social science endeavor and they find a clear place in Reason's work. Only through the detailed understanding of the real logic of human situations as lived and participated in dynamically can we reach for the larger underlying issues and causes that help us account for them.

A central tenet of AR in general is the conversion of people who would be research subjects in conventional research into coresearchers. Reason and his colleagues not only affirm this but they give more attention to the detailed discussion of the development of these collaborative relationships epistemologically and methodologically than do many others. The first-person and second-person emphasis leads to a strong focus on the constitutive elements of such relationships.

For example, John Rowan, a longtime colleague of Reason's, strongly emphasizes the need to develop the researcher's self as a part of the process of being better able to work with others. While this begins in personal growth, it is also related to the kind of personal authenticity that is necessary for AR relationships to prosper (Rowan, 2001, pp. 114–115). In particular, Rowan argues that such moves are necessary if we are to move away from alienated research and in the direction of participative research processes. Thus, the kind of self in this AR tradition is not the self of the "objectivist" researcher who fantasizes that she can reason herself completely out of the research but a vulnerable and yet healthy self authentically engaged with others in collaborative inquiry.

In describing research in this mode, John Heron states that cooperative inquiry, "being highly participative . . . has a micropolitical form and is important as an educational and politically liberating process. It empowers autonomy and co-operation among people over and against any kind of controlling, authoritarian social process" (Heron, 2001, p. 333). He calls this "transpersonal inquiry" and emphasizes the orchestration of a comprehensive process that brings about the kind of dynamics and growth that are sought. This process aims at changing state of consciousness, creating a shared language and a safe dialogical space. It also seeks to create an inquiry-oriented frame of mind, critical reflection, and to transfer power to the participants (Heron, 2001, p. 334).

As is probably evident, one of the central problems that AR must overcome is the alienation of our society. The radical individualist, commodity production kind of neoliberal mindset that underlies so much social science and social policy is evidence of this alienation, and the only path out, in this approach to AR, is through combined greater self-awareness and awareness of the self in the context of others.

In the hands of Reason, Rowan, and Heron, this desired kind of consciousness is appealing because it involves self-awareness and self-reflectiveness, is built on living in a fluid world of complex and dynamic patterns and forms, and involves the use of the imagination, the emotions, and the intellect together as tools. Human and collaborative inquiry leads the inquirer not just to conduct research differently but to live in the world as a different kind of person. This goal underlies a great deal of the attractiveness of AR in its many guises, but even that goal is poorly articulated in most written work. By stressing that human inquiry is a discipline and a practice, and that the researcher has the characteristics of a learner, these writers stress that AR involves all participants in a process of self-discovery through others.

The human inquiry tradition contains a great deal of value. Whether or not one agrees with the perspective, the approach contains a systematic epistemological and methodological development and is a good antidote to the intellectual laziness that characterizes too much AR. Often in AR, the justification that the researcher is doing good covers up the researcher's unwillingness or inability to make the intellectual effort needed to think hard about what he or she is doing and how it can be improved.

Action Inquiry and Self-Reflective Inquiry

Within this array of approaches, there clearly are different kinds of emphases. One such emphasis takes a harder-edged approach to the role of personal inquiry in making AR processes possible. Some of this work is influenced by the work of Argyris (see Chapter 15, "Action Science and Organizational

Learning"), but it also owes a good deal to the work of Kurt Lewin, other social psychologists, and to psychotherapeutic traditions. Prime exponents of these approaches are William Torbert and Judi Marshall. Torbert (2001) calls this work "action inquiry" and Marshall (2001) calls it "self-reflective inquiry." A collection of papers on these approaches can be found in the special issue of *Action Research* devoted to "Self-Reflective Practice and First-Person Action Research" (Marshall & Mead, 2005).

WILLIAM TORBERT ON ACTION INQUIRY

Although Torbert has developed these ideas in many publications and continues to develop them, we refer to the most comprehensive statement of his views, *The Power of Balance* (1991). This book opens with a rather quizzical introduction by Donald Schön, who does not ratify many of the things in the book but enjoins us to learn actively from it. Part of the reason for Schön's diffidence may be that Torbert's claims are occasionally extreme, and partly this may be due to the fact that Torbert is occasionally painfully self-revealing in making his points. While this tone of self-revelation is not foreign to human inquiry-cooperative inquiry approaches, Torbert is both more insistent and harder edged about demanding a particularly sharp focus on the self and its foibles as a central competence for an action researcher. He asserts that social transformation requires self-transformation, and he shows in most of his writing how this requires a great deal of introspection and a certain kind of openness to the personal that most other approaches seek to hide.

Of the authors discussed here, Torbert (1991) works hardest at cross-referencing participative change at the individual, group, and larger political levels. Torbert's cases routinely engage power relationships in a direct way that makes his analysis a valuable addition to this general set. He begins with the view that power as ordinarily conceived (that is, power over others) is far weaker than what he calls the "power of balance," a "self-legitimizing form of power . . . that invites mutuality, that empowers those who respond to this invitation with initiatives of their own, and that generates both productivity and inquiry, both transformation and stability, both freedom and order" (p. 2). The aim of action inquiry is to learn how to exercise this kind of power individually, in groups, and across generations.

Torbert then distinguishes four kinds of power: unilateral, diplomatic, logistical, and transforming. Blending these four types productively gives rise to the power of balance. This balance comes from what he calls "constructive rationality," which desires to achieve individual rights and fairer social relationships. Thus, the perspective is rooted in a macropolitical vision that is built on a view of group dynamics and individual action, all of which are necessary ingredients in the development of the balance. In this regard, Torbert's work is distinctive because it has a more articulated view of the macro-social and political environment.

Given Torbert's long experience of teaching in business schools and working in the private sector, most of his examples and his arguments are drawn from these settings. The work contains a long example on curriculum reform in a business school. This stands as one of a very small number of accounts of AR in curriculum change in higher education (for another, see Reynolds, 1994). The work is peppered with shorter analyses of the actions of individuals and groups that often provide vivid illustrations of his key points.

The core practice in action inquiry is what Torbert calls "the creation of liberating structures." Rather than arguing against structure, Torbert argues for structures that lead people to develop themselves and their relationships in an ongoing process of growth, confrontation, and development. In his view, without structure, there is no movement, whereas with coercive structures, there is only resistance. Liberating structures are action inquiry's way out.

Torbert lists eight essential qualities of liberating structures. First, deliberate irony attempts to move people out of conventional ways of thinking about their organizations. Second, liberating structures must define tasks that, to be completed, must be approached in ways congruent with the broader values of organizational development. Third, they involve premeditated and foretold structural change over time. Fourth, the processes must create ongoing cycles of experiential and empirical research and feedback to the participants. Fifth, leadership can use all available forms of power to achieve these goals. Sixth, the structures are always open to challenge by organizational members. Seventh, the leadership is held accountable to the same values as it espouses for the process. Eighth, the leadership aims to ferret out and fix personal and organizational incongruities.

Although these positions echo other frameworks, Torbert's combination is unique. Torbert is much more attentive to the dilemmas of the exercise of power and leadership. The dimensions arrayed earlier are played out in a long example of a curriculum reform that Torbert undertook at Southern Methodist University's business school. The vivid retelling, the ethnographic specificity, the tacking back and forth between the organizational story and the personal and existential dimensions of the process, and the macropolitics of the school make this a uniquely valuable case to read. The fits and starts, the uncertainties, the fears, depressions, highs, and errors that necessarily accompany anything so complex as major organizational change are wonderfully retold. These are gradually woven into a larger narrative about Torbert's own trajectory as an educator, husband, friend, and leader. The confessional tone of this writing provides one of the few published accounts of the existential side of AR, a telling reminder that engaged inquiry engages us on all levels, not just as trained professionals.

He has continued to develop these perspectives in a variety of writings. A brief summary of his practices is found in Torbert (2001). He has also articulated his views into a larger framing of the field of AR in an interesting essay on the many "flavors" of AR in Chandler and Torbert (2003). A particularly riveting set of case examples is found in Sherman and Torbert (2000).

JUDI MARSHALL ON SELF-REFLECTIVE INQUIRY

Judi Marshall, a longtime colleague of Peter Reason, has made first-person action research her particular focus. She provides an overview of her practices in the *Handbook of Action Research* (2001) and links her work to systems theory in an article in *Action Research* (Marshall, 2004). Her point of departure is that inquiry itself requires discipline and that what she calls "attentional disciplines" are central to successful AR processes. These attentional disciplines are not narrow prescriptions or rules but rather ways to achieve general greater growth and inquiry skill. In Marshall's framing, inquiry itself is a central piece of life. She says, "I currently prefer the notion of inquiry as life process, respecting how inquiring is a core of my being, and that my full (multiple) being is involved in any 'researching' I undertake" (Marshall, 2004, p. 438, emphasis removed).

Marshall insists that attention must be directed both inward and outward in AR and that these attentional disciplines are then placed in the context of systematic cycling between action and reflection and between both action and reception of action. Never is inquiry unintentional, despite the fiction held by some practitioners that AR should be determined by everyone else and the action researcher herself should be entirely neutral. Marshall, rightly we believe, emphasizes being deliberate and intentional while also remaining open and receptive, a skill that can only be achieved through the strengthening of a well-understood selfhood and authenticity about one's own motives and needs. Clearly, great weight in Torbert's and Marshall's work is placed on the attentional disciplines and the enhancement of self-knowledge as a prerequisite and perhaps a key motivation for doing AR.

Cooperative Inquiry

JOHN HERON ON COLLABORATIVE INQUIRY

John Heron is a collaborator as well as a friendly critic of Peter Reason (he set up the New Paradigm Research Group in London in 1978 with Reason and John Rowan). He is also a prolific writer and practitioner in his own right. While Heron's work has much in common with the work already discussed, Heron's overall emphasis on the larger processes of research and on questions of validity makes it valuable for us to treat his work here on its own.

His major book on these topics is *Co-Operative Inquiry: Research Into the Human Condition* (Heron, 1996), a comprehensive development of an epistemology and methodology for AR. The book begins by disavowing the desire to create yet another orthodoxy. Heron actively seeks to map his approach onto others, including qualitative inquiry in general, and promises to explore the paradigm of inquiry underlying his approach and compare it with others. He tries to live up to these promises, taking an inviting and nonparochial approach to a complex subject.

In cooperative inquiry, the point of departure is *participative reality*, by which Heron (1996) refers to the immanence of mind in nature (reminiscent of Bateson, 1979) and the necessarily cogenerative quality of human knowing. What sets Heron's treatment apart is his distinction between participative reality as an epistemological question and the equally important and powerful political (and ethical) values of participation and human development. These are treated as two dimensions. He does not try to derive one from the other, as is so often done. "The democratization of research management is as much a human rights issue as the democratization of government at national and local levels" (1996, p. 21).

His argument for cooperative inquiry links these two meanings of participation, and he systematically defends it against other approaches that he considers more limited. He uses the distinctions among experiential, presentational, practical, and propositional knowing throughout and to good effect; as a good action researcher, he begins the process with experiential knowing.

Heron also faces the issues of truth and validity squarely, rather than arguing that doing good excuses any methodological or epistemological sloppiness. Heron is a strong believer in the *warrant for action* view of knowledge. Heron works through the various ways inquiry processes are begun, their phases, and the variety of things that can happen at different points. Though no solution is offered to the dilemmas of coauthorship, Heron confronts these issues forthrightly.

Heron is particularly attentive to issues of validity, and he makes important contributions to the broader discussion of AR. He connects inquiry cycles, reflection, action, and other elements in the process to an overall view of what constitutes validity in this kind of work. We believe this still stands as the most comprehensive statement of an approach to validity found in the AR literatures. Among the validity procedures Heron advocates are research cycling, balancing divergence and convergence in the process, and elements of reflection. The discussion on validity has much in common with the arguments presented in Chapter 4. As always in AR, the basis for making claims for validity is whether they warrant action or create workable solutions.

Having taken us this long way, Heron (1996) then returns to the larger worldview that guides cooperative inquiry. He restates his commitment to what he calls "empiricism," but he does so subversively by insisting that empiricism means not prejudging the content of experience. Heron effectively takes on the empiricists in their lair by arguing that their own views of what is empirical are completely inadequate. He closes the work by showing how cooperative inquiry better addresses nearly all the conceptual, empirical, and political dilemmas of conventional social research.

VALIDITY

Heron's emphasis on validity is taken up by Bradbury and Reason in the concluding chapter of the *Handbook of Action Research* (Bradbury & Reason, 2001), an interesting choice and one that shows that Heron's argument for the importance of taking on the question of validity in AR has gained traction. Rather than arguing that doing research that is ethically good somehow automatically produces "good" research, it is now clear that we must make defensible arguments regarding the quality and validity of our work.

Bradbury and Reason review the multiple meanings of validity and how deeply unacceptable to AR it would be to accept the postmodern attempt at the destruction of all standards of validation and meaning. They link questions of validity to questions of quality because without judgments of what is good quality, what is valid work is impossible to determine. But goodness depends very much on the goals of the inquiry. Thus the value and "worthwhileness" of the work are key elements in validity judgments.

In AR, validity, like everything else, is dynamic, it is processual. For each kind of process and each kind of knowledge deployed, there are different ways of dealing with validity. Bradbury and Reason close the essay with a good synthetic illustration that we reproduce here:

Issues as choice-points and questions for quality in action research

Is the action research:

Explicit in developing a praxis of relational-participation?

Guided by reflexive concern for practical outcomes?

Inclusive of a plurality of knowing?

Ensuring conceptual-theoretical integrity?

Embracing ways of knowing beyond the intellect?

Intentionally choosing appropriate research methods?

Worthy of the term significant?

Emerging toward a new and enduring infrastructure?

(Bradbury & Reason, 2001, p. 454)

Conclusions

Taken together, these strands of thought give us a broad view of a particular set of related approaches to AR strongly anchored in social psychology, organizational development, and human service work. The practitioners have also done more than anyone else to try to map the fields of AR and to link discussions from the disparate sources and arenas of AR practice into a larger, worldwide conversation. This has been a major contribution and the field is very different now from what it was even 5 years ago because of this work.

That said, we also have some hopes about future directions of development that might take place under this rubric. What strikes us most clearly is that, with the exception of some elements in Torbert and Heron's work, the first-person and second-person forms of inquiry and analysis and the attentional disciplines attendant to them get the lion's share of the attention. In part, this is an outgrowth of the strong grounding of this group in social psychology, psychotherapy, and meditative practices. Certainly, this emphasis is a healthy counterpoint to the long-standing overemphasis on third-person forms of inquiry both in AR and in the conventional social sciences. But one overemphasis is not corrected with another.

By focusing so strongly on the first- and second-person, much of the writing in this field says much more about personal and interpersonal dynamics than about the larger dynamics of organizational change and transformation. Organizations seem to hover in the background as aggregates of personal and dyadic interactions rather than systems that also have their own dynamics.

Linked to this but not by any means implied in the framework either is the tendency to study small groups and to focus on social service delivery and educational organizations. The large public sector organizations, large-scale bureaucracies, industrial plants, regional development initiatives, multinational corporations, and the like do not find much attention here.

There are now significant signs that this is changing because, recently, Peter Reason and his collaborators have moved into major new arenas of application that bring their work a good deal closer to the industrial democracy threat of AR. One such project is entitled "Unlocking Low Carbon Potential: Integrated Action Research to Enable Adoption of Existing Low Carbon Technologies," and it seeks to create new understandings of ways to change carbon emissions, particularly in the food industries. In taking this on, the group focuses on organizational barriers to the solution of this "mess" and mounts an interdisciplinary effort at AR, including team building and dialogue conferences, to confront this complexity (Reason, personal communication).

A second major project focuses on the transformation of public service management in Wales specifically through attention to middle management development. It focuses on network building and participatory learning through cogenerative processes. The program has three goals: management development, creation of action learning groups with shared foci, and the transformation of the organizational culture of public service in Wales (Reason, personal communication).

15

Action Science and Organizational Learning

By singling out action science (AS) and organizational learning (OL) for an extended treatment, we argue for its significance as one line of development of the action research (AR) approach of Kurt Lewin (1935, 1943, 1948) and pragmatic philosophy and for its utility in current AR practice. We think AS embodies one of the most significant and systematic attempts to build AR in a way that respects the need for both scientific clarity and practical utility. OL and organizational development frameworks are the two important conceptual contributions to the body of social science knowledge that has emerged from AR. We are not unbiased proponents, however, as our critique will show.

AS is also important in this book because discussing it permits us to include an approach to AR that has a decidedly psychodynamic emphasis, a component of AR that has been present for at least 50 years. The principal architects of AS and OL are Chris Argyris and Donald Schön, both prolific writers and renowned teachers. Argyris has written on these themes from many different perspectives over the years (1974, 1980, 1985, 1993; Argyris & Schön, 1978, 1996; Schön 1983). We have elected to concentrate on the contents of two major works, *Action Science: Concepts, Methods, and Skills for Research and Intervention* (Argyris, Putnam, & McClain Smith, 1985), a core essay on the AS approach; and two books on OL coauthored with Donald Schön and *Organizational Learning II* (1996).[1] The latter link action science, reflective practice,[2] and organizational learning perspectives.

Action Science

We focus on the book *Action Science,* by Chris Argyris, Robert Putnam, and Diana McClain Smith (1985; also available at http://www.actiondesign.com/ action_science/index.htm) because it contains the major ingredients of the action science approach; we have been able to use the book in the classroom, where it succeeds in making the arguments clear to first-time readers. We believe that the approach deserves an extended presentation because action science is a major strand of development in action research, combining elements from systems theory, psychoanalysis, and organizational behavior perspectives in an overarching approach. It also explicitly takes on the issues of scientific knowledge in the practice of social change. To date, it is one of the best efforts to deal with the relation between AR and scientific method.

Early on in *Action Science*, the authors state their main objective clearly: "Our focus is on knowledge that can be used to produce action, while at the same time contributing to a theory of action" (p. ix). In so doing, they argue for a link between theory building and theory testing in action as a single repertoire of actions.

Argyris, Putnam, and McClain Smith (1985) recognize that this has rarely been attempted; they work to frame an explanation for this failure by discussing what they call the false conflict between "rigor" and "relevance." The authors point to the long-standing institutional habit in the social sciences to assume that what is relevant, what touches the real world in known locations, cannot be by definition the source of rigorous knowledge. They argue that rigor and relevance is a false dichotomy. Referring to Lewin's view that the best way to understand something is to try to change it, they argue that the road to rigor lies in the attempt to apply social theory to social action, a view consistent with the philosophy of AR we have laid out in previous chapters.

CONFRONTING

A key concept and method in AS is *confronting*. Confronting is a process by which social actors are forced to come to terms explicitly with their own defensive reactions to changes and perceived threats by inquiring into the causes of those reactions and analyzing the consequences of giving into them. Though Argyris et al. (1985) point out that not all defensive reactions have negative consequences, they strongly believe that defensive behaviors are the key causes for the widespread observation that groups often cycle endlessly between conflicting demands, when the only way forward is to confront and resolve the conflicts.

Theory of Change and Stasis

In Argyris et al.'s view, the aim of AS is to create "an inquiry into how human beings design and implement action in relation to one another. Hence it is a science of practice" (1985, p. 4).

But their goals are even more ambitious because they intend to inquire into (1) the variables embedded in the status quo that keep it the status quo; (2) the variables involved in changing the status quo and moving toward liberating alternatives; (3) the variables in a science of intervention that will be required if the previous propositions are ever to be tested; and finally (4) the research methodology that will make change possible and simultaneously produce knowledge that meets rigorous tests of disconfirmability (1985, p. xii).

By means of this effort, Argyris et al. (1985) seek to develop a "science of practice" (p. 4) through which individuals and groups can be assisted in "creating and maintaining behavioral worlds conducive to generating valid information [under] conditions in which agents can make free and informed choices and feel internally committed to their choices" (p. 77).

OBJECTIVITY

Action science takes on the social science bastion of objectivity directly because Argyris et al. (1985) correctly anticipate that the core objections to their formulations will center on this standard positivistic defensive routine. Their response to the objectivity argument is that it is not possible to achieve even the minimal "valid description" (p. xii) until at least some of the defensive routines of the participants have been directly engaged. Because in their view these patterns of defensive behavior can be both functional and dysfunctional, it is not possible to understand behavior until some sorting out of these elements has been undertaken. In other words, empirical description itself is impossible without intervention, a direct attack on the conventional social science position.

INTERVENTION AND SCIENCE

Argyris et al. (1985) argue for intervention as the principal source of meaningful descriptions on the basis of which a science of action can be built. They invert the conventional social science approach to rigor and relevance by arguing that the standard approach to rigor produces irrelevant, untested, and untestable propositions. "We will argue . . . that theory that intends to contribute to practice should have features that differ from those of theory responsible only to the criteria of pure science" (pp. 18–19).

In their view, what makes the human sciences unique is that they study a group of people in practice, and the action scientist is a practitioner engaged in parallel processes of practice, reflection, defensiveness, and objectification with these cosubjects (p. 22). In the end, their goal is no less than the following:

> Action science is centrally concerned with the practice of intervention. It is by reflecting on this practice that we hope to contribute to an understanding of how knowledge claims can be tested and justified in practice and of how such inquiry is similar to and different from that of mainstream science. (p. 35)

Espoused Theory and Theory-in-Use

In developing the argument for AS, Argyris uses concepts and theories developed in a host of previous works, including some written with Donald Schön (Argyris & Schön, 1978, 1996). Among them are espoused theory, theory-in-use, single-loop learning, double-loop learning, and Model I and Model II theories of action. We develop these notions briefly here because they are fundamental elements in the infrastructure of AS as a form of practice.

The espoused theory/theory-in-use terminology does not refer to newly discovered concepts, but rather names well-known ideas that are important in any kind of competent social research. *Espoused theory* refers to the account actors give of the reasons for their actions. *Theory-in-use* refers to the observer-analyst's inferences about the theory that must underlie the observed actions of the same people if their actions are to be made sense of. Often, espoused theory and theory-in-use do not coincide; occasionally, they are directly at odds with each other.

These are not new distinctions. In anthropology, they have been rendered as the distinction between *emic* and *etic* approaches. Historical materialism poses the same issue in terms of ideology and infrastructure as does Gramsci's (1975) use of the concept of hegemony. What is new about AS is that the distance between the espoused theory and theory-in-use becomes the focus of attention in a group's inquiry into its own actions as a means to try to move the group to a more liberating dynamic.

Single-loop learning refers to a situation in which people or organizations alter their behavior but do nothing to change the behavioral strategies that gave rise to the problematic situation initially. The problem situation is taken as given, and the participants improve their ability to solve specific challenges. The effect is to achieve, possibly, a brief amelioration of a problem, but because the underlying causes are not confronted, the problems return. They persist and regain strength as soon as another dilemma is encountered.

By contrast, *double-loop learning* results from responding to a problem by stepping back and examining alternative larger frames into which the problem can be put. The immediate problem is understood to be the product of a context that itself must be altered. By altering this context, a group can move to a new plane of OL and change. Action science generally views the persistence of single-loop learning as the product of defensive reactions and improper inferences about the motives of others.

The import of the single-loop/double-loop distinction is that it identifies certain kinds of problems as those toward which AS interventions should be aimed. These are "problems that persist despite efforts to solve them. . . . [They] are likely to have double-loop issues embedded in them" (Argyris et al., 1985, p. 87).

Linked to these two kinds of learning are theories of action. In what Argyris et al. (1985) call "Model I," the underlying model is based on having unilateral control over others. Few people espouse Model I, but many people practice it. Another theory of action is "Model O(rganizational)-I." This kind of theory of action gives rise to a limited learning system that corrects errors that cannot be hidden and do not threaten the group's underlying norms. Here the center is broad participation, a focus on win-win approaches, and a strong emphasis on expressing feelings while suppressing intellectual analysis.

Counterposed to these are "Model II" theories of action. In Model II, there are "minimally defensive interpersonal and group relationships, high freedom of choice, and high risk taking. The likelihood of double-loop learning is enhanced, and effectiveness should increase over time" (Argyris et al., 1985, p. 102).

Model O(rganizational)-II is the same, but the individuals making up a collectivity are acting out Model II theories-in-use. The result is the creation of a *community of inquiry* in which issues and conflicts can be opened up and in which both single- and double-loop learning occurs.

EMPIRICAL TESTING IN ACTION SCIENCE

One of the most interesting features of AS is its strong attention to methods for developing tests of interpretations. The perspective is based on an extensive development of the kinds of concepts used in attributing reasons for people's behaviors, assigning causal responsibility, and achieving intersubjective agreement about the data.

A technique called the "ladder of inference" is used to link subject dialogues, interpretations, and actions into an analyzed interpretation of interactions: "In AS we deal with this issue with the help of a conceptual device, the ladder of inference. This is a schematic representation of the steps by which human beings select from and read into interaction as they make sense of everyday life" (Argyris et al., 1985, p. 57).

In constructing this analysis, the first round is utterances from ordinary speech in a specific situation. Then the observers and participants assign meanings of the utterances (both their own and those of the people they are dealing with). These meanings are then examined and compared, and the inferences used to arrive at the meanings are analyzed. The ladder of inference refers to the connecting links of analysis between the utterance and the interpretation arrived at. Typically, most people make very powerful inferences about the aims of others on the basis of shaky data. The point is to move up and down the ladder together with the actors in the situation being examined, checking how conclusions are drawn, what is paid attention to, and what is ignored. From this, the patterns of behavior leading to a persistence of single-loop learning surface and can be examined.

Note that the ladder of inference is a technique of organizational intervention, not a mere research tool. It is applied because a group has a problem that it has commissioned an action scientist to help it try to solve. Intervention is not at the opposite end of some continuum leading from action to research.

Rather, as Argyris et al. (1985) put it, "Intervention is the AS analogue of experimentation" (p. 64). Without intervention, there is no AS! The Lewin and Dewey inheritance is clear.

A RETROSPECTIVE EXAMPLE OF ACTION
SCIENCE: THE MILGRAM EXPERIMENTS

One of the most outstanding features of Argyris et al. (1985) is a fascinating critique and reformulation of the famous experiments by the U.S. psychologist Stanley Milgram (1974) on the willingness of ordinary people to inflict harm on fellow human beings. By commenting on the Milgram experiments and distinguishing their strategy from Milgram's, Argyris et al. succeed in showing how different a science of action would be from conventional social science, even on socially relevant subjects.

Milgram used people recruited by an advertisement putatively to teach an experimental subject some word associations. Whenever the subject failed, the teacher was to administer electric shocks, and the shocks increased over the course of the experiment to dangerous levels. In fact, Milgram and the experimental subject were secretly collaborating, and no electric shocks were administered. The "teachers" did not know this, however.

Milgram interviewed the teachers beforehand, and all asserted that they would not knowingly harm a fellow human being. Though Milgram found lots of variation in people's reactions, many people were in fact willing to shock the experimental subject. From this, Milgram concludes, without a clear line to the data, that humans are not intrinsically hostile or aggressive, but rather are weak willed and prone to follow orders by those in authority. As a result of this finding, the work was dubbed the "Eichmann experiments." Milgram reported his findings almost 10 years after completing the work, but made no social intervention other than writing his book.

In commenting on Milgram's (1974) work, Argyris et al. (1985) are respectful of his accomplishments and yet distinguish their approach from his. "In order to reliably describe some phenomenon, one ought to retain its essential features and construct a situation that captures its essence" (p. 111).

In Argyris et al.'s view, Milgram did not try to alter the situation and its outcomes. This lost him the possibility of understanding the genesis of the observed behavior. As a result, his experiments could not yield knowledge that might help individuals break out of this dilemma. We never learn of alternatives that might better manage it, and we do not discover the deep structures that maintain it.

Argyris et al.'s Model II approach would have been to alter the parameters of the experiment to change the outcomes. Because what is socially desired is a population in which no one is willing to follow immoral orders, Argyris et al. argue that AR should focus on the disobedient teachers and inquire into the causes of their unwillingness to follow such orders. From this, theories can be developed about the causes of disobedience, and the experiment could be varied to increase the causes of disobedience until the maximum disobedience is achieved. In this way, a Model II inquiry both inquires into the causes of behavior and intervenes directly to promote morally desirable behavior in the research subjects. The distance between this and conventional social science is clear, and the basis of conventional social science itself is revealed to be single-loop, Model I behavior.

Practicing Action Science

Not content simply to lay out abstract theories of AS, Argyris et al. (1985) also formulate a number of *rules of practice* that guide their AR. Paralleling these are a series of rules for testing hypotheses, a subject almost never broached in the AR literature. Whatever one thinks of this version of AS, Argyris et al. are correct in making attention to scientific reasoning a higher priority.

POSITIVE FEATURES

There is much that is useful in this framework. Rather than justifying action by using some kind of ethical argument about dealing with social problems, Argyris et al. (1985) argue for AS as a better form of scientific inquiry than conventional science. They also pick up the core of Dewey's and Lewin's arguments that it is through action that learning can occur. Thus, in these authors' view, to be scientific, social research must be socially engaged. To put it in the frame that Argyris has long used, the aim of AS is to increase the possibility of unlikely but socially beneficial (liberating) outcomes. They want to achieve this through the deployment of the scientific method. The core logic of their argument is that any social research that is not interventionist cannot be scientific, an argument they make quite effectively in their analysis of the Milgram experiments.

The reverse side of this logic is a less clearly expressed but equally severe judgment of many other action researchers. In Argyris et al.'s view, too many action researchers routinely accept the separation of thought and action that characterizes conventional social science, choosing to justify their work by the urgency of the problems they study or the goodness of the goals they have. More bluntly, the greater part of AR is characterized by foggy epistemologies and incoherent or careless methodologies. By the logic of AS, this is itself a Model I single-loop behavior and will not produce a successful community of inquiry.

CRITIQUE

Psychologism, Defensive Routines, and Intervener Paternalism

For us, AS takes a very narrow cut of the complexities of human psychology, even though we welcome its analysis of motivation and behavior at this level. In the main, human psychology, as relevant to action, is reduced to the production of defensive routines leading to single-loop outcomes. It does not seem plausible to us that defensiveness is the only major psychological process relevant to these group phenomena. The richness of human motivations, the complex interactions between cultural ideas and the economics and politics of particular situations, and the complex differences among all the participants in a particular situation are not explored if the analysis focuses only on defensiveness.

It is unclear how the action scientists themselves overcome this defensiveness. According to their own view, defensiveness is the "default" form of human action (they describe the Model I responses of individuals as "natural" and "automatic"; Argyris et al., 1985, p. 151). This assumption is quite important because it creates an unexplained gulf between the facilitator and the subject.

Left to their own devices, participants would be unable to redesign the Model I predispositions that lead to repetitive failures. Rather than continue to feel frustrated and hopeless, they might decide that it is impossible to produce Model II action and thereby justify their withdrawal; or they might decide that some Model I strategies are as good as could be expected, and not focus on their counterproductive features. In other words, the defenses that enable people to remain unaware of their theories-in-use in the Model I world would reassert themselves. The task of the interventionist is to help participants begin to redesign their theories-in-use genuinely (Argyris et al., 1985, p. 338).

No justification is ever given for this state of affairs, nor is any explanation provided about the sources of the interventionists' "unnatural" human capacities to overcome these limitations. Argyris et al. appear to be natural-born action researchers in this account.

In speaking of choosing to change, they state that although individuals have no choice in their theory-in-use and the O-I learning system, they can choose to alter their theory-in-use and, hence, the OL system and culture. But such changes will not occur unless the players are committed (p. 152). But why individuals have no choice, what commitment is, and how commitment develops are not discussed.

This view is highly charged politically because it forces us to conclude that action scientists are different kinds of human beings from natural ones. Although this view might be justified through a discussion of the process of people becoming trained to be action scientists, AS does not contain such a discussion. We are left with the action scientist as an unchallenged, self-conscious, and self-contained individual capable of acting on others.

Another way of looking at this problem in AS is to note that the analysis has a strongly dyadic bias. That is to say, although many of the examples occur in group contexts and Model I and Model II refer to group behavior, the predominant image that emerges from a reading of AS is that of a skilled practitioner or teacher confronting a group member and getting that group member to inquire into and change his or her behavior.

We believe that this image of the teacher and student, the therapist and the patient, though having the merit of focusing attention on some of the psychological dimensions of group processes, also incurs significant costs. Until recently in AS, we did not see an analysis of groups as groups. Rather, groups were assumed to function well when all the dyads in them are functioning well. Notions of group structure, political economy, gender differences, ethnicity, and the like have been left out. Groups are portrayed as being constituted of individuals engaged in exchange and as ideally moving toward some kind of rational choice model. In particular, this makes the analysis insensitive to power relationships, including the power this approach bestows on the expert intervener.

This matters, not because there are no good action scientists; indeed we have both seen marvelous AS practice. Rather, it matters because we think the good practice we see arises, in part, because these practitioners have a more sophisticated social theory than they articulate in their writings and that they practice in a less hierarchical way than the model suggests. Developing a better analysis of these elements is a pending assignment for AS.

These issues of hierarchy matter a great deal because AS proceeds by identifying problems and agreeing when solutions have been found. Thus, the authority to make these decisions is central. Deciding what kind of behavior is appropriate, for instance, is crucial. Yet, for example, in referring to "brittleness" in social relationships, action scientists define it as a "predisposition to express an inappropriately high sense of despair or failure when producing error" (Argyris et al., 1985, p. 156). What is inappropriate and who decides is not discussed; this apparently is a decision to be made by the intervener. Argyris et al. also speak of "genuine organizational change" without defining what is genuine, again permitting the intervener the authoritative position of deciding what constitutes change and what does not.

The way in which the ladder of inference is used and the way segments of dialogue are separated for analysis also reveals a highly rule-based vision of culture, a view supported by Argyris et al.'s repeated use of the term *routines* to describe behaviors. Although many schools of thought do this, including componential analysis in anthropology, there are significant limitations to such a view. Behavior is more than rules, just as language is more than grammar. This is particularly important because AS's effort to be scientific requires some sort of notion of "disconfirmation" as part of the approach. But the discussions these authors give of disconfirmation rest heavily on this rule-based view of behavior, giving us little sense of the experiential difficulties of a disconfirmation strategy when the flow of human behavior is viewed in its ethnographic complexity.

HISTORY OF SCIENCE

All of us who are posing critiques of conventional social science approaches must have an explanation about why such conventional social science prevails. If we are right and conventional social science is wrong, then we must explain why it is dominant and we are not. We have already devoted attention to this issue in the present book (see Part 2). We only point out that AS lacks an explanation why the social sciences chose to mimic the natural sciences rather than Dewey and Lewin (Argyris et al., 1985, p. 5) or why there exists what Argyris et al. call "pernicious separation" of theory and practice (1985, p. 7).

In our view, this inattention to larger issues of social structure and political economy stems from the same dyadic and therapeutic view we commented on above. Action scientists assume that people are misguided and can be brought back to a better view of the matter through high-quality intervention. This ignores the existence of the whole political economy of social research that always moves in the direction of blunting the reformist and democratizing elements in social science for reasons that seem better explained by matters of power than by "defensive routines" of the members of particular groups.

None of these criticisms is unanswerable, and some of them have been addressed by action scientists in recent publications. This framework has gone farther than any other in trying to address some of the methodological and epistemological issues raised by the notion of a science of AR, and deserves close attention for this reason.

Organizational Learning

The long and fruitful collaboration between Chris Argyris and Donald Schön led to a number of books; two of the most important are *Organizational Learning* (1978) and *Organizational Learning II* (1996). Though the term OL is now common, Argyris and Schön created it in 1978, at a time when organizational behavior thinking was pointing in very different directions. Now there are hundreds of works and high-profit consulting businesses based on promises about OL (for example, Senge, 1990).

Many arguments are similar to those presented in relation to AS, but some issues of organizational dynamics are taken up only in these works. Here we deal with the second book, *Organizational Learning II* (1996). It provides an excellent critical overview of the OL literature. The authors offer their own well-grounded and nuanced view of OL, followed by an extended and clear presentation of the basic single-loop, double-loop, Model I, and Model II schemes already discussed.

What is important about this book for the overall AS perspective is that the authors strive hard to get beyond dyadic relationships in which power is not an issue. They discuss organizational politics and show an awareness of the complexities that the symbolic-cultural life of organizations creates not evident in the earlier work (Argyris & Schön, 1978). They also succeed in making inquiry-enhancing intervention a much clearer concept and process than in Argyris et al. (1985).

Particularly valuable too is the Afterword by Argyris and Schön, which is built around a robust critique of academic practice, arguing that academics are unlikely to confront theory-practice relationships. We concur with their AS analysis that universities are particularly unlikely to become learning organizations in a meaningful sense.

Few books address the complex issues of AS and OL as effectively as Argyris and Schön. Perhaps only Robert Flood and Norma Romm's (1996) *Diversity Management* shares their epistemological, methodological, and practical ambitions. Argyris and Schön advance over *Action Science* by showing that they are aware of the need to speak to the issues of organizational culture inherent in OL, an awareness not visible in the earlier work.

Yet this dimension needs more attention, because the treatment of organizational culture remains rather limited and mechanistic in contrast to their dynamic and more differentiated behavioral perspectives. The richness of cultural productivity in organizational contexts and around the kinds of processes Argyris and Schön are attempting to stimulate requires greater analytical development. This richness is one of the most enduring experiences of search conferences.

Argyris and Schön also make a number of attempts to get beyond a view of organizations as collectivities of individuals struggling with each other dyadically to a more truly social concept of organizational structure. This is important, but the issue is not well resolved.

The authors show their awareness of criticisms that their perspectives are either blind to power relations or actually reinforce certain kinds of hierarchies in organizations. Nevertheless, the fact that Model I behavior is the default for people in organizations is still treated pretty much as a law of nature rather than as a possible product of particular systems of political economy. This leaves the sources of Model I and Model II still unexplained, just as in Argyris et al. (1985). Not explaining the ultimate sources of Model I leaves us without an explanation of why certain individuals (in this case, the authors) are capable of transcending ordinary human limits and then leading others to do so. This opens up legitimations of authority and expertise that deserve more open inquiry.

Though the book is clearly in the AR tradition, just like *Action Science,* *Organizational Learning II* does not speak strongly to the issue of the normative and ethical ends of OL. The clear interest in nondefensive human behavior is positive, but no explicit connection is made between this commitment to democratization. The approach can easily be adopted by conventional consultants for whom participation and democratization are not high priorities.

The Skills Required for Action Science and Organizational Learning

Good AS practice focuses heavily on group process skills. In the interventions we have observed by some action scientists, we have been impressed by certain skills they develop. For one thing, they are very patient and persistent with the processes. The calm, persistent, clear, and supportive role interveners play does much to create the space in which the kind of AS inquiry leading to changes in group process can be developed. It is our sense that AS insists that practitioners discipline themselves to wait longer, persist more, and remain calm perhaps more than most other approaches. Perhaps this is part of the therapeutic legacy of this tradition.

Another important feature of AS intervention is the way in which practitioners learn not to feel threatened by silences and vacuums in group processes. Rather than rushing in to fill awkward spaces with sound and action, they keep uncomfortable spaces open longer, confronting the participants with the need to examine their actions in part out of the discomfort caused by the process of standing still.

At every turn, AS practitioners challenge participants to be explicit and to explain their actions, and they repeatedly make explicit their own reactions and explanations as a model for this behavior. This quasi-Socratic intervention often leads participants to make their own analytical breakthroughs rather than allowing them to hide in the interstices of group process. This requires skill in confronting people without silencing them, being strong yet open, sympathetic yet critical, and unusually attentive to the details of speech and action. Again, these are legacies of the therapeutic tradition and are worthy of study and emulation in AR processes.

Conclusions

In conclusion, AS and OL are neither perfect nor wrong. They are bold and clearly articulated attempts to bring AR into direct confrontation with conventional social science and to pursue a limited social reform agenda. That they have gaps and problems does not make them different from other approaches. They merit close study by action researchers.

Notes

1. In practice, we deal only with the second of these books because it is a complete revision of the first book, based on the authors' continued practice and the critiques they received.

2. We made the decision not to include a separate chapter on the approach most individually associated with Donald Schön, which he calls "reflective practice" (Schön, 1983, 1987, 1991), mainly because many of the organizational practice elements in this perspective emerge in the coauthored books, and some of the other key elements in the reflective practice approach center on dyadic coaching relationships and not on larger-scale organizational change.

Part 4

Action Research, Higher Education, and Democracy

W e have systematically defined, described, and justified action research (AR) and placed AR in a philosophical, technical, organizational, and political context. We have presented our own preferred approach and a sampling from the wide variety of other AR approaches. A great deal has been left out, and even the approaches we presented have been dealt with only briefly. Many important contributors to the field have not been mentioned, and thorny issues have received only brief treatments. Still, we hope that these sketches have whetted your appetite for AR and that they will serve as a beginning point for a more detailed examination of these approaches.

What remains now is to discuss the education of action researchers, the complexities of the relationship between AR and institutions of higher education, and the future deployments of AR that we hope for. This involves an examination of some of the pedagogies associated with AR, building AR into higher education, and deploying AR throughout society. To accomplish this, in Chapter 16 ("Educating Action Researchers") we review the tensions and possibilities that we see in the relationship between AR practices and ongoing change/transformation in institutions of higher education, and in Chapter 17 ("Action Research, Participation, and Democratization") we lay out concluding arguments for the potential role of AR in revitalizing democratic processes and recreating some of the characteristics of civil society that are being worn away by the onslaught of economic globalization.

16

Educating Action Researchers

Despite the existence of "educational action research" and the many action researchers who hold positions in institutions of higher education, action research (AR) lacks much of a literature on how to educate action researchers. The emphasis on adult and informal education found in the educational AR literature is not matched with similar attention to AR in higher education. Other than general analyses about the role of universities in society from an AR perspective (Brulin, 2001; Greenwood & Levin, 2000), Reason and Bradbury's *Handbook of Action Research* (2001a) lacks chapters on educating action researchers in the higher education system. Though a section of the *Handbook* is devoted to the skills necessary for doing action research, there is no systematic presentation on how to impart those skills in academic settings. Anecdotes about teaching and learning are found in many of the chapters. The *Handbook* is not unique in this regard.

This absence arises in part from the historical process of separating social science from social action and making university social researchers aloof from society's concerns (see Chapter 5). This story is well known in the United States (Furner, 1975; Madoo Lengermann & Niebrugge-Brantley, 1998; Ross, 1991), but it is repeated everywhere. It happened even in Norway, where AR is much more widely respected than in the United States and where it is well funded as an instrument of public policy.

The first AR institution in Norway was founded in the 1960s on the premises of the Norwegian Institute of Technology (NTNU). The Institute for Social Research in Industry (IFIM) focused on industrial research and on engineering education. IFIM focused on research, and it did provide a few courses to the College of Engineering. Over time, the acceptance of AR at the university grew to the point that a separate Department of Psychology and Social Research was created. However, by then, the action researchers of IFIM had left NTNU to start a new institution in Oslo, the Work Research Institute (WRI), an institute not located at an academic institution. The researchers' motivation was that being in Oslo put them closer to the political processes surrounding setting priorities for work research and improved their access to public funding. But one consequence of the move to Oslo was that it disconnected AR from daily academic life. The WRI never managed to build good relations with the University of Oslo. To the contrary, the hostility toward WRI on the part of the conventional academics was so intense that cooperation eventually became impossible.

This situation alienated AR from university life in Norway for decades. As a result, almost no university student had the opportunity to become acquainted with AR during his or her university studies, despite the centrality of Norway in international AR and the emphasis on AR in Norwegian national policy. The recruitment of action researchers occurred after the students had received conventional master's and Ph.D. degrees. This was a disastrous situation, because students were socialized and trained as conventional researchers and then given responsibility for AR projects for which they had no training.

The Tavistock Institute in the United Kingdom had no better luck connecting with English higher education. To this day, with the exception of a couple of efforts in Australia (Deakin University and Southern Cross University), there are few examples of formal AR university training or degree programs anywhere in the world, including the United States. When similar trajectories are followed in many different countries, different political systems, and different higher education structures, it is no accident.

While it is tempting to place the full blame on the universities and the conventional social scientists, part of this problem is caused by the action researchers themselves. Many action researchers have been content to excoriate our academic colleagues and to engage in posturing rather than mutually critical discourse. Our conventional academic colleagues routinely have done the same. This "dance" has permitted both sides to remain ignorant of each other and the effect has been deleterious for both AR and for conventional social science. By not engaging with each other, both sides have become intellectually weaker.

In this regard, the action researchers have done little better than the conventional researchers. At the 50th anniversary celebration of the Tavistock Institute of Human Relations in London, Levin noted that that intellectually responsible, self-critical discourse had disappeared within the ranks of action researchers. Permitting separation and not challenging each other has also let the conventional social scientists off the hook. They have not been forced to justify their autopoietic and socially irrelevant professional activities in the face of well-reasoned criticisms from action researchers, including criticism of their pretension to have created a social "science" without social praxis.

This has resulted in marginality for action researchers, but it has also left conventional social scientists in what is for them an unexpectedly vulnerable situation. The irrelevance of their work and their overwhelming attention to matters only of internal interest to their disciplines is not lost on governments and other funders. While this position worked during the decades of growth of universities and research budgets, the economic and political conditions affecting university life have changed. Public officials, private sector leaders, and academic administrators are all now aware that continued funding for higher education depends partly on universities making visible, accountable contributions to the general social welfare and economic competitiveness. To deal with these pressures, university administrators have been hiring expensive consultants to tell them about "knowledge management," "academic industrial parks," and the "creative class." They have taken this route, in part, because many have had very unproductive discussions about these issues with their own social science faculty members. Nearly every academic leader and policymaker is aware of Gibbons, Limoges, Nowotny, Schwartzman, Scott, and Trow's (1994; and Nowotny, Scott, & Gibbons, 2001) concept of Mode 2 research (research carried out in the context of application and that produces "socially robust" knowledge tested in action). They are anxious to have universities do research in the context of application, to contribute to the "knowledge economy" and to create general economic benefits by training students with relevant skills.

However, because of the long alienation between AR and the universities, most leaders do not understand that AR is the only research strategy built precisely on this way of generating knowledge and action. That conventional social researchers would not know how to contribute to such activities is not surprising, but the absence of the voices of action researchers in the movement to reform the management of higher education and to address these Mode 2 needs in a socially and politically constructive way is hard to excuse.

General Considerations

There are a few postgraduate programs in AR and, to our knowledge, no specialized undergraduate AR programs worldwide. AR lacks any kind of forum for the discussion of the pedagogical strategies and choices involved in the competent training of students in AR.

Action research can bridge the gap between universities and societies in ways that are very powerful, but only if we can make AR an integral part of higher education teaching and research. AR will not find a broader place in social and scientific life unless new cadres of professionals and researchers are well trained in universities and not just given on-the-job training after having completed a conventional social science education. Accomplishing this involves the deployment of teaching AR to undergraduates, master's, and Ph.D. students.

DEPARTMENTALIZATION VERSUS MULTIDISCIPLINARITY

A predictable university response to this challenge would be to create separate courses of study, programs, or departments of action research. This is precisely what was done with women's studies, ethnic studies, and science and technology studies and makes the typical organizational model the conventional academic department that is coterminous with a discipline and evaluated by a single professional association.

Accepting this organizational model for AR would reproduce the self-regarding professionalism and disciplinary narrowness that has caused the failure of the conventional social sciences and that now isolates feminism, ethnic studies, and science and technology studies from the disciplinary bunkers that they originally sought to break up (see, for example, Messer-Davidow, 2002).

Isolating AR in its own programs and departments would literally destroy it because AR is an integrating strategy of knowledge production built on cogenerating knowledge across disciplines and in conjunction with the local problem owners to produce practical and theoretical knowledge simultaneously. A departmental, disciplinary structure would make that impossible.

The logic of this should be clear. AR cannot operate within one specific conventional discipline because AR generates new knowledge holistically in the context of application and, as a consequence, AR must be multidisciplinary. And even trying to create a multidisciplinary department will not work, because the disciplines that are integrated in different AR projects vary according to the problem being addressed. We cannot know a priori which disciplines will be relevant.

In Tayloristic institutions like universities, this kind of spanning of fields, departments, programs, and colleges is not just unwelcome but it presents Tayloristic deans and department heads with what are, for them, impossible conundrums. Being faced with trying to match university expertise to the holistic complexity of real-world problems seems for them both impossible and undesirable. Never mind that society at large is telling them through increased demands for accountability that, like it or not, they had better find a way or they will find themselves without resources.

MULTIDISCIPLINARITY OR A MULTIDISCIPLINARY MINDSET

It is obvious that we cannot train students to be experts in all the disciplines relevant to the AR projects they will encounter during their professional lives. What we can do, however, is encourage and enable them to bridge different disciplines willingly and agilely rather than letting them become accustomed to digging one deep mineshaft in a single field of expertise. Being comfortable in a group of people with widely different forms of expertise and takes on problems is something that can be taught and learned.

Furthermore, despite the self-serving cult of expertise (Brint, 1994), we know from experience that being highly accomplished at something in particular does not require a person to be incompetent at everything else. It is possible to cultivate a broad view of education and a welcoming attitude about learning how to learn new things and learning how to share expertise with colleagues with unlike backgrounds. If we truly believe what we say about cogenerative knowledge creation and the value of having multiple knowledges represented in the process, we also have to behave this way on university campuses. In this regard, we are asking no more than that our colleagues and AR students to behave in the same way we expect the local stakeholders in AR projects to behave. We tell them to be tolerant and open to the knowledge of other stakeholders and to work together cogeneratively.

We know from long experience that our conventional academic colleagues will defend their turfs by retorting that our AR students will be poorly trained dilettantes, that they will know something about everything but nothing much about anything in particular. This is a demonstrably false argument that would be dismissed were it not currently backed up by the accumulated political power of decades of academic Taylorism. Having a broad and holistic view not only does not discourage developing deep knowledge of particular subjects; it makes it clear that deep knowledge is not only necessary in dealing with complex problems but can only be developed through cogenerative processes that combine many kinds of expertise in effective ways. And, of course, our conventional colleagues, who often have deep knowledge of something in particular, rarely are able to deploy this knowledge anywhere but in professional journals read by a small cadre of similarly trained peers. Confusing parochialism with expertise is commonplace in academia.

AR Praxis in Higher Education

The point of departure for AR in universities is a pedagogical approach that combines multiple professional knowledges (from one or more disciplines) with engagement with local problem owners in real-life problems in context. This contrasts with conventional university training that generally and purposely disconnects theory from practice, teaching from doing, and relies heavily on teaching only explicit and propositional knowledge. The "banking model" (Freire, 1970), in which the student is a passive receiver of knowledge deposited in his or her head by the teacher, reigns supreme on campuses, despite overwhelming evidence that it is ineffectual and even counterproductive.

PSEUDO-CONSTRAINTS

When any change project is proposed to a hierarchical group that does not want to change, excuses about resource constraints and administrative limitations proliferate. We call these "pseudo-constraints" to point out that the objections are no more than statements of an unwillingness to alter current behavior and distributions of power, an excellent example of Model I behavior.

One such constraint affecting AR teaching at every level is class size. At the undergraduate level at large universities, social science classes can often be given to hundreds of students gathered in one auditorium. The sheer size of classes is one important obstacle to creating a fruitful AR-based teaching that needs to be interactive and team based and linked to concrete groups of problem owners.

These are pseudo-constraints because they are the results of existing institutional choices and priorities. Where small class size is thought to be crucial, as it is in the United States in language and writing or composition instruction, art and architecture studio teaching, music teaching, and so on, most institutions manage to keep classes seminar size. A small class setting with personal connections between the professor and the students is expensive. So universities, rather than teach the social sciences properly, engage in the disreputable pedagogical enterprise of "processing" lots of students and having departments compete to increase the size of their classes by using this metric to reward them with more faculty positions, office space, and other perks.

Course and curricular structures produce other pseudo-constraints. Students take many courses at once with very little institutional coordination among them. There is no justification for students doing this. They could just as easily take one course full time for a month at a time and have the same number of courses in a year. Such intensive courses would be superior situations in which to develop AR (and most other forms of) teaching and learning. However, such reorganizations would require imagination and ambition that are generally lacking among higher education administrators.

Courses and semesters also are poor time horizons for teaching the practice of AR. It is all but impossible for a full cycle of an AR project to take place on a typical academic calendar. Longer-term involvements over an undergraduate career are possible, but little or no effort is provided by institutions to make this happen.

Clearly these pseudo-constraints on the changes necessary to enable competent AR teaching and learning at universities are a result of an unwillingness to meet the challenges of Mode 2 knowledge production. The failure to do this soon will exact a very high price on most universities, and the public and politicians show this by increasingly withdrawing both their moral and financial support from public higher education (Lyall & Sell, 2006).

Some Possibilities for Undergraduate AR Teaching

With the exception of offering some specialized programs for small groups of undergraduates, which we describe later, we think the main focus of AR undergraduate teaching should be to provide an initial understanding of what AR is, its goals, its history in the larger context of social knowledge production, and an initial understanding of the kinds of skills required to do it. Our own long teaching experience shows us that, even within the limitations of the pseudo-constraints we have mentioned earlier, AR teaching can be carried out successfully. We can give students some experience in running their own cogenerative learning environments, help them learn about projects and the role of the AR professionals in them, teach them about the ethical and political aims of AR, and give them a chance to reflect on ways their own interests and capacities might fit into AR. Such teaching can even be done in large introductory courses, though it is rare.

INTERMEDIATE UNDERGRADUATE INSTRUCTION

At the intermediate level, smaller classes focused on AR are easier to develop.

Levin's Public Planning and Administration Course

At NTNU, Levin created an experimental arena for AR teaching public planning and administration. At an engineering school such a topic attracted only a few students, but this had the advantage of permitting the creation of an interactive environment. To bring real-life problems into the classroom, Levin divided the class into teams of three to five students and had each team decide on a public planning issue in the region worth dealing with. It was easy for the students to find interesting and motivating problem areas. The student teams then had to develop their own problem focus and engage in a process of fieldwork.

Levin's role was to become a critical listener-questioner in support of the effort of creating a research question for the project, and often but not always was the source of practical entry points into the field. The students had to operate by themselves in the field and did a lot of interviewing and data gathering, though with very minimal training in data acquisition and analysis. Most of them needed new technical skills, and they learned them by concretely dealing with the real-life problems in the field situation.

The learning process was designed around the development of the students' projects, balanced against what Levin considered to be necessary substantive texts to be read and used as tools. In one of the most successful years of this course's operation, all four class projects made it to the front page of the regional newspaper.

The strong motivational mechanisms created by working on real-life problems were very clear. Students devoted so much time and energy in these assignments that they complained of not having enough time for their other courses, but they also refused to reduce their engagement in the projects. Talking to and learning from people for whom a problem situation was real created this high commitment and energy.

Greenwood's Introductory Course in Action Research

Greenwood has been teaching an introductory AR course for both under-graduate and graduate students together for 14 years. He begins it by provid-ing a day-by-day syllabus with required and recommended readings. However, the students are then required to submit a biographical statement to the class listserv and to compose a list of their "wants" and their "offers" for the course. They are asked to state what they want to accomplish and what they are able and prepared to contribute to the course. These wants and offers are collectively worked into a list of priorities for the course by means of an extended group process exercise, and the results are composed into a syllabus. Students then volunteer to take on the orchestration of particular topics according to their interests and the expertise and experience they have to offer, and, together with Greenwood, they prepare and deliver the course materials and design the group processes as part of the course's pedagogy.

Though this experience is unsettling to the students at the outset, the process takes off very quickly and students who have been expert passive learn-ers for years are able to take on the management of their own learning remark-ably quickly. Over the semester, they learn more about the complexities of their choices and designs and also a good deal about themselves. They are also tasked with developing a participatory evaluation process throughout the course and developing and administering a grading system for themselves and an evalua-tion of the professor as well.[1]

As in Levin's course, it is amazing how quickly students are able to move into this way of learning and how seriously they take it. They inevitably work harder and more willingly than in conventionally organized classes. They are aware of this, attributing this response to the fact that what they learn and do is their own choice and responsibility to themselves and others.

Levin's Course on Organizational Development

Levin created a new course on organizational development (OD) from an AR perspective using his experiences from the previously described course in planning. Rather than taking the conventional OD expert professional posi-tion, the OD process was constructed around the cogenerative model. Levin also emphasized planning for and reflecting on change processes by using a timeline-based perspective, since change does not happen in the wink of an eye, but is a process that gradually evolves.

This way of teaching AR was well received by the students and was stimu-lating for Levin as well. Student enrollments were quite high (30–50) and student evaluations were quite favorable. "You take this course in order to learn"; "You have to work as much in this course as in all the other together courses this semester"; "You will need what you learn in this course when you start your professional life."

Given these initial reactions, Levin looked for better ways to bring realism into the classroom and developed an assignment structure to support it. The students had to develop an assessment of the organization they studied, including the strengths and weaknesses. This analysis was then fed into the first development plan on which the students got simulated feedback that forced them to change or redevelop their initial plans. This modest change in structure created a dramatic change in the course because it simulated a dynamic change situation, making it clear to the students that a plan for an OD process is only a plan and not a final blueprint for how things will evolve. They had to learn to change strategies and goals as the process developed.

Building on this experience, Levin looked for a way to present a case without an a priori focus of attention in order to have the students also learn how to set problems and not just to solve them. Computerized streaming of video opened up new possibilities. Levin taped a number of conversations with people in an organization and then made them accessible on a computer so that the students could listen, take notes, and discuss what they saw and heard.

In addition, members from the "case" organization were invited to give a guest lecture in the class, which gave them a chance to present their experiences and perspectives on their own organization. This was done in a 2- or 3-hour session. Then, some weeks into the semester, Levin either arranged for a video conference or, if the company was local, invited the local people back to clarify and discuss issues that the students came across as they worked on the project.

The students' assignment was simply stated as "Develop an OD plan that improves this organization's operation." This simple and purposely imprecise problem statement frustrated many students. On the other hand, the experiential situation reflected how messy and unclear are real-life situations. Since an important element in professional action is to make sense of a holistic and complex real-life situation and to be able to formulate a grounded understanding of what key issues need to be dealt with, this was realistic teaching. A demanding and time-consuming part of this assignment was to analyze the interviews. This was problematic and challenging, as the students had only rudimentary knowledge of data analysis. It was necessary to offer a crash course module on data analysis.

The focus of intervention was negotiated with local stakeholders, and students had to seriously think through and argue for the kinds of learning arenas they suggested to make organizational change take place. At the end of the course, members of the organization were invited to participate in the students' final presentation, and direct and grounded feedback was given by the problem owners. The students' work was always well received by the local stakeholders, even when the work took a critical stance toward the local organization.

The most evident disconnection from an AR process was the lack of direct exposure to the field. It was impossible to send 30–50 students out to a single location because they would overwhelm it. And the students could not take responsibility for running an AR-based change process themselves.

Many other AR teachers have developed similar cogenerative learning arenas, and there is little that is special about what we have just described. Rather, we want to emphasize that, despite the institutional hegemony of the banking model, it is remarkably easy to engage students as colearners. Of course, it is up to the professor to make the first moves and to know how to support such a learning process.

Experience-Based Courses for Undergraduates

For advanced undergraduate students with an expressed interest in AR, special programs built around smaller classes that take on AR in more detail are possible. For three years, Greenwood, together with a group of volunteer colleagues (Nimat Hafez Barazangi, Ken Reardon, Paula Horrigan, and Leonardo Vargas Méndez) and the Cornell Public Service Center, ran the Bartels Undergraduate Action Research Fellows Program. With a grant from a Cornell donor, we set up a competition for undergraduate fellowships in AR. The applicants had to have a local project underway, have a letter of support from a local stakeholder, and be willing to take an AR seminar with the other fellows all year. In return, those with financial aid needs received scholarships, and all got some funding to support their projects.

The premise was that a much better link between service and learning could be created if the individual project work of the students was discussed and presented in a seminar and that training in AR was given in the seminar and matched to the needs of the projects. The program was quite successful, evaluated rigorously (Hafez Barazangi, Greenwood, Burns, & Finne, 2004), and popular with the students and the local problem owners. But Cornell was unwilling to reallocate its existing financial aid packages to support such a program or officially to second the faculty to the program by relieving them of some teaching duties in their home departments. This did not require new money, just the administrative will to allocate existing resources around this activity. As a result, when the donor's gift was consumed, the program disappeared. Such a case demonstrates that merely having an AR pedagogy that works does not assure its survival in the academy.

Kenneth Reardon, who is a major national figure in both AR and service learning, runs the Cornell Urban Scholars Program. With support from a foundation, he annually gives more than 20 Cornell undergraduates from six colleges, together with a smaller group of graduate students, the chance to work in the summer with community-based organizations in New York City.

To prepare, they have an on-campus AR and planning seminar during the regular academic year. In addition to giving students this experience, the program is aimed at encouraging more students to elect careers in public service by giving them both the tools and experience needed to understand such a future (more information is available at http://www.cusp.cornell.edu).

There are lots of other examples of what is called "service learning" at U.S. universities. The quality of these experiences varies a great deal. In some cases, the students simply are employed as volunteers in local agencies and the experience is called service learning. In others, faculty members have ongoing projects locally that students join, and, in a few cases, courses are taught that have a service learning component. Not all service learning is "learning," and most of it is not oriented around an AR research strategy but takes the form of conventional, expert-driven consulting.

The space to develop an AR focus in such activities exists, as Greenwood's and Reardon's undergraduate programs demonstrate, but garnering regular institutional support and recognition for such activities is an uphill battle. These experiences show that it is possible to create undergraduate teaching that can prepare students for doing AR.

Ph.D. Training in Action Research

In our view, the most promising educational arena for AR is found in Ph.D. training. The students are more mature, can focus their attention on a particular set of interests, and the Ph.D. program is of sufficient duration for major change projects to be possible. This creates a situation in which the students can be engaged in the field for a substantial period and can, accordingly, be exposed to regular and systematic AR activity.

INDIVIDUALIZED Ph.D. PROGRAMS

The most direct way to do this is to create individual AR projects, where the advisor directly supports and guides the student both in the field and in academic reflection and writing. This mode of advising, both on change activity and on academic work, creates the conventional one-to-one relationship found in most Ph.D. programs. It is easy to move this relationship into the craft mode of teaching and learning, both in the field and in the reflection and research process. This kind of alliance, characterized by in-depth cooperation, can be very valuable, but it is also a very demanding training activity requiring a great deal of the professor's personal and economic resources. There is an obvious limit to how many supervisions and field sites a single advisor can handle. There also often is a problem of defending such students against the hostile reactions of disciplinary colleagues who dislike AR, create course and examination requirements that are useless for AR students, and tend not to distribute departmental largess to the graduate students they have purposely marginalized.

GROUP-BASED Ph.D. PROGRAMS

At NTNU, Levin has created a succession of Ph.D. training programs in AR (Levin, 2003). Since the core of an AR intervention is to create opportunities for collective learning by integrating local members and action researchers in the same reflection and learning process, this kind of Ph.D. training can only take place in real-life situations. Students and advisors share responsibility for the design of the learning processes and for enabling both reflection in action and reflection on action (Schön, 1983).To make such a program possible, Levin had to raise external funds to admit a cohort of Ph.D. students who then passed through the whole program together (Levin, 2003). These Ph.D. programs were linked to ongoing field projects with systematic interaction among fieldwork, seminars, and training on the university campus. The heart of the teacher-learner relationship in these programs was the creation of learning possibilities directly linked to concrete praxis either through mutual engagement in the fieldwork or in reflecting on shared work experiences. For this to be possible, Levin had to have the freedom and ability to be concretely engaged in the field project and be able to manage the art of reflection in action, making it possible for students to see and understand why and how actions were taken.

These programs were successful in the sense that they have created a new generation of well-trained action researchers in Norway, but there is a way in which such Ph.D. cohorts remain isolated. The broader reflections among more heterogeneous groups of students and advisors found in conventional Ph.D. programs are missing. Rather, the process is dominated by one-to-one relationships.

AN INTERNATIONAL Ph.D. PROGRAM: EDWOR

With funding from the Norwegian Research Council, Levin moved beyond the limitations of the local cohort-based Ph.D. program in AR to an international Ph.D. program. Linked to the module structure of the Norwegian Value Creation 2010 Program (funded by the Norwegian Science Foundation), a Ph.D. program was created. Levin selected a faculty of nine, including four non-Norwegians who were appointed adjunct professors at NTNU and five Norwegian faculty members from various research institutes around Norway. The Norwegian faculty accepted applications and admitted 24 students, including an American, a Dane, and three Turks.

Each of the applicants was expected to bring to the program an AR project already in progress. The teaching was divided into 4 years of four 1-week hyper-intensive teaching and advising sessions in which the full required number of course hours for a Norwegian Ph.D. was met. The faculty created the curriculum and delivered course work on theory of science, method, work research, innovations systems, and writing. All writing was to be done in English. Each student selected two Ph.D. advisors from within the program. At this point (mid-2006), the program is in its final year.

Since all of these students are in their thirties and forties and have full-time jobs, finding and making time for the Ph.D. work and keeping a sustained focus has been difficult for many. In addition, the limitations of sixteen 1-week meetings in terms of the social solidarity and social learning that happens with other kinds of cohort-based Ph.D. programs are clear. However, EDWOR has been successful enough that the program has been funded for another Ph.D. cycle, and the lessons learned are being applied in redesigning the process.

ACTION RESEARCH DISSERTATIONS

For too long, action researchers were silent about the problems of writing an AR dissertation and getting it accepted. Fortunately, now, more constructive responses are available. One of the most helpful documents to appear in recent years is *The Action Research Dissertation* (Herr & Anderson, 2005); we recommend it to all thesis and dissertation writers as a practical guide to negotiating the complexities of writing an AR dissertation.

As good as *The Action Research Dissertation* is, a single book is not enough. Developing our own shared conventions regarding what constitutes high-quality AR writing belongs on the international network of action researchers' agenda, as Bradbury and Reason (2001a) point out. All of the issues of voice, multimode writing, intellectual property, and confidentiality that vex AR processes in university environments require the collaborative development of sensible responses from us on behalf of the students we train.

Situating Action Research Within the University

Teaching is one but not the only way of situating AR within the university. Universities are structured to suit the convenience of those who earn their livings there and who manage them. Having an array of separate departments, each putatively encompassing a discipline with no ambiguity at the borders, as if the disciplines had been separately created by a clockmaker deity, is the academic bureaucrat's and the academic disciplinarian's wish. The department chairs, college deans, and university leaders (president, provost, vice chancellor, rector) become respectively the foremen, division managers, and CEOs of an aesthetically pleasing Tayloristic work organization. Whatever else they do, such organizational structures assure universities of hierarchical political structures internally and "structurally produced irrelevance" to the problems of the world, except insofar as those problems interest powerful business and political elites who demand and pay for work on them. So long as nobody much cared what university researchers studied, this kind of Taylorism could survive, but now that universities are being called to account and to demonstrate their value, not to the careers of academics and academic administrators but to society at large, this situation is untenable.

There is an increasing emphasis on research and discovery processes, particularly in the social sciences, not in the test tube but in the "context of application" (Nowotny et al., 2001). However, proposing Mode 2 knowledge production in the abstract is not the same as having organizational mechanisms for achieving it in real universities. Mode 2 knowledge production demands that the knowledge of subjects and methods at universities be easily and quickly mobilized around problems external to the academic professions, in the context of application, and in collaboration with the societal stakeholders whose problems they "are."

At present, most universities have hierarchical, compartmentalized structures with gatekeepers at every level from the department to the college to the university as a whole. The opportunistic gathering of expertise and interest from faculty and students all over the structure and the creation of a work organization that supports engagement in Mode 2 work is a major challenge. Many academics oppose making such changes, and many administrators believe that such changes are impossible to achieve without a radical increase in hierarchical administrative authority, the curtailment of academic freedom and tenured appointments, and the realignment of departmental structures. In other words, we hear all the excuses that business and union leaders gave in the 1970s and 1980s for being unable to improve their performance.

The whole process of creating "entrepreneurial universities" (Marginson & Considine, 2000; Slaughter & Leslie, 1997) is one kind of administrative and policymaker's response to this challenge. It achieves greater flexibility by making all units accountable to external authorities, by separating research and teaching into enterprises with different staffs, by imposing quality assurance schemes—all efforts that consolidate central power. Whatever one thinks of the larger meaning of this process of hierarchization, as longtime work researchers and experts in organizational development, we know this is counterproductive to the creation of Mode 2 processes in higher education.

There is a direct analogy here to the recent history of the reorganization of manufacturing industries. Under the impact of global competition, those Tayloristic companies that did not go bankrupt have been transformed in fundamental ways. The boundaries between the firms and their external customers have been lowered and the relationships have been rebuilt on a more cooperative basis. The internal organizational hierarchies have been flattened significantly and decision making has been moved as far down toward the point of production as possible. Multiskilled and interconnected teams have become the preferred production system, and information circulates much more fluidly through the whole system. A much greater portion of the workforce participates in a detailed understanding of the business strategies and challenges and contributes ideas and experience to the resolution of company problems (see, for example, Womack et al. 1990).

Obviously this is an idealized picture, but it is not irrelevant to our argument. What currently are claimed to be more businesslike practices at most universities are nothing like what we have just described. If universities were reconstructed around this new manufacturing model, authority would be redistributed downward along with the right to act, to interact with external stakeholders, and teamwork and multiskilling would all be prominent. If this were done, universities could indeed engage effectively in Mode 2 processes.

We are now in a position to point out that AR research strategies are coterminous with Mode 2 knowledge production. Collaborative, multiskilled teams with good communication with external stakeholders study and act on problems "in the context of application" and produce "socially robust knowledge." How then would universities have to be reorganized to make Mode 2 knowledge production the dominant research form?

Universities would have to clearly identify the external stakeholders whose problems and claims should be addressed by the university rather than by some other kind of research organization. Because many faculty and external stakeholders already have relationships and ideas about potentially valuable collaborations, internal communicative arenas would have to be created to bring this information to the university's attention. Once the key stakeholders and problems have been identified, as in any AR project, it would be necessary to find out what kind of professional expertise would be of value in working on the problem. This would have to be an interactive process with the external stakeholders.

Having identified the valuable internal university people, university management would have to restructure work organization to allow them to form an ad hoc team, to relieve them of some other duties, and to give them the flexibility to be both on and off campus, to interact with other team members and local stakeholders regularly, and to train themselves more fully in areas that emerge in the course of the projects. The time horizon for such activities would need to be revisited annually until the project ended and the academic people returned to their units, perhaps to be called up again for other projects.

This process would give rise to a wide variety of short-term AR groups and, if properly handled, could also contribute greatly to the academic life of the university. Creating internal university arenas for reports to the community on the projects, taking suitable students along in relevant roles in the projects as part of their undergraduate and graduate training, and using administrative personnel to continue the process of finding external problem owners and sources of support for these activities all seem quite possible.

Conclusions

The virtue of what we have just described is that it not only meets the demand for Mode 2 research through AR but that it truly is possible. However, being possible and being enacted are two different things. None of this is easy, nor do we believe it will take place without a struggle. There are real adversaries, those powerful elites who currently profit from the exploitative, extractive approach to knowledge generation and management, those who cannot imagine any world other than the one they know, and the lazy and cynical who don't want to be bothered. However, it is not clear that there is a choice. Universities appear to us to be the last of the major public institutions to be converted into neoliberal arenas for the play of competitive self-interest (Lyall & Sell, 2006).

Rather than giving in, we think that AR should try to orchestrate a coun-termovement aimed at the promotion of what Ronald Barnett (2003) calls "virtuous ideologies," that is, ideologies that center on the neopragmatic bal-ancing of divergent positions in democratic dialogues rather than the annihi-lation of all opposition and the substitution of the bottom line for democracy. We action researchers have been very good at telling other local stakeholders how to cogeneratively transform their situations, but we seem less skilled and courageous in taking these lessons home to our own institutions.

We suspect that, until the external pressure and hostility toward universi-ties that is mounting by the day reaches the boiling point, our academic col-leagues and university administrators will continue to follow familiar paths and engage in Mode 1 knowledge production and Model I defensive routines while the action researchers wring their hands.

Note

1. This experience is documented by the students and Greenwood in Elvemo, Grant Matthews, Greenwood, Martin, Strubel, and Thomas (1997).

17

Action Research, Participation, and Democratization

In this closing chapter, we turn our attention to some of the broader issues surrounding participation and democratization. These words and concepts are much in use these days in action research (AR) circles and well beyond, but too often the concepts are used as ideological weapons. To locate AR in the broader picture of participation and democracy, we need a sober clarification of our use of these terms.

Participation and democratization themselves are not panaceas; they will not solve all the problems of the world. They do not have magical effects in transforming the world into a fairer, better, and more sustainable place. Participation is always attached to politics. Participation can support the power holders' oppression by being used as a token without content or it can be a vehicle for real social transformation. Participation does not prepare the ground for democracy unless it creates real and sustainable venues for power sharing that increases the local participants' ability to control their own situations.

We are strong promoters of both participation and democratization, but we want to avoid being captured by the dichotomous logics of moral argument. We know from the work of many writers that radical dichotomies are almost always morally charged and substitute for thoughtful argument. The binary cultural logics always privilege one pole as the ideal and demonize the other as the source of all evil, oversimplifying the world in a morally coercive way. Mary Douglas (2002) so effectively pointed out long ago, believing unabashedly in such dichotomies condemns us to a lifetime of sweeping up the "dirt"—that is, the vast number of things in life that do not neatly fit into the dichotomous framework.

Because there are explicit moral agendas in AR, action researchers are quite vulnerable to such moralizing. Since action researchers oppose authoritarianism and unjustified hierarchies and favor redistributing power and respect more widely, it is easy for us to fall into railing against authoritarianism and hierarchy by uncritically celebrating participation, democratization, and even equality and claiming that AR is always on the side of the angels. Too often participation is idealized while the hierarchical systems within which participation always occurs are overlooked. While some useful conceptual clarification may be achieved by contrasting concepts in a polar way, such polarities are useless when designing actions. Action occurs always on murkier terrain, and our aim here is to differentiate the terrain a little more fully.

We think that particular kinds of participation are vital to successful AR work and that, without participation, social problems cannot be solved effectively. But participation itself is not a cause of a good AR process; it is an instrument of a broader process of cogenerative knowledge creation, action design, and evaluation. Participation is not a "thing" or a "quantum"; it is a process that often is complexly differentiated and uneven and occasionally even contradictory. And participation is always located within broader hierarchical social and political boundaries.

Democratization, in the sense of increasing the self-determination of the broadest possible array of stakeholders in search of social designs that are fairer, more healthful, more liberating, and more sustainable, is the broader aim of AR. Particular kinds of participatory processes serve this aim, but participation alone does not produce democratization.

Participation

Because participation is often treated too generally, it is worthwhile both to differentiate and contextualize the concept in ways that can help action researchers triangulate the overall direction of their projects. Participation can be viewed from different perspectives. We have chosen three: the first is built on power and control, the second framed in light of an epistemology of political positioning, and the third is structured around the pragmatics of workplace realities.

ARNSTEIN: POWER AND CONTROL

As a point of departure, we think a good source is the analytical typology on participation created in 1969 by Sherry Arnstein. Its multiple dimensions are depicted in Figure 17.1.

A valuable contribution of Arnstein's analysis is to treat participation broadly by including everything from manipulation to citizen control and then to differentiate the effects on power relationships. For example, people can be said to participate in manipulative situations but, from the point of view of

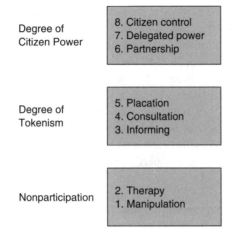

Figure 17.1   Forms and Levels of Participation

power, they are nonparticipants in the social outcomes created. Whatever else it does, this typology makes it clear that participation is not always a virtue.

Arnstein's typology begins with manipulation and therapy. There is an expert or a power holder present, and the people subjected to their will are participants in a set of situations. However, from the political point of view, these are nonparticipative approaches because the goal is for the experts or leaders to get the "participants" to do as they are told. The emphasis is on authority and public relations (and often on patriotism, civic pride, and other such hot button feelings).

The first step toward political inclusion involves what Arnstein calls "informing." This can be developed in many ways. At the lower limit, it involves authorities and leaders in meeting or otherwise communicating with their employees or constituencies and telling them what is happening. In many cases, this kind of communication is a one-way street. An example of informing could be the chief executive officer of a major corporation gathering the employees and informing them that 5,000 jobs will be cut over a period of time.

The next kind of participation is "consultation." Here, either voluntarily or by legal mandate, those in authority engage in a "consultation" with the legitimate stakeholders. This can involve meetings, public inquiry forums, meetings with citizen's committees, and so on. While this kind of consultation makes those in authority more available to questions from their constituencies, for the most part such meetings are heavily orchestrated and controlled. They often have an adversarial tone and involve a good deal of "spinning" of information by all the parties.

In Arnstein's model, the next kind of participation is "placation," in which certain members of the affected stakeholder groups are picked out and incorporated into the communication networks of those in power. This channels stakeholder opinion through individuals selected by those in power and also often co-opts potential leaders of stakeholder groups into the plans of those holding power. Power holders can learn a good deal this way, and some information about what they are doing and thinking can pass on to the stakeholders as well, but the role of the stakeholders in making determinations about what is to be done generally is minimal.

In a more robust form of participation, there is a "partnership" between the stakeholders and the power holders. They have made a choice to jointly constitute working groups and to otherwise share information, analysis, and power with each other. In this case, there is a redistribution of power from the apex to much broader levels of the system, and decision making takes on joint characteristics.

Arnstein's next type of participation is called "delegated power," and this involves actually giving stakeholders the majority position in making decisions that affect their interests and welfare. This not only puts the stakeholders in charge of the process but also makes them accountable to themselves, the leaders, and others in the community for the quality or rightness of their decisions and actions.

Finally, Arnstein describes a situation of "citizen control," in which those directly affected by any decision, condition, or action are completely in charge of planning, making policies, and taking actions to affect their own situation and that of the broader collectivity of which they are a part.

GREENBERG: POLITICAL POSITIONING

In an article entitled "The Consequences of Worker Participation: A Clarification of the Theoretical Literature," Greenberg (1975) forms another taxonomy that is useful for understanding participation in work organization. Greenberg integrates participation, attitudinal and behavioral effects, and social and political consequences in his discussion. He creates four typologies he identifies as different schools of thought.

The first strand is management-centered thinking, in which participation is expected to be low intensity and narrow in scope. The focus would be on enhancing morale and increasing the efficiency of the operation. The goals for participation are identical to the company's, and the result would be to improve the overall operation of the plant.

The second strand of thinking is humanistic psychology. The intensity of participation is expected to be very high, but with a fairly narrow scope. The effects are seen in improved mental health and in the well-being of the participants. The effects are also seen in improved performance of the organization.

Third, Greenberg points out that in democratic theory, the intensity of the participation is expected to be very high and to span a wide range of social and political issues. Participation is anticipated to bring about increased interest in and understanding of public affairs. In addition. participation could lead to a greater tolerance for the viewpoints of others and for diverse ways of being. The broadest effect is the development of a civic-minded citizenry.

His fourth category is the "participatory left," which expects participation to be of high intensity and to span a broad spectrum of societal and political issues. Participation would bring about a healthy work life, a growing desire for control, higher levels of economic activity, but combined with hostility to bureaucratic centralization and hierarchy. The ultimate effect of participation would be a nonelitist, mass-based revolution.

LEVIN: REAL-WORLD PRAGMATICS

These distinctions are useful in real-world contexts. In a study by Levin (1984), the issue was to investigate the situation of participation in Norwegian industry. Instead of commissioning a survey-based study, the research was done in major companies in Norway's dominant process industries and was based on in-depth interviews. The study revealed that the individual's concept of participation was a consequence of his or her role and position in the organization. Management believed that participation was important and useful because it was an effective move to pass information on to workers. It was also important because it provided management a knowledge base as it gave them insights into the workers' way of thinking and acting.

This was a pure practical approach to participation, stripped of all ideological commitments to democratic institutions. On the other hand, workers at the shop-floor level had a very limited perspective on participation, believing that participation was mainly useful in having an impact on the immediate and local working conditions. They reasoned from their experiences that, through participation, it was possible to influence concrete physical design of workplaces, how the canteen should be designed and run, and so on.

A third view on participation was held by the trade unionists. Their position had ideological overtones; they argued that participation was an important source of remedial actions that could move companies toward industrial democracy. At the same time, in their daily work, this group was fully engaged in concrete, practical participation projects to improve the companies' efficiency and in projects to improve general working conditions. The trade unionist combined a view of participation that spanned from practical, everyday participative issues to dealing with the larger political issues in the companies.

The small sample of conceptualizations we have presented so far clearly shows that participation is a protean concept. Co-optation is an important issue both in Arnstein's and Greenberg's classificatory schemes, while this element is disguised in Levin's conceptualization. We always need to ask whether a particular participatory process can be understood as co-optive. Ideological blindness will result if participation operates only at the level of talk (Brunsson, 1989) and not as action. Participation does not mean a thing if it does not lead to concrete results from creating enough power in the group to facilitate change according to the participants' priorities.

These many dimensions of participation find their way throughout AR processes. No AR process is homogeneously perfect or uniformly carried out at the "best" level of participation. At every juncture there are weaknesses, and there is always room for enhancement. We think it is important for action researchers to keep an analytical eye on the variety of participatory processes taking place in their projects and to work strategically to keep enhancing the depth and scope of participation and to understand its genuineness in terms of concrete actions.

Though participation is generally lauded as a good thing, there are many voices raising legitimate criticisms of participation. Part of the problem is resolved when we understand that all of the different activities in Arnstein's, Greenberg's, and Levin's models have flown under the flag of participation, and manipulative and cynical uses of what we would consider to be pseudo-participatory processes are quite legitimately criticized. When a group is told that an organization or government is engaged in a participatory process and their "input" is requested but that the decisions will be made after the "participants" have made their input, this process not only does not lead to democratization but often attempts to hide manipulation under the rhetoric of participation. For this reason, there have been many moments in recent labor history when labor unions, struggling with employers in a negotiation, have withdrawn from company-mandated schemes of participation (for example, work circles, total quality management, and so on) as a weapon in their negotiations. Union leaders recognize that such participation is, in fact, not about power sharing at all but merely about increasing efficiency, competitiveness, and the corporate bottom line.

Coerced pseudo-participation is commonplace in many situations and leads away from democratization. We have already mentioned Cooke and Kothari's views on participation in this sense as a new form of tyranny (Chapter 13), and, though we find their arguments oversimplified, we think their picture of manipulative pseudo-participation in many international and community development schemes is accurate. Under such coercive conditions, resistance to participation can itself be a pro-democratization action. AR needs to take these critiques seriously and be less confident that participation by itself is an unabashed good thing. The specter of co-optation is always present.

Democratization

If understanding the diverse meanings of participation is complex, the concept of democratization offers even more challenges because its referents are even broader. This is a term that refers to structures, processes, governments, decision making, and moral goals, and no short treatment will do it justice. Despite the importance action researchers ascribe to it, sustained discussions of the meaning of democratization in AR are rare. They are much needed.

In organizing our thinking about democratization, we developed a brief typology that highlights different elements in the process. Key to all of them is the notion of collaboration. Democratization requires collaboratively setting the problems to be addressed. Deciding what is to be decided is one of the most fundamental points in any kind of democratic process. Democracy is a collective good, and as a consequence it cannot be achieved through the vehicle of radical individualism. Democracy either is based on representative models or on participative models built on people's ability to make collective decisions. The rules used for reaching a decision can and will vary in different contexts, but the fundamental issue is that decisions be based on collective constructions of meaning and on collaboration and conflict between members who together shape a decision.

Once the problems have been collaboratively set, then collaboration once again is essential in developing the solutions. Here too democratization has multiple meanings. It involves developing the requisite knowledge base for understanding the contours of the problems. This also often means giving the collaborators necessary tools and training so that they can carry on the research on the problems they have set for themselves. In all these cases, the responsibility for acquiring the necessary knowledge is democratized rather than being lodged in the hands of the experts.

Once the knowledge has been developed, the process of analysis is also collaborative, taking advantage of the multiple perspectives of the diverse stakeholders and their experiences with the problems. And from here, the collaboration extends to the design of actions that will help resolve the problems that motivated the work from the outset. This step of action design is shared and does not rely solely on the experts to design programs. Finally, the collaboration extends to applying the actions designed and evaluating the results.

Throughout the base of collaboration is broad and the role of participation is one in which a high degree of codetermination is central. Though this kind of democratization of research implies it, we think it worthwhile to emphasize that it is premised fully on respect for the knowledge and experiences of all problem owners. The democratic assumption here is that every human being knows more about his or her own life situation than anyone else and that everyone, given reasonable support, is capable of contributing knowledge and analysis to a collaborative social process if we collectively are skillful enough in creating the arena for collaboration.

One thing too often lost sight of in the talk about democracy and AR is that both consensus models and majoritarian models of democracy are inimical to the conception of democracy that guides AR. Except in the unusual situation in which everyone has an identical interest (that is, that the meteor coming our way not hit the Earth), consensus decision making usually involves dominant voices and perspectives tyrannizing subordinate ones. Majority rule strikes us as even more hostile. In this case, the majority wins and the minority is crushed.

In our view, the only approach to democracy consistent with AR is democracy as the harmonization of positions (Lijphart, 1977). AR processes are not about erasing difference but about mapping them and mapping possible ways forward that respect the differences that the stakeholders either cannot or will not give up. Often this means restricting actions to those areas where there is enough overlap of interests to permit action, though successes with such actions may eventually lead to the possibility of tackling more divisive issues. What we reject is the notion that a decision rule be used to ignore or crush the legitimate interests of any stakeholder group. In this sense, our notion of democracy is fully in accord with the neopragmatist view that the goal of these activities is "keeping the conversation going" (Rorty, 1980).

Finally, we think that democratization requires a kind of ultimate vigilance about the fairness of the process in conjunction with the fairness of the outcomes. That is, as AR projects proceed, we must be concerned to question the openness and fairness of the day-to-day processes that take place but also to see about fairness of the outcomes. These must not be separated. It is possible to have an open and fair process and end up with a poor outcome. It is also occasionally possible to achieve a good outcome by a bad process. In AR, we try to be attentive and consistent in our concern for democracy both along the road and at the end of the day.

Venues for Participation and Democratization

To this point, we have talked about participation and democratization in a fairly abstract way. Another strategy is to think contextually about the conditions of possibility that we find in the situations we work in. Conditions for participation and democratization differ in manufacturing, process, and service industries, and these conditions differ from those in service organizations, educational institutions, governmental agencies, international development agencies, and nongovernmental organizations. And, of course, they also differ within each of these sectors according to the specific activities, organizational structures, histories, and organizational cultures.

Since both authors have worked in industry, community development, educational institutions, and service organizations, we are aware of the different conditions of possibility for participation and democratization in these different settings. We have experienced the dismissal of our work by some action researchers who believe that any work in industry, universities, and governmental agencies is inherently co-opted and that maintaining a coherent AR position requires staying out of "the belly of the beast." While we accept the right of colleagues to have views different from ours, we are under no obligation to agree.

In our view, it is more productive for AR to take an open-minded view of all human situations and to learn how AR can make contributions to human betterment in all contexts. We do not believe that any institutional context is inherently off limits to AR, though we certainly recognize that particular projects in any sector may operate under conditions that are so inimical to AR that nothing meaningful happens.

So we are asserting that democracy is context bound, always operating within particular contexts, power structures, and environments. The Faroe Islands, for example, have their own, self-controlled democratic system, but, on certain issues related to foreign policy, they have to coordinate their efforts with Denmark, which again will have to follow decisions in the European Union. And, finally, the European Union has to struggle to achieve and implement its own democratically derived decisions. Thus, democracy will always operate under certain boundary conditions, either on the national or on the local level.

In AR, this often seems to be ignored. A good illustration of the complexity of these relationships is the Norwegian Industrial Democracy Project. The idea was to support democratization on the shop-floor level; it started with a negotiated truce between the national confederation of employers and trade unions. What turned out to be a significant contradiction in this democratic effort was a schism between the trade unions' power position in companies built on a high level of membership and collective representation toward management and the local democratic processes at the shop-floor level. These shop-floor decisions could make the local trade union superfluous as the basis for influence is eroded, and in turn, this would make the trade unions hostile to democratization at the shop-floor level. In short, democracy at one level has to be in balance with the conditions on the other system levels. Different levels demand different modes of democratization to be effective.

Another way to state our point is to say that AR is always contextually relative. As we have stated repeatedly in this book, AR processes can always be improved, always opened up more than where we find them on any given day. But this necessarily also means that what constitutes an improvement means measuring what is accomplished today against what was accomplished the day

264 HIGHER EDUCATION, AND DEMOCRACY

before. This is not an absolute scale but an ongoing process of attempting to deepen and enhance the conditions for participation and thereby a broader democratization of a situation.

To give an example, AR work in an industrial setting, where the ownership of the means of production is in the hands of a group of stockholders external to the workforce or is in the hands of the founder of the firm or his or her family, involves a complex process of increasing the capacity of the full array of stakeholders to affect work conditions and benefits and eventually to achieve a fairer distribution of the benefits of the work. But *fairer* is quite unlikely to mean equal shares or anything even close to it. However, it can mean significant improvements in work safety, job satisfaction, and perhaps compensation or even some equity in the business. While engaging in such work is always an individual moral choice, we believe that no one has the right to dismiss such work as outside the boundaries of AR simply because inequality remains and because capitalist organizations have not been overturned completely.

We also believe that, without more democratized workplaces, the future of political democracy in general is bleak. Working in coercive, authoritarian workplaces and then going to vote democratically for a group of leaders mainly financed by big business is hardly a recipe for serious democratic governance. Thus, we understand industrial work as a slow and painful process of winning ground for democracy itself.

Similar arguments can be made for work in service organizations, governmental agencies, and the many other institutions in which currently authoritarianism, co-optation, and antidemocratic practices reign. While it is certainly true that action researchers who are so appalled by such conditions that they cannot abide to be present in these places should not do this kind of work, it is not true that such work is out of bounds for AR. To accept that would be to condemn AR to the poverty-stricken margins of the world system and strikes us as a co-opted position in its own right, a domestication of AR to the margins of advanced capitalism.

Co-optation is always the central risk in any AR process, but just what constitutes co-optation is by no means easily ascertainable. One person may see possibilities in a situation where another sees none. To the one who sees none, trying to do AR in such a situation is condemned to co-optation, and to the one who sees possibilities, a failure to take action seems to be a co-opted form of passivity. In our view, every single AR situation contains the elements of co-optation, pseudo-participation, and manipulation. The only solutions are continuing personal vigilance and an active discussion among AR practitioners to keep clarifying the scope and contours of these issues.

Conclusions: Action Research and Democratic Processes

The aim of action research is to support democratization processes. Now the question is whether there is a general AR perspective that supports this. Reviewing our previous arguments, we have said that to achieve democratic decision making, processes have to be built on participation by the involved problem owners. We have also said that democratic decisions are not synonymous with consensus-based processes. Decisions should build on the diversity and multidimensionality of the stakeholders. At the same time, the process has to enable creation of reframed positions that emerge as a consequence of the knowledge generation processes in the AR activity.

In our view, the essence of the democratic process is the cogeneration of knowledge. The kind of "political" pseudo-deliberation that usually is based on ideological posturing is, in AR, replaced by collective knowledge generation processes built on active and practical experimentation aimed at solving pertinent problems. This knowledge generation process is different from ideological political debate, even if it is impacted by ideologies, because the sense-making process is directly tied to a concrete, shared situation. Because of this, the sense making will be both contextualized and practical.

Further, this grounding of sense making in context and practical choices creates the possibility of overcoming "the hegemony of the ruling class," as Gramsci so forcefully put it (Ransome, 1992). Gramsci argued that the underprivileged classes took up the models of society held by the power holders and thus were unable to sort out their own best interests. This is a formidable problem, but AR makes some small but significant inroads here by creating processes that give rise to knowledge and action designs that are authentically in accord with a broad array of stakeholders' interests. Thus, despite all the risks of co-optation, we argue that the cogenerative knowledge creation processes of AR are a promising way of supporting democracy.

References

Adams, J. (2004, July). *Scientific teams and institutional collaborations: Evidence from U.S. universities, 1981–1999* (Working Paper no. 10640). Cambridge, MA: National Bureau of Economic Research.

Alinsky, S. (1946). *Reveille for radicals.* Chicago: University of Chicago Press.

Amabile, T. M. (1996). *Creativity in context.* Boulder, CO: Westview.

Argyris, C. (1974). *Theory in practice.* San Francisco: Jossey-Bass.

Argyris, C. (1980). *Inner contradictions of rigorous research.* New York: Academic Press.

Argyris, C. (1985). *Strategy, change, and defensive routines.* Boston: Pitman.

Argyris, C. (1993). *On organizational learning.* Cambridge, MA: Blackwell.

Argyris, C., Putnam, R., & McClain Smith, D. (1985). *Action science: Concepts, methods, and skills for research and intervention.* San Francisco: Jossey-Bass.

Argyris, C., & Schön, D. (1978). *Organizational learning.* Reading, MA: Addison-Wesley.

Argyris, C., & Schön, D. (1996). *Organizational learning II.* Reading, MA: Addison-Wesley.

Arnstein, S. R. (1969, July). A ladder of citizen participation. *Journal of the American Planning Association, 35*(4), 216–224.

Barnes, B. (1977). *Interests and the growth of knowledge.* London: Routledge & Kegan Paul.

Barnes B., & Shapin, S. (1979). *Natural order.* Beverly Hills, CA: Sage.

Barnett, R. (2003). *Beyond all reason: Living with ideology in the university.* Buckingham, England: Society for Research into Higher Education and Open University Press.

Bateson, G. (1979). *Mind and nature: A necessary unity.* New York: Dutton.

Belenky, M., Bond, L., & Weinstock, J. (1997). *A tradition that has no name.* New York: Basic Books.

Belenky, M., Clinchy, B., Goldberger, N., & Tarule, J. (1997). *Women's ways of knowing.* New York: Basic Books.

Belshaw, D. (1981). A theoretical framework for data-economizing appraisal procedures with applications for rural development planning. *IDS Bulletin, 12,* 12–22.

Benson, L., Harkavy, I., & Puckett, J. (2000). An implementation revolution as a strategy for fulfilling the democratic promise of university-community partnerships: Penn-West Philadelphia as an experiment in progress. *Nonprofit and Voluntary Sector Quarterly, 29*(1), 24–45.

Berger, P., & Luckmann, T. (1966). *The social construction of reality.* Garden City, NY: Doubleday.

Bowers, C. A., & Apffel-Marglin, F. (Eds.). (2004). *Rethinking Freire: Globalization and the environmental crisis.* Mahwah, NJ: Lawrence Erlbaum Associates.

Bradbury H., & Reason, P. (2001). Conclusion: Broadening the bandwidth of validity: Issues and choice-points for improving the quality of action research. In P. Reason & H. Bradbury (Eds.), *Handbook of action research* (pp. 447–455). London: Sage.

Bradley, K., & Gelb, A. (1983). *Cooperation at work: The Mondragón experience.* London: Heinemann Educational Books.

Brint, S. (1994). *In an age of experts: The changing role of professionals in politics and public life.* Princeton, NJ: Princeton University Press.

Brokhaug, I., Levin, M., & Nilssen, T. (1986). *Tiltaksarbeid på dugnad* [Collective work for community development]. Trondheim, Norway: IFIM/ORAL.

Brookfield, S. (1986). *Understanding and facilitating learning: A comprehensive analysis of principles and effective practices.* San Francisco: Jossey-Bass.

Brookfield, S. (1987). *Developing critical thinkers: Challenging adults to explore alternative ways of thinking and acting.* San Francisco: Jossey-Bass.

Brown, L. D., & Tandon, R. (1993). Ideology and political economy in inquiry: Action research and participatory research. *Journal of Applied Behavioral Science, 19*(3), 277–294.

Brulin, G. (2001). The third task of universities or how to get universities to serve their communities. In P. Reason & H. Bradbury (Eds.), *Handbook of action research* (pp. 440–446). London: Sage.

Brunner, I., & Guzman, A. (1989). Participatory evaluation: A tool to assess projects and empower people. In R. Conner & M. Hendricks (Eds.), *International innovations in evaluation methodology* (New Directions in Evaluation no. 42; pp. 9–18). San Francisco: Jossey-Bass.

Brunsson, N. (1989). *The organization of hypocrisy: Talk, decisions and actions in organizations.* Chichester, England: Wiley.

Burke, T. (1994). *Dewey's new logic: A reply to Russell.* Chicago: University of Chicago Press.

Bråthen, S. (1973). Model monopoly and communication systems: Theoretical notes on democratization. *Acta Sociologica, 16*(2), 98–107.

Carr, W., & Kemmis, S. (1985). *Becoming critical: Education, knowledge and action research.* London: Falmer.

Chambers, R. (1981). Rapid rural appraisal: Rationale and repertoire. *Public Administration and Rural Development, 2*(2), 95–106.

Chambers, R. (1994a). The origins and practice of participatory rural appraisal. *World Development, 22*(7), 953–966.

Chambers, R. (1994b). Participatory rural appraisal (PRA): Analysis of experience. *World Development, 22*(9), 1253–1268.

Chambers, R. (1994c). Participatory rural appraisal (PRA): Challenges, potentials and paradigms. *World Development, 22*(10), 1437–1454.

Chambers, R. (1997). *Whose reality counts? Putting the first last.* London: Intermediate Technology.

Chambers, R. (2002). *Participatory workshops: A sourcebook for 21 sets of ideas and activities.* London: James & James/Earthscan.

Chambers, R. (2005). *Ideas for development.* London: James & James/Earthscan.

Chandler, D., & Torbert, W. (2003). Transforming inquiry and action: Interweaving flavors of action research. *Journal of Action Research 1* (2), 133–152.

Chávez, C. (1975). *César Chávez: Autobiography of La Causa* (with J. E. Levy). New York: Norton.

Chessler, M., & Chesney, B. (1995). *Cancer and self-help: Bridging the troubled waters of childhood illness.* Madison: University of Wisconsin Press.

Clifford, J., & Marcus, G. (Eds.). (1985). *Writing culture.* Berkeley: University of California Press.

Cooke, B., & Kothari, U. (Eds.). (2001). *Participation: A new tyranny?* London: Zed Books.

Crane, B. (2000). *Building a theory of change and a logic model for an empowerment-oriented family support training and credentialing program.* Unpublished doctoral dissertation, Cornell University, Ithaca, NY.

Cronbach, L. J., & Suppes, P. (1969). *Research for tomorrow's schools: Disciplined inquiry for education.* London: Macmillan.

Cummings, T. G., & Worley, C. G. (2001). *Organization development and change.* Cincinnati: South-Western.

Dahl, R. (1989). *Democracy and its critics.* New Haven, CT: Yale University Press.

Davis, L. E., & Taylor, J. C. (1972). *Design of jobs.* Harmondsworth, England: Penguin.

Deming, W. E. (1983). *Out of the crisis: Quality, productivity, and competitive position.* Cambridge, MA: MIT Center for Advanced Engineering Technology.

Dewey, J. (1900). *The school and society.* Chicago: University of Chicago Press.

Dewey, J. (1902). *The child and the curriculum.* Chicago: University of Chicago Press.

Dewey, J. (1976). *Essays on logical theory, 1902–1903* (A. Boydston, ed.). Carbondale: Southern Illinois University Press.

Dewey, J. (1991). *Logic: The theory of inquiry.* Carbondale: Southern Illinois University Press.

Dewey, J. (1991/1927). *The public and its problems.* Athens: Ohio University Press. (Original work published 1927).

Diggins, J. (1994). *The promise of pragmatism.* Chicago: University of Chicago Press.

Douglas, M. (2002). *Purity and danger: An analysis of the concepts of pollution and taboo.* London: Routledge.

Dreyfus, H., & Dreyfus, S. (1986). *Mind over machine.* New York: Free Press.

Eikeland, O. (1992). *Erfaring, dialogikk og politikk* [Experience, dialogue and politics]. Oslo: Work Research Institute.

Elden, M. (1979). Three generations of work democracy experiments in Norway. In G. Cooper & E. Mumford (Eds.), *The quality of working life in Western Europe* (pp. 226–257). London: Associated Business Press.

Elden, M., & Levin, M. (1991). Co-generative learning: Bringing participation into action research. In W. F. Whyte (Ed.), *Participatory action research* (pp. 127–142). Newbury Park, CA: Sage.

Elliott, J. (1991). *Action research for educational change.* Buckingham, England: Open University Press.

Elster, J. (Ed.). (1986). *Rational choice.* Oxford, England: Basil Blackwell.

Elvemo, J., Grant Matthews, L., Greenwood, D., Martin, A., Strubel, A., & Thomas, L. (1997). Participation, action, and research in classroom. *Studies in Continuing Education, 19*(1), 1–50.

Emery, F., & Emery, M. (1974). *Participative design: Work and community life.* Canberra: Australian National University Centre for Continuing Education.

Emery, F., & Thorsrud, E. (1976). *Democracy at work.* Leiden, Netherlands: Martinus Nijhoff.

Emery, F., & Trist, E. (1973). *Towards a social ecology.* London: Plenum.

Emery, F. E., & Oeser, O. A. (1958). *Information, decision, and action.* Melbourne: Melbourne University Press.

Emery, M. (1982). *Searching.* Canberra: Australian National University Centre for Continuing Education.

Emery, M. (1993). *Participative design for participative democracy.* Canberra: Australian National University Centre for Continuing Education.

Emery, M. (1998). *Searching.* Amsterdam: John Benjamins.

Engelstad, P. H., & Haugen, R. (1972). *Skjervøy i gar, i dag og i morgen* [Sjervøy, yesterday, today and tomorrow]. Oslo: Work Research Institute.

Eurich, N. (1985). *Corporate classrooms: The learning business.* Princeton, NJ: Princeton University Press.

Fals Borda, O. (1969). *Subversion and social change in Colombia* (J. D. Skiles, trans.). New York: Columbia University Press.

Fals Borda, O., & Rahman, M. (Eds.). (1991). *Action and knowledge: Breaking the monopoly with participatory action research.* New York: Apex.

Fetterman, D., Kaftarian, S. J., & Wandersman, A. (1995). *Empowerment evaluation: Knowledge and tools for self-assessment and accountability.* Thousand Oaks, CA: Sage.

Filley, A. C., & House, R. J. (1969). *Managerial process and organizational behavior.* Glenview, IL: Scott, Foresman.

Fine, M. (1992). *Disruptive voices: The possibilities of feminist research.* Ann Arbor: University of Michigan Press.

Finger, M., & Asún, J. M. (2001). *Adult education at the crossroads: Learning our way out.* New York: National Institute of Adult Continuing Education.

Finne, H., Levin, M., & Nilssen, T. (1995). Trailing research: A model for useful evaluation. *Evaluation, 1*(1), 11–32.

Flood, R., & Romm, N. (1996). *Diversity management.* Chichester, England: Wiley.

Fox Keller, E. (1985). *Reflections on gender and science.* New Haven, CT: Yale University Press.

Frege, G. (1956). The thought: A logical inquiry. *Mind, 65,* 289–311. (Original work published 1918).

Freire, P. (1970). *The pedagogy of the oppressed.* New York: Herder & Herder.

Freire, P. (1998a). *Pedagogy of the heart.* New York: Continuum International.

Freire, P. (1998b). *Teachers as cultural workers: Letters to those who dare.* Boulder, CO: Westview.

Fuller, S. (2000). *The governance of science: Ideology and the future of the open society.* London: Open University Press.

Furner, M. (1975). *Advocacy and objectivity: A crisis in the professionalization of American social science, 1865–1905.* Lexington: University of Kentucky Press.

Gabarrón, L., & Hernández-Landa, L. (1994). *Investigación participative* [Participatory research]. Madrid: Centro de Investigaciones Sociológicas.

Gadamer, H. G. (1982). *Truth and method* (2nd ed.). New York: Crossroads.

Gallagher, R. A. (2001). *T-Groups.* Available at http://www.orgdct.com/more_on_t -groups.htm

Gaventa, J. (1982). *Power and powerlessness: Quiescence and rebellion in an Appalachian valley.* Urbana and Chicago: University of Illinois Press.

Gardner, K., & Lewis, D. (1996). *Anthropology, development and the post-modern challenge.* London: Pluto.

Geertz, C. (1973). *The interpretation of cultures.* New York: Basic Books.

Gerhardsen, E. (1932). *Tillitsmannen* [Becoming a union official]. Oslo: Tiden Forlag.

Gibbons, M., Limoges, C., Nowotny, H., Schwartzman, S., Scott, P., & Trow, M. (1994). *The new production of knowledge: The dynamics of science and research in contemporary societies.* London: Sage.

Gilligan, C. (1982). *In a different voice.* Cambridge, MA: Harvard University Press.

Giles, D., Stanton, T., & Cruz, N. (1999). *Service-learning: A movement's pioneers reflect on its origins, practice, and future.* San Francisco: Jossey-Bass.

Gramsci, A. (1975). *Letters from prison* (L. Lawner, trans.). London: Jonathan Cape.

Greenberg, E. S. (1975, September). The consequences of worker participation and control: A clarification of the theoretical literature. *Social Science Quarterly, 2,* 225–242.

Greenwood, D. (1980). *Community-level research, local-regional-governmental interaction and development planning: A strategy for baseline studies* (Rural Development Occasional Paper no. 10). Ithaca, NY: Cornell University, Center for International Studies.

Greenwood, D. (1985). *The taming of evolution: The persistence of nonevolutionary views in the study of humans.* Ithaca, NY: Cornell University Press.

Greenwood, D. (1989). Paradigm-centered versus client-centered research: A proposal for linkage. In *Proceedings of the forty-second annual meeting, Industrial Relations Research Association* (pp. 273–281). Madison, WI: Industrial Relations Research Association.

Greenwood, D. (2002). Action research: Unfulfilled promises and unmet challenges. *Concepts and Transformation, 7*(2), 117–139.

Greenwood, D. (2004a). Action research: Collegial responses fulfilled. *Concepts and Transformation, 9*(1), 80–93.

Greenwood, D. (2004b). Feminism and action research: Is "resistance" possible and, if so, why is it necessary? In M. Brydon-Miller, P. Maguire, & A. McIntyre (Eds.), *Traveling companions: Feminism, teaching, and action research* (pp. 157–168). Westport, CT: Praeger.

Greenwood, D., et al. (1990). *Culturas de Fagor: Estudio antropológico de las cooperativas de Mondragón.* San Sebastian, Spain: Editorial Txertoa.

Greenwood, D., et al. (1992). *Industrial democracy as process: Participatory action research in the Fagor Cooperative Group of Mondragón.* Assen-Maastricht, Netherlands: Van Gorcum.

Greenwood, D., & Levin, M. (1998). Action research, science, and the co-optation of social research. *Studies in Cultures, Organizations and Societies, 5*(1), 237–261.

Greenwood, D., & Levin, M. (2000). Reconstructing the relationships between universities and society through action research. In N. Denzin & Y. Lincoln (Eds.), *Handbook of qualitative research* (2nd ed.; pp. 85–106). Thousand Oaks, CA: Sage.

Greenwood, D., Whyte, W., & Harkavy, I. (1993). Participatory action research as a process and as a goal. *Human Relations, 46*(2), 175–192.

Guba, E., & Lincoln, Y. (1981). *Effective evaluation: Improving the usefulness of evaluation results through responsive and naturalistic approaches.* San Francisco, CA: Jossey-Bass.

Guba, E., & Lincoln, Y. (1985). *Naturalistic inquiry.* Newbury Park, CA: Sage.

Guba, E., & Lincoln, Y. (1989). *Fourth generation evaluation.* Newbury Park, CA: Sage.

Guba, E., & Lincoln, Y. (2005). Paradigmatic controversies, contradictions, and emerging confluences. In N. Denzin & Y. Lincoln (Eds.), *Handbook of qualitative research* (3rd ed.; pp. 191–215). Thousand Oaks, CA: Sage.

Gunder Frank, A. (1970). *Latin America: Underdevelopment or revolution: Essays on the development of underdevelopment and the immediate enemy.* New York: Monthly Review Press.

Gustavsen, B. (1985). Work place reform and democratic dialogue. *Economic and Industrial Democracy, 6,* 461–479.

Gustavsen, B. (1992). *Dialogue and development.* Assen-Maastricht, Netherlands: Van Gorcum.

Gustavsen, B., & Engelstad, P. H. (1986). The design of conferences and the evolving role of democratic dialogue in changing working life. *Human Relations, 39*(2), 101–116.

Habermas, J. (1984). *The theory of communicative action: Reason and the rationality of society* (T. McCarthy, trans.). Boston: Beacon.

Hafez Barazangi, N., Greenwood, D., Burns, M., & Finne, J. (2004). Evaluation model for an undergraduate action research program. In B. Hall & M. del Carmen Rodríguez de France (Eds.), *Learning the world we want* (pp. 152–159). Proceedings of the conference "Intersecting Conversations on Education, Culture, and Community," Victoria, British Columbia, November 2003.

Hall, B. (1975). Participatory research: An approach for change. *Convergence, 8*(2), 24–32.

Hall, B., Gillette, A., & Tandon, R. (Eds.). (1982). *Creating knowledge: A monopoly? Participatory research in development.* New Delhi: Society for Participatory Research in Asia.

Hanssen Bauer, J., & Aslaksen, K. (1991). *Rett sats* [Correct start]. Oslo: SBA.

Hemmati, M., Dodds, F., & Enayati, J. (2002). *Multi-stakeholder processes for governance and sustainability.* London: James & James/Earthscan.

Herbst, P. (1976). *Alternatives to hierarchies.* Leiden, Netherlands: Martinus Nijhoff.

Herbst, P. (1980). Community conference design: Skjervøy, today and tomorrow. *Human Futures* (2), 1–6.

Heron, J. (1996). *Co-operative inquiry: Research into the human condition.* London: Sage.

Heron, J. (2001). Transpersonal co-operative inquiry. In P. Reason & H. Bradbury (Eds.), *Handbook of action research* (pp. 333–339). London: Sage.

Herr, K., & Anderson, G. L. (2005). *The action research dissertation.* Thousand Oaks, CA: Sage.

Herzberg, F. (1966). *Work and the nature of man.* Cleveland: World.

Hess, D. (2001). *Science studies: An advanced introduction.* New York: New York University Press.

Hinsdale, M., Lewis, H., & Waller, S. (1995). *It comes from the people.* Philadelphia: Temple University Press.

Horton, M. (with J. Kohl & H. Kohl). (1990). *The long haul: An autobiography.* New York: Doubleday.

Horton, M., & Freire, P. (1990). *We make the road by walking: Conversations on education and social change.* Philadelphia: Temple University Press.

House, E. (1972). The conscience of educational evaluation. *Teachers Colleges Record, 73*(3), 405–414.

House, E. (1993). *Professional evaluation: Social impact and political consequences.* Thousand Oaks, CA: Sage

Ishikawa, K. (1976). *Guide to quality control.* Tokyo: Asian Productivity Organization.

Jacob, F. (1982). *The possible and the actual.* Seattle: University of Washington Press.

James, W. (1948). *Essays in pragmatism.* New York: Hafner.

James, W. (1995). *Essays in radical empiricism.* Lincoln: University of Nebraska Press.

Johannesen, K. S. (1996). Action research and epistemology: Some remarks concerning the activity-relatedness and contextuality of human language. *Concepts and Transformation, 1*(2/3), 281–297.

Joyappa, V., & Martin, D. (1996). Exploring alternative research epistemologies for adult education: Participatory research, feminist research and feminist participatory research. *Adult Education Quarterly, 47*(1), 1–14.

Juran, J. M. (1980). *Quality planning and analysis.* New York: McGraw-Hill.

Kasmir, S. (1996). *The myth of Mondragón*. Albany: State University of New York Press.

King, J. (1998). Making sense of participatory evaluation practice. *New Directions for Evaluation, 80*, 57–67.

Knowles, M. (1990). *The adult learner: A neglected species* (rev. ed.). Houston: Gulf Publishing.

Knowles, M., and others. (1984). *Andragogy in action: Applying modern principles of adult education*. San Francisco: Jossey-Bass.

Kuhn, T. (1962). *The structure of scientific revolutions*. Chicago: University of Chicago Press.

Lather, P. (1991). *Getting smart: Feminist research and pedagogy with/in the postmodern*. New York: Routledge.

Latour, B. (1987). *Science in action*. Cambridge, MA: Harvard University Press.

Latour, B., & Woolgar, S. (1979). *Laboratory life*. Beverly Hills, CA: Sage.

Levin, M. (1984). Worker participation in the design of new technology. In T. Martin (Ed.), *Design of work in automated manufacturing systems* (pp. 97–103). Oxford, England: Pergamon.

Levin, M. (1988). *Lokal mobilisering* [Local mobilization]. Trondheim, Norway: IFIM.

Levin, M. (1993). Creating networks for rural economic development in Norway. *Human Relations, 46*(2), 193–217.

Levin, M. (1994). Action research and critical systems thinking: Two icons carved out of the same log? *Systems Practice, 7*(1), 25–42.

Levin, M. (1998). Book Review—PAR/Action and Knowledge. *Systemic Practice and Action Research, 11*(2), 207–211.

Levin, M. (2003). Ph.D. programs in action research: Can they be housed in universities? *Concepts and Transformation, 8*(3), 3–23.

Levin, M., & Klev, R. (Eds.) (2000). *Forandring som praxis* [Change as praxis]. Bergen, Norway: Fagbokforlaget.

Levin, M., & Martin, A. (1995). *Power differences in discourse*. Unpublished manuscript.

Levin, M., et al. (1980a). *Hitterværinger vi kan vil vi?* [Citizens of Hitra, we can but will we?]. Trondheim, Norway: IFIM.

Levin, M., et al. (1980b). *Teknisk utvikling og arbeidsforhold i aluminiumselektrolyse* [Technical development and quality of working life in aluminum smelting]. Trondheim, Norway: IFIM.

Lewin, K. (1935). *A dynamic theory of personality* (D. Adams & E. Zener, trans.). New York: McGraw-Hall.

Lewin, K. (1943). Forces behind food habits and methods of change. *Bulletin of the National Research Council, 108*, 35–65.

Lewin, K. (1948). *Resolving social conflicts*. New York: Harper.

Lewis, D. (2001). *The management of non-governmental development organizations: An introduction*. London: Routledge.

Lijphart, A. (1977). *Democracy in plural societies: A comparative exploration*. New Haven, CT: Yale University Press.

Lyall, K., & Sell, K. (2006). *The true genius of America at risk: Are we losing our public universities to de facto privatization?* New York: American Council on Education/Praeger.

Madoo Lengermann, P., & Niebrugge-Brantley, J. (1998). *The women founders: Sociology and social theory, 1830–1930*. Boston: Mc-Graw-Hill.

McIntyre, A. (2004). *Women in Belfast: How violence shapes identity.* Westport, CT: Greenwood.

Maguire, P. (1987). *Doing participatory research: A feminist approach.* Amherst: University of Massachusetts, Center for International Education.

Maguire, P. (1994). Participatory research from one feminist's perspective: Moving from exposing androcentricism to embracing possible contributions of feminism to participatory research and practice. In I. de Koning (Ed.), *Proceedings of the international symposium on participatory research in health promotion* (pp. 5–14). Liverpool, England: Liverpool School of Tropical Medicine, Education Resource Group.

Maguire, P. (1996). Considering more feminist participatory research: What has congruency got to do with it? *Qualitative Inquiry, 2*(1), 106–118.

Mansbridge, J. (1983). *Beyond adversary democracy.* Chicago: University of Chicago Press.

Marginson, S., & Considine, M. (2000). *The enterprise university: Power, governance, and reinvention in Australia.* Cambridge, England: Cambridge University Press.

Markova, I., & Foppa, K. (1991). *Asymmetries in dialogue.* Herfordshire, England: Harvester Wheatsheaf.

Marshall, J. (2001). Self-reflective inquiry practices. In P. Reason & H. Bradbury (Eds.), *Handbook of action research* (pp. 433–439). London: Sage.

Marshall, J. (2004). Living systemic thinking. *Journal of Action Research, 2*(3), 305–325.

Marshall, J., & Mead, G. (Eds.). (2005). Self-reflective practice and first-person action research. Special Issue of the *Journal of Action Research 3*(3).

Martin, A. (2000). *Search conference methodology and the politics of difference.* Unpublished doctoral dissertation, Columbia University Teachers College.

Martin, A., Hemlock, N., & Rich, R. (1994). *Saskatchewan highways and transportation traffic safety search conference.* Ithaca, NY: Cornell University Programs for Employment and Workplace Systems.

Martin, A., & Rich, B. (1994). *Seneca Nation of Indians search '94.* Ithaca, NY: Cornell University Programs for Employment and Workplace Systems.

Martin, A. W. (1995, November). *Power differences in discourse.* Unpublished proceedings from Power Difference in Discourse, Ithaca, NY.

Maslow, A. (1943). A theory of human motivation. *Psychological Review, 50,* 370–396.

Miles, B., & Huberman, M. (1994). *Data analysis: An expanded sourcebook.* Thousand Oaks, CA: Sage.

Mayo, E. (1933). *The human problems of industrial civilization.* New York: Macmillan.

Messer-Davidow, E. (2002). *Disciplining feminism: From social activism to academic discourse.* Durham, NC: Duke University Press.

Mezirow, J. (1991). *Transformative dimensions of adult learning.* San Francisco: Jossey-Bass.

Mezirow, J. (1996). Contemporary paradigms of learning. *Adult Education Quarterly, 46*(3), 158–173.

Mies, M. (1990). Women's studies: Science, violence and responsibility. *Women's Studies International Forum, 13,* 433–441.

Milgram, S. (1974). *Obedience to authority.* New York: Harper & Row.

Mills, C. Wright. (1959/1976). *The sociological imagination.* New York: Oxford University Press.

Monden, Y. (1983). *The Toyota production system: A practical approach to production management.* Norcross, GA: Industrial Engineering and Management Press.

Monk, R. (1990). *Ludwig Wittgenstein: The duty of genius.* London: Jonathan Cape.

Mosse, D. (1993). *Authority, gender and knowledge: Theoretical reflections on the practice of participatory rural appraisal* (ODI Network Paper 44). London: ODI.

Nash, N. S., & Hawthorne, E. M. (1988). *Corporate education* (ERIC Digest no. ED301142). Available at http://www.ericdigests.org/pre-9210/corporate.htm

Negt, O. (1977). *Sociologisk fantasi og eksemplarisk indlæring* [Sociological fantasy and exemplary learning]. Roskilde, Denmark: Roskilde Universitetsforlag.

Noffke, S. (1994). Action research: Towards the next generation. *Educational Action Research, 2*(1), 9–21.

Nowotny, H., Scott, P., & Gibbons, M. (2001). *Re-thinking science: Knowledge and the public in an age of uncertainty.* London: Polity.

Nørgaard, A. (1935). *Grundtvigianismen* [The Grundtvid way]. København, Denmark: Gyldendal.

Park, P., Brydon-Miller, M., Hall, B., & Jackson, T. (Eds.). (1993). *Voices of change: Participatory research in the United States and Canada.* Westport, CT: Bergin & Garvey.

Parsons, T. (1951). *The social system.* Glencoe, IL: Free Press.

Pateman, C. (1970). *Participation and democratic theory.* Cambridge, England: Cambridge University Press.

Patton, M. Q. (1986). *Utilization-focused evaluation.* Beverly Hills, CA: Sage.

Patton, M. Q. (1997). *Utilization-focused evaluation* (3rd ed.). Thousand Oaks, CA: Sage.

Peirce, C. (1950). *Philosophy: Selected writings.* New York: Harcourt Brace.

Pelletier, D., Kraak, V., McCullum, C., Uusitalo, U., & Rich, R. (1999). The shaping of collective values through deliberative democracy: An empirical study from New York's North Country. *Policy Sciences, 32,* 103–131.

Pelletier, D., McCullum, C., Kraak, V., & Asher, K. (2003). Participation, power and beliefs shape local food and nutrition policy. *Journal of Nutrition, 133,* 301–304.

Peters, S. (2001). The civic mission question in land-grant education. *Higher Education Exchange, 6,* 25–37.

Peters, S., Hittleman, M., & Pelletier, D. (2005). The North Country community food and economic security project case study. In S. Peters, N. Jordan, M. Adamek, & T. Alter. (Eds.), *Engaging campus and community: Public scholarship in the state and land-grant university system.* Dayton, OH: Kettering Foundation Press.

Peters, S., Jordan, N., Adamek, M., & Alter, T. (Eds.). (2005). *Engaging campus and community: The practice of public scholarship in the state and land-grant university system.* Dayton, OH: Kettering Foundation Press.

Philips, Ä. (1988). *Eldsjälar* [Burning souls]. Doctoral dissertation, Stockholm School of Economics.

Polanyi, M. (1964). *Personal knowledge.* New York: Harper & Row.

Polanyi, M. (1966). *The tacit dimension.* Gloucester, MA: P. Smith.

Porter, T. (1995). *Trust in numbers: the pursuit of objectivity in science and public life.* Princeton, NJ: Princeton University Press.

Pretty, J. N., & Vodouhê, S. D. (n.d.). *Using rapid or participatory rural appraisal.* Available at http://www.fao.org/docrep/w5830e/w5830e08.htm

Pålshaugen, Ø. (1998). *The end of organization theory?* Amsterdam: John Benjamins.

Pålshaugen, Ø. (2000). Dialogkonferanser som metode i bedriftsutvikling [Dialogue conferences as method in enterprise development]. In M. Levin & R. Klev (Eds.). *Forandring som praxis* [Change as praxis] (pp. 187–195). Bergen, Norway: Fagbokforlaget.

Pålshaugen, Ø. (2002). Discourse democracy at work. *Concepts and Transformation, 7,* 141–192.

Price, D. (2004). *Threatening anthropology.* Durham, NC, and London: Duke University Press.

Rabinow, P. (1996). *Making PCR.* Chicago: University of Chicago Press.

Rabinow, P., & Sullivan, W. (Eds.). (1987). *Interpretive social science.* Berkeley: University of California Press.

Ransome, P. (1992). *Antonio Gramsci: A new introduction.* Hemel Hempstead, Hertfordshire, England: Harvester Wheatsheaf.

Rapoport, A. (1974). *Conflict in man-made environments.* Harmondsworth, England: Penguin.

Readings, B. (1996). *The university in ruins.* Cambridge, MA: Harvard University Press.

Reardon, K. (1997). Participatory action research and real community-based planning in East St. Louis. In P. Nyden et al. (Eds.), *Building community: Social science in action* (pp. 233–239). Thousand Oaks, CA: Pine Forge Press.

Reason, P. (Ed.). (1994). *Participation in human inquiry.* London: Sage.

Reason, P. (Ed.). (1988). *Human inquiry in action.* London: Sage.

Reason, P., & Bradbury, H. (Eds.). (2001a). *Handbook of action research.* London: Sage.

Reason, P., & Bradbury, H. (2001b). Introduction: Inquiry and participation in search of a world worthy of human aspiration. In P. Reason & H. Bradbury (Eds.), *Handbook of action research* (pp. 1–14). London: Sage.

Reason, P., & Rowan, J. (Eds.). (1981). *Human inquiry: A sourcebook of new paradigm research.* Chichester, England: Wiley.

Reinharz, S. (1992). *Feminist methods in social research.* New York: Oxford University Press.

Reynolds, M. (1994). *Democracy in higher education: Participatory action research in the Physics 101–102 curriculum revision project at Cornell University.* Doctoral dissertation, Cornell University, Ithaca, NY.

Rolfsen, M., & Torvatn, H. (2005). How to" get through" communication challenges in formative evaluation, *Evaluation, 11*(3), 297–309.

Rorty, R. (1980). *Philosophy and the mirror of nature.* Princeton, NJ: Princeton University Press.

Ross, D. (1991). *The origin of American social science.* Cambridge, England: Cambridge University Press.

Rowan, J. (2001). The humanistic approach to action research. In P. Reason & H. Bradbury (eds.), *Handbook of action research* (pp. 114–123). London: Sage.

Russell, B. (1903). *The principles of mathematics.* Cambridge, England: Cambridge University Press.

Ryle, G. (1949). *The concept of mind.* London: Hutchinson.

Schafft, K., & Greenwood, D. (2003). Promises and dilemmas of participation: Action research, search conference methodology, and community development. *Journal of the Community Development Society, 34* (1), 18–35.

Schön, D. (1983). *The reflective practitioner.* New York: Basic Books.

Schön, D. (1987). *Educating the reflective practitioner.* San Francisco: Jossey-Bass.

Schön, D. (Ed.). (1991). *The reflective turn.* New York: Teachers College Press.

Schumacher, E. (1973). *Small is beautiful: A study of economics as if people mattered.* New York: Harper & Row.

Schwandt, T. (1997a). *Qualitative inquiry: A dictionary of terms.* Thousand Oaks, CA: Sage.

Schwandt, T. (1997b). *Towards a new science of action research.* Paper presented at the Tavistock conference "Is Action Research Real Research," London.

Scriven, M. (1991). *Evaluation thesaurus.* Thousand Oaks, CA: Sage.

Scriven, M. (1995). The logic of evaluation and evaluation practice. *New Directions for Evaluation, 68,* 49–70.

Scott, J. (1995). *Sociological theory: Contemporary debates.* Cheltenham, England: Edward Elgar.

Senge, P. (1990). *The fifth discipline: The art and practice of the learning organization.* New York: Doubleday.

Shor, I., & Freire, P. (1987). *A pedagogy for liberation: Dialogues on transforming education.* South Hadley, MA: Bergin & Garvey.

Sherman, F., & Torbert, W. (Eds.). (2000). *Transforming social inquiry, transforming social action.* Boston: Kluwer Academic.

Sims Feldstein, H., & Poats, S. (Eds.) (1990). *Working together: Gender analysis in agriculture.* West Hartford, CT: Kumarian.

Skjervheim, H. (1974). *Objektivismen og studiet av mennesket* [Objectivity and the study of man]. Oslo: Gyldendal.

Slaughter, S., & Leslie, L. (1997). *Academic capitalism: Politics, policies and the entrepreneurial university.* Baltimore: Johns Hopkins University Press.

Stringer, E. (2004). *Action research in education.* Thousand Oaks, CA: Sage.

Swantz, M. L. (1985). *Women in development: A creative role denied? The case of Tanzania.* London: Hurst.

Sørensen, Å. B. (1992). Aktionsforskning i om arbejdslivet [Action research in work life]. *Tidsskrift for samfunnsforskning, 33* (s.), 213–230.

Taylor, C. (1985). *Philosophy and the human sciences.* Cambridge, England: Cambridge University Press.

Taylor, F. W. (1911). *The principles of scientific management.* New York: Harper Bros.

Thomas, H., & Logan, C. (1982). *Mondragón: An economic analysis.* London: Allen & Unwin.

Thomson, J., & Schoonmaker Freudenberger, K. (1997). *Crafting institutional arrangements for community forestry.* Rome: Food and Agriculture Organization of the United Nations (Forests, Trees and People Community Forestry Field Manual 7). Available at http://www.fao.org/docrep/w7483e/w7483e00.htm#contents

Tocqueville, A. de. (2001). *Democracy in America.* New York: New American Library, Signet Classic. (Originally published in two volumes, 1835 and 1840).

Torbert, W. (1991). *The power of balance: Transforming self, society, and scientific inquiry.* Newbury Park, CA: Sage.

Torbert, W. (2001). The practice of action inquiry. In P. Reason & H. Bradbury (Eds.), *Handbook of action research* (pp. 250–260). London: Sage.

Toulmin, S. (1996). Concluding methodological reflection: Elitism and democracy among the sciences. In S. Toulmin & B. Gustavsen (Eds.), *Beyond theory* (pp. 203–225). Amsterdam and Philadelphia: John Benjamins.

Toulmin, S., & Gustavsen, B. (Eds.). (1996). *Beyond theory.* Amsterdam and Philadelphia: John Benjamins.

Traweek, S. (1992). *Beamtimes and lifetimes.* Cambridge, MA: Harvard University Press.

Trist, E. (1981). *The evolution of socio-technical systems* (Occasional Paper No. 2). Toronto: Ontario Quality of Work Life Council.

Trist, E., & Bamforth, K. W. (1951). Some social and psychological consequences of the longwall method of coal getting. *Human Relations, 4,* 3–38.

Uphoff, N. (1992, 1996). *Learning from Gal Oya: Possibilities for participatory development and post-newtonian social science.* Ithaca, NY: Cornell University Press, 1992. (Paperback edition with new introduction, Intermediate Technology Publications, 1996).

Usher, R. B., Bryant, I., & Johnston, R. (1997). *Adult education and the postmodern challenge: Learning beyond the limits.* London: Routledge & Kegan Paul.

van den Hombergh, H. (1993). *Gender, environment, and development: A guide to the literature.* Utrecht: Institute for Development Research, International Books.

Van Eijnatten, F. M. (1993). *The paradigm that changed the work place.* Assen, Netherlands: van Gorcum.

Ver Beek, K. (1996). *The pilgrimage for life, justice and liberty: Insights for development.* Doctoral dissertation, Cornell University, Ithaca, NY.

von Bertalanffy, L. (1966). *Modern theories of development.* London: Oxford University Press.

von Bertalanffy, L. (1968). *General systems theory.* New York: Braziller.

Weber, M. (1958). *The city* (D. Martindale & G. Neuwirth, trans.). Glencoe, IL: Free Press.

Weisbord, M. (1987). *Productive workplaces: Organizing and managing for meaning and community.* San Francisco: Jossey-Bass.

Weisbord, M. (1992). *Discovering common ground.* San Francisco: Berrett-Koehler.

Weiss, H., & Greene, J. (1992). An empowerment partnership for family support and education programs and evaluations. *Family Science Review,* 5(1 and 2), 131–149.

Westbrook, R. (1991). *John Dewey and American democracy.* Ithaca, NY: Cornell University Press.

Whyte, W. F. (1991). *Participatory action research.* Newbury Park, CA: Sage.

Whyte, W. F. (1994). *Participant observer: An autobiography.* Ithaca, NY: ILR Press.

Whyte, W. F., & Alberti, G. (1976). *Power, politics, and progress: Social change in rural Peru.* New York: Elsevier-North Holland.

Whyte, W. F., & Boynton, D. (Eds.). (1983). *Higher yielding human systems for agriculture.* Ithaca, NY: Cornell University Press.

Whyte, W. F., & Whyte, K. K. (1991). *Making Mondragón* (2nd ed.). Ithaca, NY: ILR Press.

Wittgenstein, L. (1953). *Philosophical investigations.* Oxford, England: Basil Blackwell.

Womack, J. P., et al. (1990). *The machine that changed the world.* New York: Rawson Associates.

Young, I. M. (1990). *Justice and the politics of difference.* Princeton, NJ: Princeton University Press.

Zabusky, S. (1995). *Launching Europe.* Princeton, NJ: Princeton University Press.

Zeichner, K. (2001). Educational action research. In P. Pearson & H. Bradbury (Eds.), *Handbook of Action Research* (pp. 273–284). London: Sage.

Index

Action and Knowledge: Breaking the Monopoly with Participatory Action Research (Fals Borda and Rahman), 13

Action research (AR)
action element of, 7–8
cogenerative learning focus of, 17
collaborative knowledge development, 1, 53
defined, 1–2, 3–4, 12*n. 1*
friendly outsider concept, 52
general systems theory, 57–59
Kurt Lewin and, 16
as multi-method research, 17
mutual learning process of problem owners and researchers, 26–27, 51
ongoing dialogue focus of, 17
as research strategy and reform practice, 1
scientific method and, 52
social science revitalization by, 1–2
thought and action relationship, 60, 65–66, 68, 73, 78–79
See also Action research (AR): diversity and democracy; Action research (AR): historical perspective; Action research (AR): participation and democratization; Action science (AS) and organizational learning (OL); Case studies from practice; Cogenerative model of AR process; Credibility and validity; Democracy focus, of AR; Democratization; Educating action researchers; Educational

AR; Epistemological foundations for AR; Feminism and AR; The Friendly outsider; Human inquiry research method of AR; Industrial democracy; Knowledge generation in AR; Norwegian Industrial Democracy Project; Participatory evaluation; Participatory rural appraisal; Power and social reform; Pragmatic AR; Pragmatic philosophy; Scientific method and AR; Social science research techniques, work forms and strategies in AR; Southern participatory action research (PAR)

Action research (AR): diversity and democracy
action element of, 6–7
applied research and, 5–6
assumptions regarding readers, 12
book organization, 11
collaborative knowledge development, 3, 5–6
definitions regarding, 3–4, 12*n. 1*
democratic inclusion, 3, 9–11, 26, 106–107, 116, 265
disciplines and coverage, 7–8
diversity focus, 11
elements of, 6–7
in higher education environment, 7–8
liberation agenda, 6–7, 15
overviews regarding, 4–5, 8
participation element of, 7
pragmatic action research, 9–11

qualitative *vs.* quantitative
research, 5–6
research element of, 7
social change agenda, 3, 5–6, 9–11
social research quality, 3
stakeholders as coresearchers, 3,
12*n. 2,* 51
Action research (AR): historical
perspective
human inquiry and cooperative
inquiry, 14, 32–33
industrial democracy, intellectual
content of, 27–29
industrial democracy (Northern,
Western) focus, 14–29
Kurt Lewin, early work, 15–18
liberationist movement focus, 14
literature review regarding, 13–14
short *vs.* long term change process
and, 17
sources of, 2
"South" in the "North," 31–32
"Southern" participatory action
research (PAR), 14, 29,
30–31, 34
Tavistock Institute of Human
Relations, 18–23
See also Industrial democracy; Lewin,
Kurt; Norwegian Industrial
Democracy Project; Tavistock
Institute of Human Relations,
London, England
Action research (AR): participation and
democratization
AR moral agenda, 255–256
clarification of terms, 255–256
democratic process and, 265
democratization, 256, 261–262
participation, 255–256
participation, criticism of, 260–261
participation, from political
positioning perspective, 258–259
participation, from power and control
perspective, 256–258, 257*fig.*

participation, from real-world
pragmatics perspective, 259–260
venues for, 262–264
See also Democracy focus, of AR;
Democratic inquiry process, AR
epistemological foundation;
Democratization; Participatory
evaluation; Participatory
research
The Action Research Dissertation
(Herr & Anderson), 251
Action Research for Educational Change
(Elliott), 167*n.* 3
Action Research in Education
(Stringer), 171
Action Research publication, 32
Action researcher. *See* The friendly
outsider
*Action Science: Concepts, Methods, and
Skills for Research and Intervention*
(Argyris, Putnam, & McClain
Smith), 223–224, 234
Action science (AS) and organizational
learning (OL), 210, 215–216
Chris Argyris' work on, 223
change and stasis theory, 224–225
conclusions regarding, 234–235
confronting process, 224
criticism of, 230–232
defensive routines, 230
double-loop learning concept,
226, 233
empirical testing in, 227–228
espoused *vs.* theory-in-use, 226–227
group process skills and, 234
history of science and, 232
intervention and science, 225–227
"ladder of inference" concept, 228
Milgram experiments examples of,
228–229
Model I, II theories of action,
226–227, 229–230, 233
Model O(rganizational)-1 theory of
action, 227

objectivity, 225
organizational learning, 232–234, 234
positive features of, 229
psychologism, 230–231, 234
"rigor" *vs.* "relevance" conflict, 234
Donald Schön's work and,
   223, 235*nn. 1–2*
scientific knowledge focus, 233, 234
single-loop learning concept,
   226, 230, 233
skills required for, 234
systems theory, 234
See also Human inquiry research
   method of AR
Activism, 179
Adamek, M., 172
Adams, H., 72
Adams, J., 86
Adult education. *See* Community
   development and adult education;
   Educational AR; Southern
   participatory action research (PAR)
*Adult Education and the Postmodern
   Challenge: Learning Beyond the
   Limits* (Bryant and Johnston),
   168–169
*Adult Education at the Crossroads:
   Learning Our Way Out*
   (Finger and Asún), 168
African Americans, exploitation of, 29
Alberti, G., 198
Alfa Laval plants (Sweden), 23
Alinsky, S., 159
Alter, T., 172
Amabile, T. M., 65
American Anthropological
   Association, 111
American Sociological
   Association, 111
Anderson, G. L., 251
Andragogy, 174–175
Antioch University, 173
Apffel-Marglin, F., 152, 179
Appalachia AR activity, 31–32
Applied research *vs.* AR, 5–6

Appraisal. *See* Participatory evaluation;
   Participatory rural appraisal
   (PRA), in international
   development
AR. *See* Action research
Argyris, C., 47, 58, 88*n. 5,* 125, 169
   action inquiry work, 210, 215
   AS work of, 223–224, 229
   empirical testing, 227–228, 229
   espoused theory and theory-in-use,
      226–227
   intervention and science, 225–227
   ladder of inference technique,
      228, 231
   Migram experiments and, 228–229
   objectivity issue, 225
   organizational learning work of,
      223, 232–234
   "science of practice" concept of,
      224–225, 229
Aristotle, 105
Arnstein, S., 256–258, 257*fig.*
AS. *See* Action science (AS) and
   organizational learning (OL)
Asher, K., 144
Aslaksen, K., 139
Asún, J. M., 168, 169, 175, 176, 177, 183
Australian National University, 138
Australian search conference
   experiences, 139–140

Bamforth, K. W., 18–19, 22
Barnes, B., 78, 81
Bartels Undergraduate Action Research
   Fellows Program (Cornell
   University), 248–249
Bateson, G., 212, 219
Becoming a Union Official
   (Gerhardsen), 161
Becoming Critical (Carr and Kemmis),
   167*n. 3,* 174
Beinum, H. van, xi
Belenky, M., 31, 32, 166, 176
Belshaw, D., 201
Benson, L., 31, 32

Berea College, 173
Berger, P., 68, 104, 105
Beyond Adversary Democracy
    (Mansbridge), 10
Bond, L., 32, 176
Bowers, C. A., 152, 179
Boynton, E., 198
Bradbury, H., 12*n. 2*, 13, 33, 251
    human/cooperative inquiry work
        of, 32, 208, 209, 211
    skills for AR, 239
    validity focus of, 220
Bradley, K., 42
Bråthen, S., 97
Brazil. *See* Freire, Paolo
Breenburg, E. S., 258–259
Brint, S., 242
British Postgraduate Medical
    Federation, University of
    London, 33
Brokhaug, I., 37, 139
Brookfield, S., 169, 174
Brown, L. D., 157
Brulin, G., 239
Brunner, I., 190
Brunsson, N., 260
Bryant, I., 168, 170, 177, 183
Brydon-Miller, M., 157
Burke, T., 65
Burns, M., 248

Carr, W., 103, 167*n. 3*, 174
Case studies from practice
    application of, 2
    conclusions regarding, 51
    Cornell University School of
        Industrial and Labor
        Relations, 48–51, 133
    heterogeneity emphasis, 35
    Mondragón organization problems
        in industrial cooperatives,
        42–48, 51, 133
    Stongforden: Village development
        in Western Norway,
        36–42, 51, 133

Center for Community Partnerships,
    University of Pennsylvania, 31
Chambers, R., 15, 31, 201
    participatory rural appraisal work
        of, 195, 199, 200, 204, 207*n. 3*
Chandler, D., 218
Chávez, C., 159
Chesney, B., 181
Chessler, M., 181
The Child and the Curriculum
    (Dewey), 60
Civil rights movement, 30, 31
Clifford, J., 77
Clinchy, B., 31, 166
*Co-Operative Inquiry: Research Into
    the Human Condition* (Heron),
    219–220
Co-optation
    AR and, 264
    authority of evaluation and, 186
    feminism and, 152–153, 163
    method of searching, 141–142
    North-South co-optation
        and, 157–158
    participation dimensions and, 260
    by PRA, 194, 204
Cogenerative model of AR process,
    17, 72, 94*fig.*
    communication arenas, 94–96, 108
    creating arenas, 97
    democratization in, 107, 116, 265
    "double-blind" research methods
        and, 97
    feedback, 96–97
    insider and outsider mutual learning,
        93–94, 102–103, 106–107
    insider *vs.* outsider differences,
        93, 94*fig.*, 97
    integrity importance, 127
    Levin's organizational development
        course, 246–248
    liberating outcomes and, 135–136
    linking theory and local
        understanding, 119–121
    maintaining differences and, 107

"model monopoly" concept, 97
narratives of experiential learning
and, 111–112
power relationships and, 95–96
practical and context-bound problem
solving, 108
in pragmatic AR, 133
problem definition, 93–94
technique and work form
choices, 108–109
what action researchers may not
do, 97–98
See also The friendly outsider;
Knowledge generation in AR;
Search conferencing; Search
conferencing steps (time
sequential order)
Cohen, J., 199
Collaborative knowledge development,
1, 3, 5–6
collaborative human inquiry
research, 218–220
in democratization, 261–262
See also Cogenerative model of AR
process; Knowledge generation
in AR
Communication arenas, in AR process,
94–96, 94fig., 108
Community development and adult
education
as a framework for AR, 176–177
Paolo Freire's work and, 178–179
international development agencies,
179–180
missions and evangelization, 182
NGOs (nongovernmental
organizations), 181–182
popular education in the South,
176–178
study circles, 181
support groups, 180–181
Concepts and Transformation
publication, 32
Conscientization technique, of PAR,
30–31, 64, 179

Considine, M., 252
Constructivism
constructivist participatory
evaluation and, 188–189
interpretive researcher autonomy
and, 91–92
knowledge as socially constructed
concept, 68
participatory evaluation and, 188
social constructivism, 105, 110, 120
Context-bound inquiry, of AR
foundation, 63–64, 66, 108
Convergence journal, 167n. 3
Cooke, B., 205, 260
Cooperative Inquiry (Heron), 33
Cooperative inquiry research method
of AR, 32–33
Cooperatives. See Mondragón
cooperatives
Corey, S., 171
Cornell University, x, 9, 43
AR case examples, 2, 48–51
experience-based undergraduate
course at, 248–249
Davydd Greenwood's work at, 48–51,
52n. 3, 133, 207n. 3, 248–249
international development
work at, 195
Kurt Lewin's work at, 14–15
models of organizational
change, 49–50
organizational effect of new
manufacturing systems, 49–50
participatory rural appraisal and,
198, 199
philosophy of science case example,
80–86
research vs. extension conflict case,
48–51
School of Industrial and Labor
Relations case study, 48–51, 141
See also Case studies from practice
Corporate classrooms, 175–176
Crane, B., 173
Credibility and validity

credibility, defined, 67
ideal type concept, 70, 75*n. 3*
internal *vs.* external credibility, 67
of local knowledge, 106
sense making, 68–69
in social science research, 66–68
transcontextual credibility, 69–70
workability, 63–64, 68
Cronbach, L. J., 99
Cruz, N., 173
Cummings, T. G., 17, 28, 92

Davis, L. E., 24
Deconstruction, 72, 78
Deming, W. E., 25
Democracy focus, of AR, 9–11,
    106–107, 265
cogenerative research and, 107, 265
mutualism between researchers
    and participants, 64, 95
political positioning, 258–259
power relationships and,
    73–74, 95–96
social improvement and, 61–62
See also Action research (AR):
    diversity and democracy; Action
    research (AR): historical
    perspective; Action research
    (AR): participation and
    democratization;
    Democratization; Educational
    AR; Pragmatic AR; Pragmatic
    philosophy
Democratic inquiry process, AR
    epistemological foundation, 64–65
Democratization, 106–107, 116
AR process and, 237, 265
collaboration importance in, 261–262
educational reform focus, 160, 182
fairness of process and outcomes, 262
harmonization of positions concept
    and, 262
land grant universities and, 172–173
as liberation, Southern PAR and,
    154–157

missionary groups and, 182
participatory evaluation and,
    190–191
of research development, 219
venues for, 262–264
See also Action research (AR):
    participation and
    democratization
Denmark adult education field, 160–161
Dewey, J., 13, 79, 183*n. 2*
critique of education by, 72
democracy and social improvement,
    59–62, 61, 159
diversity and conflict in democratic
    society, 61
knowledge generation, 104
learning as an action process, 60–61
pragmatism and, 59–60, 72, 169
reflective practice and, 122
scientific research and democratic
    social action, 61, 64
service learning, 173
thought and action relationship,
    59–62, 65–66, 68, 73, 228, 229
works of, 60
See also Pragmatic AR; Pragmatic
    philosophy
Dialectical knowledge generation.
    See Knowledge generation in AR
Dialogue conferences employee
    participation concept, 29, 139
Diggins, J., 68, 71, 72–73
Disruptive Voices (Fine), 165–166
Distributive justice model, 10, 164
Diversity focus, of AR, 11, 65
See also Action research (AR):
    diversity and democracy
Diversity Management (Flood and
    Romm), 233
Dodds, F., 194
*Doing Participatory Research: A Feminist
    Approach* (Maguire), 165
"Double-blind" research methods, 97
Double-loop learning, 226, 233
Douglas, M., 255

Dreyfus, H., 123, 124*table*
Dreyfus, S., 123, 124*table*

East St. Louis redevelopment
    project, 31
Edifying philosophy, 71
Educating action researchers, 237
    AR and social science disengagement,
        240–243
    AR dissertations, 251
    AR praxis in higher education,
        243–244
    AR within the University, 251–254
    cogenerative knowledge building, 243
    conclusions regarding, 254
    departmentalization *vs.*
        multidisciplinarity, 241–243
    "entrepreneurial universities"
        concept, 252–254
    literature review regarding, 239
    Norwegian history of, 239–240
    Ph.D. programs, group-based, 250
    Ph.D. programs, individualized,
        249–250
    Ph.D. programs, international,
        250–251
    research and discovery processes
        focus, 252
    service learning example, 248–249
    social science *vs.* social action, 239
    Tavistock Institute, U.K. and, 240
    undergraduate AR teaching
        possibilities, 244–249
Educational AR, 152
    adult education, 168, 174–175
    adult education, and community
        development, 176–182
    adult education, at crossroads,
        169, 183
    adult education, in industrialized
        countries, 173–175
    adult education, international
        development agencies, 179–180
    andragogy, 174–175

corporate classrooms, 175–176
critical thinking components,
    174–175
educational arenas and functions, 159
folk high schools and popular
    education, 160–161, 162–163
frameworks, 168–170
Paolo Freire and, 178–179
in higher education, ix
within higher education institutions,
    171–173
Highlander Research and Education
    Center, Tennessee, 162–163, 176
land grant universities and, 172–173
literature regarding, 167*n. 3*, 168–169,
    174–175, 183*n. 1*, 183*n. 2*
Marxism and, 169
missions and evangelization, 182
nongovernmental organizations
    (NGOs), 181–182
popular education, 162–163
popular education, in the South,
    176–178
postmodern challenge, 170
power in a learning situation, 175
public school alternatives, 171
reforming education in the North,
    170–173
reformist and social change
    orientation, 159–160
in the schools and teaching
    professions, 170–171
scope of subject, 168, 183*n. 1*
service learning, 173
Southern PAR *vs.* Northern
    andragogy, 175
study circles, 181
support groups, 180–181
trade union education, 161–162
transformational learning, 174–175
See also Community development
    and adult education; Educating
    action researchers; Southern
    participatory action research

Effective Evaluation (Guba and
   Lincoln), 188
Egalitarianism, 10, 47
Eikeland, O., 105
Einar Thorsrud Memorial Conference, x
Elden, M., 17, 26, 27, 138
Eldon, M., x
Elliott, J., 171
Ellott, J., 167*n. 3*
Elster, J., 59
Elvemo, J., 255*n. 1*
Emery, F., 19, 20, 21, 21*fig.*, 29, 136,
   137, 138, 139–140
Emery, M., 137, 138, 139–140, 141
Empowerment
   participatory evaluation, 190–192
   vs. democracy, 28
   See also Feminism and AR;
      Participatory evaluation
Enayati, J., 194
Engelstad, P. H., 26, 138
Epistemological foundations for AR, 51
   AR process, 62–63, 71–73
   cogenerative learning and, 72
   context-bound inquiry, 63–64,
      66, 108
   core characteristics of, 62–63
   credibility and validity, 63, 66–70
   democratic inquiry process,
      63, 64–65, 66
   diversity as opportunity, 63, 65
   general systems theory, 57–59
   inquiry process/action link, 63, 65–66
   language enabling discourse,
      communication, 66
   making sense, 68–69
   political economy and social structure
      of science, 73–75
   power relationship ideas and,
      73–74, 95–96
   pragmatism and neopragmatism
      philosophies, 59–62
   pragmatist framework for philosophy
      and, 71, 72–73

real-life practical problem solving,
   63–64
scientific research defined, 55–57
systematic *vs.* edifying philosophy
   and, 71
transcontextual credibility, 69–70
workability, 63–64, 68
   See also Scientific research
Eurich, N., 175
Evaluation Thesaurus (Scriven), 187
Evangelization, 182
Experiential learning, narratives
   of, 111–112
External credibility, 67

FAGOR cooperative group, Spanish
   Basque Country, 43, 44–45, 48
Fals Borda, Orlando, 13, 14, 31, 34*n.*
   2, 157, 159, 177
FAO. *See* Food and Agriculture
   Organization
Faucheux, Claude, xi
Feedback, in cogenerative model
   of AR, 96–97
Feminism and AR, 30, 31
   AR co-optation of, 152–153, 163
   authoritarianism of social science
      and social programs, 164
   democracy and social justice
      focus, 163
   diversity valued by, 164
   ending gendered and class-based
      silence, 164
   gender responsible research focus, 164
   gendered oppression focus, 163–164
   impact of, 152
   linking feminism and AR, 164–165
   local knowledge emphasis, 164, 206
   participatory rural appraisal and, 197,
      200, 204, 205, 206
   radical feminism and, 154
   Southern PAR criticized by, 152
   value-free research and social
      oppression, 164

Fetterman, D., 188, 191
Fifth discipline, 58
Filley, A. C., 18
Fine, M., 160, 165, 191
Finger, M., 168, 169, 175, 176, 177, 183
Finne, M., 192, 248
Flood, R., 58, 59, 69, 130*n. 1*, 233
Folk high schools, 160–161
   See also Highlander Research and
      Education Center, Tennessee
Food and Agriculture Organization
   (FAO), 194
Foppa, K., 95
Fourth Generation Evaluation
   (Guba and Lincoln), 188
Frank, A. G, 29
Freire, Paolo, 30, 64, 152, 157, 163, 167*n.*
   3, 169, 175, 176, 178–179, 200, 243
The friendly outsider (action
   researcher), 52
   actual *vs.* possible concept, 117–119
   analytical, comparative, contextual
      framework of, 120–121
   conclusions regarding, 130
   creating possibilities *vs.* reinforcing
      limits, 116–119
   critique and support skills, 125
   irony and humor in thoughtful
      action, 127–128, 130*n. 1*
   knowing what *vs.* knowing how,
      121–122
   linking theory and local
      understanding, 119–121
   local and researcher partnership
      focus, 117, 178
   local resources assessments skills, 126
   not trying to overcome an unruly
      world, 115–116
   outsider link skills, 126
   patience, 128
   planning and spontaneity, 129–130
   possible-actual human relationships
      concept, 118–119, 128
   process skills of, 126–129

reflective practice concept, 122
risk taking by, 127
scientific method used by, 119–120
security of open-mindedness, 128
self-confidence and integrity
   of, 126–127
skill development stages, 123, 124*table*
skills acquisition by, 121–124
skills required of, 124–130
social skills, 129
speaking the locally unspeakable, 125
tacit knowledge acknowledgment, 125
Fuller, S., 87*n. 1*
Furner, M., 239

Gadamer, H. G., 13, 68, 69, 71, 72
Gallagher, R. A., 16
Gardner, J, 196
Gateson, G., 58
Gaventa, J., 31, 176
Geertz, C., 77
Gelb, A., 42
Gender-responsible research, 126, 148,
   160, 163, 164–165, 200, 205–206,
   212, 231
General systems theory (GST), 57–59
   AR relationship with, 59
   closed *vs.* open systems concept, 58
   holistic concepts of interacting
      systems, 57–58
   nature-culture issue, 58
   systems as units of analysis, 58
Gerhardsen, E., 161
*Getting Smart: Feminist Research and
   Pedagogy Within the Postmodern*
   (Lather), 165
Gibbons, M., 54, 77, 99, 241, 252
Giles, D., 173
Gillette, A., 157
Goldberger, N., 31, 166
González, J. L., 43
Gramsci, A., 265
Grant Matthews, L., 255*n. 1*
Great Britain

trade unions in, 19
WWII rebuilding of, 18
See also Tavistock Institute of Human
    Relations, London, England
Greenberg, E. S., 258–259
Greene, J., 191
Greenwood, D., x–xii, 9, 31, 42, 44, 48,
    52*n. 3*, 109, 118, 152, 248, 255*n. 1*
baseline development for PRA work
    of, 201
Cornell University work of, 48–51,
    52*n. 3*, 207*n. 3*, 248–249
experience-based undergraduate
    courses of, 248–249
human inquiry, 213
introductory AR course of,
    246, 254*n. 1*
Mondragón Cooperative project
    and, 43–48
physical and biological science as
    iterative cycles of thought and
    action, 80–86
universities in society, 239
Group dynamics, 16–18, 85, 148,
    150, 216
Grundtvig, Bishop, 160
GST. *See* General systems theory
Guba, E., 188
Gustavsen, B., 17, 19, 26, 29, 59, 139
Guzman, A., 190

Habermas, J., 13, 174
ideal speech, 26, 68–69, 139
Hafez Barazangi, N., 248
Hall, B., 157, 167*n. 3*, 176, 177
Handbook of Action Research
    (Marshall), 218
Handbook of Action Research (Reason
    and Bradbury), 12*n. 2*, 13, 32,
    208–209, 211, 220, 239
Hanssen Bauer, J., 139
Harkavy, I., 31, 32, 213
Harmonization of positions concept,
    of democratization, 262

Haugen, R., 138
Hawthorne, E. M., 176
Heidegger, M., 71
Hemlock, N., 138
Hemmati, M., 194
Herbst, P., 22, 137, 138, 142, 143*fig.*
Hermeneutics, 56, 68, 72
participatory evaluation and, 189
Heron, J., 15, 32, 33
collaborative inquiry work of, 208,
    209, 218–220
democratization of research
    management focus of, 219
empiricism commitment of, 219–220
participative reality concept of, 219
Peter Reason and, 218
truth and validity issues, 219, 220
warrant for action view of
    knowledge, 219
Herr, K., 251
Herzberg, F., 22
Hess, D., 81
Highlander Research and Education
    Center, Tennessee, 31, 161,
    162–163, 176
Hinsdale, M., 31, 176
Historical perspective. *See* Action
    research (AR): historical
    perspective
Hittleman, M., 144, 172
Horton, M., 31, 159, 161, 162–163, 175
House, E., 187
House, R. J., 18
Human inquiry research method of AR,
    14, 32–33, 34
action inquiry, 210, 215–218
central perspectives of, 209–211
collaborative inquiry concept,
    218–220
conclusions regarding, 221–222
cooperative inquiry concept, 209–210
first/second/third-person research
    and, 210–211, 231
Freire's work and, 179

John Heron's collaborative inquiry
    work, 218–220
Judi Marshall's self-reflecting inquiry
    work, 218
"participatory worldview"
    concept, 209
Peter Reason's work on, 208–215
self-reflective inquiry, 216, 218
William Torbert's action inquiry
    work, 210, 216–218
validity focus, 209, 220
See also Heron, John; Marshall, Judi;
    Reason, Peter; Torbert, William
Human rights violations, 29

Ideal speech concept, 26, 68–69, 139
Ideal type concept, 70, 75n. 3
IMF. See International Monetary Fund
Industrial democracy, 27, 34, 264
    change process concept in, 28–29
    development of underdevelopment
        concept, 29
    "dialogue conferences" concept,
        29, 139
    Eastern then Western diffusion of,
        23–27
    empowerment vs. democracy, 28
    ethics of ideal speech concept,
        26, 68–69, 139
    individual direct participation, 27–29
    intellectual content of, 27–29
    in Japan, 25
    liberationist work and, 15
    mutual learning process of problem
        owners and researchers, 26–27
    participant control, 27
    production technology and work
        organization link and, 18–19
    Peter Reason's work and, 221–222
    representative and participatory
        democracy relationship, 27, 264
    research networking and, 25–26
    "search conferences" concept,
        29, 37–38

social change as three-stage
    process, 16
"sociotechnical reorganization" of
    work, 16, 19, 24, 25, 26
stable social states concept, 16–17
T-group concept and, 16, 45, 52n. 2
"Taylorism" concept and, 15, 19, 20,
    21, 34n. 1
union busting and, 24–25
See also Lewin, Kurt; Mondragón
    cooperatives; Norwegian
    Industrial Democracy Project
Industrial Democracy Project (Lewin,
    Norway), 15, 19–23, 23fig.
    See also Lewin, Kurt; Norwegian
    Industrial Democracy Project
Inquiry. See Democratic inquiry process,
    AR epistemological foundation;
    Human inquiry research
    method of AR
Institute for Development Studies at
    Sussex, 195
Institute for Social Research in Industry
    (IFIM, at Norwegian Institute of
    Technology), 239
Intellectual foundations of AR, ix
Internal credibility, 67
International development agencies
    adult education focus, 179–180
    See also Participatory rural appraisal;
        Southern participatory action
        research
International Institute for Environment
    and Development (London), 201
International Journal of Action
    Research, 32
International Monetary Fund (IMF),
    180, 197
International Potato Center
    (Peru), 195
Ishikawa, K., 25

Jackson, T., 157
Jacob, F., 69, 117, 118, 128

James, W., 59, 71
Japanese reindustrialization process, 25
Johannesen, K. S., xi, 68
Johnston, R., 168, 170, 177, 183
Jordan, N., 172
Journal of Action Research (Sage
  Publications), 32, 208, 209,
  216, 218
Joyappa, V., 165
Juran, J. M., 25
"Just-in-time" production technique
  (Japan), 25
Justice and the Politics of Difference
  (Young), 164

Kaban (Toyota production
  management system), 25
Kaftarian, S. J., 188
Karlsen, J, I., 49
Kasmir, S., 42
Keller, F., 164
Kemmis, S., 103, 167*n. 3*, 171, 174
King, J., 192
Klev, R., 92, 101*n. 1*
Knowledge generation in AR,
  53, 102–103
  action as sources of (Dewey), 60, 65
  cogenerative learning and, 72, 92–98,
    94*fig.*, 104
  conclusions regarding, 113–114
  democratic ideals, 106–107, 265
  democratic inquiry processes,
    64–65, 116
  dialectical relationship between local
    and scholarly knowledge,
    104–105, 109, 113
  inquiry process linked to action
    and, 65–66
  insider's reflections, 112
  language enabling discourse,
    communication, 66
  linking theory and local
    understanding, 119–121
  local *vs.* scholarly, 102–103, 103–106

maintaining differences, 107
multi-method research of, 51
narratives of experiential learning,
  103, 106, 109, 110–112
practical and context-bound problem
  solving, 108
pragmatist framework for philosophy
  and, 71, 72
process of, 106–109
research *vs.* practical knowledge, 51
scientific method application
  and, 52
social research constructed
  knowledge, 105–106
socially constructed knowledge and,
  68, 75*n. 1*
technique and work form selection,
  108–109
time investments, 108
writing process, 103, 109–113
See also Action science (AS) and
  organizational learning (OL);
  Cogenerative model of AR
  process; Credibility and validity;
  The friendly outsider; Scientific
  method and AR
Knowles, M. 169, 174
Kolb, D., 169
Kothari, U., 205, 260
Kraak, V., 144
Kuhn, T., 81

Land grant universities, 172–173
Lather, P., 32, 164, 165, 191
Latour, B., 57, 81, 86, 87*n. 1*, 118
Leslie, L., 252
Levin, M., x–xii, 9, 13, 17, 26, 92,
  101*n. 1*, 112, 123, 139, 175, 192
  group-based Ph.D. programs of
    (NTNU), 250
  international Ph.D. program of,
    250–251
  organizational development course
    of, 246–248

participation in Norwegian industry
  study of, 259–260
public planning and administration
  AR course of, 245
sociotechnical thinking introduced
  to, 24
Stongfjorden project, 37, 39, 42
universities in society, 239
See also Stongfjorden village
  development, Western Norway
Lewin, K., 13, 28, 59, 79, 138
action research work of, 16, 223,
  228, 229
change process work of, 16–17,
  28, 224
Cornell University work of, 14–15
early work of, 15–18
education AR, 171
mottos of, 18
natural experimentation and, 16, 19
Norwegian Industrial Democracy
  Project, 16
pragmatism and, 169
stable social states concept, 16–17
T-group technique of, 16, 17–18,
  45, 52*n*. 2
See also Norwegian Industrial
  Democracy project
Lewis, D., 196
Lewis, H., 31, 176
Liberation agenda, of AR, 6–7,
  14, 15, 175
democratization and, 154–157
Paolo Freire and, 175, 179
participatory evaluation and,
  191–192
participatory rural appraisal, 15, 31
in participatory rural appraisal, 196
William Torbert's work on, 217
trade unions and, 30
See also Feminism and AR
Lijphart, S., 262
Limoges, C., 54, 241
Lincoln, Y., 188

Local knowledge. *See* Knowledge
  generation in AR
Local Mobilization (Levin), 42
Logan, C., 42
Logical positivism, defined, 56
Luckmann, T., 68, 104, 105
Lyall, K., 172, 244

Madoo Lengermann, P., 78, 239
Maguire, P., 32, 152, 165
Mansbridge, J. 10
Marcus, G., 77
Marginson, S., 252
Markova, L., 95
Marshall, J.
  "attentional disciplines"
    concept of, 218
  human inquiry work of, 208, 210
  self-reflective inquiry work of, 218
Martin, A., 138, 141, 146, 147, 175,
  255*n*. 1
Martin, D., 165
Marx, Karl, 13
Marxism, 121
  Paolo Freire and, 178–179
  adult education and, 169, 177, 178
  neo-Marxism and, 8, 154, 164,
    178, 198
  participatory rural appraisal and, 197,
    198, 199, 200
  political economy and social
    transformation, 7
Maslow, A., 22
Massachusetts Institute of Technology
  (MIT), 14
McClain Smith, D., 88*n*. 5, 210, 223–233
McCullum, C., 144
McIntyre, A., 32
McTaggart, R., 171
Mead, G., 216
Messer-Davidow, E., 78, 153, 242
Methodology, defined, 90
Mezirow, Jack, 169, 174
Mies, M., 164

Milgram, S., 228
Mills, C. W., 78
Minimum critical specifications, 22
Mission organizations
    international development agencies
        and, 180, 182
Modernization theory, of PRA, 197
Monden, Y., 25
Mondragón Cooperatives, x, 2, 51,
    93, 133
    AR Process, 44–46, 48
    cooperatives, history of, 42–43,
        52n. 1
    disaffected members analysis, 46, 47
    governance organizational behavior
        in, 46–47
    as industrial democracy success
        example, 42
    as a narrative, 110
    organization problems in industrial
        cooperatives case study,
        35, 42–48
    reflection, 46–48
    shared values of members and, 47–48
    T-group process and, 45, 52n. 2
Monk, R., 55
Mosse, D., 204, 205

Narrativity, 103, 106
    of experiential learning, 111–112
    writing up AR experiences, 109,
        110–111
Nash, N. S., 176
National Training Laboratory,
    University of Michigan, 18
Native Americans, exploitation of, 22
Natural experimentation, 16, 19
Naturalistic Inquiry (Guba and
    Lincoln), 188
Naturalistic paradigm, of participatory
    evaluation, 188–189
Negt, O., 161
New Paradigm Research Group,
    London, 32–33, 218

NGOs. See Nongovernmental
    organizations
Niebrugge-Brantley, J., 78, 239
Nilssen, T., 37, 139, 192
Noffke, S., 167n. 3
Nongovernmental organizations
    (NGOs), 181–182
    international development agencies
        and, 180
    participatory rural appraisal and, 194,
        196, 197, 200, 201, 206
NORAD, of Norway, 180
Northern participatory AR
    activity, 31–32
    education reforming, 170–173
    North-South co-optation, 157–158
Northern andragogy, 175
Norway. See Norwegian Confederation
    of Employers; Norwegian
    Enterprise 2000 Program;
    Norwegian Industrial Democracy
    Project; Norwegian University of
    Science and Technology (NTNU),
    Trondheim; Stongfjorden village
    development, Western Norway
Norwegian Confederation of
    Employers, 19, 27
Norwegian Enterprise 2000
    Program, xi
Norwegian Industrial Democracy
    Project, 133, 138–139
    democratic and idealistic tenets of,
        22–23, 263
    Kurt Lewin and, 19
    "minimum critical specification"
        concept and, 21
    old vs. new work organization
        paradigms, 23fig.
    participant control, 27
    "psychological job demands" concept
        and, 20–21, 21fig.
    "redundancy of functions"
        concept, 21–22
    "redundancy of tasks" concept, 21–22

"semiautonomous groups" concept and, 20
"sociotechnical reorganization" work of, 19–22, 23*fig.*
Norwegian Institute of Technology, 26, 239
Norwegian University of Science and Technology (NTNU), Trondheim, x, 9, 26, 37, 141, 250
Norwegian Value Creation 2010 Program, 250
Nowotny, H., 54, 77, 99, 241, 252
Nørgaard, A., 161
NTNU. *See* Norwegian University of Science and Technology

Objectivity and the Study of Man (Skjervheim), 64–65
Oeser, O. A., 138
Organizational development
Morten Levin's college course on, 246–248
short-term change process and, 17
See also Action science (AS) and organizational learning (OL)
Organizational learning. *See* Action science (AS) and organizational learning (OL)
Organizational Learning (Argyris & Schön), 232
Organizational Learning II (Argyris & Schön), 223, 232–234, 235*nn. 1–2*
Owens, Ted, 198–199, 199

PA rådet organization (Sweden), 24
Pålshaugen, Ø., 26, 29, 139
The Paradigm That Changed the Work Place (Eijinatten), 22
Park, P., 157
Parsonian role pattern variable model, 24, 120
Participation. *See* Action research (AR): participation and democratization; Democracy focus, of AR;

Democratic inquiry process,
AR epistemological foundation;
Democratization; Participatory evaluation; Participatory rural appraisal (PRA), in international development; Southern participatory action research (PAR)
Participation: A New Tyranny? (Cooke and Kothari), 205
Participation and Democratic Theory (Pateman), 27
Participation element of AR, 8
Participation in Human Inquiry (Reason), 211
Participatory Action Research (Whyte), 13
Participatory Community Development, 29
Participatory Evaluation: A Tool to Assess Projects and Empower People (Brunner and Guzman), 190–191
Participatory evaluation (PE)
accountability to authority and, 184
AR in, 192
authority of evaluation and, 186
co-optation possibilities, 186
conclusions regarding, 192–193
constructivist evaluation, 188–189
conventional evaluation criticism, 184–187
emergence of, 186–187
empowerment evaluation, 190–192
local stakeholder focus in, 184–185, 187, 188–192
modes of, 187–192
naturalistic paradigm of, 188–189
utilization-based evaluation, 189–190
See also Action research (AR): participation and democratization; Participatory rural appraisal
"Participatory Learning Analysis" liberationist work, 15
Participatory learning and action (PLA)

terminology, 207n. 1
  See also Action research (AR):
    participation and
    democratization
Participatory learning and analysis. See
  Participatory rural appraisal
Participatory research, 29, 30
  feminism and, 165–166
  See also Action research (AR):
    participation and
    democratization; Participatory
    evaluation; Participatory rural
    appraisal; Southern participatory
    action research (PAR)
Participatory rural appraisal (PRA), in
  international development, 180,
  194, 195–199, 207n. 2
  AR and, 205–206
  Robert Chambers' work in, 195,
    200–201, 204, 207n. 3
  competitive individualist market
    theory and, 197
  conclusions regarding, 206
  critiques of, 204–205, 260
  history of, 196–198
  human rights issues and, 300
  interview and sampling methods of,
    202–203figs.
  large development agencies
    context, 198–199
  liberationist work and, 15, 31, 300
  literature review, 195–196
  local knowledge and participation,
    203–204, 205
  modernization theory and, 197
  nomenclature used, 195, 207nn. 1–2
  participatory learning and action
    term (PLA), 207n. 1
  poverty as product of capitalism, 198
  power relationships and,
    205–206, 260
  rapid rural appraisal (RRA), 15, 198,
    201–204, 202–203figs., 207n. 1
  rural vs. urban work in, 198–199

Southern PAR and, 201
  sustainability of, 199–200
  in sustainable environmental
    practices, 194
  technology and development, 197
  See also Action research (AR):
    participation and
    democratization
Pateman, C., 27
Patton, M. Q., 188, 189, 192
PE. See Participatory evaluation
Parsons, T., 24
A Pedagogy for Liberation (Shor and
  Freire), 175
Pedagogy of the Oppressed (Freire),
  167n. 3, 178–179
Pelletier, D., 144, 172
Peters, S., 144, 172, 183n. 1
PEWS. See Programs for Employment
  and Workplace Systems
Philips, A., 37
Philosophy and the Mirror of Nature
  (Rorty), 71
Phronesis concept (Aristotle), 105
Pierce, C. S., 59, 71
Poats, S., 164
Polanyi, M., 121, 122
Political economic foundations
  of AR, ix
Popular education. See Educational AR
Porter, T., 76, 77
The Possible and the Actual (Jacob), 117
Postmodern challenge, 170
Power and social reform
  AR power relationships, 28,
    73–74, 95–96
  conclusions regarding, 166
  educational strategies, 158–163
  feminist analyses of inequality and
    development, 163–166
  ideological and methodological
    differences, 151–152
  participation issues of power and
    control, 256–258, 257fig.

participatory research and Southern
  PAR, 153–158, 166*n. 1*
power relationship imbalances, 152
See also Educational AR; Feminism
  and AR; Participatory research;
  Participatory rural appraisal;
  Southern participatory action
  research
The Power of Balance (Tolbert),
  216–218
PRA. *See* Participatory rural appraisal
Pragmatic AR
  Australian experiences, 139–140
  case study references, 133
  co-optation, 141–142
  cogenerative research, 134
  conclusions regarding, 150
  dialogue arenas, construction of,
    134, 135–136
  group process as a search,
    142–143, 143*fig.*
  liberating outcomes goal, 135–136
  multi-method techniques and work
    forms, 134
  the Norwegian experiences,
    138–139
  "pragmatic" as used here, 134, 150*n. 1*
  search conferences, 136–149
  U.S. search conferencing, 140–141
  See also Pragmatic philosophy;
    Search conferencing; Search
    conferencing steps (time
    sequential order)
Pragmatic philosophy, 9–11, 62–63,
  71–73, 134
  democracy and social
    improvement, 61
  John Dewey and, 59–62
  search conference technique, 29,
    37–38, 108
  See also Dewey, John; Pragmatic AR
Pretty, J., 195, 207*n. 2*
Price, D., 74
Productive Workplace (Weisbord), 140

Programs for Employment and
  Workplace Systems (PEWS),
  Cornell University, 48–51, 141
The Promise of Pragmatism (Diggins), 71
"Psychological job demands" concept of
  industrial democracy, 20–21, 21*fig.*
The Public and Its Problems (Dewey), 60
Puckett, J., 31, 32
Putnam, R., 88*n. 5*, 210, 223–233

Qualitative research, 5–6
Quality circles, problem solving groups
  (Japan), 25
Quantitative research, 5–6
Quine, W., 71

Rabinow, P., 77, 81, 87*n. 1*
Rahman, M., 157, 177
Ransome, P., 265
Rapid rural appraisal. *See* Participatory
  rural appraisal (PRA), in
  international development
Readings, B., 160
Reardon, K., 31, 32, 173, 248
Reason, P., 12*n. 2*, 13, 15, 32, 33, 251
  collaboration, 213–214, 215
  dominant conventional social
    research and, 212
  experience and engagement
    focus of, 211
  facilitation skills and group processes
    knowledge, 214
  John Heron and, 218
  human consciousness evolution
    concept of, 212
  human/cooperative inquiry work of,
    32, 208, 209, 210, 211–215
  "human flourishing" concept of, 209
  industrial democracy and, 221
  knowledge types and stages, 212–213
  narratives/stories focus of, 214
  "participatory worldview" concept of,
    209, 212, 214
  researcher's personal growth, 214

skills for AR, 239
  validity focus of, 220
"Redundancy of functions" concept of
  industrial democracy, 21–22
"Redundancy of tasks" concept of
  industrial democracy, 21–22
Reinharz, S., 165
Research-based knowledge. See
  Knowledge generation in AR
Research element of AR, 8
Researcher. See The friendly outsider
Reynolds, M., 217
Rich, R., 138, 144, 146
Rogers, Carl, 169
Rolfsen, M., 192
Romm, N., 58, 59, 69, 130n. 1, 233
Ropoport, A., 58
Rorty, R., 13, 71–72, 130n. 1, 133, 262
Ross, D., 78, 239
Rowan, J., 32
  human/cooperative inquiry work of,
    208, 215
  researcher's personal growth, 214
Rural Development Participation Review
  (Cornell University), 199
Russell, B., 64
Ryle, G., 121, 122

Saab-Scania plants (Sweden), 23–24
Scandinavian Action Research
  Development Program, xi
Schafft, K., 31
Schön, D., 47, 58, 109, 122–123, 125, 169
  action inquiry work, 210
  action science work of, 223
  espoused theory and theory-in-use,
    226–227
  group-based Ph.D. programs and, 250
  organizational learning work of,
    232–234
  "reflective practice" approach of,
    235n. 2
  Torbert's work reviewed by, 216
The School and Society (Dewey), 60

School of Industrial and Labor
  Relations, Cornell University,
  48–51
Schoomaker Fruedenberger, K.,
  202, 203fig.
Schumacher, E., 199
Schwandt, T., 90, 103, 105
Schwartzman, S., 54, 241
Scientific method and AR, ix, 52
  AR and scientifically meaningful
    results, 77–79, 87n. 3
  AR as "storytelling" criticism,
    79, 87n. 4
  conclusions regarding, 87
  linking theory and local
    understanding, 119–120
  misunderstanding of science and,
    78–79, 87n. 3
  philosophy of science case example,
    80–86
  physical and biological sciences as
    iterative thought and action
    cycles, 80–86
  "reliable" vs. "socially robust"
    knowledge, 77
  science is humans in action, 85–87,
    86–87
  science is humans in action, case
    example, 80–86, 88n. 6, 88n. 7
  social science criticism and, 77–78
  social science research and, 76–77, 79,
    87n. 1, 87n. 2, 88n. 5
  thought and action relationship,
    78–79, 80–86
  See also Scientific method and AR,
    stages of (in time-sequence
    order); Scientific research
Scientific method and AR, stages of
  (in time-sequence order)
  generate a problem to study, 81–82
  how to study problem, 82
  how to document information, 82–83
  deciding when data collection is
    complete, 83

accounting for distribution or
structure of data, 83
testing hypotheses against data,
84, 88n. 6
when no hypothesis is proven, 84–85
prediction element, 85–86, 88n. 7
Scientific research
defined, 55–57
democratic social action and, 61
general systems theory, 57–59
hermeneutics and, 56, 68, 72
introductory texts inadequacies,
56–57
logical positivism and, 56
political power relationships and, 74
qualitative vs. quantitative, 5–6
transcontextual credibility, 69–70
See also Scientific method and AR
Scott, J., 199
Scott, P., 54, 59, 77, 99, 241, 252
Scriven, M., 187
Search conferencing, 136–137
arenas for dialogue, construction of,
135–136
elements of, 142–143, 143fig.
employee participation concept,
29, 37–38, 108
historical roots of, 137–138
participatory planning and, 136, 138
planning and execution of, 144–149
preparation for, 143–144
as structured change processes, 141
in the US, 140–141
See also Search conferencing steps
(time sequential order)
Search conferencing steps (time
sequential order)
commissioning the search
conference, 144
identifying the participants, 144–145
inviting the participants, 145
logistical support, 145–146
stages in, 146
creating a shared history, 146–147

creating a shared vision, 147–148
identifying action plans, 148
prioritizing ideas, 148–149
concrete change activity through
volunteer action teams, 149
Self-reflecting human inquiry
research, 218
Sell, K., 172, 244
"Semiautonomous groups" concept of
industrial democracy, 20
Senge, P., 58, 175, 232
Sensitivity groups, 17–18
Shapin, S., 78, 81
Sherman, F., 218
Sims Feldstein, H., 164
Single-loop learning, 226, 230, 233
Skjervheim, H., 64
Slaughter, S., 252
Social change agenda, of AR,
3, 5–6, 9–11
management tools as, 15
See also Power and social reform;
Southern participatory action
research (PAR)
The Social Construction of Reality
(Berger and Luckmann), 104
Social reform. See Educational AR;
Feminism and AR; Power and
social reform; Southern
participatory action research (PAR)
Social science research, 66–68, 76, 87n. 1
accountability to authority and, 184
conventional evaluation criticism,
184–186
See also Knowledge generation in AR;
Social science research
techniques, work forms and
strategies in AR
Social science research techniques, work
forms and strategies in AR, 89–90
bureaucratic ideology and
practices, 116
cogenerative model, 93–98, 94fig.
communication arenas, 94–96, 108

conventional social research
   vs., 90–93
creating arenas, 97
feedback, 96–97
impartiality focus and failure, 116
methodology, defined, 90
narratives and, 110, 111
problem definition, 93–94
"qualitative" vs. mixed method
   research, 98–99
research strategies, of AR, 91, 92–93
research strategies, of social research
   strategies, 91–92
researcher training imperatives
   and, 89–90
social sciences separated from
   action, 89
techniques, of AR, 90, 92
techniques, of social research
   strategies, 91
what action researchers may
   not do, 97–98
workability and explanation, 63–64,
   68, 100–101
workforms, of AR, 90–91, 92, 101n. 1
workforms, of social research
   strategies, 91
See also Cogenerative model of
   AR process; Knowledge
   generation in AR
Society for International
   Development, 199
"Sociotechnical reorganization" work of
   industrial democracy, 16, 19–22,
   23fig., 24, 25, 26
Southern participatory action research
   (PAR), 29, 34
cogenerative dialogue in, 155–156
conscientization concept, 30–31, 64
democratization, adult education
   focus, 160, 176–179
democratization as liberation,
   154–157
diversity within, 151

Orlando Fals Borda's Latin American
   work, 157
feminism and, 152–153
Freire's work and, 179
local knowledge focus of, 155, 179
Marxism foundation of, 169, 177
North-South co-optation, 157–158
outsider distrust and, 156–157
participatory rural appraisal
   and, 201
poor and oppressed focus of,
   153–154, 177–179
popular education and, 177–179
power and money factors, 154,
   177–179, 183n. 3
PR vs. PAR, 153–154, 157–158,
   166–167n. 2
public institution distrust, 154
research focus of, 156
"South" designation and, 153–154,
   166–167n. 2, 166n. 1
vs. Northern andragogy, 175
Sørensen, Å., 99
Sørmarka trade union education facility
   (Norway), 161
Spain. See Mondragón Cooperatives
Sri Lanka irrigation systems project, 199
Stanton, T., 173
Stenhouse, L., 171
Stongfjorden village development,
   Western Norway, 36–42, 51
communication arenas, 41
community solidarity evidence,
   36, 38–39, 41
entrepreneurial efforts, 39
facilitator role shift, 40–41
industrialization history of, 36–37
municipal administration, 39–40
revitalization program, 35, 37–39
social structure, 41
sustaining development effort, 38
Stringer, E., 171
Strubel, A., 255n. 1
Study circles, 181

Sullivan, W., 77
Suppes, P., 99
Support groups, 180–181
Swantz, M. L., 164
Swedish Confederation of Employers, 24
Swedish industrial democracy, 23–24
Systematic philosophy, 71
Systemic Practice and Action Research
    publication, 32
Systems. *See* General systems
    theory (GST)

T-group praxis, of Kurt Lewin, 16,
    17–18, 45, 52*n. 2*
Tandon, R., 157
Tarule, J., 31, 166
Tavistock Institute of Human Relations,
    London, England, 15, 26, 27, 137,
    140, 240
    educational AR and, 171
    natural experiments in work life, 19
    production technology and work
        organization link and, 18–19
    See also Industrial democracy;
        Norwegian Industrial
        Democracy Project
Taylor, C., 71
Taylor, F. W., 15, 34*n. 1*
    See also "Taylorism"
Taylor, J. C., 24
"Taylorism"
    academic Taylorism and, 243, 252
    vs. industrial democracy, 15, 19,
        20, 21, 34*n. 1*
Thomas, H., 42
Thomas, L., 255*n. 1*
Thomson, J., 202, 202*fig.*, 203*fig.*
Thorsrud, E., 19, 20, 21*fig.*
Tocqueville, A. de, 10–11
Torbert, W., 33
    action inquiry work of, 208, 210,
        216–218
    constructive rationality concept of,
        216–217

curriculum reform in business
    school, 217
liberating structures focus of, 217
power, types of, 216–217
power and leadership focus
    of, 217
Torvatn, H., 192
Toulmin, S., 59, 105
Toyota, 25
Trade Union Council (Norway), 19
Trade unions
    in Great Britain, 19
    individual influence, workplace
        representation issues, 28
    liberationist concepts, 30
    participatory research projects
        of, 32, 260
    study circle concept and, 181
    trade union education, 161–162
Transcontextual credibility, 69–70
Transformational learning, 174–175
Traweek, S., 81
Trist, E., 18–19, 21, 22, 23*fig.*, 140
Trodenheim, x
Trow, M., 54, 241
Truth and Method (Gadamer), 69

UCLA, 24
Ulgor founding cooperative, Spanish
    Basque Country, 42, 43
Union busting, 24–25
University of Bath, 208
University of California in Los
    Angeles (UCLA), 24
University of London, 33
University of Michigan, 18
University of Pennsylvania, 31, 140
Uphoff, N., 198–199
U.S. Agency for International
    Development (USAID), 180,
    194, 198–199
USAID. *See* U.S. Agency for
    International Development
Usher, R., 168, 170, 177, 183

Utilization-based participatory
    evaluation, 189–190
Utilization-Focused Evaluation
    (Patton), 189
Uusitalo, U., 144

Validity in AR
    John Heron's work in, 219
    See also Credibility and validity
van den Hombergh, H., 164
van der Vlist, R., xi
Van Eijnatten, F. M., 22
Ver Beek, K., 182
Verbalism, 179
Vodoubê, Simplice, 195, 207*n. 2*
Volvo (Norway plants), 20, 23–24
von Bertalanffy, L., 58

Waller, S., 31, 176
Wandersman, A., 188
We Make the Road by Walking (Horton
    and Freire), 175
Weber, M.
    "causal interpretation of history"
        work of, 70
    ideal type concept of, 70, 75*n. 3*
    pragmatist framework for
        philosophy and, 71
Weinstock, J., 32, 176
Weisbord, M., 138, 139, 140, 141
Weiss, H., 191

Westbrook, R., 60, 159
WHO. *See* World Heath Organization
*Whose Reality Counts? Putting the First
    Last* (Chambers), 200–201, 204
Whyte, K. K., 42, 141, 166*n. 2*, 198
Whyte, W., 213
Whyte, W. F., 13, 42, 43, 49, 141,
    166*n. 2*, 198
Wilson, A., 183*n. 1*
Wittgenstein, L., 55, 66, 71
Womack, J. P., 25, 253
Woolgar, S., 81, 86, 87*n. 1*
Work organization, paradigms,
    22–23, 23*fig.*
"Work Place Australia," 140
Work Research Institute, Oslo, Norway,
    138, 139
Work Research Institute (WRI, Oslow,
    Norway), 239–240
Workability issue of AR, 63–64, 68,
    100–101
World Bank, 180, 197
    PRA and, 194
World Heath Organization
    (WHO), 180
Worley, C. G., 17, 28, 92

Young, I., 10, 164

Zabusky, S., 81, 86, 87*n. 1*
Zeichner, K., 171

About the Authors

Davydd J. Greenwood is the Goldwin Smith Professor of Anthropology and Director of the Institute for European Studies at Cornell University, where he has served as a faculty member since 1970. He has been elected a Corresponding Member of the Spanish Royal Academy of Moral and Political Sciences. He served as the John S. Knight Professor and Director of the Mario Einaudi Center for 10 years and was President of the Association of International Education Administrators. He also has served as a program evaluator for many universities and for the National Foreign Language Center. His work centers on action research, political economy, ethnic conflict, community and regional development in Spain and the United States. His current work focuses on the impact of corporatization on higher education with a particular emphasis on the social sciences. His published works include *Unrewarding Wealth: The Commercialization and Collapse of Agriculture in a Spanish Basque Town; Nature, Culture, and Human History; The Taming of Evolution: The Persistence of Non-evolutionary Views in the Study of Humans; Las culturas de Fagor; Industrial Democracy as Process: Participatory Action Research in the Fagor Cooperative Group of Mondragón; Introduction to Action Research: Social Research for Social Change* (with Morten Levin), and two edited books.

Morten Levin is a professor at the Department of Industrial Economics and Technology Management in the Faculty of Social Sciences and Technology Management at the Norwegian University of Science and Technology in Trondheim, Norway. He holds graduate degrees in engineering and in sociology. Throughout his professional life, he has worked as an action researcher with a particular focus on processes and structures of social change in the relationships between technology and organization. His action research has taken place in industrial contexts, in local communities, and in university teaching where he has developed and been in charge of three successive Ph.D. programs in action research. He is author of a number of books and articles, including *Introduction to Action Research: Social Research for Social Change*, and he serves on the editorial boards of *Systemic Practice and Action Research, Action Research International, Action Research,* the *Handbook of Qualitative Inquiry,* and the *Handbook of Action Research.*